W9-BOQ-201

Eastern
Pennsylvania

Eastern Pennsylvania

Includes Philadelphia, Gettysburg, Amish Country & the Pocono Mountains

Laura Randall

with photographs by the author

The Countryman Press ✳ Woodstock, Vermont

SECOND EDITION

Explorer's Guide Eastern Pennsylvania
978-0-88150-993-9

Interior photographs by the author unless otherwise specified
Maps by Erin Greb Cartography, © The Countryman Press
Book design by Bodenweber Design
Composition by PerfecType, Nashville, TN

Published by The Countryman Press, P.O. Box 748, Woodstock, VT 05091

Distributed by W. W. Norton & Company, Inc., 500 Fifth Avenue, New York, NY 10110

Printed in the United States of America

10 9 8 7 6 5 4 3 2 1

For my parents, Bill and Rosemarie Randall.

EXPLORE WITH US!

Welcome to the second edition of *Eastern Pennsylvania: An Explorer's Guide*, the definitive guide to Philadelphia and the large and diverse regions that surround it. It's the ideal companion for exploring the Brandywine Valley, Bucks County, Amish Country, Gettysburg, and the Pocono Mountains. Here you'll find thorough coverage of big cities and small towns, plus everything in between, with detailed listings on the best sightseeing, outdoor activities, restaurants, shopping, and B&Bs. Like all other Explorer's Guides, this book is an old-fashioned, classic traveler's guide, where an experienced and knowledgeable expert helps you find your way around a new area or explore some fascinating corners of a familiar one.

WHAT'S WHERE

In the beginning of this book, you'll find an alphabetical listing of special highlights and important information that you may want to reference quickly. You'll find advice on everything from navigating the complicated state liquor laws to ordering cheesesteaks.

LODGING

We've selected lodging places for inclusion in this book based on merit alone; we do not charge innkeepers for their inclusion. Prices: Please don't hold us or the respective innkeepers responsible for rates listed as of press time in late 2011. Changes are inevitable. At the time of this writing, the state room tax was 6 percent (plus an additional 1 percent in Philadelphia) and city and county room tax was 6 percent.

RESTAURANTS

In most chapters, please note the distinction between Eating Out and Dining Out. By their nature, restaurants included in the Eating Out group are generally inexpensive. A range of prices is included for each entry.

KEY TO SYMBOLS

  ✎ Child-friendly. The crayon denotes a family-friendly place or event that welcomes young children. Most B&Bs prohibit children under 12.

  &. Handicapped access. The wheelchair icon denotes a place with full ADA—Americans with Disabilities Act—standard access, still distressingly rare in these remote areas.

  ☂ Rainy day. The umbrella icon points out places where you can entertain yourself but still stay dry in bad weather.

☙ Pets. The dog's paw icon identifies lodgings that allow pets—still the exception to the rule. Accommodations that accept pets may still charge an extra fee or restrict pets to certain areas, as well as require advance notice.

❦ Special value. The blue-ribbon symbol appears next to selected lodging and restaurants that combine quality and moderate prices.

Ⴁ Good bars. The martini glass icon appears next to restaurants and entertainment venues that have them.

⚭ Weddings. Listings with the ring symbol have the skill and capacity to host wedding ceremonies and receptions.

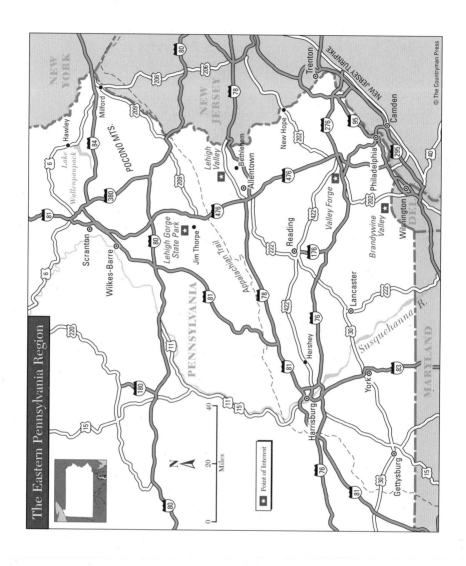

The Eastern Pennsylvania Region

Point of Interest

© The Countryman Press

CONTENTS

LIST OF MAPS

ACKNOWLEDGMENTS

First, I want to send heartfelt appreciation to each business, chamber of commerce, convention-bureau staff member, historian, and park ranger who contributed information, offered assistance, and patiently answered my many, many questions about their towns and attractions.

It's impossible to name everyone, but a few stand out. Mary Linkevich at Hawk Mountain Sanctuary for steering me toward local shops and B&Bs in addition to all the tips on visiting her beloved mountain. The folks at Hopewell Furnace, Independence Hall, and Eisenhower National Historic Sites for loving their jobs so much and conveying that to everyone who visits. Nadine and Carl Glassman, of Wedgwood Inn in New Hope, quintessential innkeepers and invaluable fonts of information about their lovely river town. Nina Kelly, for making my visit to West Chester so easy, and tirelessly showing off the town's beauty and culture.

This book also wouldn't have been possible without my network of friends and family who were always on hand to recommend and describe their favorite places to eat, stroll, shop, and sightsee in the Keystone State. Ayleen Stellhorn, Deborah and Laine Kasdras, Karen and Tom Condor, and Sherri Schmidt—your tips and opinions are always spot-on and useful. The high standards of the voracious and devoted folks at Chowhound must also be acknowledged here. The Pennsylvania food threads inspired me to scope out many new farm markets and restaurants—and they never steered me wrong. Finally, grateful thanks go to Lynn Williams and Tracey Molettiere for being game to try any type of meal or road trip with relish and laughter—here's to friendship.

Thanks and sincere appreciation must also go to my parents, Bill and Rosemarie Randall, for their tireless reconnaissance work, which in this edition involved everything from sampling chicken potpies and butter brickle ice cream to tracking down the trailhead to a hidden waterfall deep in the Pocono Mountains. The always-accessible Kim Grant, as well as Kermit Hummel and Lisa Sacks at The Countryman Press, also deserve a shout for their editorial guidance and infectious enthusiasm for travel.

12

ACKNOWLEDGMENTS

And, as always, thanks to my husband, John Kimble, for his ever-calming presence, and to our sons, Jack and Theo, for their willingness to visit parks, diners, out-of-the-way museums, and Italian ice stands with me at all hours of the day and night. Here's to a future of many more fun family adventures.

INTRODUCTION

With its abundant natural resources and central role in early American history, eastern Pennsylvania attracts a wide swath of travelers to its cities and rural towns. It is home to the Liberty Bell and Independence Hall, the country's second-largest Amish community and one of its biggest shopping malls, and more than 100 lakes, rivers, and state parks. Philadelphia may be the area's anchor and urban soul, but it is surrounded by miles of rolling green farmlands, forested mountains, and villages that haven't changed much since the king of England bequeathed the state to William Penn. Within an hour or two's drive from the city's center, you can tour a dozen historic battlefields, shop for antiques, go tubing along a pristine stretch of the Delaware River, visit a chocolate factory straight out of Willie Wonka, and eat chicken corn soup and chow-chow in an 18th-century farmhouse. The area really does offer something for everyone.

I am a native Pennsylvanian who grew up near Valley Forge National Historical Park and went to college within cannon-firing distance of the battlefields of Gettysburg. I spent summers cycling the Schuylkill River, devouring lemon water ice at Rita's, cheering on the Phillies (during those halcyon Mike Schmidt days), and hiking and swimming in the Pocono Mountains. As an adult, I lived in a corner of a converted sugar mill in Old City, Philadelphia, just as the area was beginning to explode into the vibrant neighborhood it is today, and got married amid the B&Bs and quirky shops of New Hope, Bucks County. My husband and I chose to marry there because it represented to us an idyllic (yet accessible) place where our friends and family could kick back, explore at their leisure, and leave with a happy memory or two. In putting together a guide to the area for out-of-town guests, we coaxed local acquaintances into divulging their favorite haunts, walked the river towpath to check out the trails and views ourselves, and banged on doors of small Colonial inns.

That's also the way I have treated this guide—by relying on word of mouth, conversations with long-time residents, and my own research and instincts rather than on Web sites or paid media advertisements. The second edition also acknowledges that everyone likes a good bargain these days. You may notice that there are more low-cost eating and sleeping options included in this guide, as well as more suggestions for scenic drives, quiet walks, discounted museum days, and happy hours. If a listed hotel or restaurant seems overly expensive or decadent, it is very likely worth the splurge.

I also bring to this guide 20 years of experience as a travel writer and globetrotter who appreciates a four-star dining experience as much as the discovery of a bargain hotel room that's as clean and attractive as the significantly more expensive chain place around the corner. I have traveled extensively in the Caribbean, Latin America, and Europe, writing dispatches for the *Washington Post*, the *Los Angeles Times*, the *Christian Science Monitor*, and *National Geographic News Service*. I have lived and worked in Washington, D.C., Puerto Rico, New Jersey, and Los Angeles, yet I still consider Pennsylvania home and return several times a year to see family and friends and get my fix of cobblestones, 18th-century architecture, and, yes, cheesesteaks. No matter what they tell you, they just aren't as good west of the Susquehanna.

Another significant way this guide stands out from the pack is that it devotes as many pages to the areas surrounding Philadelphia as it does to the city itself. The covered bridges of Bucks County and hex signs of northern Berks County will get as much attention as Constitution Hall and the Mummers Parade. I understand that visitors to the area are as interested in hiking a forest trail, hearing the *Gettysburg Address* at its original site, and shopping for Amish-made farm tables as much as they are in seeing the Liberty Bell, and I have applied that knowledge accordingly. This book is written for Pennsylvania residents who enjoy taking short excursions in their home state throughout the year, and it is written for those who own or rent vacation homes in places like the Pocono Mountains and want to gain a better understanding of their adopted neighborhoods. It's also written for American history lovers and for parents who want to introduce their children to names such as Hershey, Crayola, and Daniel Boone.

Most of all, however, this book aims to introduce eastern Pennsylvania's beauty and diversity to the many people who assume that the region is defined only by the nation's fifth-largest city. As much as I love Philadelphia and take great pleasure in profiling it for this book, there is much more to the region than the city and its immediate surroundings. There is a whole "idyllic and accessible" side of eastern Pennsylvania that's also well worth a visit.

WHAT'S WHERE IN EASTERN PENNSYLVANIA

AMISH COUNTRY Lancaster County is home to one of the country's largest Amish populations. They don't drive, but you will undoubtedly see them out and about in horse and buggy or walking to and from shops. Please respect their wishes and don't snap photos. The best ways to learn more about their culture and lifestyle are via buggy rides that wind through backcountry roads and farms or by joining an Amish family for dinner in their home, which can often be arranged by B&B owners.

ANTIQUES Quaint shopping districts abound in this part of the state. Serious antiques buyers flock to **Adamstown** near Reading, **Hawley** and **Honesdale** in the Pocono Mountains, and **Chadds Ford** and other small towns in the Brandywine Valley. You'll also find a good concentration of antiques shops in the Bucks County villages of New Hope, Lahaska, and Kintnersville.

CAVES There is nothing like a cave to make you feel your mortality, and eastern Pennsylvania has at least three fine ones that are open to tourists. **Indian Echo Caverns** near Hershey is a favorite, and **Crystal Cave** and **Lost River Caverns** are the ones to hit if you're in the Reading/Kutztown area or the Lehigh Valley.

CHEESESTEAKS It's one word in Philadelphia. And the favorite way to order it is with Cheez Whiz and fried onions. **John's Roast Pork** near the waterfront has been the king of the steak sandwich in

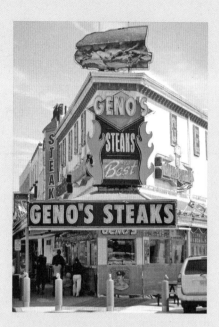

recent years, garnering rave reviews of food critics, though many Philadelphians remain loyal to the two South Philadelphia institutions, **Pat's** (215-468-1546; 1237 E. Passyunk Avenue) and **Geno's** (215-389-0659; 1219 S. Ninth Street).

CIVIL WAR The Battle of Gettysburg yielded the largest number of casualties of any battle of the American Civil War and is often cited as the war's turning point. Today, thousands of Civil War buffs come to south-central Pennsylvania to visit the solemn battlefield site and the countless other attractions that have sprung up around it. In Harrisburg, the **National Civil War Museum** takes pains to tell the story of the Civil War without taking sides. Numerous other smaller battles

were also fought here in towns such as Hanover, Fairfield, and Carlisle.

CONVENIENCE STORES Once you get past the funny name, you'll realize that Wawa is the Toyota Prius of convenience stores. If you're driving around the state and looking for a pick-me-up Tastykake or hoagie, this is the place to go. Everything here is fresh, the prices are reasonable, and the clerks are usually polite, if not downright friendly. Many branches sell gas at a discount, and the ATMs are surcharge-free. There are more than 500 Wawa stores in Pennsylvania, New Jersey, Delaware, and Maryland.

COVERED BRIDGES Forget the Bridges of Madison County. More than 200 covered bridges dot the Pennsylvania landscape between Philadelphia and Pittsburgh. Entire Web sites are devoted to their beauty and preservation. The places to find them in the eastern part of the state are Bucks

County, especially the central and upper parts, Lancaster County, and the back roads of the Brandywine Valley.

DINERS Nobody does diners better than Pennsylvania, in my humble opinion. Expect homemade soups, hearty servings, efficient (if brusque) service, and low prices. It's hard to find a bad one in the state, but **Daddypops** in Hatboro (near the Bucks County line), **Saville Diner** in Boyertown, and **Hawley Diner** in the Pocono Mountains are three of the best.

FESTIVALS Eastern Pennsylvania loves a good party, especially if it involves Ben Franklin, fireworks, or green beer. Some of the state's best annual events can be found in small towns such as Kutztown (the **Kutztown Folk Festival**), Kennett Square (**Mushroom Festival**), and Bethlehem (**Bach Festival**). In Philadelphia, the feather-and-sequins Mummers Parade on New Year's Day is like no other costume parade you'll ever experience. Lancaster hosts the world's largest chicken barbecue in late summer at Long's Park, and Shawnee in the Pocono Mountains pays homage to the garlic bulb every Labor Day Weekend.

FISHING A license is required to fish in Pennsylvania's rivers, lakes, and streams. For more information, go to www.www.pgc.state.pa.us. Another good source for the state's best fishing spots is www.paflyfish.com.

FLEA MARKETS They are rampant around here, and offer terrific people-watching opportunities, not to mention the chance to buy such things as handmade quilts and sticky buns. Two of the biggest and oldest are **Zern's** near Reading and **Rice's** in New Hope. Renninger's markets, with locations in Adamstown and Kutztown, and Root's Country Market in Manheim (Lancaster County) are also worth a special trip.

GAMBLING The state opened its first slot parlor in 2006; it now has 10 full-scale casinos paying an annual $1.3 billion in taxes, with more in the works. The **Sugar-House Casino** in northeast Philadelphia is one of the newest. For updated info, go to www.visit pacasinos.com.

GARDENS Philadelphia and its outlying areas are home to dozens of world-class gardens. Head to **Longwood Gardens** in Kennett Square for seasonal perfection, or to **Chanticleer** in Wayne for a quiet meander. For a comprehensive list, pick up *A Guide to the Great Gardens of the Philadelphia Region* by Adam Levine (2007, Temple University Press).

HUNTING The forests and fields of Pennsylvania are open to hunting during established seasons. Common game species are deer, rabbit, pheasant, ruffed grouse, bear, squirrel, and waterfowl. Hunters are expected to follow the rules and regulations of the state game commission. For more information, go to www.www.pgc.state.pa.us or www.huntingpa.com.

ITALIAN ICE If you visit eastern Pennsylvania in the late spring or summer, chances are you'll see lines of people gathered at small stands selling Italian ices. Also called water ice, it's a dessert made from shaved ice and flavored with concentrated syrup (lemon is a favorite). **Rita's Water Ice** is a homegrown chain with stands throughout the state.

LIQUOR LAWS As anyone who has spent any time here knows, Pennsylvania has some of the most restrictive laws in the country concerning the purchase of alcohol. Ironically, Philadelphia also has more BYO restaurants than just about any other city. You can buy wine and spirits only in stores operated by the state-run Liquor Control Board. This book includes a BYO section at the end of each Where to Eat section to help you find Wine & Spirits stores in the area. For a complete list of stores in the state, go to www.lcb.state.pa.us.

MUSEUMS You'll find all kinds represented here, from the diverse offerings of the free **State Museum** in Harrisburg to niche facilities devoted to woodcarving, 19th-century quilts, and Ben Franklin's inventions. Don't miss the **Mütter, Chemical Heritage,** or **Rodin** Museums if you're in Philadelphia. Elsewhere, the **Brandywine River Museum** and **Christian C. Sanderson Museum** in Chadds Ford, **Dorflinger Glass Museum** in Honesdale, and **Wharton Esherick Museum** in Malvern are all worth a special trip. Children will love the new and improved **Please Touch Museum** in Philadelphia and the **National Canal Museum** and **Crayola Factory** in Easton.

PENNSYLVANIA DUTCH FOOD If you see chow-chow, chicken corn soup, or shoofly pie on a menu, chances are you're within spitting distance of Lancaster County. Chow-chow is a sweet and sour relish made up from end-of-summer garden leftovers. Shoofly pie is a crumb-topped pie with a sticky molasses bottom. Other not-to-be-missed Pennsylvania Dutch delicacies:

whoopie pie, an oversized cakelike Oreo, and funnel cake, fried dough topped with powdered sugar sold often at carnivals and festivals. The strong-of-stomach may also want to try scrapple, a pan-fried slab of cornmeal mush and pork byproducts, and "church spread," an Amish invention of corn syrup or molasses, marshmallow cream, and peanut butter.

PRETZELS You can have them for breakfast, tour factories that produce them by the ton, and watch them being hand-twisted by Amish grandmothers—all in a single day in the Reading or Lancaster areas. Life isn't complete until you have sampled a soft pretzel that's butter-brushed and fresh from the oven.

RAILROAD Eastern Pennsylvania was a leader in rail travel during the 1800s, and today you will find many, many places here that celebrate that heritage. You can still view the rolling hills and farmland from restored passenger cars on the Strasburg Railroad, the Stourbridge Lion in Honesdale, and M&H Railroad in Hummelstown. Train lovers of all ages also shouldn't miss the Railroad Museum of Pennsylvania in Strasburg or Scranton's **Steamtown National Historic Site,** which ranks among the best in the country.

SMOKING Smoking is prohibited in most public places and work-

places (except casinos) throughout the state.

STATE PARKS You'll find dozens of state parks in this part of the state; many offer camping, swimming, boating, and hiking, and horseback riding options. **Promised Land** in the Pocono Mountains, **French Creek** between Reading and Valley Forge, and **Nockamixon** in Upper Bucks County are a few favorites.

THEME PARKS With its wide appeal, reputation for cleanliness, and chocolate connection, **Hershey Park** dominates in this department. The state also has some smaller amusement parks that are worth a look: **Dutch Wonderland** in Lancaster is great for preschoolers, and **Knoebels**

way up in Elysburg is known for its free admission, old-fashioned roller coasters, and good food.

WATERFALLS The Pocono Mountains have some of the best cascades this side of Niagara. **Bushkill** Falls is probably the most famous, but there are also many free ones that are also worth a visit, including Raymondskill Falls, **Dingmans Falls,** and Shohola Falls.

WINERIES The state's wineries may be light years away from matching the Rhone or Napa Valleys in terms of quality, but its boutique wineries have expanded and upgraded in recent years and the number of wineries in the state has grown to 130. Bucks County, the Brandywine Valley, Lancaster, and York County all boast serious wineries that often combine events and fun activities with tastings.

Philadelphia

1

CENTER CITY EAST &
SOUTH PHILADELPHIA

CENTER CITY WEST &
UNIVERSITY CITY

CHESTNUT HILL, GERMANTOWN &
MANAYUNK

INTRODUCTION

E ver since William Penn landed on its shores in 1682 and dubbed it the City of Brotherly Love, Philadelphia has been a place of contrasts. It gave the world Grace Kelly and Rocky Balboa. Its cheesesteak stands garner as much attention as Le Bec Fin, one of the country's finest French restaurants. In Center City, sleek skyscrapers coexist next to neighborhoods of neat brick rowhouses, where residents still throw block parties.

First and foremost, Philadelphia is the nation's birthplace, home to countless historic sites, pioneering architectural styles, and American firsts. It was here that the U.S. Constitution and Declaration of Independence were signed, the first stock exchange opened, and the first urban planning experiment was set in motion. History is evident on just about every block, whether it's a plaque commemorating the Founding Fathers, an 18th-century Federal townhome, or a gravestone with the name Franklin etched on it. It's here that you will find the country's oldest mint, art museum, post office, lending library, zoo, and continuously occupied public street.

Yet you don't have to be a history buff to visit Philadelphia. You will find things to enjoy if you like good food, soulful jazz, high-end shopping, and top-tier art museums. Philly, as it's often called, is home to top-notch restaurants, dozens of colleges, a terrific urban park larger than New York City's Central Park, and scores of restaurants, shops, hotels, and theaters. Reading Terminal Market, a massive indoor marketplace directly across from the Pennsylvania Convention Center and a few blocks from City Hall, unites locals and tourists alike with its fresh-cut flowers, vibrant produce, Amish-made breads and apple butter, and two-fisted pork sandwiches.

Observers and tourism officials like to say the city truly came into its own as a standalone travel destination in the late 1990s and early 2000s, with the openings of a 1-million-square-foot convention center, the $250-million Kimmel Center for the Performing Arts, two new sports stadiums, and the National Constitution Center. They have a point, but as someone who has spent time here since the 1970s, I like to think many of the right elements were in place long before that. The city, despite a host of urban problems like crime and graffiti that continue to this day, has always had good food, loud and loyal locals, and a walkable, easy-to-navigate downtown. It has always had Independence Hall, the Liberty Bell, and Ben Franklin's spirit.

First-time visitors should also expect experiences that they might not have elsewhere in the country, for better or for worse. You will hear "Yo!" more often than you can imagine. You will probably be called "hon," whatever your gender, by everyone from the curbside hot dog vendor to the stylish clerk at your boutique hotel. You may get snarled at, or at least a raised eyebrow, if you ask for anything but fried onions and Cheez Whiz on your cheesesteak. And anyone who spends time at a sporting event here in which the hometown is losing will question why it deserves its City of Brotherly Love title.

The easiest and most satisfying way to see Philadelphia is to walk. It is laid out in a grid pattern of wide, straight streets that cross at right angles (thank you, Mr. Penn). Those in moderately good shape can walk or jog from the University of Pennsylvania campus all the way to the Delaware River, via Walnut or Spruce streets, passing by Independence Hall, Washington Square Park, and many cobblestoned alleys along the way. Detour over a few blocks to the north and you'll find yourself climbing the steps of the Philadelphia Art Museum, where Rocky Balboa took his famous victory lap.

Philly is home to more than 100 neighborhoods. Center City is its core, anchored by City Hall and split to the east and west by Broad Street. South Philadelphia is home to multigenerational families, the bustling Italian market, and some of the best trattorias around. The University of Pennsylvania's influence is strong amid West Philadelphia's corner stores and brownstones, while the Philadelphia Art Museum and other first-class museums dominate the Benjamin Franklin Parkway Area to the north. Much of the historic district, including Independence Hall and the Liberty Bell, lies in or around Old City, a once-industrial area that has been transformed in recent years to a hip neighborhood with some of the city's best restaurants, nightlife, and art galleries. On the outskirts, Chestnut Hill, Germantown, and Manayunk have some of the city's best boutique shopping and examples of preserved 18th-century architecture.

Whatever your reason for visiting, Philadelphia is an important part of travel within the eastern Pennsylvania region, a place that can serve as a base for day or overnight trips to Gettysburg or Pennsylvania Dutch Country or spark your interest in visiting them independently.

CENTER CITY EAST & SOUTH PHILADELPHIA

AREA CODE The area code for Philadelphia is 215.

GUIDANCE Independence Visitor Center (800-537-7676 or 215-965-7676; www.independencevisitorcenter.com), Sixth and Market Streets, is a must for anyone visiting the historic district. It's the place to pick up free timed tickets to Independence Hall, as well as paid tickets to other attractions, plus it offers a café, gift shop, and a huge selection of publications and maps of the city and its surrounding counties. Volunteers and National Park Service employees are on hand to answer questions.

GETTING THERE By car: Several major interstate highways lead through Philadelphia. From the north or south, take I-95 to I-676 (Vine Street Expressway), which cuts right through Center City. From the west, I-76 (the Schuylkill Expressway) branches off the Pennsylvania Turnpike and follows the river to South Philadelphia.

By air: **Philadelphia International Airport** (215-937-6800) is about a 20-minute drive from Center City, and served by all major airlines. The Southeastern Pennsylvania Transportation Authority (SEPTA) R1 line offers direct service between Center City and the airport.

By bus: **Greyhound** (800-231-2222; www.greyhound.com) and **Peter Pan** (800-343-9999; www.peterpanbus.com) offer service between Philadelphia, New York, and dozens of major cities, operating out of the Greyhound terminal next to Reading Terminal Market.

By train: **Amtrak** stops at 30th Street Station on its Northeast Corridor route between Richmond, Virginia, and Boston. SEPTA's R7 suburban train runs to Trenton, New Jersey, where New Jersey Transit trains run to New York's Penn Station. The R7 stops at the Market Street East station, about four blocks from Independence Hall.

PHILADELPHIA

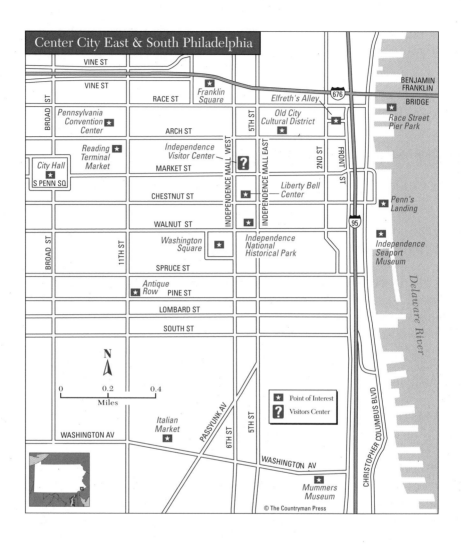

Center City East & South Philadelphia

VINE ST

VINE ST

BROAD ST

RACE ST

Franklin Square ★

Elfreth's Alley

676

BENJAMIN FRANKLIN BRIDGE

Pennsylvania Convention Center ★

ARCH ST

5TH ST

Old City Cultural District ★

★

Race Street Pier Park ★

City Hall ★

Reading Terminal Market ★

Independence Visitor Center ?

MARKET ST

INDEPENDENCE MALL WEST

INDEPENDENCE MALL EAST

2ND ST

FRONT ST

S PENN SQ

CHESTNUT ST

★

Liberty Bell Center ★

Penn's Landing ★

WALNUT ST

★

95

BROAD ST

11TH ST

Washington Square ★

SPRUCE ST

Independence National Historical Park

Independence Seaport Museum ★

Antique Row ★ PINE ST

LOMBARD ST

SOUTH ST

N

0   0.2   0.4
Miles

Italian Market ★

WASHINGTON AV

PASSYUNK AV

6TH ST

5TH ST

★ Point of Interest

? Visitors Center

CHRISTOPHER COLUMBUS BLVD

Delaware River

WASHINGTON AV

Mummers Museum ★

© The Countryman Press

GETTING AROUND SEPTA municipal buses run all over the city, though they can be daunting for first-time visitors. The Market–Frankford Line is a rapid-transit line that stops in Old City (Second and Market) and near the University of Pennsylvania's campus, ending in the city's far northwest corner. If you're staying in Center City, the most rewarding way to get from one destination to another is by walking. If it's late or you're tired, it's fairly easy to flag down a taxi in Center City, especially on main thoroughfares like Market and Walnut Streets.

The purple **Phlash** bus (215-599-0776; www.phillyphlash.com) runs a continuous loop between the city's major attractions, including the historic district and Penn's Landing. Buses stop every 12 minutes at designated purple lampposts and operate daily May through October. Cost is $2 a ride, or $5 for an all-day pass.

PARKING There is restricted metered parking available on the street throughout Center City. If you're spending the day, your best bet is to park in one of the many parking garages in the city's historic area and near City Hall. **Central Parking Auto Park** at Independence Mall (Sixth Street between Market and Arch), lets you enter Independence Visitor Center without having to go outside. Convenient to both the historic district and the convention center is the Philadelphia Parking Authority's **Auto Parking Plaza** (215-925-4305), 801 Filbert Street, which offers early-bird specials to cars entering before 10 AM. For the best rates, go online to philapark.org/locator or Philadelphia.bestparking.com and type in the address of your destination.

MEDICAL EMERGENCY Pennsylvania Hospital (215-829-3000) 800 Spruce Street, Philadelphia.

WHEN TO GO Philadelphia's many museums, theaters, and shops make it a good place to visit year-round. The lines at many of its historic sites, such as Independence Hall and the Liberty Bell, tend to be shortest in January and February. If you prefer warmer weather and lots of activities, try to plan your visit in the summer, when Penn's Landing and the city's squares are alive with all kinds of entertainment and festivities.

✳ Neighborhoods

Old City. At the edge of Independence National Historical Park, Old City has its share of worthy historic sites including Ben Franklin's grave and Elfreth's Alley. It's best known, however, for its lively nightlife and gallery scene, the result of a gentrification in the 1990s that transformed its dilapidated warehouses and factories into loft apartments and art studios.

Society Hill. This neighborhood between Old City and South Street is known for its preserved Federal and Georgian row homes and cobblestone streets. The only high-rises are three apartment towers designed by I. M. Pei in the 1970s to help revitalize the area.

South Street/Queen Village. South Street between 10th and Front Streets is a commercial strip of nightclubs, cheesesteak stands, and shops that sell everything from leather pants and Goth hair dye to antique armoires and Reeboks. To the south is Queen Village, a quieter neighborhood of narrow streets, antiques shops, and neighborhood BYO cafés that always seem to be buzzing.

Washington Square West. The sprawling neighborhood between Independence Hall and Broad Street contains the shopping districts of Jeweler's

BEN FRANKLIN WATCHES OVER AN OLD CITY STREET.

Row and Pine Street Antiques, several hospitals, and a mix of high-end restaurants, cheap electronics stores, and old taverns. It's also home to Gayborhood, the city's small but thriving gay community and a handful of bars and B&Bs.

Waterfront/Columbus Avenue. Once a busy port area, it is now known for its warm-weather festivals and wide-open views of the Benjamin Franklin Bridge. Penn's Landing, several big-box stores, and a couple of huge river-view bars like Dave and Buster's are the main anchors, but it's also home to Philly treasures like John's Roast Pork, a family-owned cheesesteak stand that has been around for decades. I-95 divides the waterfront from Old City and South Philadelphia, but there are two pedestrian bridges that lead to Penn's Landing.

✱ To See

MUSEUMS ♿ ☂ **Chemical Heritage Foundation Museum** (215-925-2222; www.chemheritage.org) 315 Chestnut Street. Free. Open Monday through Friday 10–4, until 8 PM on first Friday of the month. The periodic tables have never looked so good. This small two-story museum showcases chemistry's impact on our lives in sleek exhibits that combine fine art and high-tech images with antique tools and professorial explanations. A cool and tranquil respite from the tourist-filled historic sites that surround it, this may be Old City's least-known free attraction.

↑ **National Liberty Museum** (215-925-2800; www.libertymuseum.org), 321 Chestnut Street, Old City. Open daily in summer, Tuesday through Sunday the rest of the year; $7 adults, $2 ages 5–17. This eclectic museum is dedicated to promoting the ideals of freedom and diversity. Exhibits include a showcase of glass sculptures by Dale Chihuly, memorials to America's Nobel Peace Prize winners, and a gallery featuring frank images and statistics on youth violence. Tucked away in a corner on the upper levels you will find John Lennon's handwritten lyrics to "Beautiful Boy."

& ↑ **National Museum of American Jewish History** (215-923-3811; www.nmajh.org), 101 South Independence Mall East. Closed Monday and most Jewish holidays; $12 adults, $11 seniors and ages 12–21. Let other museums effectively cover the Holocaust, this large five-story building on Independence Mall instead focuses on 350 years of Jewish life in the U.S. There are films, interactive displays, and artifacts such as a pipe that belonged to Albert Einstein, a baseball glove owned by Sandy Koufax, and a Torah from Colonial times. It's hard to take it all in, in one visit.

& ↑ **Mummers Museum** (215-336-3050; www.mummersmuseum .org), 1100 S. Second Street (at Washington Avenue), South Philly. Closed Monday; $3.50 adults. Philadelphia's version of Madame Tussaud's, featuring wax figurines dressed in the feathered and spangled costumes that characterize the city's raucous New Year's Day parade. There's also an exhibit explaining the parade's history, as well as live string-band concerts in the summer (call for dates and times). This is the way to experience the Mummers Parade without having to endure the cold weather or the smell of hops.

HISTORIC SITES Carpenter's Hall (215-925-0167), 320 Chestnut Street. Open 10–4 daily; closed Monday and Tuesday, January and February; free. This redbrick Georgian building was the original home of a guild of

LIBERTY BELL, INDEPENDENCE HALL, SKYSCRAPERS

Independence Hall (215-497-8974), Chestnut Street, between Fifth and Sixth. Open 9–5 daily. If you have time to visit only one historic attraction in Philly, this is quite possibly the best choice. It's hard not to step inside and immediately sense the building's monumental significance and hear the echoes of "We the People" within its walls. Free guided tours of the restored Georgian building include a stop in the regal blue Assembly Room, where the Declaration of Independence was adopted in 1776 and the U.S. Constitution was drafted in 1787. Artifacts on display include the "rising sun" chair used by George Washington during the Constitutional Convention and the silver inkstand used in the formal signing of the Declaration of Independence and the Constitution. Between March and December, all visitors must pick up free timed tickets at the Independence Visitor Center. The 30-minute tours run every 15 minutes, but they do fill up, especially during the summer months. Outside the hall, you can take a guided horse and buggy ride through the historic district or grab a bench under a tree in Independence Square, site of the Declaration's first public reading. Across the street sits the Liberty

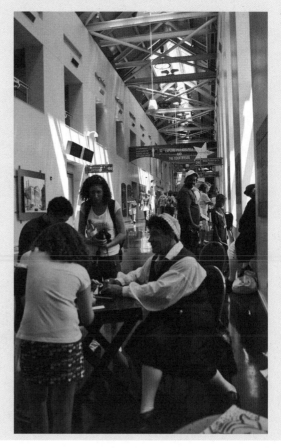

COSTUMED GUIDE POSES FOR PHOTOS AT INDEPENDENCE VISITOR CENTER.

INDEPENDENCE VISITOR CENTER

Bell Center (215-597-8974), Sixth and Market Streets, home to the 2,080-pound bronze bell that heralded the country's most significant achievements before cracking and becoming unusable in 1846. It's worth a brief stop, though it can be challenging to get a clear photo of the bell. Expect shoulder-to-shoulder crowds on weekends during the summer. It's free, but all visitors must pass a security screening. From April to October, the park hosts the Lights of Liberty Show, an audio-visual spectacular that takes visitors into the heart of the American Revolution through hand-painted images projected onto the buildings around the Independence National Historical Park, while a musical score composed for the show and performed by musicians of the Philadelphia Orchestra is played through special headphones. Get tickets at the visitor center.

carpenters and architects and served as the site of the First Continental Congress in 1774. It was also the site of the nation's first bank robbery. On display are some of the original Windsor chairs on which the representatives sat, as well as displays of carpenters' tools, and a parade float built to celebrate the ratification of the U.S. Constitution. It's easy to miss with all the other historic sites around but worth seeking out.

✿ **Franklin Court** (215-965-2305), 314-322 Market Street, Old City. Fans of Ben Franklin won't want to miss this fascinating complex of buildings and exhibits that pay homage to the city's wittiest and most influential inhabitant. Enter through a brick archway on Market Street to a courtyard where Franklin's original house once stood, now outlined by a steel frame "ghost sculpture" designed by architect Robert Venturi. The nearby underground museum, which underwent an $18 million renovation in 2011, displays Franklin's many inventions, plus a couple of oddities such as a motorized diorama depicting Franklin's career as a diplomat and a hall of mirrors featuring his most famous phrases. On the way out, stop by Franklin's small printing office and bindery, 320 Market Street, and take a postcard to get hand-stamped at the B Free Franklin Post Office two doors down.

OUTSIDE FRANKLIN COURT IN OLD CITY

✿ **Elfreth's Alley** (215-574-0560; www.elfrethsalley.org), Second Street, between Race and Arch, Old City. This narrow block of 32 row homes built between 1728 and 1836 is believed to be America's oldest continually occupied residential street. It is named for a blacksmith who once lived here, alongside carpenters, pewter makers, and other craftspeople of the period. Today, all but two of the homes are privately owned and occupied. No. 126 is a small museum that offers daily 15-minute tours, perhaps to

&. ♪ **Macy's,** in the fabled Wanamaker's building at Market and South 13th Streets, is home to the first and only pipe organ ever to be designated a National Historic Landmark. Its 28,000 pipes debuted in 1911 and still rattle the rafters of the grand old building two or three times a day, Monday through Saturday. Shows are at noon Monday through Saturday, 5:30 PM Monday, Tuesday, Thursday, and Saturday, and 7 PM Wednesday and Saturday. Many suburban Philadelphia kids (myself included) have fond memories of getting dressed up and taking the train into the city to watch the annual Christmas Light Show in the courtyard atrium—a light and sound extravaganza of dancing reindeer and snowflakes accompanied by organ music. The shows run hourly from the day after Thanksgiving through December 25. For more info, visit www.wanamakerorgan.com or call the store at 215-241-9000.

dissuade visitors from peeking into the windows of the other homes as residents try to cook supper. It's open year-round, but be sure to call ahead first. Many residents also throw open their doors to the public every June (see Special Events).

Christ Church Burial Ground (215-922-1695), Fifth and Arch Streets. $2 adults. Throw a good-luck penny on Benjamin Franklin's gravestone, located within the brick walls of this small cemetery that also holds the remains of Franklin's wife Deborah and several other signers of the Declaration of Independence.

♈ **Portrait Gallery** in the Second Bank of the United States (800-537-7676), 420 Chestnut Street. Open Tuesday through Saturday 11–4. Free. See the original portraits of the 18th-century luminaries you have been learning about at other historic sites in this magnificent Ionic-columned building. Highlights include George Washington's death mask and a small replica of Charles Willson Peale's natural-history collection in the back.

♈ **Masonic Temple** (215-988-1910) 1 N. Broad Street. Tours $8; $5 ages 12 and under. This stunning Norman-style structure near City Hall was a meeting place for 28 Philadelphia-based Masonic organizations in the 18th century. Guided tours of the seven extravagantly decorated lodge halls are given daily; call for exact times. A small first-floor exhibit includes George Washington's Masonic apron, a fragment of mahogany taken from his coffin, a collection of historic walking sticks, and many, many portraits of solemn white men.

✻ To Do

FOR FAMILIES ✏ ♿ ♈ **National Constitution Center,** open daily, except Thanksgiving, Christmas, and New Year's Day; $12 adults, $8 ages 4–8. It's easy to spend several hours in this sleek and spacious building on Independence Square. Begin your visit in the theater, where a live costumed actor tells the "We the People" story with the help of 360-degree multimedia images, then head to the high-tech exhibit hall where interactive, in-depth displays will appeal to both novice history students and serious historians. Older kids will have fun reciting the presidential oath of office from a podium and donning the robes of Supreme Court justices before rendering their opinions of key cases. Don't miss Signers' Hall, featuring life-size bronze statues of all 42 Constitution signers as they may have been seated or standing during the convention. The statue designers studied each delegate's height, weight, and facial features and made them so realistic you may feel the urge to strike up a conversation with George Washington or Ben Franklin.

✏ ♿ ♈ **Money in Motion** at the Federal Reserve Bank (866-574-3727; philadelphiafed.org). Open Monday through Friday 9:30–4:30 March through December and weekends throughout the summer. Free. See a $10,000 bill, exchange old quarters for the latest ones, learn how to identify counterfeit bills, and test your knowledge of the U.S. currency system via high-tech kiosks. Housed in the nation's first Federal Reserve Bank, this small kid-friendly exhibit requires a full body scan of all visitors, but is well worth a stop if you're in the vicinity of Independence Hall. Everyone is handed a small bag of shredded money on the way out.

✏ **Franklin Square** (215-629-4026; historicphiladelphia.org), Sixth and Race Streets. When the kids are about to wig out from history-lesson overload, this 7.5-acre park is where you want to go. An easy walk from Independence Hall and Constitution Center, it was completely overhauled in 2006 and features a carousel, playground, Philly-themed mini-golf featuring Independence Hall, the Liberty Bell, Boathouse Row, and other local icons ($8 adults), and vintage marble fountain. The SquareBurger kiosk (215-629-4026) sells good burgers, hot dogs, and Tastykake shakes; hours vary by season.

✏ **Penn's Landing** stretches along the Delaware River between Vine and South Streets and includes the spot where William Penn first arrived from England in 1682 aboard the ship Welcome. Once the center of Philly's maritime activities and a thriving commercial district, it's now a waterfront park with a promenade, outdoor events plaza, and nice views of the Benjamin Franklin Bridge. It's also home to **Independence Seaport Museum,** (215-413-8655; www.phillyseaport.org), a drab concrete building that belies the interesting exhibits on local and national shipping history inside.

MAGIC GARDENS

The little girl isn't sure whether she wants to have her photo taken below the bicycle spokes and empty green bottles, or beside the sun-dappled mosaic of a man's face; a passerby eventually captures her and her mother grinning and surrounded by an ethereal swirl of turquoise pottery shards and mirror triangles. Welcome to Philadelphia's kookiest and most endearing attraction. Artist Isaiah Zagar began tiling South Street in the 1960s with discarded factory porcelain and glass—and never stopped. The community stepped in to save the buildings from demolition in the 1990s, and the half-block complex is now run by a non-profit group (with Zagar making frequent appearances to teach workshops and answer questions). Anyone can gape at the floor-to-ceiling-tiled courtyard from the street, but to fully experience this folk-art masterpiece, pay $5 and wander through the labyrinthine rooms, closets, and basement. Watch a movie (made by his son) on Zagar's life and technique, then wander some more. Trained guides lead tours of the buildings and nearby street murals most Saturday mornings for $8–10 a person. Magic Gardens (215-733-0390; www.phillymagic gardens.org), 1020 South Street, $5 admission. Open daily.

A PEDESTRIAN SOAKS UP SOUTH STREET'S INDOOR-OUTDOOR ARTWORK

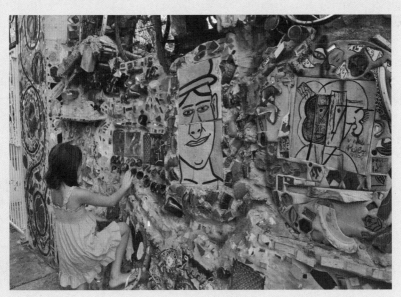

The museum also manages the USS *Olympia,* the oldest steel warship and only U.S. vessel remaining from the Spanish-American War and the USS *Becuna,* a submarine that patrolled the South Pacific during World War II. Admission to the museum is $9 and includes tours of both ships. The area hosts outdoor concerts, fireworks, and movies throughout the summer; go to www.pennslandingcorp.com for more information. It can be accessed by walking across the pedestrian bridge at Walnut and Front Streets or by car via I-95 at the Columbus Boulevard exit.

✳ Green Space

⌁ ♟ **John Heinz National Wildlife Refuge** at Tinicum (215-365-3118; www.fws.gov/northeast/heinz/), 8601 Lindbergh Boulevard. Open daily; free. This 1,200-acre refuge is just a mile from Philadelphia International Airport and home to the largest remaining freshwater tidal wetland in the state. Once threatened by plans to reroute I-95, it was saved by local environmentalists and the late senator for whom it's named. Today, you can hike, bike, canoe, and fish here. Wildlife includes muskrats, fox, deer, turtles, and 280 species of birds. The hiking trails are wide and flat and great for families and leashed dogs. Pick up a map at the Cusano Environmental Education Center near the entrance.

Race Street Pier, Race Street at Delaware Avenue. Walk over the Market Street pedestrian bridge to Penn's Landing and follow the waterfront sidewalk north about 0.5-mile to reach the city's newest and coolest park. Designed by the team behind Manhattan's High Line park, it's now a cantilevered recreational space with grass, trees, and benches with commanding views of the Ben Franklin Bridge. There's even WiFi access. It's about a 20-minute walk from Old City.

✳ Outdoor Activities

BOAT EXCURSIONS Ride the Ducks (215-351-9989; www.phillyducks .com) offers 80-minute tours of the historic district and Penn's Landing using World War II–era amphibious vehicles, from May to December.

RiverLink Ferry (215-925-5465), Penn's Landing. Open May through September; $7 adults, $6 kids. Ferries depart from Penn's Landing every hour, 9–6, and head across the river to the revitalized Camden, New Jersey waterfront, where there's the USS *New Jersey* battleship, and the kid-friendly Adventure Aquarium. The trip takes 15 minutes and offers terrific views of the Philly skyline. They also run express rides during, before, and after popular concerts at Susquehanna Bank Center.

BASEBALL The **Philadelphia Phillies** (215-463-1000; 1 Citizen Bank Way), 2008 World Series champs, play all their home games at the mod-

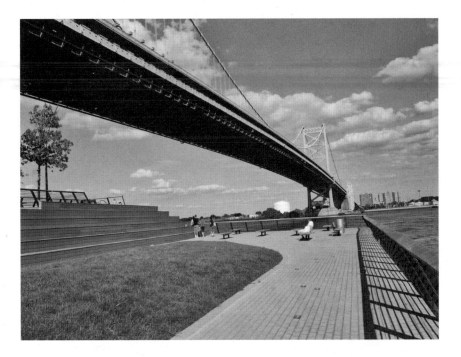

RACE STREET PIER'S PARK HAS VIEWS OF THE BEN FRANKLIN BRIDGE.

ern, fan-friendly Citizens Bank Park, which replaced Veterans Stadium in 2004. Year-round 90-minute tours are offered Monday through Saturday; call for times and reservations.

BASKETBALL The **76ers** (215-339-7676; 3601 S. Broad Street) play hoops at the Wachovia Center near Citizens Park. College basketball is big here: the **Drexel University Dragons** play at Daskalakis Athletic Center in University City (866-437-3935; Market Street between 33rd and 34th), while the **University of Pennsylvania's Quakers** play at the venerable Palestra Gymnasium (215-898-6151; 215 S. 33rd Street).

HORSE-DRAWN CARRIAGES, led by guides in Colonial garb, wind their way through the historic district on most days and evenings. Many local couples have become engaged during a romantic moonlit ride. Tours last anywhere from 15 minutes to an hour and cost from $25–70 for up to four people. Carriages line up on Chestnut and Sixth Streets near Independence Hall most days and at South and Second Streets most evenings.

ICE SKATING Blue Cross **RiverRink** (215-925-7465), Columbus Boulevard. at Market Street, is open for public skating late November through early March. A two-hour session is $6, skate rental $3.

✳ Lodging

HOTELS & INNS & **Alexander Inn** (215-923-3535, www.alexander inn.com), 12th and Spruce Streets. You can walk to Reading Terminal Market, the Broad Street theaters, and Old City historic sites from this attractive and efficient seven-story inn. It's often filled with a wide range of travelers, who like the discreet European-style service, stylish rooms, and reasonable rates. A practical breakfast of yogurt, cereal, fruit, and boiled eggs is served daily in a dining room off the lobby. There's a tiny gym in the basement. Rooms $119–169.

& **Omni Hotel** at Independence Park (215-925-0000; www.omni hotels.com), 401 Chestnut Street. History-minded visitors love the location of this sleek multi-story chain near Independence Hall and Constitution Center. Other perks: a small indoor pool, spa and fitness center, and complimentary shoeshines. Request a room on an upper floor for great views of the city and ask about packages that include tickets to local attractions and valet parking, which costs $37 a day. Rooms $125–199.

& **Penn's View Hotel** (215-922-7600; 800-331-7634; www.penns viewhotel.com), Front Street. This small family-owned hotel has a prime Old City location, elegant rooms, and dignified Old World vibe. The 27 rooms and suites are large and decorated in Colonial style; many have Jacuzzi tubs, fireplaces, or balconies. Try to snag one on the top floor facing the Benjamin Franklin Bridge (though that also means you'll have a distant view of I-95). It's an easy walk to Independence Hall, Penn's Landing, and Old City's nightlife. Another bonus: one of the city's best wine bars is downstairs (see Dining Out). Rooms and suites $159–259, including continental breakfast.

Morris House Hotel (215-922-2446; www.morrishousehotel .com), 225 S. Eighth Street, between Walnut and Locust Streets. This attractive 1787 Federal mansion was once home to Philadelphia mayor Anthony Morris. The 15 opulent rooms have modern amenities such as DVD players and complimentary wireless Internet access; extended suites with kitchens, living areas, and Jacuzzi tubs were added in 2005 in a separate wing. Afternoon tea is served daily by a roaring fireplace or in the peaceful back garden. Children are welcome. This is one of the few non-chain hotel alternatives in this area of the city, and it's a good one. Rooms $179–249, including continental breakfast. Parking in a garage across the street is extra.

✦ & ❀ **Loew's Philadelphia** (215-627-1200; www.loewshotels .com), 1200 Market Street. Yes, it's a chain that caters to convention crowds, but this 581-room hotel is housed in a beautiful Art Deco building that was renovated in 2000 and has many charms, including a large gym, friendly staff, and over-the-top pet services. Pets are allowed for an extra $25 per stay. The downside is it's on a busy, characterless section of Market Street. Rooms $159–300.

BED & BREAKFASTS The **Bed and Breakfast Connection** (800-448-3619; www.bnbphiladelphia .com), acts as a liaison for many private homes and small B&Bs in Center City, Valley Forge, and outlying areas including Bucks County and Lancaster. Rates usually range $80–200 a night and include breakfast. Some allow pets. Photos and descriptions of many of the homes are posted on the Web site.

Thomas Bond House (215-923-8523; www.thomasbondhouse bandb.com), 129 S. Second Street. Ben Franklin probably didn't sleep in this 1769 townhouse, but he surely knocked back a few within its walls with Mr. Bond, his friend and a prominent local physician. Now owned by the National Park Service, it sits next to a parking garage and is surrounded by many of Old City's top bars and restaurants. The 12 rooms are decorated in Colonial style with four-poster beds, working fireplaces (in some rooms), and Chippendale-period furniture; there are complimentary wines and cheeses in the evening and fresh-baked muffins at breakfast. It's not the most luxurious choice in the area, but it is a unique and affordable B&B option right in the heart of the city. Rooms $115–190.

✳ Where to Eat

DINING OUT ♿ ❢ **Buddakan** (215-574-9440; www.buddakan .com), 325 Chestnut Street. Lunch Monday through Friday, dinner daily. Sit next to the city's most beautiful people and enjoy edamame ravioli or tuna carpaccio pizza under the watchful eye of a gargantuan golden Buddha. Lunch $15–20, dinner $19–39.

Chloe (215-629-2337; chloebyob .com), 232 Arch Street. Dinner Wednesday through Saturday. Reliable BYO near Elfreth's Alley that is ideal for a quiet romantic dinner. The menu is simple but creative—grilled Caesar salad, tuna with soy-banana-ginger sauce, coffee-rubbed rib eye with house-made Worcestershire. No reservations. Entrées $17–29.

❢ **City Tavern** (215-413-1443; www.citytavern.com), 138 S. 2nd Street. Lunch and dinner daily. John Adams called it "the most genteel tavern in America." It still makes the most of the fact that the Founding Fathers dined here, catering to tour buses and having its servers channel Betsy Ross. The menu includes Colonial classics such as cornmeal-fried oysters, West Indies pepper pot soup, and turkey potpie. Yes, it has its own gift shop. Lunch $10–20, dinner entrées $18–33.

❢ **Fork** (215-625-9425), 306 Market Street. Lunch and dinner daily; brunch Sunday. This stylish bistro was one of the first upscale restaurants to open in Old City in the late 1990s and has outlasted many places that followed it. Owner Ellen Yin is a fixture in the handsome dining room, which has a visible kitchen and large *Cheers*-like bar. Look for innovative dishes such as penne with chervil-hazelnut pesto and garlic-crusted rib eye with guajillo-pepper coulis. For Old City club-goers, there's a late-night menu served Thursday through Saturday. Reservations recommended. Next door, Fork Etc. has gourmet prepared foods to go and a sitting area with WiFi access. Lunch $13–18, dinner entrées $19–30.

Kanella (215-922-1773), 1001 Spruce Street. Breakfast and lunch Thursday through Sunday, dinner Tuesday through Saturday. This blue-awning Greek BYO was named one of 59 best breakfast places in America by *Esquire* magazine in 2009. Dinners get frequent praise, too, but don't expect a tourist-friendly Greek taverna menu; instead you'll find sheep cheese pan-fried in ouzo, braised rabbit with butter beans and pasturma, and dorado grilled in grape leaves. It often closes for vacation in late August.

Koo Zee Doo (215-923-8080; www.koozeedoo.com), 614 N. 2nd Street, Northern Liberties. Dinner Wednesday through Sunday. Wonderfully authentic Portuguese dishes served in a cozy row home north of Old City. I suggest sitting at the kitchen counter if there's room, and saving room for dessert.

BYO. Entrées $24–36; tasting menu $50 per person.

Mercato (215-985-2962; www .mercatobyob.com), 1216 Spruce Street. Dinner daily. This is the place to go when you crave home-made papardelle or exquisite veal Parmesan before a Broad Street theater performance and don't want to drive to South Philly. It's tiny, and they only take pre-theater reservations (5–6:30 PM), but you can head down the street for a drink at **Valanni** and they'll call you when a table opens. Cash only, BYO. Entrées $19–26.

&. ⟨ **Ristorante Panorama** (215-922-7800), Front and Market Streets. Dinner daily. This Old World Italian restaurant in the Penn's View Hotel is known for its legendary wine bar, which offers more than 150 wines by the glass, flight, or bottle. The food is traditional and reliably good, as is the service. All the pasta is homemade and you may order appetizer sizes of any entrée. There's a divine triple-cream tiramisu for dessert. Entrées $22–29.

⟨ **Serrano** (215-928-0770), 20 S. 2nd Street. I have a soft spot for Serrano, as it was one of the first restaurant meals I had after moving to Old City in the late 1990s; bacon-wrapped meat loaf never tasted so good. It's not overly fancy or creative, just international comfort food (from seafood paella to chicken potpie) in a brick-walled dining room with good music upstairs at the Tin Angel. Entrées $16–29.

Ỿ **Vetri** (215-732-3478), 1312 Spruce Street. Closed Sunday. Marc Vetri's original Italian restaurant has been showered with praise by experts from Mario Batali to *Gourmet.* His intimate 35-seat dining room provides one of the city's most sensational culinary experiences. The $135 tasting menu might include crispy octopus with red-pepper soup, spinach gnocchi with shaved ricotta and brown butter, and foie gras-stuffed quail with cantaloupe. The 5,000-bottle wine cellar specializes in regional wines. Reservations required.

South Philly

Fond (215-551-5000; www.fond philly.com), 1617 E. Passyunk Avenue. Dinner Tuesday through Saturday. Le Bec Fin alum Lee Styer turns out salt-and-sugar-cured pork belly, crispy veal sweetbreads with caramelized fennel, and other creative dishes at this warm, yellow-walled café. You're a better person than I am if you can leave without sampling the malted-chocolate ice cream with peanut butter ganache. BYO. Dishes $9–26.

Tre Scalini (215-551-3870), 1915 E. Passyunk Avenue. Dinner Tuesday through Sunday. This veteran neighborhood BYO moved to bigger digs near Broad Street in 2010, but Franca DiRenza (now a nonna), is still the chef and the menu is still straightforward Italian inspired by her hometown of Molise. You can't go wrong with

the homemade gnocchi or veal piccante. Dishes $15–26.

Ỿ **Villa di Roma** (215-592-1295), 936 S. Ninth Street. Lunch Friday through Sunday; dinner daily. For a true South Philly experience, head to this family-run "gravy" trattoria in the center of the Italian market area. You'll forget about the no-frills ambiance and wagon-wheel chandeliers as soon as you whiff the oregano-spiked marinara sauce simmering in the kitchen or look at the reasonably priced menu. Regulars get misty-eyed over the fried asparagus in scampi butter; there are also steamed mussels marinara, spaghetti and meatballs, and sausage cacciatore. Dishes $11–27.

EATING OUT Brauhaus Schmitz (267-909-8814), 718 South Street. German beer hall in the heart of the South Street scene with a solid menu of bratwurst, crispy pork schnitzel, and Bavarian pretzels to die for. Dishes $6–12, entrées $16–28.

✿ **Dimitri's** (215-625-0556) 795 S. Third Street, Queen Village. Dinner daily. This popular BYO two blocks off South Street is known for its fresh Greek-style seafood. It doesn't take reservations, and you might wait up to 90 minutes for a table, but the food is worth it. Favorites include tender grilled octopus, spicy shrimp pil pil, and an appetizer of marinated olives and hummus. To kill time when there's a wait, hang out at the bar at the **New Wave Café** across the street, where the staff will fetch you when a table is ready. Cash only. Entrées $15–25.

Eulogy Belgian Tavern (215-413-1918; www.eulogybar.com), 136 Chestnut Street. Lunch and dinner daily. A fine place for a beer (choose from 300 brands) and a burger after catching a film at the Ritz 5.

Y ℰ **Jones** (215-223-5663; www .jones-restaurant.com), 700 Chestnut Street. Restaurateur Stephen Starr's latest crowd-pleaser serves fried chicken and waffles, beef brisket, Jell-O parfaits, and imaginative cocktails a block from Independence Hall.

♀ Y **Vietnam** (215-592-1163), 221 N. 11th Street, Chinatown. Lunch and dinner daily. Good food, reasonable prices, and a relaxing wood-paneling and bamboo ambiance. Try the crispy duck or anything that comes with a dipping sauce. Head upstairs to Bar Saigon for a Flaming Volcano or Mai Thai before dinner. There's also a branch in University City. Dishes $8–20.

Sabrina's Café (215-574-1599), 910 Christian Street. Breakfast and lunch daily, dinner Monday through Saturday. Tucked into three cozy rooms in a South Philadelphia row house, Sabrina's serves lunch and dinner, but is best known for its good and hearty breakfasts. The weekend brunch menu might include challah French toast stuffed with cream cheese or a three-egg frittata. No

reservations; expect a wait on weekends. BYO. There's another location at 1802 Callowhill Street in the Fairmount neighborhood. Breakfast and brunch $4–12; lunch and dinner $10–18.

Carman's Country Kitchen (215-339-9613), 1301 S. 11th Street. Breakfast and lunch Friday through Monday. Kentucky-born Carman Luntzel cooks according to season and whim in her tiny and colorful eatery in South Philly. The small menu might include cornflake-crusted French toast with Georgia peaches or wild game chili with fried eggs. Breakfast is usually terrific, if pricey for the neighborhood. Expect a wait on weekends. Dishes $12–15.

ℰ **Little Italy Pizza** (215-922-1440), 901 South Street. Stop here for a baked pizza roll or "bacon, chicken, and ranch" slice before or after a night out on South Street. There's plenty of indoor seating. Large pizzas start at $11.

COFFEE, SANDWICHES, & DESSERT ℰ **The Bourse** (215-625-0300), 111 S. Independence Mall, site of the first U.S. commodities exchange, is a good option for anyone looking for a quick meal that will allow you to resume your sightseeing agenda as quickly as possible. The first-floor food court has nearly a dozen counter-service options, including Sbarro and Bain's Deli, and seating is plentiful and pleasant.

Bean Café (215-629-2250), 615 South Street. La Columbe coffee, art on the walls, and a vibe that encourages you to linger over your laptop or latte.

Capogiro Gelato (215-351-0900; www.capogiro.com), 119 S. 13th Street (at Sansom). No flavor combination is too bold at this world-famous gelataria. Butterscotch intermingles with Wild Turkey bourbon, cilantro and lime make a fine sorbetto, and Lancaster County white peaches meet prosecco; it's a different menu every day, always fabulous. There are also branches in Rittenhouse Square (117 S. 20th Street), University City (3925 Walnut Street), and South Philly (1325 Passyunk Avenue). Check the Web site for hours. Did I mention that there are cappuccino and panini as well?

Cosmi's (215-468-6093; www .cosmideli.com), 1501 S. 8th Street, South Philly. Open daily. Folks line up for the cheesesteaks, which come with wiz, long hots (peppers), broccoli rabe, and more at this tiny corner deli. There are also authentic hoagies (from prosciutto to veggie), chili, pizza fries, and just about every other deli standard on the menu. The only seating is a fold-up table and chair on the sidewalk outside, so get it to go and enjoy it elsewhere.

Ishkabibble's (215-923-4337), 337 South Street. A popular spot for late-night chicken cheesesteaks, gravy fries, and water ice. Seating is limited to a few bar stools or the curb out front. Dishes $3–8.

Jim's Steaks (215-928-1911), 400 South Street. My personal favorite cheesesteak spot. Order on the first floor, watch the smooth line chefs assemble your sandwich, and bring it on up to the dining room, where you can watch the South Street scene unfold below.

♿ **John's Roast Pork** (215-463-1951), 14 Snyder Avenue (near Columbus). Open for breakfast and lunch Monday through Saturday. Outdoor seating only. Don't go for the ambiance, go for the excellent cheesesteaks, fried egg sandwiches, and hot pork sandwiches. Dishes $4–7.

JOHN'S ROAST PORK

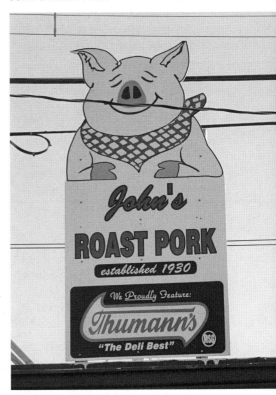

Old City Coffee (215-629-9292), 221 Church Street. Tucked off a cobblestone alley about three blocks from Independence Hall, this small shop serves the best coffee east of Broad Street. There's an attached seating area, and a few tables outside.

BYO Where to buy wine in Center City and South Philadelphia: **Wine & Spirits Shoppe** (215-560-6900; 724 South Street) offers a wide selection of wines and liquors in the heart of the South Street scene. In Old City, just south of Market, is **State Liquor** (215-625-0906; 32 S. Second Street). Closer to City Hall and the convention center is **State Liquor Super Store** (215-560-4381; 1218 Chestnut Street). You'll find a wine boutique with knowledgeable clerks inside the gourmet **Garces Trading Co.** complex (215-923-2261; 1111 Locust Street).

✳ Entertainment

MUSIC ♉ **Tin Angel** (215-928-0770; tinangel.com), 20 S. Second Street, attracts top acoustic and singer-songwriter acts that perform in an intimate café-style setting. Seating is unreserved, unless you dine at the excellent Serrano restaurant downstairs before the show (See Dining Out). Cover $10–20.

Painted Bride Art Center (215-925-9914; www.paintedbride.org), 230 Vine Street. A multifaceted

Old City gallery with changing art exhibits and a variety of cutting-edge dance, jazz, and spoken-word performances.

MOVIES/FILMS Ritz 5 (215-925-7900; www.landmarktheatres.com), 214 Walnut Street, opened in 1976 and is one of the best places to see first-run art and independent films in Philly. Now owned by Landmark Theatres, it's still a delightfully grown-up way to see a film; no kids under 6 are allowed and latecomers (15 minutes or more) are turned away. **Ritz at the Bourse,** a couple of blocks away at 400 Ranstead Street, has an additional five screens, and the **Ritz East** at 125 S. 2nd Street has two screens.

THEATER ♿ **Arden Theatre** (215-922-1122; www.ardentheatre.org), 40 N. Second Street, stages classic and cutting-edge dramas, comedies, and children's shows. It has a slew of awards to show for its work and has been named "Theatre Company of the Year" four times by the *Philadelphia Inquirer.*

♿ **Forrest Theatre** (215-923-1515; www.forrest-theatre.com), 1114 Walnut Street. The place to catch such touring Broadway productions as *Les Miserables* and *Jersey Boys.*

Society Hill Playhouse (215-923-0210; www.societyhillplayhouse.com), 507 S. 8th Street. Catch a new or long-running comedy like *Nunsense* in a beautiful

Victorian house off South Street. The downstairs Red Room hosts cabaret and British pub-style theater.

St. Stephen's Theater (215-829-0395; www.lanterntheater.org), 10th and Ludlow Streets. "Impressively diverse in genre and style" is how one local paper describes the Lantern's selection of classic, modern, and original plays.

&. **Walnut Street Theatre** (215-574-3550; www.walnutstreettheatre .org), 825 Walnut Street, is the city's oldest theater, serving as the debut stage for Ethel Barrymore and Edwin Forrest. It often features big Broadway musicals on its main stage.

NIGHTLIFE The Old City and South Street area are packed with nightspots that appeal to a variety of crowds.

Y **Lucy's Hat Shop** (215-413-1433), 247 Market Street. There's never a cover charge at this laid-back Old City joint. Pool tables, pinball machines, rock and roll DJs, and late-night happy hour specials keep the crowds coming.

Y **The Continental** (215-923-6069), 134 Market Street. Beautiful people sip espresso martinis and snack on tapas under olive-shaped halogen lamps in this diner-turned-cutting-edge nightspot. Weekday happy hours feature $6 cocktails.

Y **The Dark Horse** (215-928-9307), 421 S. Second Street. Formerly the Dickens Inn, this dark-walled English tavern just off South Street has four bars, a hearty pub menu, and TVs tuned to rugby and soccer matches.

Nick's Roast Beef (215-928-9411), 16 S. 2nd Street. Cheap bar food, beer bucket specials, and karaoke on weekends.

Standard Tap (215-238-0630), Northern Liberties. One of Philly's first craft brewpubs (with upscale snacks to match), it attracts a diverse crowd of artists, locals, and suits.

Center City
Dirty Frank's (215-985-9600), 347 S. 13th Street. Philly's finest dive bar, with a Sopranos pinball machine, darts, wood paneling, and cheap, strong drinks.

Y **McGillin's Old Ale House** (215-735-5562), 1310 Drury Street. Philly's oldest (and hardest to locate) pub is tucked in an alley between 13th and Juniper Streets. The brick-walled downstairs room is decorated with American flags, black-and-white cityscape photos, and framed liquor licenses that date back to the 1800s. The crowd tends to be young and festive; there's karaoke on Wednesday nights.

Y **Woody's** (215-545-1893), 202 S. 13th Street. Popular nightclub in the heart of Philly's small gay community. Theme nights include Latin music on Thursday and country line dancing on Friday. It's open to anyone, but expect a high male ratio.

✳ Selective Shopping

Philly has several quaint districts featuring a dozen or more stores that specialize in similar items. **Antiques Row** runs on Pine Street where you'll find shops selling grandfather clocks, estate jewelry, hand-carved cabinets, and more. **Jewelers' Row** is the place to go for discounted diamonds; its shops line a red-bricked block of Sansom Street between Seventh and Eighth Streets. In Old City, many art galleries stay open late on the first Friday of the month, when the area is a packed with art lovers and partyers (for more info, visit www.phillyartgalleries.com).

Old City

AIA Bookstore and Design Center (215-569-3188), 1213 Arch Street. One of the oldest chapters of the American Institute of Architects sells Philadelphia-centric gifts (neckties, miniature LOVE statues), children's toys, and an impressive selection of books on historic architecture, urban planning, Frank Lloyd Wright, and landscape design.

Art Star Gallery and Boutique (215-238-1557; www.artstarphilly .com), 623 N. 2nd Street. Whimsical jewelry, clothes, ceramics, and hostess gifts—most at very reasonable prices. The shop orchestrates a fabulous art bazaar with live music at Penn's Landing every May.

Clay Studio (215-925-3453; www.theclaystudio.org), 139 N. Second Street. Innovative selection of ceramic cups, bowls, vases, and tiles. There are all kinds of pottery-making classes and workshops for adults and kids.

Giovanni's Room (215-923-2960), 1145 Pine Street. Best selection of gay, lesbian, bisexual, and transgender literature in the city.

Scarlett Alley (215-592-7898), 241 Race Street, Old City. Stylish gifts for the person who has everything: designer cutting boards, ceramic bowls, cashmere robes, creative baby mobiles, and much more.

Viv Pickle (215-922-5904), 21 N. Third Street. A unique and colorful assortment of handbags, wallets, backpacks, and diaper bags. Or design your own with the help of a consultant.

Book Trader (215-925-0511), 7 N. Second Street. A reader's haven of used books, comfy old chairs, and friendly cats, just up the street from Elfreth's Alley. There's an especially strong cookbook section, and no one cares how long you linger (except maybe the cats who want your chair).

Robin's Books and Moonstone Arts Center (215-735-9600), 110 S. 13th Street, Center City. This venerable independent bookstore was forced to downsize and move upstairs during the recession, but it still offers a great selection of bargain books and a strong African American studies section. The arts center hosts poetry readings, book signings, and film screenings.

MARKETS ♿ **Reading Terminal Market** (215-922-2317; www.readingterminalmarket.org), 12th and Arch Streets. Open 8–6 daily, though some stalls are closed on Sunday and the Amish-owned stalls are closed Sunday through Tuesday. This fabulous indoor collection of food, flower, and produce stalls has been operating since 1893 on the lower level of the Reading Terminal, home to the largest single-arch train shed in the world. It's a great introduction to Philadelphia's flavors and people, and an excellent place to get a quick lunch if you're in the area. In the northwest corner, Amish women serve up scrapple, home fries, and eggs at the counter of the **Dutch Eating Place.** Across the way, you can take home Lancaster County baked goods such as whoopie pies, sticky buns, and shoofly pies, and sample soft pretzels still warm from the oven at **Fisher's.** Ice cream lovers won't want to miss **Basset's,** a venerable local ice cream company that serves the richest vanilla double dip around, and hungry omnivores should check out **DiNic's** for juicy roast pork sandwiches. Tucked in between the food stalls are vendors selling everything from used cookbooks to dried flower arrangements. **Taste of Philly** store sells chocolate-covered scrapple, Goldenberg peanut chews, and fun Philly-themed gift baskets. Saturday morning is the best time for people watching and for finding all the stalls open, though expect shoulder-to-shoulder crowds if a convention is in town (the

READING TERMINAL MARKET

SCRAPPLE

Along with soft pretzels, cheesesteaks, pork roll, and Italian water ice, scrapple will go down in history as a beloved local food that sets the Philadelphia area apart from the rest of the planet. You will find it on the menus and breakfast platters of most diners around here: a pan-fried gray slice of cornmeal mush and pork by-product that has been made fun of by outsiders more often than Johnny Carson dissed the city of Burbank. In reality, it's no worse, and arguably tastier, than a hot dog when made properly—a crisp exterior and soft creamy inside that tastes more like seasoned mashed potatoes than pig parts. Perhaps the best way to experience scrapple is at Reading Terminal's annual Scrapplefest (215-922-2317; www.readingterminalmarket.org). Held in March or April, it features scrapple-making demonstrations (not for the weak of stomach), tastings, a towering gray wedding cake fashioned out of scrapple, and an *Iron Chef*-like scrapple competition.

SCRAPPLE, A POPULAR PENNSYLVANIA BREAKFAST

convention center and several large hotels are nearby). **Italian Market,** Ninth Street between Washington and Christian, South Philadelphia. Closed Monday. Anyone who has seen *Rocky* will remember the boxer's famous training run through this indoor-outdoor street market on his way to the steps of the art museum. It's loud, rude, chaotic, and fascinating—a mix of outdoor stalls offering fresh produce, live seafood, bootleg CDs, and T-shirts, and brick-and-mortar stores selling spices, cheeses, homemade ravioli, and pastries. Several Mexican taco stands and Vietnamese grocers have opened in recent years and added to the area's vibrancy. **Tallutto's** (215-627-4967), a legendary Italian gourmet

shop known for its homemade pasta and imported meats, olive oils, and vinegars, anchors one end at 944 S. 9th Street, while **Fante's Kitchen Wares Shop** (215-922-5557; 1006 9th Street) is a chef's paradise of micro-graters and cavatelli makers.

✳ Special Events

January: **Mummers Parade** (New Year's Day), Broad and Market Streets—raucous string-band parade that began in the 1700s and features thousands of men (and a few women) strutting and strumming their way up Broad Street in outrageous sequined and feathered costumes.

March: **Philadelphia International Flower Show** (first and

SOUTH PHILLY'S ITALIAN MARKET

second week), Pennsylvania Convention Center—the world's largest indoor flower show with elaborate exhibits, expert lectures, and culinary demos, all of which are centered around an annual theme like the Legends of Ireland or Islands of Hawaii.

May: **Jam on the River** (Memorial Day), Penn's Landing—three-day waterfront festival featuring a diverse group of headliners that might include a Grateful Dead tribute band, reggae singers, progressive electronic bands, and rap groups, plus crafts displays and food vendors selling everything from cheesesteaks to crawfish pasta.

June: **Fete Day** (first Saturday), Elfreth's Alley—residents of America's oldest continually occupied street throw a block party and invite the public to partake of house and garden tours, live music, and crafts demonstrations (see also Historic Sites).

July: **Independence Day Celebration** (July Fourth), Historic District—series of events that begins with the awarding of the prestigious Liberty Medal in front of Independence Hall and capped by an evening concert and fireworks across town on the Benjamin Franklin Parkway.

September: **Live Arts Festival/ Philly Fringe** (first two weeks)—cutting-edge performances by dancers, acrobats, actors, clowns, and performance artists on stages all over the city. For more info, visit www.livearts-fringe.org.

October: **Outfest** (first weekend), Spruce and Pine streets, between 11th and 13th Streets—Philly's four-day National Coming Out Day festival has grown to be one of the largest in the world, with more than 150 vendors, performers, and community groups filling the city's "Gayborhood."

CENTER CITY WEST & UNIVERSITY CITY

GUIDANCE An information center in the east portal of **City Hall** (215-686-2840; Broad Street) has local guides and brochures, a retail store, and a video monitor showing continuous footage of local attractions. Purchase tickets for City Hall tours here (see also To See). There is also a visitor center for **Fairmount Park** at 16th Street and JFK Boulevard, in the spaceship-like building on the northeast corner, which has park maps and other info. Both are open 9–5 weekdays.

GETTING THERE By car: Several major interstate highways lead through Philadelphia. From the north or south, take I-95 to I-676 (Vine Street Expressway), which cuts right through the Center City area. From the west, I-76 (the Schuylkill Expressway) branches off the Pennsylvania Turnpike and heads to South Philadelphia, with exits for the Benjamin Franklin Parkway and 30th Street Station.

By air: **Philadelphia International Airport** (215-937-6800) is about a 20-minute drive from Center City Philadelphia, and served by all major airlines. SEPTA's R1 line offers direct service between Center City, University City, and the airport.

By bus: **Greyhound** (800-231-2222) and **Peter Pan** (800-343-9999) offer frequent service between Philadelphia and dozens of major cities.

By train: **Amtrak** (800-USA-RAIL) stops at 30th Street Station on its Northeast Corridor route between Richmond, Virginia, and Boston. SEPTA's R7 suburban train runs to Trenton, New Jersey, where New Jersey Transit trains run to New York's Penn Station. The R7 stops at Suburban station, about four blocks from Rittenhouse Square, and 30th Street Station.

GETTING AROUND SEPTA municipal buses run all over the city, though they can be daunting for first-time visitors. The Market–Frankford Line is a rapid-transit line that stops outside City Hall (Broad and Market) and near the University of Pennsylvania's campus, ending in the city's far

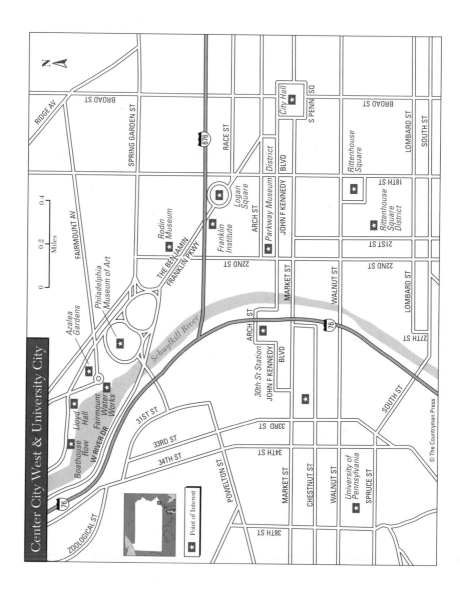

Center City West & University City

northwest corner. The purple **Phlash** bus (215-599-0776; www.philly phlash.com) runs a continuous loop between the city's major attractions, from Penn's Landing to the Parkway museums. Buses stop every 12 minutes at designated purple lampposts and operate daily May through September. Cost is $2 a ride, or $5 for an all-day pass.

MEDICAL EMERGENCY **Hospital of the University of Pennsylvania** (215-662-4000) 3400 Spruce Street, University City.

☀ Neighborhoods

Logan Square anchors the northeast end of the Benjamin Franklin Parkway and is one of five original planned squares laid out on the city grid. Originally called Northwest Square, the park has a somewhat macabre history of being a site of public executions and burial plots until the early 19th century. In 1825, it was renamed Logan Square after Philadelphia statesman James Logan. Among the sites you'll find nearby are the Academy of Natural Sciences, the Franklin Institute, the Free Library of Philadelphia, and the Roman Catholic Cathedral-Basilica of Saints Peter and Paul. It's also close to the art museum area, a pretty and walkable neighborhood of urban row homes, high-rise apartment buildings, and good local watering holes.

Rittenhouse Square. This affluent pedestrian-friendly neighborhood takes its name from the tree-filled square that anchors it. It is named after David Rittenhouse, the astronomer and descendent of Philadelphia's first papermaker, William Rittenhouse, and home to many of the city's top restaurants, hotels, and shops. Walnut Street between Broad and 21st Streets is its commercial pulse, but don't be afraid to wander; the historic architecture along residential streets like Spruce and Delancey are delightful. Residents vary widely, from silver-haired doyennes to young families and Penn graduate students.

RITTENHOUSE SQUARE

University of Pennsylvania, at 30th and Walnut Streets in West Philadelphia, is the city's oldest and most prestigious university. Founded by Benjamin Franklin and others in 1740, it boasts the nation's first medical, law, and business schools. While the neighborhood surrounding Penn has undergone a revitalization, the campus itself is worth a visit, whether you have a connection to it or not. Anyone may stroll across its attractive quadrangle and admire the Gothic-style buildings and centuries-old trees. Don't miss the three statues of Franklin on campus—one depicts the school's founder as a carefree teenager newly arrived from Boston, another as a portly statesman, and a third, seated on a bench engrossed in the *Pennsylvania Gazette.* Also worth checking out while here is the University Museum of Archaeology and Anthropology (215-898-4000; 3260 South Street; $10 adults; $6 children), home to a 12-ton sphinx, Egyptian mummies, and other artifacts the university has acquired through over 400 sponsored archaeological expeditions. Finally, art lovers should check out the latest exhibit at the bold Institute for Contemporary Art (215-898-5911; icaphila.org; 118 S. 36th Street), which hosted the first-ever museum shows of Andy Warhol and Laurie Anderson. Closed Monday and Tuesday; free.

BENJAMIN FRANKLIN AT PENN

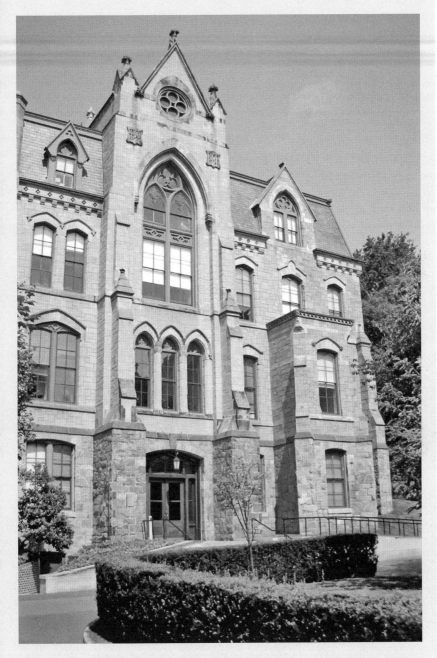

PENN'S GOTHIC ARCHITECTURE

University City. This West Philly neighborhood got its start in the late 1880s when the University of Pennsylvania moved across the Schuylkill River from Center City, though no one really referred to it by its current name until the 1960s. Life here still revolves around the Ivy League school (as well as nearby Drexel University). Though the area has struggled with blight and crime problems, you will find streets lined with beautiful old Victorian row homes, a luxury movie theater, national retailers, and many hip restaurants.

✵ To See

HISTORIC SITES Eastern State Penitentiary (215-236-3300; www .easternstate.org), 2124 Fairmount Avenue. Open daily April through November; $12 adults, $8 ages 7–12. Willie Sutton and Al Capone were among the inmates who slept in the vaulted, skylit cells of this 1829 prison, whose wagon-wheel design (and belief in reform through isolation) served as a model for dozens of other 19th-century prisons. Admission

---

WALKING PHILADELPHIA

For several years when I lived in Los Angeles, I was a contributor to the arts and entertainment section of the *Philadelphia Daily News.* That meant interviewing actors and directors about their work and lives. If they had ever spent any time in Philly, I also would ask about their best memories of the city. Sarah Jessica Parker remembered a mime who performed near her dad's place at the old Headhouse Square, Nicolas Cage liked the pizza at Tacconelli's, and Elizabeth Banks has fond memories of catching a show at the Theatre of Living Arts after a dinner date in South Philly. All good stories, but my favorite answer came from Rick Yune, who played a villain in the James Bond film *Die Another Day.* As a University of Pennsylvania student in the 1990s, he recalled his favorite running route: beginning at 40th and Chestnut in West Philly, east to the Delaware Avenue waterfront, then back. Whether you run, walk or stroll it, it's a fantastic way to experience the city—32 blocks that take you by historic sites, beautiful old churches, unexpected murals, top restaurants, brick homes, and gates that lead to secret gardens or alleys. Take Walnut one way and follow Chestnut back past Independence Hall, Washington Square, and City Hall, or zigzag between them and other parallel streets such as Spruce or Pine. The grid layout means you'll

includes a 30-minute guided tour of the decrepit cellblocks (including Capone's), plus interesting details on life as an inmate. The prison's popular "Terror Behind the Walls" event, held evenings in October, features five separate haunted houses, complete with howling prisoners and sadistic guards, and a DJ-hosted Monster Mash.

🐾 **Edgar Allen Poe National Historic Site** (215-597-8780; www.nps.gov /edal), 532 N. Seventh Street. Open 9–5 Wednesday through Sunday; free. The 19th-century horror author penned *The Tell-Tale Heart, The Fall of the House of Usher,* and more in this small brick house north of Old City. Ranger-led tours include a trip to the basement that's said to be the inspiration for *The Black Cat,* and engaging anecdotes about Poe's writing habits and family. The Park Service has deliberately left the rooms empty and the floorboards creaky, making the visit all the more creepy and reminiscent of the former resident. It's a little off the beaten path, but it's a must for Poe fans and literary buffs.

A MURAL NEAR RITTENHOUSE SQUARE

never get lost (though you may have to share the sidewalk with many pedestrians in some places), and you'll end with a better sense of the city's eclectic mix of academia, history, and blue-collar pride.

Laurel Hill Cemetery (215-228-8200; www.thelaurelhillcemetery.org), a national historic landmark whose tenants include astronomer David Rittenhouse, 40 Civil War–era generals, and 6 victims of the *Titanic* sinking. It's a peaceful place for a stroll or jog, with a bluff-side setting overlooking the Schuylkill River. The office sells a map and guide for $5, or you can take a guided theme tour, such as "Ghosts Among Our Graves" or "Sinners, Scandals, and Suicides" for $10–20. Call for days and times.

City Hall (215-686-2840), Broad Street ($10 adults; $8 ages 3–18). Tours Monday through Friday at 12:30. This granite monolith in the center of town, capped by a 37-foot statue of William Penn, has the distinction of being the country's largest and most costly municipal building. It's also a beautiful example of Victorian architecture, when it's not hidden by scaffolding. The 90-minute tour details the building's history, architecture, and sculpture, and includes a visit to the tower observation deck. Tours of only the observation deck, which affords one of the best panoramic views in the city, run every 15 minutes 9:30–4 for $5. All tours leave from the information center near the east entrance.

CITY HALL

MUSEUMS ઠ **Philadelphia Museum of Art** (215-763-8100), 2600 Benjamin Franklin Parkway. Closed Monday; $16 adults, $12 ages 13–18. Park in the garage for $10 with validation, or seek out a free space on the streets off the parkway. This grandiose Greco-Roman temple is America's third-largest art museum and home to more than 225,000 works of art, including important collections of Pennsylvania German and French impressionist paintings and 18th- and 19th-century furniture. The third floor features a stunning reconstructed Hindu stone temple that dates back to 1550, a Medieval French cloister with a massive Romanesque fountain, and a cedar-thatched Japanese teahouse designed by Ogi Rodo and purchased by the museum in 1928.

GREAT HALL OF THE PHILADELPHIA MUSEUM OF ART

Allow for at least several hours to tour the 200 galleries; one of my favorite spots to rest is the Resnick Rotunda in the European Art section, where masterpieces by Van Gogh, Cezanne, and Renoir surround benches and a gurgling fountain. If you don't have time to go inside, you can jog, Rocky-style, up the steps of the grand old building, or just settle for posing next to a bronze statue of the Italian Stallion at the foot of the steps at the east entrance. The museum throws a big "Art after 5" cocktail party every Friday evening with live music, movie screenings, and mingling events. In 2007, the museum opened the Ruth and Raymond G. Perelman Building across the street at 2501 Benjamin Franklin Parkway. It features special exhibits, as well as the museum's photography and textiles collections. Shuttles run every 15 minutes, though it's an easy walk between the two buildings. Food options include the elegant Granite Hill café or the busy cafeteria, which serves healthy (though expensive) lunches.

PHILADELPHIA MUSEUM OF ART AND WATER WORKS

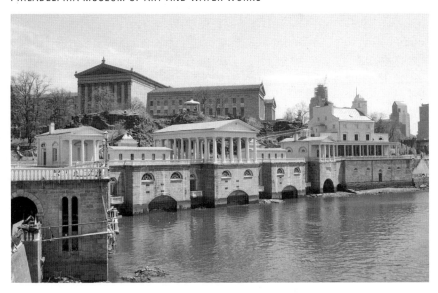

 Rodin Museum (215-763-8100; www.rodinmuseum.org), Benjamin Franklin Parkway at 22nd Street. Open Tuesday through Saturday; $5 suggested donation. Home to the largest collection of Auguste Rodin sculpture outside of France, including his most notable works, *The Thinker* and *The Burghers of Calais*. The museum closed in late 2011 for a major overhaul and was expected to reopen in mid-2012, though its gardens were to remain open during renovations.

 Rosenbach Museum & Library (215-732-1600; www.rosenbach.org), 2010 Delancey Place. $10 adults, free Tuesday. Bibliophiles will love the intriguing literary treasures found in this 1863 double townhouse off Rittenhouse Square: James Joyce's handwritten manuscript for *Ulysses*, a lock of Charles Dickens's hair, and Bram Stoker's notes and outlines for *Dracula*, to name a few. The owners and brothers, A. S. W. and Philip Rosenbach, were 19th-century art and book dealers; there are also personal letters penned by George Washington, the reassembled Greenwich Village living room of poet Marianne Moore, and more than 10,000 illustrations and manuscripts by Maurice Sendak. Tours are given several times a day.

 & Pennsylvania Academy of Fine Arts (215-972-7600; www.pafa .org), 118 N. Broad Street. Open Tuesday through Sunday; $10 adults, $8 ages 5–18. An impressive collection of American paintings and sculpture by Benjamin West, Mary Cassatt, Thomas Eakins, Winslow Homer, and others housed in an exquisite Victorian Gothic building that served as the nation's first art museum and school. Next door, the contemporary Samuel M. V. Hamilton building displays works by Georgia O'Keefe, Roy Lichtenstein, and Mark Rothko.

 Mütter Museum (215-563-3737; www.collphyphil.org), 19 S. 22nd Street. $14 adults, $10 ages 6–17. In 1858, Thomas Dent Mütter, a retired professor of surgery, donated his spectacular collection of cancerous tumors, skeletons, and other anatomic specimens and medical artifacts to the College of Physicians of Philadelphia. Today, they're on display in all their gruesome glory in several large rooms off the school's lobby. The 8-foot colon is always a jaw-dropper; you'll also find skeletons that demonstrate the lasting effects of corsets on the torso and a display of book bindings made out of human skin. A new Civil War Medicine exhibit includes a piece of Lincoln assassin John Wilkes Booth's thorax and the dried, bloodied arm of Major Henry Rathbone, who was stabbed while trying to keep Booth from fleeing the Ford Theatre. The small gift shop is chock full of fun, macabre gifts such as cadaver soaps and crocheted skulls.

✳ To Do

FOR FAMILIES & 🖉 Franklin Institute Science Museum (215-448-1200; www.fi.edu), 222 N. 20th Street. Open 9:30–5 daily. Adults $15.50,

THE ENTRANCE TO ONE OF PHILLY'S ODDEST MUSEUMS, THE MÜTTER

seniors and children 4–11, $12. Kids and grown-ups alike will find many things to enjoy at this favorite Parkway attraction. Founded in 1824, it has a planetarium, an IMAX theater, and many hands-on exhibits that celebrate and teach the wonders of science, from sports to trains to Isaac Newton. A walk through the giant papier-mâché replica of a beating heart is a must—so is a stop in the Franklin Gallery, where you'll find many of Ben's own inventions and models, including his lightning rod and a reproduction of his bifocals.

✣ ♿ **Academy of Natural Sciences** (215-299-1000; www.ansp.org), 1900 Benjamin Franklin Parkway. Adults $12, ages 3–12, $10. Open daily. Another Philly attraction that was the first of its kind (it's the nation's oldest natural history museum), this neighbor to the Franklin Institute is the place to go for dinosaurs and enormous mounted-animal dioramas. Future paleontologists can dig for fossils in Dinosaur Hall (weekends only) and mingle with live butterflies (for an additional $2) in a re-created rain forest.

✣ ♿ **Please Touch Museum** (215-963-0667; www.pleasetouchmuseum .org), 4231 Avenue of the Republic. Children and adults $15. It's expensive, especially for large families, but it's a magical place for the under-eight set in the grand setting of Fairmount Park's Memorial Hall. Six interactive zones are divided by theme: City Capers, Flight Fantasy, Wonderland, Roadside Attractions, River Adventures, and Rainforest Rhythm.

Covering 9,200 acres that resemble the shape of an elephant's head, **Fairmount Park** (215-683-0200; www.fairmountpark.org) is one of the nation's oldest and largest urban parks. It lines either side of the Schuylkill River from the Philadelphia Museum of Art north to Manayunk, then snakes west and north through the leafy Wissahickon Valley. You could spend days here and not cover all of its diverse attractions. Maps are usually available at Lloyd Hall, the modern two-story community center that has a café with limited hours and a bike rental outfit. The lower section (from Falls Bridge south to the art museum) is the part that's easiest to access from Center City. It includes Boathouse Row, a line of Victorian boathouses along Kelly Drive that make up a group called the Schuylkill Navy. (East River Drive was renamed Kelly Drive in 1985 after local oarsman Jack, who also happened to be Grace Kelly's brother.) Each boathouse is decorated with strings of lights, creating a festive gingerbread-house-style display at night; I've passed Boathouse Row at night hundreds of times and never fail to be awed by the sight. Below is a collection of the lower park's best attractions. For information on the upper section of Fairmount Park, see Chestnut Hill, Germantown, and Manayunk.

✐ **Philadelphia Zoo** (215-243-1100; www.philadelphiazoo.org), 3400 W. Girard Avenue. Open year-round. $18 adults, $15, ages 3–11. The country's oldest zoo is a compact 42 acres that is home to 1,800 species of animals, including polar bears, red pandas, camels, and two rare white African lions. Kids will love the $6 camel rides and swan boats (also $6). Its newest attraction is the Zooballoon, a hot-air balloon ride that gives you a bird's-eye view of the animals. Parking will set you back another $12.

Nearby is the **Smith Civil War Memorial Arch,** 4231 N. Concourse Drive, which honors the state's Civil War heroes. At its base are the whispering benches, developed in a way that a whisper into the wall at one end will carry all the way to the other end. It's also a popular local spot to get engaged or steal a first kiss.

After the yellow fever epidemic in 1793, many city dwellers built country homes along the Schuylkill River to escape the heat and disease. Today, many of these **Fairmount Park Mansions** remain intact and about a dozen are open several days a week for tours. The neoclassical **Lemon Hill** (215-235-1776; 7201 N. Randolph Drive) in the park's eastern section was meticulously restored in 2005 and has three stacked oval rooms with curved doors and floor-to-ceiling Palladian windows. **Strawberry Mansion** (215-228-8364; 2450 Strawberry Mansion Drive) so named because it once served as a restaurant with a signature dessert of strawberries and cream, is known for its antique toy and doll collection and array of Federal and Empire furniture.

The park's most interesting and unsung mansion has got to be the **Ryerss Museum and Library** (215-685-0544; 7370 Central Avenue), about a 20-minute drive from Center City in the city's Fox Chase section. Robert Ryerss, president of the Tioga Railroad and an avid collector of Asian art and artifacts, scandalized society when he married his housekeeper eight months before he died and willed her his family's Italianate summer home with the stipulation that she eventually leave it to the city to run as a public museum. She did, but not before traveling around the world and adding to her husband's 25,000-piece collection with such treasures as an 11th-century Buddha from Japan and a Chinese papier-mâché puppet theater.

SWAN RIDES AT THE PHILADELPHIA ZOO

FAIRMOUNT PARK'S RYERSS MUSEUM AND LIBRARY

Don't miss the family's beloved pet cemetery. Tours are free (Friday through Sunday), also at the behest of Mr. Ryerss.

Wissahickon Valley Park (215-685-9285) is part of the Fairmount Park system and stretches northwest along the Wissahickon Creek past Chestnut Hill. It's home to breathtaking natural settings and some of the best hiking and biking trails in the city. Maps and free trail permits are available at the **Wissahickon Environmental Center** (215-685-9285, 300 Northwestern Avenue), located at the north corner of the park and a short drive from the Morris Arboretum. On the site of a former nursery, it's worth a stop alone for its huge wildlife mural, aquarium, and helpful staff.

Other top attractions include **Rittenhouse Town** (215-438-5711, 206 Lincoln Drive), the site of the first paper mill in North America, built in 1690 by William Rittenhouse (great grandfather of David, the scientist for whom Rittenhouse Square is named). By the late 18th century, the area grew into a small self-sufficient community with more than 40 buildings. Today, seven buildings remain, including a barn that houses a papermaking studio and the original Rittenhouse family homestead and bakehouse. Pick up a self-guided walking map at the visitor center, or try to visit on a weekend in the summer, when guided tours are given. Call for specific hours. Even when the buildings aren't open, its creek-side setting just off Lincoln Drive is a pleasant place to read or let the kids run around.

Forbidden Drive is the park's top hiking, biking, and equestrian trail, a wide gravel road that parallels Wissahickon Creek. It has been closed to car traffic since the 1920s (hence the name) and begins off Lincoln Drive near RittenhouseTown, winding 5 miles one way past WPA shelters from the 1930s, a covered bridge, and dense woodland to Northwestern Avenue at the city's limits. A local rite of passage is brunch at the Valley Green Inn (see also Eating Out), a full-service restaurant with a front porch that over-looks the trail. There's even a place to hitch your horses while you eat.

WISSAHICKON'S FORBIDDEN DRIVE TRAIL

Philadelphia-born parents will appreciate the preserved set and props from *Captain Noah and his Magical Ark,* a favorite TV show shot locally in the 1970s. It is $8 to park in the museum's lot, or there's usually plenty of street parking.

🐾 **Smith Memorial Playground** (215-765-4325; www.smithkidsplayplace .org), 33rd and Oxford Streets. Free. Open 10–4 Tuesday through Sunday, April through October. The average plastic playground will never look the same again after you've taken the kids to this fabulous 6-acre space in east Fairmount Park just above Kelly Drive. There's a wooden slide, a giant spider web for climbing, and a three-story play mansion for kids five and under, full of toys, tricycles, and a kid-friendly kitchen.

SCENIC DRIVES A pleasant urban drive begins at the Museum of Art and follows Kelly Drive north past Boathouse Row. Turn right at Hunting Park Avenue and look for Laurel Hill Cemetery on the bluff to your left, cross Ridge Avenue, and then turn left onto Henry Avenue and follow it about a mile to 3901 Henry Avenue, site of the childhood home of Grace Kelly. Continue north on Henry Avenue about 3 miles past neighborhoods of brick and stone row houses and make a right onto Wise's Mill Road, which will bring you back into Fairmount Park. Follow the narrow tree-lined road as it winds next to the Wissahickon River to the **Valley Green Inn** (215-247-1730), where you can have a leisurely lunch or brunch on its front porch overlooking the creek and bicycle path.

✳ Outdoor Activities

BICYCLING/RENTALS The **Schuylkill River Trail** is a paved bicycle and jogging trail that follows the Schuylkill River 23 miles from Center City to Norristown. A popular 9-mile loop for walkers, joggers, and cyclists begins at the art museum, runs north past Boathouse Row and up the east bank of the Schuylkill, crosses the river at Falls Bridge, and works its way back to the museum along the west side of the river.

Bike rentals are available near the path's Center City portion from **Trophy Bikes** (215-222-2020), 3131 Walnut Street (in the Left Bank apartment building). Bikes are $20 for 4 hours, $25 for 24 hours. Over near the art museum, you can rent bikes and rollerblades on weekends from **Drive Sports 2** (215-232-7900), 1 Boathouse Row, next to Lloyd Hall, or from **Fairmount Bicycles** (267-507-9370), 2015 Fairmount Avenue.

The city closes the 4-mile stretch of Martin Luther King Drive west of the Schuylkill River to vehicular traffic on weekends between April and October; it fills up fast with cyclists, runners, and in-line skaters.

ALONG BOATHOUSE ROW

BOATING Rowing along the Schuylkill near Boathouse Row is reserved for trained athletes, but anyone can play spectator on the river's banks. April through September, you can watch regattas on the Schuylkill River, which have been held for more than a century. Contact the **National Association of Amateur Oarsmen** (215-769-2068) or the **Boathouse Association** (215-686-0052) for a complete schedule of races.

FISHING You can fish for bass and catfish behind the Philadelphia Museum of Art at the **Water Works** pier, and along the river north of **Boathouse Row.** A required license of $21 for Pennsylvania residents, or $25 for out-of-staters, is available weekdays at the Municipal Services Building, 1401 John F. Kennedy Boulevard, near the visitor center.

GOLF Cobbs Creek Golf Club (215-877-8707), 7200 Lansdowne Avenue, a well-maintained course on the northwest edge of the city, offers a challenging par-71 course.

HORSEBACK RIDING Chamounix Equestrian Center (215-877-4419; www.worktoride.net), 98 Chamounix Drive, Fairmount Park. Riding lessons are available Wednesday and Friday through Sun. April through November. It's $140 for 4 one-hour lessons. Nearby bridle trails.

✳ Green Space

Bartram's Gardens (215-729-5281; www.bartramsgarden.org), 54th Street and Lindbergh Boulevard. Open daily 10–5, except holidays. John Bartram planted what would become the nation's oldest living botanical garden here in 1728. It's a beautiful property despite its location in the middle of an industrialized neighborhood near the airport, with a boardwalk trail, 15-acre meadow, and the world's oldest gingko tree. Guided tours of Bartram's original 1731 house and garden are available for $10 a person Friday through Sunday, April through October; admission to the grounds is free. There's also a boat ramp with access to the Schuylkill River.

Clark Park (www.friendsofclarkpark.org), 43rd Street at Baltimore Avenue, University City. A life-size bronze statue of Charles Dickens oversees 9 acres of welcome green space, trees, and a playground. In February, the park throws a party in honor of Mr. Dickens's birthday; it also hosts outdoor movies, youth soccer, flea markets, and Shakespeare in the summer. There's a very popular farmers' market on Saturday mornings and Thursday evenings from April through November.

Penn Park, 31st Street between South and Walnut Streets. In 2011, the University of Pennsylvania in 2011 transformed an old Post Office parking lot into a lush 24-acre park beneath the Walnut Street Bridge, calling it a "gateway between Center City and West Philadelphia." It has tennis courts, jogging paths, two athletic fields, and stellar views of the Philadelphia skyline.

✳ Lodging

HOTELS & INNS & **Rittenhouse Hotel** (215-546-9000; www.rittenhousehotel.com), 210 W. Rittenhouse Square. If you're looking to splurge on accommodations, this is the place to go. Overlooking one of the city's best public squares, it has 98 elegant and spacious rooms, luxurious marble bathrooms, and attentive service. The amenities are endless: plush bathrobes, twice-daily maid service, an indoor pool, fitness center, and TVs in the bathrooms. It's also home to LaCroix, one of the city's top French restaurants and brunch spots. Rooms $299–480, suites $640–2,500.

& ✿ **Sofitel** (215-569-8300), 120 S. 17th Street. Hip and businesslike at once, this 306-room hotel was once home to the Philadelphia Stock Exchange and is in a prime location near Rittenhouse Square's best bars and restaurants. The handsome rooms were renovated in 2000 and have cloudlike king beds and modern cherry-wood furniture. Rooms $295–420.

& **Club Quarters** (215-282-5000; www.clubquarters.info), 1628

Chestnut Street. This private hotel for business travelers opens its doors to nonmembers on weekends (and occasional weekdays) through Internet booking services such as Orbitz and Hotels.com. The rooms are on the small side, but spotless and attractively decorated with mahogany furniture and colorful linens. There is free high-speed Internet access throughout the hotel, a small fitness center, and 24-hour room service. The inviting lobby is stocked with magazines, comfy couches, and brewed coffee. Rooms $89–119 (weekday rates are more).

&. **Hotel Palomar** (215-563-5006) 117 S. 17th Street. The hip boutique hotel chain opened near Rittenhouse Square in 2010. Its 230 rooms and suites blend luxury with a bit of Zen (high-end Frette linens, free yoga products to borrow, evening wine hour for guests). Pets are welcome and even treated like royalty at no extra charge. Rooms and suites $179–409.

&. **Independent Hotel** (215-772-1440, www.theindependenthotel .com), 1234 Locust Street. The 24 rooms and suites in this historic hotel are comfortable, spacious, and art-filled and come with mini-fridges and microwaves. Other reasons to stay here: the service is excellent, and it tends to be quiet in spite of its location in the center of the theater district. A Continental breakfast is included,

though parking is not. The queen loft suite is ideal for families. Rooms $149–179, suites $189–209.

BED & BREAKFASTS

La Reserve (215-735-1137; www.lareservebnb.com), 1804 Pine Street. Centrally located in a residential neighborhood a few blocks from Rittenhouse Square, this 19th-century townhome has six comfortable rooms, some with shared baths, and one efficiency apartment. Guests are encouraged to play the baby grand piano in the lobby or read in the elegant library. Parking is challenging around here, but there is a small discount at a nearby parking lot. Rates $80–175 (includes breakfast).

University City

&. **Inn at Penn** (215-222-0200; www.theinnatpenn.com), 3600 Sansom Street. Just as the name implies, this 238-room inn caters to those with connections to the University of Pennsylvania, which sits just across the street. It is run by the Hilton chain, but maintains an independent and polished academic air. Rooms are large and elegant and include coffeemakers, plush robes, and high-end bath amenities. There's also a fitness center, a restaurant, and a clubby lounge called the Living Room, where coffee, tea, and cocktails are served. Rooms start at $169, but can skyrocket during graduation time.

Gables (215-662-1918; www .gablesbb.com), 4520 Chester Avenue. Built in 1889, this beautiful Victorian building with its wraparound porch and gardens is a less expensive and homier alternative to the big hotels surrounding Penn. It's near Spruce Street, about six blocks from Penn's campus. Owners Don Caskey and Warren Cederholm bought and restored the place in the early 1990s; many of the 10 rooms feature antique brass beds and fireplaces; 2 have shared baths. Breakfast might include baked almond French toast or sausage and veggie strata. Rooms $115–185.

HOSTELS Chamounix Mansion (215-878-3676; www.philahostel .org), 3250 Chamounix Drive, Philadelphia. This 1802 country estate in Fairmount Park attracts a wide mix of frugal travelers for its leafy setting and close proximity to Center City. Each dormitory-style room has between 4 and 16 beds and little else. The elegant parlor in the main house, however, will make you feel like a privileged guest of the original owners. There are also laundry and kitchen facilities, and Internet access. Beds $20–23.

✳ Where to Eat

DINING OUT Audrey Claire (215-731-1222), 20th and Spruce Streets. Dinner Tuesday through Sunday. This terrific corner bistro near Rittenhouse Square serves Mediterranean-influenced dishes such as roasted chicken with lemon and feta, and garlic-crusted rack of lamb. Don't miss the amazing selection of appetizers, especially the grilled flatbreads and spicy hummus. No reservations; be prepared for a long wait on weekends. BYO. Entrées: $14–20.

Le Bec Fin (215-567-1000; www.lebecfin.com), 1523 Walnut Street. Open since 1970 and still the finest special-occasion restaurant in the city. Georges Perrier impresses newcomers and regulars alike with his exquisite French cuisine and near-perfect service. Whatever you do, do not miss the dessert cart: It is life changing. Tasting menus: lunch, $35–55, dinner $80–185.

🍸 **Nineteen** (215-790-1919), 200 S. Broad Street. Open daily for lunch and dinner, Sunday brunch. This 19th-floor restaurant in the Park Hyatt at the Bellevue has panoramic views of the city, fabulous cuisine, and an elegant dining room featuring a raw bar and a huge pearl chandelier. The menu emphasizes simple seafood and steaks, with such dishes as Boston cod fish and chips, steak frites, and bouillabaisse with garlic aioli. The $20 three-course café lunch is a bargain. Don't miss the signature dessert: lemon-foam carrot cake served with cream cheese sorbet. Dinner entrées: $18–36.

🍸 **Osteria** (215-763-0920; www .osteriaphilly.com), 640 N. Broad Street. Lunch Thursday and Friday, dinner daily. Marc Vetri's ode to rustic Italian country food opened in the Fairmount area in 2007 and quickly became a local favorite. The food is indisputably spectacular: Go for the black-pepper ravioli with peaches and guancalier or the rosemary-marinated veal with mushrooms and cherries, or keep things simple with a thin-crusted margherita pizza. Pizzas $15–19, entrées $24–35.

  Ɫ ℟ **Rouge** (215-732-6622), 205 S. 18th Street. Open daily for lunch and dinner. When it opened in 1998, this stylish late-night bar and restaurant was the first to take advantage of the stellar views of Rittenhouse Square. Its patio is always hopping. The food tends to be American with a French influence: monkfish in tomato-saffron broth, crispy oyster salad, and pommes frites. Extensive wine list. Small dishes $10–16, entrées $23–33.

  ℟ **Tria** (215-972-8742; www.tria cafe.com), 123 S. 18th Street. Sleek and stylish, it's perfect for an after-dinner drink and light meal. The excellent wine list is longer than the menu, and the cheese list (ranked by stinky, approachable, stoic, and racy) is longer than an average grocery list. A fine selection of local and imported beers, too. There are two other locations at Washington Square West and University City. Dishes $4–10.

University City
℟ **White Dog Café** (215-386-9224), 3420 Sansom Street. Open for lunch and dinner daily, Sunday brunch. This gourmet hub for social activists is Philadelphia's version of Berkeley's Chez Panisse. Its menu pushes locally grown and raised produce; you might find Kung Pao tofu with toasted peanuts and free-range Lancaster County chicken for dinner, and smoked salmon sandwiches with caper cream cheese for lunch. The piano parlor features live music on Friday and Saturday nights, and there are regular lectures and film events. Lunch and brunch $10–15, dinner entrées $16–29.

Marigold Kitchen (215-222-3699; www.marigoldkitchen byob.com), 501 S. 45th Street. Serves a small, appealing Mediterranean-influenced menu in a cozy Victorian brownstone on a quiet residential street a few blocks from Penn's campus. Dinner highlights include squab with chocolate foie gras ragout, and Berkshire pork tenderloin with white bean puree, pretzel crumbs, and Guinness suds. Reservations recommended. BYO. Entrées $20–36.

  Ɫ ℟ **Distrito** (215-222-1657; www.distritorestaurant.com), 3945 Chestnut Street. Lunch and dinner daily. Go for the modern Mexican cuisine (pork belly mole, yellowtail ceviche); stay for the superb margaritas and neon-hued party ambiance. Request the Volkswagen table even if you don't bring the kids. Dishes $8–12, entrées $19–33.

✿ **Sycamore** (484-461-2867; www.sycamorebyo.com), 14 S. Lansdowne Avenue, Lansdowne. A "cocktail-loving BYO" just over the West Philadelphia border with tasty, creative dishes such as molasses cumin-brined pork chop with macerated plums, and shiitake-stuffed pierogi with smoked paprika oil. Weekday specials include chef's tastings and a $25 Movie Night Special in partnership with Cinema 16:9 down the street. Entrées $20–29.

EATING OUT The Market at Comcast Center (215-496-1810), 1701 John F. Kennedy Boulevard. The tallest building in Philadelphia also boasts its fanciest food court. Sushi, crab cakes, croissants, and fresh fruit and produce are among your options. Don't leave without checking out the giant high-def video wall in the lobby. Rainy day tip: The building can be accessed underground from City Hall and Suburban Station.

Υ **Monk's Café** (215-545-7005) 264 S. 16th Street. Lunch and dinner daily. This narrow neighborhood tavern regularly wins "Best of Philly" awards for its huge Belgian beer selection. It also has swell burgers (beef and veggie), beer-braised mussels, and pommes frites served with bourbon mayonnaise. Dishes $7–25.

& Υ **Oyster House** (215-567-7683; www.oysterhousephilly .com), 1516 Sansom Street. Lunch and dinner Monday through Sat-urday. Original owners rescued this Philly institution from disrepute in 2009 and turned it into a noisy, whitewashed palace to the bivalve. Expect sweet crab salad, classic snapper turtle soup, and entrées such as oyster stew and sautéed flounder with spinach and potatoes. It's the place to get lobster rolls in summer, and the daily Buck a Shuck Oyster Hour is great fun. Lunch and small plates $10–16, entrées $21–32.

Υ ✿ & **Pietro's Coal Oven Pizzeria** (215-735-8090), 1714 Walnut Street. Lunch and dinner daily. This casual trattoria serves thin-crust pizza with gourmet toppings like goat cheese and prosciutto, and a wide selection of pastas and salads. It's good for families looking for a reasonable meal in Rittenhouse Square. Full bar. Dishes $9–16.

Darling's (215-545-5745), 2100 Spring Street. Locals and Franklin Institute visitors flock to this cute café for breakfast, lunch, and cheesecake. Besides an assortment of omelets, salads, and sandwiches on home-baked bread, there are 10 different kinds of cheesecake daily, from classic to Bananas Foster—all divine. Look for Bailey's Irish Cream cheesecake around St. Patrick's Day. Lunch $5–7.

& **Di Bruno Brothers** (215-665-9220), 1730 Chestnut Street. Lunch daily. This outpost of the Italian Market cheese shop has an upstairs café that's perfect for a quick gourmet lunch (try the Mamma Mia panini with prosciutto, fresh mozzarella, and roasted peppers). Afterward, browse the selections of imported olives, pates, and specialty cheeses. BYO. Sandwiches $8.

University City

Abner's (215-662-0100), 3813 Chestnut Street. If you need a cheesesteak fix west of Broad, this is the place to go; it's usually packed with Penn students. Sandwiches $4–8.

Lovers and Madmen, 40th Street (at Lombard). The coffee comes in real mugs, the WiFi is free, and the couches are soft and inviting at this Shakespeare-loving coffeehouse. There are sandwiches, too.

🍴 **Saad's Halal Palace** (215-222-7223), 4500 Walnut Street. It's a little off the beaten path (about five blocks west of Penn's campus) but a great find for a cheap, filling meal of falafel, shawarma, and other Middle Eastern dishes. Dishes $5–7.

Rittenhouse Square

COFFEE La Colombe Torrefaction (215-563-0860), 130 S. 19th Street. Open daily. No lattes, teas, or attitude—just fabulous house-blend coffee served in an art-filled room with large windows.

Walnut Bridge Coffeehouse (215-496-9003), 2319 Walnut Street. Penn students living in Center City fill up their carry mugs with Illy brand coffee before crossing the Schuylkill to West Philly.

BYO Where to buy wine west of City Hall: Around Rittenhouse Square there is a **Wine & Spirits** store at 1913 Chestnut Street (215-560-4215). In University City, there's a state store at 4049 Walnut Street (215-823-4709).

✴ Entertainment

MUSIC & THEATER Academy of Music (215-893-1999), Broad and Locust Streets. One of the oldest opera houses in the U.S., and a gorgeous setting for performances by the Pennsylvania Ballet and Philadelphia Opera Co.

Chris' Jazz Café (215-568-3131; www.chrisjazzcafe.com), 1421 Sansom Street. Cover charge $10–30. Decades-old jazz joint near City Hall.

Curtis Institute of Music (215-893-5261), 1726 Locust Street, Rittenhouse Square. This prestigious conservatory holds free student recitals every Monday, Wednesday, and Friday October through May. Arrive early; seating is on a first-come basis.

&. **Kimmel Center** (215-790-5800; www.kimmelcenter.org), 260 S. Broad Street. The city's newest performing arts center is home to the 2,500-seat Verizon Hall, where you can catch the Philadelphia Orchestra and other musical performances. Tours are given daily at 1 PM.

Y **Natalie's Lounge** (215-222-5162), 4003 Market Street. This narrow, smoky jazz club in West Philly has hosted John Coltrane,

Grover Washington Jr., and other jazz and blues legends. It's still going strong after 60 years.

Prince Music Theater (215-569-9700; www.princemusictheater .org), 1412 Chestnut Street. Musical theater—opera, cabaret, experimental—in a 450-seat movie palace.

Ⴅ **World Café Live** (215-222-1400), 3025 Walnut Street. This smoke-free club and restaurant near Penn is the best place in town to catch cutting-edge indie artists. A smaller upstairs stage features new and local talent.

MOVIES Ⴅ Ⴅ **Rave Cinemas** (215-386-9600; www.ravemotion pictures.com), 40th and Walnut Streets. Six screens with stadium seating, showing first-run films.

Ⴅ **International House** (215-387-5125; www.ihousephilly.org), 3701 Chestnut Street. The place for spaghetti westerns, John Carpenter triple features, and avant-garde cinema. There's always an interesting art exhibit you can check out before a screening.

Roxy Theater (215-923-6699), 2023 Sansom Street. You'll find two small screens, lower-than-average ticket prices, and a refreshing lack of multiplex sterility at this Rittenhouse Square institution.

Cinema 16:9 (484-461-7676), 35 N. Lansdowne Avenue, Lansdowne. Independent and hard-to-find films are screened in a

historic theater just over the West Philly border. Terrible Tuesdays showcase bad films (*Schoolgirl Hitchhikers*) and encourage audiences to heckle.

NIGHTLIFE Ⴅ **Alma de Cuba** (215-988-1799), 1623 Walnut Street, Rittenhouse Square. Comfy chairs, dim lighting, and splendid pomegranate martinis make this two-level restaurant a worthy late-night stop if you're in Rittenhouse Square. There's live Cuban jazz on Wednesday nights.

Ⴅ **The Bards** (215-569-9585), 2013 Walnut Street, Rittenhouse Square. An agreeable mix of barflies, professionals, and Penn graduate students share Guinness on tap and shepherd's pie at the long bar of this friendly Irish pub. Its weeknight happy hour is very popular, and there's live Irish music on Sunday evenings.

Ⴅ **Bob and Barbara's** (215-545-4511), 1509 South Street. Live jazz until 2 AM Friday and Saturday and a legendary Drag Night every Thursday.

Ⴅ Ⴅ **City Tap House** (215-662-0105; www.citytaphouse.com), 3925 Walnut Street (in the Radian Building). Everything you'd want in a gastropub: 60 craft ales on tap, good grub (from burgers to striped bass), and future stockbrokers (Penn's Wharton School is next door). Regulars can keep track of the beer they sample on cards that are then entered into an online database.

Ⱶ **Franklin Mortgage and Investment Co.** (215-467-2677), 112 S. 18th Street. Perfectly executed cocktails in a subterranean speakeasy environment.

Ⅎ Ⱶ **JG Domestic** (215-222-2363), 2929 Arch Street in Cira Center next to 30th Street Station. Iron Chef Jose Garces' farm-to-table restaurant has great happy hour specials between 3 and 7 PM weekdays. Phillies games. It's not an easy walk from Center City, but you can take the Frankford Line to 30th Station and walk over from there.

Ⱶ **Jollys Piano Bar** (267-687-1161; www.jollyspianobar.com), 1420 Locust Street. It's impossible not to have fun. Expect Billy Joel and Neil Diamond sing-alongs, sports on the TV, and lots of happy bachelorette parties.

Ⱶ **Misconduct Tavern** (215-732-5797), 1511 Locust Street. Open 11 AM–2 AM daily. A favorite place to catch a Phillies game—or celebrate their win afterward with craft beers and blue-cheese burgers.

Ⱶ **Pod** (215-387-1803), 3636 Sansom Street, University City. A college bar for students with trust funds (or at least some extra cash) and a taste for sake martinis and conveyor-belt sushi. Its futuristic all-white decor and hip sound system make this a fun alternative when you're not in the mood for the city's 19th-century beer taverns.

✳ Selective Shopping

Rittenhouse Square has a multi-story **Barnes & Noble** store (215-665-0716) overlooking the north side, an **Apple Store,** and many upscale designer clothing and gift boutiques along Walnut Street, plus several hidden gems like **Joseph Fox Bookshop** (215-563-4184; 1724 Sansom Street), an independent bookseller with a great architecture selection. Chestnut Street (between 16th and 17th) is home to the **Shops at Liberty Place,** where you'll find Nine West, J. Crew, and other upscale chains, and **Daffy's** (215-568-9664; 1700 Chestnut Street), a longtime purveyor of discount designer dresses, men's Italian suits, and lingerie in the old Bonwit Teller building.

In University City, **Sansom Common** (215-573-5290) at 36th and Sansom, has dozens of specialty, fashion, music, book, and gift shops, including Urban Outfitters and Barnes & Noble, all catering to collegiate tastes. Nearby, the **Black Cat** (215-386-6664), 3424 Sansom Street, features an eclectic collection of handmade jewelry, books, folk art, and lovely handicrafts from Asia, Latin America, and Africa. Owned by the adjacent White Dog Café, it stays open late most nights.

In the Fairmount district near the Art Museum are two wonderful used bookshops: **Book Haven** (215-235-3226; 2202 Fairmount

Avenue), two well-stocked stories across from Eastern State Penitentiary, and **Book Corner,** run by the Friends of the Free Library (215-567-0527; 311 N. 20th Street, behind the Central Library), a vast collection of used and nearly new books at low prices.

✳ Special Events

April: **Penn Relays** (last weekend), University of Pennsylvania—America's first intercollegiate and amateur track event takes over Franklin Field. Besides the races, you'll find food stands, live music, and other activities around campus.

June: **Bloomsday** (June 16), Rosenbach Library, Rittenhouse Square—the home of James Joyce's original Ulysses manuscript celebrates the famed literary holiday with Irish music, food provided by nearby pubs, and a series of readings by local celebrities on Delancey Place. Inside, there's a special exhibit of Joyce materials.

CHESTNUT HILL, GERMANTOWN & MANAYUNK

C hestnut Hill, Germantown, and Manayunk all lie outside Philadelphia's original boundaries and have a slightly suburban feel, each in its own separate way. Because they are outside Center City, they often aren't included in maps or travel stories on Philadelphia, but they are well worth a visit, especially if you like boutique shopping, cobblestoned streets, and preserved Victorian houses. Germantown sits the closest to Center City and was once one of Philadelphia's most affluent communities. Today, it has a grittier feel and is less pedestrian-friendly than its neighbors to the north, but its historical monuments are well preserved and among the finest and least crowded in the city, most notably the elegant and bullet-riddled Cliveden, site of the Battle of Germantown in 1777. Chestnut Hill is just a 10-minute drive north up Germantown Avenue, with its thriving main drag of boutique shops, sidewalk cafes, and attractive architecture. Once a farming community, it is now a sought-after address for many young Philadelphia families who like its easy access to Center City, wide tree-lined streets, and Queen Anne–style homes. You're bound to spot plenty of Bugaboo strollers and four-figure pocketbooks as you stroll along Germantown Avenue in Chestnut Hill, but the snobbish attitude you might find in other well-to-do areas isn't as evident here. Manayunk, a former textile-manufacturing center perched above the Manayunk canal a bit farther north, has transformed its main street into a happening string of restaurants, loft apartments, boutiques, and tattoo parlors, though the hilly streets above it still have the feel of a tight working-class community. Its name is, fittingly, a Native American expression for "where we go to drink." If you like a lively night out that is sure to include young Yuengling-guzzling crowds and parking challenges, then this is the place for you. Others might want to stick with a daytime visit, when shopping and strolling are easiest, or make an early dinner reservation and leave before the late-night gridlock takes over Main Street.

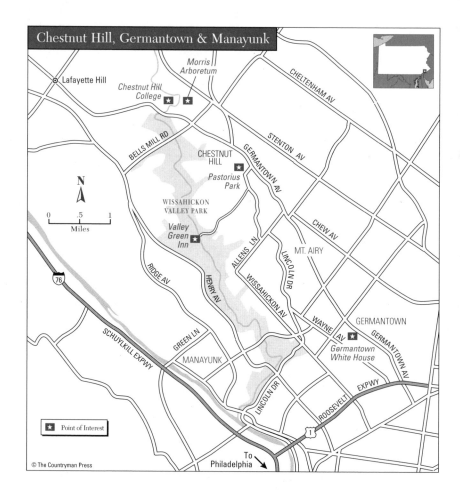

Chestnut Hill, Germantown & Manayunk

Morris Arboretum

Lafayette Hill

Chestnut Hill College

CHELTENHAM AV

BELLS MILL RD

STENTON AV

CHESTNUT HILL

GERMANTOWN AV

Pastorius Park

N

0   .5   1
Miles

WISSAHICKON VALLEY PARK

Valley Green Inn

CHEW AV

ALLENS LN

LINCOLN DR

MT. AIRY

76

RIDGE AV

HENRY AV

WISSAHICKON AV

WAYNE

GERMANTOWN

SCHUYLKILL EXPWY

GREEN LN

MANAYUNK

AV

Germantown White House

GERMANTOWN AV

LINCOLN DR

EXPWY

ROOSEVELT

1

Point of Interest

© The Countryman Press

To Philadelphia

GUIDANCE The **Germantown Historical Society and Visitor Center** (215-844-1683), 5501 Germantown Avenue, serves as a local museum as much as a venue for maps and brochures. On display are cannonballs from the Battle of Germantown, paintings by Charles Wilson Peale, and old photographs and etchings of the town. In **Chestnut Hill,** stop by the small visitor center (215-247-6696) at 8426 Germantown Avenue, for a walking map of town and information on surrounding attractions.

GETTING THERE By car: For Chestnut Hill and Germantown, take I-76 to Lincoln Drive and follow it east to Germantown Avenue in Mount Airy; head right (south) for Germantown or left for Chestnut Hill. Manayunk is also off I-76; exit at Manayunk (No. 338), turn right and follow Greene Lane Bridge to Main Street. Turn right and follow it into the heart of town.

By bus: SEPTA bus route 61 runs along Ridge Avenue between Manayunk and Center City.

By train: SEPTA regional R7 and R8 lines (215-580-7800; www.septa.org) run regularly between 30th Street Station and Chestnut Hill, with stops in Germantown and Mount Airy. The Chestnut Hill West station is within walking distance of the town's main drag.

Manayunk is on the R6 line, which runs from Center City out to Norristown.

GETTING AROUND Ridge Avenue and Germantown Avenue are the main north-south thoroughfares between Center City and its northern neighborhoods.

Manayunk and Chestnut Hill are terrific walking towns with thriving main streets. In Manayunk, pick up the canal towpath behind Main Street and follow the route that was originally used by mules pulling boats loaded with coal to the textile mills that lined the river.

The Chestnut Hill Historical Society (215-247-0417; 8708 Germantown Avenue) sells detailed maps and offers walking tours of Chestnut Hill in spring and fall.

CHESTNUT HILL STREET SCENE

MEDICAL EMERGENCY Chestnut Hill Hospital (215-753-2000) 8835 Germantown Avenue, is at the north end of Chestnut Hill.

✳ To See

MUSEUMS ♿ ⚲ **Woodmere Art Museum** (215-247-0476; www .woodmereartmuseum.org), 9201 Germantown Avenue, Chestnut Hill. Free. Closed Monday. This fine small art museum is located in a stately stone mansion just north of Chestnut Hill's main drag. It features the work of Philadelphia-area artists such as N. C. Wyeth, Benjamin West, Daniel Garber, and Violet Oakley.

HISTORIC SITES Cliveden (215-848-1777; www.cliveden.org), 6401 Germantown Avenue, Germantown. Open 12–4 Thursday through Sunday, $10 adults, $8 ages 6–12. More than 100 British troops holed up in the home of Pennsylvania's first chief justice in 1777 as General Washington's army attacked the home unsuccessfully before retreating. As legend has it, the Brits didn't surrender because they feared the bluecoats, still fuming over their failure at the Battle of Paoli, would kill them anyway. So while the Battle of Germantown was unquestionably a defeat for the Americans, it served to boost morale and was a significant turning point in the Revolutionary War. Today, docents give regular tours of the bullet-riddled mansion, which contains many of original 18th-century furnishings

CLIVEDEN, GERMANTOWN

of the Benjamin Chew family. A free reenactment of the battle is held on the grounds every October (see also Special Events).

🍲 **Germantown White House** (215-842-1798; www.nps.org/demo), 5442 Germantown Avenue. Open 1–4 Friday through Sunday, April through December; free. George Washington really did sleep, eat, and drink here. They have his personal silver tankard to prove it. The first president and his family stayed here in 1793, to escape the yellow fever epidemic that ravaged the city, then they returned for vacation during the summer of 1794. Now run by the National Park Service, it is the oldest presidential residence still in existence in the U.S. Formerly called the Deshler-Morris House, the property underwent an extensive renovation in 2008.

🍲 **Johnson House** (215-438-1768; www.johnsonhouse.org), 6306 Germantown Avenue, Germantown. Open Thursday and Friday by appointment, Saturday for tours at 1:15, 2:15, and 3:15; $5 adults, $2 ages 2–11. Built in 1768, this two-story home that belonged to a local family of abolitionists was a stop on the Underground Railroad and is believed to have sheltered and fed Harriet Tubman and William Still as they guided hundreds of slaves to freedom. The 40-minute tour includes a visit to the third-floor hiding place and exhibits on American slavery and abolitionism.

Stenton (215-329-7312; www.stenton.org), 6026 Germantown Avenue. Open for tours Tuesday through Saturday 1–4 PM, April through December. The Web site urges you to "Visit Stenton. Ben Franklin thought it was worth the trip." The 18th-century Georgian-style mansion was once home to James Logan, William Penn's secretary who eventually became mayor of Philadelphia and acting governor of the state. Franklin reportedly sought the book-loving Logan's advice as he prepared to open the nation's first library. Staff members have taken great care in assembling and displaying furniture and clothing that belonged to the Logan family. Check out the cool collection of reconstructed porcelain pots and cups, taken from shards found on the property.

Wyck (215-848-1690; www.wyck.org), 6026 Germantown Avenue. Tours 1–4 Tuesday, Thursday, and Saturday and by appointment; $5 adults. The formal garden, featuring more than 30 varieties of old roses (in bloom May and June), is the star of this 2-acre Germantown property, but the house, which doubled as a field hospital during the Battle of Germantown and was home to nine generations of one Quaker family, is also worth exploring. It is full of original furniture (including a piece once owned by Ben Franklin) and has an extensive collection of early horticultural books.

✷ To Do

🐾 ♿ **Morris Arboretum** (215-247-5777; www.upenn.edu/arboretum), 100 Northwestern Avenue, Chestnut Hill. Open daily year-round; $16 adults,

$6 ages 3–18. The official state arboretum bills itself as "a tree place" and is indeed known for its collection of old and rare specimens, including one of the largest Japanese katsura trees in the United States. John and Lydia Morris, wealthy Quaker siblings who never married, deeded their 92-acre summer property to the University of Pennsylvania in 1932. In May and June, the walled rose garden is a popular spot, and the property is covered with brilliant foliage in the fall. For kids, there's a miniature Garden Railway that runs past naturally made bridges, buildings, and trestles, May through October. I like to combine a visit here with a stop at the nearby Woodmere Art Museum or an afternoon of shopping in downtown Chestnut Hill. The grounds stay open late and host outdoor concerts in the summer.

MORRIS ARBORETUM

Pastorious Park (215-248-8810), W. Hartwell Lane and Roanoke Street. A welcome bit of green space just off Germantown Avenue with 16 dog-friendly acres, a pond, and a natural amphitheater that hosts free Wednesday night concerts in summer.

SCENIC DRIVES Germantown Avenue is one of the oldest streets in America, and home to dozens of historic buildings and churches, upscale shops, and vibrant pedestrian-friendly communities. Begin your drive near Vernon Park in Germantown and follow the cobblestones north past the Johnson House, Cliveden, and other historic sites that played a role in the Battle of Germantown during the Revolutionary War. Have a delicious veggie burger at **Flower Café at Linda's** (48 W. Maplewood Mall) or continue through Mount Airy, a neighborhood of beautiful old row homes where you can stop for fish tacos at **Avenida** (7402 Germantown Avenue). Then head into Chestnut Hill for some window-shopping and perhaps an ice cream cone at **Bredenbeck's**

(7402 Germantown Avenue). The drive is less than 8 miles, but could take you a full afternoon if you brake at all the interesting sites and shops along the way.

✴ Outdoor Activities

BICYCLING/RENTALS The **Manayunk Towpath** connects with the 22-mile Schuylkill River Bicycle Trail. It can be accessed from several spots along Main Street. **Human Zoom** (215-487-7433), 4151 Main Street, in Manayunk rents standard adult hybrids and road bikes. Prices start at $8 an hour, or $30 for 24 hours.

FISHING The Pennsylvania Fish and Boat Commission stocks **Wissahickon Creek** with rainbow and brown trout in the spring, summer, and early fall. Small- and largemouth bass can also be caught in the creek.

ICE SKATING Wissahickon Skating Club (215-247-1759. www.wiss skating.com), 550 W. Willow Grove Avenue, Chestnut Hill. Open skate sessions on Friday evenings for $9 plus skate rental.

KAYAKING Kayak tours of the Manayunk Canal and Schuylkill River are offered in the summer by **Hidden River Outfitters.** Call 215-482-8220 or visit www.manayunkkayaktours.com for a schedule. They usually include all equipment rental, paddling instruction, and lunch or brunch at the Manayunk Brewery (see Eating Out). Cost is $55–65.

✴ Lodging

Lodging options are limited in Germantown and Manayunk, but Chestnut Hill has a few small and friendly inns.

Anam Cara (215-242-4327; www .anamcarabandb.com), 52 Wood-dale Avenue. Anam Cara means "soul friend" in the Celtic language. Indeed, you'll feel like you're staying at the very clean and hospitable home of a good friend here. Located in a quiet neighborhood and an easy walk to downtown Chestnut Hill, it has two small comfortable rooms and five adjacent apartments available for weekly or monthly rental.

Chestnut Hill Hotel (215-242-5905; www.chestnuthillhotel.com), 8229 Germantown Avenue. This rambling 19th-century inn in the middle of downtown has been a hotel since before the town of Chestnut Hill existed (it was rebuilt in the 1800s). Today, it attracts more business travelers than vacationers. Its 36 smoke-free rooms have pencil-post double beds, plasma TVs, wireless access, and showers or baths. The adjacent Chestnut Hill Grill has outdoor seating and is always hopping with lively crowds. Rooms $149–169, include a continental breakfast.

Silverstone (215-242-3333; www.silverstonestay.com), 8840 Stenton Avenue, Chestnut Hill. This imposing Victorian Gothic home has six spacious rooms that look like a grandmother (with stylish taste and meticulous housekeeping habits) might have decorated them. Guests can make their own breakfast (eggs, bacon, bread, and all cookware provided) in the kitchen; there are laundry facilities, a luggage elevator, and a back garden. It's a short walk on a curb-less road from the Chestnut Hill East train station. Ask for a room that doesn't face busy Stenton Avenue. Kids are welcome. Rooms $115–155.

✳ Where to Eat

DINING OUT ♿ ✐ **Avenida** (215-385-6857, www.avenida restaurant.com), 7402 Germantown Avenue, Mt. Airy. Lunch Tuesday through Friday, dinner Tuesday through Sunday, Sunday brunch. Husband-and-wife team Edgar and Kim Alvarez took over the former Cresheim Cottage in 2009 and turned it into a child-friendly restaurant with Latin American flair. Cresheim fans will be pleased to know the romantic backyard patio and circa-1700 stonework remain. The menu is influenced by the chef's Guatemalan heritage: pork pibil with green mole, yucca fries, cilantro-grilled shrimp with roasted peppers and quinoa. The kids menu (flat iron steak, chicken and cheese tostados, roasted chicken

with steamed rice—all $9 and under) will make foodie parents weep. Sandwiches $9–10, dinner entrées $15–19.

Cafette (215-242-4220; www .cafette.com), 8136 Ardleigh Street, Chestnut Hill. Lunch Monday through Saturday, dinner Tuesday through Sunday, Sunday brunch. This stylish bistro a block off Germantown Avenue is known for its creative vegetarian options (jerk tofu with jicama-mango relish, crabmeat tilapia) and romantic flower-framed patio. Corkage fee $5. Lunch $7–10, dinner $18–23.

Ɏ **Jake's** (215-483-0444; www .jakesrestaurant.com) 4365 Main Street, Manayunk. Lunch and dinner Monday through Saturday, brunch and dinner Sunday. If you want a special-occasion meal in Manayunk, this is the place to go. Consistently good food and service make it a local favorite. It now shares a kitchen and chef with the adjacent Cooper's Wine Bar. The contemporary American menu changes seasonally and might include flat iron steak with Vidalia onion confit, basil gnocchi and rock shrimp, and wood-fired pizzas with gourmet toppings such as spicy meatballs or Black Mission figs. Reservations recommended. Pizzas and small plates $11–16; dinner entrées $22–32.

Ɏ **Mica** (267-335-3912; www.mica restaurant.com), 8609 Germantown Avenue, Chestnut Hill. Dinner Tuesday through Sunday. Lunch Saturday and Sunday. Blackfish Chef Chip Roman's first venture into the city's toniest neighborhood is an elegant, if expensive, dining experience with entrées such as braised short-rib ravioli and house-cured pork loin with pickled fennel, and a thoughtful wine list. Entrées $31–50.

EATING OUT Cake Bakery & Bistro (215-247-6887), 8501 Germantown Avenue. Closed Monday. Dine on roasted beet and mango salad, specialty sandwiches, and chocolate ganache alongside fountains and brick floors in this charming former nursery. It's open for dinner (BYO) Thursday and Friday and very popular for Sunday brunch.

Flower Café at Linda's (215-991-6514), 48 W. Maplewood Mall, Germantown. A friendly spot to grab a veggie burger and peach cobbler and within easy reach of Germantown Avenue's historic houses. Dishes $6–15.

❦ **Geechee Girl Rice Café** (215-843-8113), 5496 Germantown Avenue, Germantown. Dinner Tuesday through Saturday; brunch Sunday except in summer. Dine on delicious Southern comfort food amid tangerine walls and rotating art exhibits. You can't go wrong with the creamy shrimp and grits or the fried chicken. Cash only. BYO. Entrées $15–23.

❦ ❢ **McNally's Tavern** (215-247-9736), 8634 Germantown Avenue, Chestnut Hill. Lunch and dinner daily. The specialty of this hole-in-the-wall bar is the Schmitter, a pumped-up version of the Philly cheesesteak that includes fried onions, tomato, salami, and Russian dressing. They also serve chicken Caesar salad and ham, turkey, and roast beef sandwiches. Daily specials might include crab cakes or prime rib. Dishes $6–15.

❢ ❧ ⅋ **Manayunk Brewery** (215-482-8220), 4120 Main Street, Manayunk. Lunch and dinner daily. Daily happy hour specials, a huge crowd-pleasing menu (homemade potato chips, Angus beef burgers, lobster crab cakes, sushi), and one of the best waterfront decks in the city. Ask about the weekday brewery tours. Sandwiches $9–14, dinner entrées $15–25. (See also Nightlife.)

Tommy Gunn's (215-508-1030; www.tommygunns.net), 4901 Ridge Avenue, Manayunk. Lunch and dinner daily. Philly isn't known as a barbecue town, but this mustard-yellow shack at the edge of Fairmount Park does its 'cue up right. On the menu are a variety of classics such as Kansas City baby backs, Carolina-style pulled pork, Texas beef brisket, and Philly-style spare ribs. Vegetarians will love the portobello mushroom sandwich with fresh mozzarella. Sides include sweet and smoky baked beans, deep-fried mac 'n' cheese, and Carolina coleslaw. Eat in the small dining room or outside on the deck, or get it to go like most locals do. Sandwiches $6–8; platters $8–22.

⅋ ❧ **Valley Green Inn** (215-247-1730; www.valleygreeninn.com),

Valley Green at Wissahickon. Lunch and dinner Monday through Saturday, brunch and dinner Sunday. Known for its elaborate Sunday brunches, this former 19th-century hotel sits in the middle of Wissahickon Valley Park overlooking a lovely creek. The brunch menu borders on the obscene, with offerings that include Brie-stuffed French toast, smoked salmon Benedict, and lobster, shrimp, and scallop hash. Lunch is a typical assortment of salads, burgers, and sandwiches. Dinner could be duck with goat cheese-potato croquettes, or cornmeal-coated catfish, or filet mignon. Try to get a table on the front porch for a front-row view of the bikers, hikers, and nature lovers who meander by. Lunch $7–14, dinner $22–31, brunch $19–23. ·

BYO Where to buy wine:

There's a premium **Wine & Spirits** store (215-753-4520), 8705 Germantown Avenue, in the Top of the Hill Shopping Center behind Borders.

BAKERIES & FARM MARKETS

Chestnut Hill
Bredenbeck's Bakery and Ice Cream Parlor (215-247-7374), 7402 Germantown Avenue. Delicious butter cookies and hand-dipped ice cream and milk shakes.

Chestnut Hill Farmers' Market (215-254-4900), 8829 Germantown Avenue. Open Thursday through Saturday. The area's first farmers' market features more than a dozen vendors selling fresh flowers, produce, free-range chicken, and several tasty lunch

VALLEY GREEN INN

options inside an old warehouse behind the Chestnut Hill Hotel. Free parking is available off Southampton Avenue.

Night Kitchen Bakery (215-248-9235), 7725 Germantown Avenue. This small white cottage serves lemon-curd cake, sticky buns, and other high-quality baked goods.

Manayunk
Main Street Market (215-482-9500), 4345 Main Street (at Grape). Full-service upscale market with a deli in the back. Pick up a chocolate croissant or Agiato Bread Co. baguette and bring them down to the canal. There's usually good barbecue on hand on summer weekends.

Whirled Peace (215-487-0489), 4321 Main Street, Manayunk. Make your own kosher frozen yogurt combinations (the exotic flavors include Tahitian vanilla, lychee, and red velvet cake) for 50 cents an ounce.

✳ Entertainment

MUSIC Grape Street Philadelphia (215-483-7084), 4100 Grape Street, Manayunk. This two-story nightspot dropped "pub" from its name and underwent a renovation in 2001, but it hasn't lost its mellow, neighborhood-bar vibe. The small downstairs stage attracts folk and rock bands. Upstairs, there's hip-hop music together with spinning DJs.

THEATER Sedgwick Cultural Center (215-248-9229), 7137 Germantown Avenue, Mount Airy. Gorgeous 1,600-seat Art Deco movie theater that is now a showplace for dance, music, and other performing arts.

Stagecrafters (215-247-8881; www.thestagecrafters.org), 8130 Germantown Avenue, is an all-volunteer community theater in Chestnut Hill that stages several comedies and dramas a season. David Lindsay-Haire's *Kimberly Akimbo* was a recent one. Reasonable prices and quality performances make this worth a trip out of the city.

NIGHTLIFE Manayunk Brewery (215-482-8220), 4120 Main Street, Manayunk. This former textile mill packs them in on summer weekends. The multiroom interior has live music and DJs on weekends and some weeknights (see also Eating Out).

Pitchers Pub (215-482-2269), 4328 Main Street, Manayunk. This unpretentious bar is where to go if you want to avoid the "scene" at Manayunk Brewery up the street. The weekly Wednesday beer pong tournaments (starting at 9 PM) are a big draw.

✳ Selective Shopping

Chestnut Hill
Caleb Myer Studio (215-248-9250), 8520 Germantown Avenue. Everything in this beautiful shop

was made by hand—from the delicate gold and silver earrings to the clay serving bowls.

Kilian Hardware (215-248-3733), 8450 Germantown Avenue. Besides the usual assortment of tools, garden supplies, and paint, this old-fashioned corner hardware store sells unique gifts such as Liberty Bell showerheads and antique telephones from the early 1900s.

Penzey's Spices (215-247-0770), 8528 Germantown Avenue. One of two brick-and-mortar stores in the state (the other's in Pittsburgh) from the Wisconsin-based spice empire. A chef's nirvana of Madagascar vanilla and smoked paprika.

Monkey Business (215-248-1835), 8624 Germantown Avenue. You'll find everything from vintage gowns to barely scuffed Manohlo Blahniks in this upscale consignment shop at the north end of Chestnut Hill. It is one of Chestnut Hill's longest-running shops, in business for more than 55 years.

Manayunk
Bias (215-483-8340), 4442 Main Street. This very hip clothing boutique changes its look and merchandise each season and is known for feminine frocks by owner Andre Mitchell and other local designers.

Main Street Music (215-487-7732), 4444 Main Street. All the genres are represented at this independent and well-stocked music shop. It also has a good used CD section.

Spiral Bookcase (215-482-0704), 112 Cotton Street. A true neighborhood bookshop with a wide selection of literature and regular author events and poetry readings. Jewelry made with sustainable materials is also for sale, and there's live jazz and blues some evenings.

✳ Special Events

May: **Manayunk Bike Race** (third weekend), Manayunk. Officially known as the Philadelphia International Championship, this race goes all over the city, but Manayunk is one of the best places to cheer and serenade the cyclists on as they head up the steep wall on Lyceum Avenue.

June: **Manayunk Arts Festival** (third weekend), Manayunk—huge outdoor street festival featuring live music, food by local restaurants, and handmade arts and crafts by more than 250 artists from all over the country.

October: **Battle of Germantown Reenactment** (first weekend), Germantown—live bagpipe music, lectures by historians, and an actual reenactment of the famous Revolutionary battle by more than a thousand costumed volunteers in and around the gates of Cliveden (see Historic Sites).

Southeastern Pennsylvania

2

THE MAIN LINE & VALLEY FORGE

THE BRANDYWINE VALLEY

THE MAIN LINE &
VALLEY FORGE

The Main Line is an affluent western suburb of Philadelphia comprised of a handful of towns along or near US 30 (Lancaster Avenue). There are no skyscrapers or malls or industrial centers; what you'll find are mansions fit for European aristocrats, some of the country's top private colleges, and more families listed on the Social Register than just about anywhere else in the country.

The Main Line takes its name from the local rail line that has run between Center City, Harrisburg, and Pittsburgh since the 19th century. Someone came up with the phrase "Old Maids Never Wed and Have Babies, Period" as a way to remember the names of the station stops between Center City and Malvern. They are Overbrook, Merion, Narberth, Wynnewood, Ardmore, Haverford, Bryn Mawr, and Paoli. Bala Cynwyd, Gladwyne, Radnor, Wayne, Villanova, and Malvern are also considered a part or adjacent to the Main Line, and mentioned in this chapter.

Many travel guides and articles mention the Main Line within context of Philadelphia, but it's a destination that increasingly deserves standalone coverage, with stellar shopping and restaurant options and exquisite public gardens. Despite a lingering Philadelphia Story-type snobbishness that borders on caricature and golf and cricket clubs that ooze exclusivity, the area offers much to enjoy. Colleges such as Villanova and Bryn Mawr have excellent art galleries, gardens, and theaters that are open to the public, and its restaurants and delis are good enough to motivate Philadelphians to abandon the city for an evening or afternoon. Until 2011, it was home to the Barnes Foundation, a large gallery and arboretum in Overbrook with an extraordinary collection of impressionist, post-impressionist, and early modern paintings by Picasso, Matisse, Cézanne, and others. After years of controversy, the original Barnes property shut its doors (though its gardens remain open) and the collection was relocated to a new facility on Benjamin Franklin Parkway in Philadelphia.

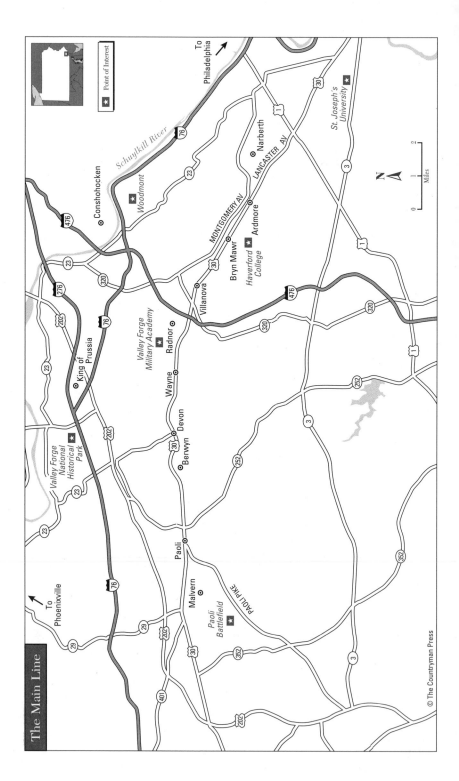

The Main Line

Point of Interest

To Phoenixville

To Philadelphia

Schuylkill River

Conshohocken

Woodmont

King of Prussia

Valley Forge National Historical Park

Valley Forge Military Academy

Radnor

Wayne

Devon

Berwyn

Paoli

Malvern

Paoli Battlefield

PAOLI PIKE

Narberth

LANCASTER AV

MONTGOMERY AV

Ardmore

Bryn Mawr

Haverford College

Villanova

St. Joseph's University

N

0 1 2
Miles

© The Countryman Press

Just a few miles away from the Main Line is Valley Forge, an unincorporated part of Chester County that is best known for lending its name to the encampment of George Washington's Continental army during the winter of 1777–78. Its 3,600-acre national historic park is undoubtedly the area's most famous attraction, though the nearby King of Prussia Court and Plaza, which claims to be the country's largest shopping mall, draws the most visitors and groupies each year (a whopping 18 million).

King of Prussia takes its name from a local 18th-century tavern called the King of Prussia Inn, which was named for the Prussian King Frederick II, possibly due to his support of George Washington during the American Revolution (another educated guess is the name was a way of attracting the German soldiers who were fighting nearby alongside the Americans). The tavern long ceased operating (it was moved from its original location in 2002 and is now home to the Chamber of Commerce), replaced by rampant commercial and residential development that grew up around the mall.

The Valley Forge area is close enough to Philadelphia to make it a reasonable day trip, but it has enough lodging, eating, and recreational options to spend a night or two. The King of Prussia Court and Plaza are cities unto themselves with hundreds of upscale stores and restaurants. Two of the Philadelphia area's most popular jogging and biking trails, the Perkiomen and Schuylkill River, converge here. And a couple of villages within easy reach of Valley Forge, Skippack and Phoenixville, offer quaint small-town shopping and dining alternatives.

AREA CODE The western Main Line lies within the 610 area code. The eastern edge uses 215. The Valley Forge area lies within the 610 and 484 area codes.

GUIDANCE The **Welcome Center at Valley Forge National Historical Park** (610-783-1077; 1400 N. Outer Line Drive), is one of the best sources for brochures and maps of the southeastern Pennsylvania area. For online information, go to www.inwayne.com, an independent Web site with good information on local events, parks, restaurants, and shopping.

GETTING THERE By car: US 30 (Lancaster Avenue) cuts an east-west route through the Main Line between Philadelphia and Paoli. From I-76 (the Schuylkill Expressway), exit at City Avenue for the eastern towns of Merion, Bryn Mawr, and Ardmore and follow US 1 to US 30 west. For the western end of the Main Line and Valley Forge, take I-76 south to the King of Prussia interchange and follow US 202 south. From the Blue Route (I-476), exit at Villanova.

By air: **Philadelphia International** (215-937-6800) is the closest airport.

By train: SEPTA's R5 rail line trains to Paoli/Thorndale (215-580-7800; www.septa.org) run regularly between Center City and the Main Line, with stops in Merion, Ardmore, Bryn Mawr, Villanova, Radnor, Wayne, and other towns. **Amtrak** trains also run along the same line.

By bus: SEPTA bus route 44 to Merion, Ardmore, Narberth, and other Lancaster Avenue towns. **Capitol Trailways** (800-721-2828) buses run four times a day between King of Prussia and Philadelphia's **Greyhound** terminal. They stop about 2 miles from the mall and 5 miles from Valley Forge at 234 E. DeKalb Pike (US 202). Buses also run regularly between King of Prussia and York, Harrisburg, and Lancaster.

GETTING AROUND You can ride the SEPTA R5 rail line between Merion and Paoli. It's also easy to get around the Main Line by car. Lancaster and Montgomery Avenues are major east-west thoroughfares that are often choked with traffic; avoid them during rush hour if possible.

Free trolleys run continuous loops through Ardmore, Haverford, and Bryn Mawr from 5–10 PM on the first Friday of every month. For more information, visit www.firstfridaymainline.com.

MEDICAL EMERGENCY Bryn Mawr Hospital (610-526-3000), 130 S. Bryn Mawr Avenue, Bryn Mawr. Closer to Valley Forge is **Montgomery Hospital** (610-270-2000), 1301 Powell Street, Norristown.

WHEN TO GO Anytime, really. It's quietest on the Main Line in late July and August, when most college students are gone and residents have left for the Jersey Shore. Spring and fall are good times to visit Valley Forge National Historical Park; there are fewer crowds than in the summer, and its hills and meadows are ablaze with orange and yellow foliage in the fall and tall grass and wildflowers in the spring. The shops and restaurants of King of Prussia, Skippack, and Phoenixville thrive year-round.

✳ Villages

Ardmore. Formerly known as Athensville, Ardmore is only 3 miles from Philadelphia and, like Narberth (see below), tends to be more laid-back than other Main Line towns. It's home to one of the country's first malls, Suburban Square, which was turned into an open-air complex of shops and restaurants in the 1970s. It also has a good farmers' market selling everything from sushi and gourmet cheese to Lancaster County produce.

Bryn Mawr. Katharine Hepburn would fit right in dining or shopping in this upscale enclave, where ladies still wear proper suits to lunch. Home to Bryn Mawr College and some of the area's wealthiest citizens, it also has businesses that cater to student budgets and tastes, like pizza joints

BRYN MAWR'S ALUMNAE HOUSE

and The Grog tavern. With its train station, hospital, and proximity to Haverford and other colleges, it is one of the busiest towns along the Main Line; expect gridlock and allow plenty of time to find street parking.

Gladwyne. Gladwyne still feels like the quiet, walkable country village it was a century ago. Its center at the intersection of Youngs Ford and Righters Mill Roads, historically known as Merion Square, includes small shops and single or double houses that were once tenant housing for the laborers or mill workers of nearby Mill Creek Valley. It's home to several parks and historic mansions, including Woodmont Palace.

Narberth is a dinner-and-movie sort of place. Its pretty tree-lined downtown, centered around Narberth and Haverford Avenues, has many good restaurants, a historic one-screen movie theater, and hip boutiques and consignment shops that seem to always rate a "Best of Philly" award for something or other.

Wayne. Named after "Mad" Anthony Wayne, a brigadier general known for his insomniac ways, this lively town makes a good base for visiting both the Main Line and nearby Valley Forge, especially if you want a nonchain lodging option. It's home to the handsome Wayne Hotel and lovely Chanticleer pleasure garden. You can easily spend an afternoon shopping and eating in its downtown, which was glammed up in the 1990s and now includes lots of shops selling home furnishings and scented candles.

PHOENIX IRON COMPANY
Established in 1783 and incorporated in 1855, the Phoenix "works" produced nails, rail, Civil War cannons, weaponry for 20th century wars, and structural steel. Among its well known products were the Griffen Gun, 1861, and the Phoenix Column, 1862. Closed in 1987.
PENNSYLVANIA HISTORICAL AND MUSEUM COMMISSION 2000 B

DOWNTOWN PHOENIXVILLE

Phoenixville. This small town on the northwest edge of Valley Forge underwent a transformation in recent years from blue-collar steel town to edgy urban neighborhood. Bridge Street, its main thoroughfare, is (so far, at least) a happy coexistence of art galleries, BYO bistros, old-time barber shops, and faded diners. Anchoring the downtown area is the restored Colonial Theater, famous for its role in the sci-fi film The Blob.

Skippack. Once a stop on a 1900s rural trolley route, Skippack added village to its name in the 1990s, opened some antiques shops and nice restaurants, and waited for the people to come. They did, and now it is the area's version of Peddler's Village (see Central Bucks County) and rarely described without the adjective quaint. It is a nice shopping alternative for those who aren't in the mood for the nearby King of Prussia mall. Its main street, however, is busy Skippack Pike, which makes it less pedestrian-friendly than you might expect.

✳ To See

MUSEUMS & GALLERIES ↑ **Wharton Esherick Museum** (610-644-5822), 1520 Horseshoe Trail Road, Malvern. Open March through December; one-hour tours on weekends; group tours weekdays; $9 adults, $4 ages 12 and under. You'll never look at a piece of timber the same again after visiting the studio and home of one of America's greatest and perhaps least appreciated woodworkers. Wharton Esherick was a Philadelphia-born artist who turned his attention to woodcraft after failing at a string of illustrating jobs. Lucky us. His stone and wood home and studio, just as he left it since his death in 1970, is located along a crest overlooking Valley Forge and is a hobbitlike wonderland of irregular plank floors, drop-leaf oak desks, sculptures, and hand-carved coat hooks. Three of the four levels are connected by a stunning spiral staircase made from massive pieces of red oak.

&. ⑳ **Philip and Muriel Berman Museum of Art** (610-409-3500; www .ursinus.edu/berman), 601 E. Main Street, Collegeville. Closed Monday; free. This gem of a small art museum on the campus of Ursinus College features paintings and prints by Charles Willson Peale, Walter Baum, Andy Warhol, Roy Lichtenstein, and Susan Rothenberg; Japanese block prints; and Pennsylvania German artifacts such as almanacs, pottery, and quilts. An impressive collection of more than 40 outdoor sculptures peppers the liberal arts college campus, where J. D. Salinger studied for four months in 1938.

&. ⑳ **Cantor-Fitzgerald Gallery** (610-896-1287; www.cantorfitzgerald gallery.com), 370 Lancaster Avenue, Haverford. Open daily September through May, weekdays June through August; free. The founder of the Wall Street company helped finance this sleek gallery space on the campus of Haverford College (in the Whitehead Campus Center). Exhibits change monthly and feature sculpture, photography, printmaking, and other media by professional artists.

&. ⑳ **Lawrence Art Gallery at Rosemont College** (610-526-2967; www.rosemont.edu), 1400 Montgomery Avenue, Rosemont. Open 9–5 weekdays; free. Situated against the picturesque backdrop of Rosemont

ODE TO LARRY, CURLY & MOE

Stoogeum (267-468-0810; www.stoogeum.com), 904 Sheble Lane (near Bethlehem Pike), Ambler. Open one Saturday or Sunday a month; free. Tough to believe, but this unassuming office building 30 minutes north of Philadelphia holds the largest public display of Three Stooges memorabilia in the world. Owner and founder Gary Lassin is president of the Three Stooges Fan Club and married to a grandniece of the Philadelphia-born Larry Fine; in 2004 he set about fashioning a museum dedicated to the legendary comedy trio out of the thousands of items he had accumulated over the years. The result is most *soitenly* fabulous, whether you're a fan or not. The crowds who fill the place when it's open are a nice mix of young and old—with everyone showing equal appreciation for the 1980s Stooges pinball machine, computerized Stoogeology 101 exhibit (which urges participants to give Curly an eye poke to proceed), and old photos and comic books. The third floor is devoted to artwork of and by the Stooges. The museum is lamentably only open once a month, but plans are in the works to add more days. Check the Web site for updates.

College, this gallery has quality exhibitions, featuring artists of local and international renown.

GARDENS Barnes Foundation (610-667-0290; barnesfoundation.org), 300 North Latch's Lane, Merion. Although much of the art once housed in the original mansion was moved to a new facility on the Benjamin Franklin Parkway, the lush arboretum and horticultural programs remained at the Main Line property and were slated to reopen to the public in late summer 2012. Check the Web site for details.

Jenkins Arboretum (610-647-8870; www.jenkinsarboretum.org), 631 Berwyn Baptist Road, Devon. Open 8–sunset daily. Elisabeth Phillippe Jenkins received part of this natural woodland property as a wedding present from her father in 1926. Her husband helped turn it into a public arboretum after her death in 1965. Now 46 acres, it is known for its big-leaved rhododendrons and evergreen azaleas and usually hits its colorful peak April through June. It has 1.2 miles of winding paved paths and a 2-acre pond framed by day lilies, wildflowers, and white pines. You'll come away from here with a newfound appreciation for leaves and twigs, since gardeners leave them where they fall to act as a sort of natural mulch.

Haverford College Arboretum (610-896-1101; www.haverford.edu /arboretum), 370 Lancaster Avenue, Haverford. Open daily dawn to dusk. Rolling lawns, a 3-acre pond, and hundreds of majestic old trees can be found in this small arboretum on the campus of Haverford College. A 2.2-mile walking and jogging nature trail circles the campus. Maps and self-guided brochures are available at the arboretum office near the main visitors parking lot.

HISTORIC SITES John James Audubon Center at Mill Grove (610-666-5593), 1201 Pawlings Road, Audubon. Closed Monday. Self-guided house tours, $6 adults. Audubon lived in this rambling stone farmhouse when he first moved to America from Europe in the early 1800s; it was here that he started studying and painting the birds that would shape his career. Mill Grove attracts a fraction of the traffic that nearby Valley Forge National Historical Park does, but it's worth an hour-long stop. Situated on a hill with an inviting back porch overlooking Perkiomen Creek, it is filled with original paintings and books by Audubon, including a complete four-volume set of *The Birds of America,* Audubon's famous portrayal of nearly 500 distinct species of birds. Picnic areas and 5 miles of hiking trails surround the house.

Woodmont Palace (610-525-5598), 1622 Spring Mill Road, Gladwyne. Open 1–5 Sunday, April through October; free. You've got to see this massive French Gothic–style manor to believe it. Built by a local steel magnate in the 1800s, it's now home to the International Peace Mission

JOHN AUDUBON'S HOME AT MILL GROVE

Movement, a religious group founded in the early 20th century by an African American man who renamed himself Father Divine and claimed to be the embodiment of Jesus. His widow, known as Mother Divine, still lives in the manse and allows the public to tour the house or stroll the bucolic grounds one afternoon a week. Tours take about an hour and include a visit to the "Shrine of Life" where Father Divine is buried. Modest dress is required (no shorts or sleeveless shirts).

🍁 **Merion Friends Meetinghouse** (610-664-4210), 615 Montgomery Avenue, Merion. One of the oldest Quaker meetinghouses in America, this 17th-century building counts William Penn among its worshippers. The cherry trees that dot its burying ground have a great backstory: Japanese and American horticulturalists planted them in the early 1900s as a test to ensure that the cherry trees Japan intended to give to Washington, D.C., would survive the climate. They did, and they're still a beautiful sight in the spring. There are worship services on Sunday and rummage sales and art exhibits throughout the year.

Valley Forge Military Academy (610-989-1509), 1001 Eagle Road, Wayne. This prestigious boarding school, whose graduates include retired Army General Norman Schwarzkopf and author J. D. Salinger, played a major role in the 1981 film *Taps* and is home to a Battle of the Bulge monument dedicated to the soldiers who fought in the significant World War II battle. Visitors are welcome to view the monument, located near the parade field next to Eisenhower Hall.

Paoli Battlefield (no phone, www.ushistory.org/paoli) Wayne and Monument Avenues, Malvern. Open daily mid-May through mid-October, weekends November through April. During the night of September 20, 1777, the British launched a surprise attack against General Anthony Wayne's troops that is now known as the Paoli Massacre. Using bayonets and swords, they killed between 50 and 100 men and wounded about 150 more. The battlefield is surrounded by development, but has been preserved in its original form as woodland and farm fields. There is no visitor center, but an easy 0.5-mile walking trail leads you past interpretative signs and significant sites.

✍ **Peter Wentz Farmstead** (610-584-5104), Shearer Road, off PA 73, Worcester. Open 10–4 Tuesday through Saturday, 1–4 Sunday; free. George Washington stayed on this Pennsylvania German farm twice in 1777, before and after the Battle of Germantown. Tours include a glimpse at the room in which he was believed to have slept. Front desk service can be laid back, but it's worth a brief stop if you're looking for a dose of history after a morning of shopping and eating in nearby Skippack.

✳ **Outdoor Activities**

BICYCLING The **Radnor Trail** is a paved 2.4-mile path with graded shoulders for walkers and horses. It begins at Radnor–Chester Road south of Lancaster Avenue and follows an old railroad line to Sugartown Road.

Valley Forge National Historical Park has several miles of moderate bike trails. City bikes for kids and adults are available for rent in the lower parking area of the welcome center and the **Betzwood Picnic Area** (610-783-4593).

The **Schuylkill River Trail** follows the river 25 miles west from Philadelphia's Fairmount Park, crosses through Valley Forge, and ends at Lower Perkiomen Valley Park, where it links with the 19-mile Perkiomen Trail, which continues west through the towns of Collegeville, Schwenksville, and Green Lane. Several bike shops near the route rent bikes and can offer guidance, including **Bikesport** (610-489-7300; 325 W. Main Street, Trappe) and **Indian Valley BikeWorks** (215-513-7550; 500 Main Street, Harleysville).

FISHING The lower half of **Little Valley Creek** near Washington's headquarters at Valley Forge National Historical Park is stocked with brown trout and popular for fly-fishing, though all caught fish must be released back into the creek.

Skippack Creek is stocked with brown and rainbow trout March through Memorial Day and warm-water fish such as smallmouth bass, catfish, and

Chanticleer (610-687-4163; www.chanticleergarden.org), 786 Church Road, Wayne. Open Wednesday through Sunday, April through October; $10 adults; children under 12 free. Grounds stay open until 8 on Friday in the summer. Hip meets elegant at this 35-acre estate and garden tucked into a tony neighborhood south of Lancaster Avenue. To give you a sense of its pedigree, the family residence of Hope Montgomery Scott, the Main Line heiress on whom Katharine Hepburn's character is based in *The Philadelphia Story,* is nearby. Once the estate of pharmaceutical mogul Adolph G. Rosengarten, it is now a pleasure garden with wisteria-draped arbors, a babbling brook, and rolling green hills. In the spring, fields surrounding the main house are awash with 150,000 white and yellow daffodils. There are few signs (plant lists are available in small, whimsical kiosks), and Adirondack chairs and stone couches with cushions are placed invitingly around the premises to take advantage of the lovely views. When the horticulturalists aren't tending to the flora and fauna, they are creating furniture, sculptures, and metal bridges for placement around the property. No child, and few adults, will be able to resist rolling down the lush sloping hillside near the main house (it's even encouraged). House tours are given at 11 AM for an additional $5 on Friday.

CHANTICLEER ESTATE AND GARDENS

eel throughout the year. An accessible fishing dock is on Lewis Road in **Evansburg State Park** (see Green Space).

GOLF Jeffersonville Golf Course (610-539-0472), 2400 W. Main Street, Jeffersonville. A well-maintained 18-hole, par-72 municipal course designed by architect Donald J. Ross.

Pickering Valley Golf Club (610-933-2223), 450 S. White Horse Road, Phoenixville. A no-frills yet challenging 18-hole course featuring 6,572 yards of golf from the longest tees with a par of 72.

Valley Forge National Historical Park (610-783-1077; www.nps.gov /vafo), 1400 N. Outer Line Drive, Valley Forge. Welcome center open 9–5 daily, until 6 in summer), grounds open year-round 6 AM–10 PM. No battles were fought here, but this 3,600-acre property is considered a critical turning point of the Revolutionary War. It's where George Washington chose to settle his weary and ill-equipped army for the winter of 1777–78. Despite the fact that as many as 2,000 Continental soldiers (out of a total 12,000) died of hunger, disease, and frostbite while here, it's also where Washington, with the help of Prussian drill master Friedrich von Steuben, eventually shaped his beleaguered army into a force to be reckoned with that would go on to defeat the British. Today the area is marked by rolling hills and woodlands, earthen forts, reconstructed log cabins, towering war memorials, and miles of hiking and biking trails.

Begin your visit at the welcome center, where you can catch a short film and talk to Park Service staffers about what's going on that day. The whole park and its highlights can be covered in a couple of hours by car (self-guided driving tours are available), or you may opt to take a ranger-led walking tour (offered three times daily in summer). There are also daily narrated open-air trolley tours in summer and weekends in September and October for $16 per adult or $8 per child, and after-hours picnics with actors playing George and Martha Washington and Continental soldiers. Call the welcome center for details.

My favorite way to experience the park is by walking its well-maintained paths. Leave your car at the visitor center or the **Washing-**

HORSEBACK RIDING Greylyn Farm (610-889-3009; www.greylyn farm), Sugartown Road and Paoli Pike, Malvern. Private or group instruction in showing horses starting at $35.

Red Buffalo Ranch (610-489-9707), 1093 Anders Road, Collegeville. Leads one- to four-hour guided trail rides through adjacent Evansburg State Park (see also Green Space). They also give lessons to all levels of riders. Rates start at $35.

ton Memorial Chapel on the north side of the park and pick up the easily accessible 5-mile loop trail. The chapel itself, built in 1917 and home to an active Episcopalian church, is worth a stop for its soaring stained-glass windows and hand-carved choir stalls. It also features a carillon of 58 bells that represent the U.S. states and territories (concerts are held every Sunday and weekday evenings during summer) and the **Justice Bell**, a replica of the Liberty Bell that was used to promote the women's suffrage movement in the early 1900s.

Behind the chapel are a tiny used bookshop, and a gift and snack shop that sells homemade soup, sandwiches, and shoofly pie for reasonable prices. From here you can pick up the main park trail for a short hike to the fields where Washington trained his army, and the Isaac Potts house (see below), one of the park's top attractions.

The area around the **Isaac Potts House**, which served as Washington's headquarters during that fateful winter, underwent a large renovation in 2007 that included restoring a 1911 train station near the house and adding exhibits aimed at better capturing the misery and pressure that permeated the encampment and Washington's state of mind, according to park officials.

With nearly 30 miles of moderate trails, Valley Forge is also a haven for bicyclists, equestrians, and walkers. On spring and summer evenings, the 5-mile Multi-Use Trail, which begins on Outer Line Drive near the welcome center and passes rows of log cabins, the **National Memorial Arch**, and the chapel, is filled with exercise hounds. The Web site has good downloadable trail maps.

✳ Green Space

Evansburg State Park (610-409-1150), 851 Mayhall Road, Collegeville. These 3,300 acres of woodlands and meadows were first settled by Mennonite farmers; remnants of water mills can still be found along the creek that runs through the property. You'll also find four baseball fields, dozens of picnic tables, fishing and hunting options, a golf course, and 26 miles of hiking, biking, and equestrian trails. The visitor center, in an early 18th-century Mennonite farmhouse, is a great place for bird watching.

Lower Perkiomen Valley Park (610-666-5371), 101 New Mill Road, Oaks. The Perkiomen and Schuylkill River trails intersect in this landscaped 107-acre park near the John James Audubon Center at Mill Grove. Besides hiking and biking trails, it also has a kids' playground, picnic areas, and basketball courts. Fishing is allowed in Perkiomen Creek.

Saunders Woods (610-520-9197), 1020 Waverly Road, Gladwyne. Open daily dawn to dusk. A 25-acre nature preserve with hiking and dog-walking trails, open meadows and forested valleys, and good bird-watching opportunities. Pick up a trail map at the information kiosk near the Waverly Road entrance.

♂ **The Willows** (610-964-9288), 490 Darby-Paoli Road, Villanova. Open daily dawn to dusk. Weddings take up much of this grand old estate most weekends, but anyone is welcome to stroll the 47 acres of grounds, which are dotted with stately trees, flowering plants, and a small pond that comes with lots of geese.

✳ Lodging

You'll find many chain hotels in St. Davids, near Radnor, and a few miles away in the King of Prussia area.

BED & BREAKFASTS General Warren Inne (610-296-3637; www.generalwarren.com), Old Lancaster Highway, Malvern. This historic inn off US 202 was a popular stage stop and Tory stronghold during the American Revolution. It has eight comfortable Colonial-style suites with sitting areas, private baths, and TVs. There's a well-regarded restaurant and tavern on the ground floor (see also Dining Out). No children or pets. Suites $130–200, including a light breakfast.

Great Valley House (610-644-6759; www.greatvalleyhouse.com), 1475 Swedesford Road, Valley Forge. Also near US 202 and a mile from Valley Forge Park, this 17th-century stone farmhouse has three guest rooms, each with quaint Victorian touches such as claw-foot bathtubs and canopy beds, as well as TVs, refrigerators, and wireless Internet access. The downstairs common areas are filled with owner Pattye Benson's collections of antique dolls, quilts, and vintage clothes from the late 1800s. Breakfast is served in the pre-Revolutionary kitchen in front of a walk-in stone fireplace. The 4 acres of grounds are a nice touch, and the tree-fringed swimming pool makes you feel like you are lounging at a friend's home. Rooms $94–129, two-night minimum on weekends with some exceptions.

Morning Star Bed and Breakfast (610-935-3289; www.morningstarbandb.net), 610 Valley Forge Road, Phoenixville. You'll share common areas with owner Rebekah Ray, her husband and teenage daughter, city folk (a.k.a. Philadelphians) who bought this rambling 19th-century house about 3 miles from Valley Forge Park in 2004. The four rooms are large and attractive with queen beds (two of them have private baths), and there's a pool table in the living room, along with fabulous old woodwork everywhere. Ray will tailor breakfast accordingly to guests with allergies or on special diets. Rooms start at $105, or you can reserve two rooms with a shared bath for $150. There's a two-night minimum for most weekends.

HOTELS & INNS ⟨ **Hotel Fiesole** (610-222-8009; www.hotelfiesole.net), 2046 Skippack Pike, Skippack. This attractive 16-room luxury inn opened in 2006 as Skippack's only upscale lodging option. Located along its thriving main street, it was once a popular restaurant known as the

Trolley Stop. All that's left is the original trolley that now serves as a dining room for one of the hotel's three restaurants. Its rates are on the high side for this area, but rooms are large and have marble baths, flat-screen televisions, and sitting areas. Try to get one facing Perkiomen Creek. Rooms $179–375, includes continental breakfast.

Radnor Hotel (610-688-5800; www.radnorhotel.com), 491 E. Lancaster Avenue (PA 30), St. Davids. A full-service four-story hotel at the Main Line's west end near the Schuylkill Expressway and PA 30. Rooms are on the bland side, but the service and convenience get high marks from the business folks who frequent it. Rates drop considerably on the weekend. Rooms $109–189, two-room suite $209–269.

Wyndham (610-526-5236; www.brynmawr.edu/wyndham), 235 N. Merion Avenue, Bryn Mawr. Housed in a quaint stone farmhouse that serves as Bryn Mawr's alumnae headquarters, this seven-room inn is one of the best lodging deals you'll find on the Main Line. Rooms are immaculate and decorated in a restrained Colonial style; all have private baths and include a continental breakfast. It's within walking distance of the Bryn Mawr train station and many shops and restaurants. Reserve early; the inn often fills up fast with visiting parents and graduates; it closes for a week in November, three weeks in

December, and a couple of weeks in August. Rooms $123, with discounts for alumnae and staff.

Bryn Mawr Suites (610-520-1664), 31 Morton Road, Bryn Mawr. Parents with kids at Bryn Mawr College, Haverford, and other nearby schools like this small guesthouse run by Ann Marie Woods. The two suites share access to a full kitchen, balcony, and backyard. It is within walking distance of the Bryn Mawr train station and an easy light-rail ride into Philadelphia. Light sleepers might not like the early morning train noise. Suites $150 for two, $30 for each extra person.

♿ **Wayne Hotel** (610-687-5000; www.waynehotel.com), 139 E. Lancaster Avenue, Wayne. This four-story Tudor Revival building in the center of Wayne's shopping and restaurant district was a retirement home and synagogue before new owners bought it in 1985 and restored it to the handsome inn it was when it opened in 1906. Its 37 rooms and 3 suites have a Victorian feel with comfortable mahogany beds, lace curtains, and flowery wallpaper. Guests have access to a gym and seasonal swimming pool at the Radnor Hotel a few miles away. Rooms $169–229, includes a light breakfast.

♿ ♿ **French Creek Inn** (610-935-3838; www.frenchcreekinn .net), 2 Ridge Road, near PA 23 and 724, Phoenixville. A good option for budget travelers, this family-owned motel has 22 large, sparsely furnished rooms with refrigerators, microwaves, and

HISTORIC WAYNE HOTEL

TVs. It's 5 miles to Valley Forge and 2 miles to Phoenixville's Main Street. Rooms $70.

✳ Where to Eat

DINING OUT ♿ 𝖸 **333 Belrose** (610-293-1000), 333 Belrose Avenue, Wayne. Lunch and dinner Monday through Friday, dinner Saturday. This stylish restaurant has a contemporary American menu that features innovative seafood dishes such as sriracha-spiked tuna tartare, mussels bouillabaisse, and wood-grilled salmon with crab butter. There are good burgers, too, which come with garlic fries and will set you back $14. The bar is often packed during happy hour. Extensive wine list. Lunch $11–17, dinner entrées $24–34.

Mediterranean Grill, 870 W. Lancaster Avenue, Bryn Mawr. Attractive BYO near the Bryn Mawr train station that is the go-to place for lamb kebabs, tahdeg (crispy rice and pita), oven-roasted baby eggplant, and all things Persian. Conveniently, there's a wine shop a few doors away (see BYO).

♿ **Teresa's Café** (610-293-9909), 124 N. Wayne Avenue, Wayne. This popular neighborhood bistro just off Lancaster Avenue serves gourmet pizzas, pastas, and Italian entrées such as veal medallions in a lemon-caper wine sauce and mushroom risotto. You can't go wrong with anything made with the house-made pesto. The restaurant serves wine, but you can also bring your own. Dinner entrées: $17–28.

White Dog Café (610-225-3700), 200 W. Lancaster Avenue, Wayne. The first outpost of West Philadelphia's original with the same tasty, locally sourced food and typically long waits. The difference is the location (Main Line opulence instead of hip city townhouse) and people (country clubbers instead of college professors). The dog-themed art remains the same. Dishes $20–25.

♿ **Wyndham** (610-526-5236; www.brynmawr.edu/wyndham), 235 N. Merion Avenue, Bryn Mawr. Lunch Monday through Friday. Closed July and August, and the last week of December. This small restaurant at the alumnae house of Bryn Mawr College exudes a "Ladies Who Lunch" vibe, but it's open to anyone and well worth a visit if you're in the area. The buffet is a great value at $13 and includes a choice of soups, salads, and changing entrées such as coconut curry chicken and beef bourguignon. There are also a la carte dishes such as pecan-crusted chicken and hot roast beef. Try to get a table on the covered patio overlooking the lawn. You may bring your own wine for a small fee. Dishes $8–14.

Phoenixville
♿ 𝖸 **Black Lab Bistro** (610-935-5988), 248 Bridge Street. Lunch Tuesday through Friday, dinner Tuesday through Sunday. The

food is consistently fabulous at this upscale bistro near the Colonial Theatre. The dinner menu might feature braised short ribs, artichoke-crusted salmon, and pepper-seared ostrich fillet. Lunch includes butternut squash gnocchi, lump crab omelet, as well as tasty sandwiches. BYO. No reservations are taken Friday and Saturday. Lunch $8–15, dinner entrées $18–32.

♣ **Majolica** (610-917-0962, www.majolicarestaurant.com), 258 Bridge Street. Critically lauded BYO next door to the Black Lab. The changing menu might include fried squash blossoms with smoked salmon, pasta with rabbit confit ragu, and braised short ribs with caramelized onions. For dessert. try the warm Nutella crepes or spiced cardamom-coffee doughnuts. Three-course, $30 prix fixe meals on Wednesday, Thursday, and Sunday. Dinner entrées $18–24.

Skippack

& ℉ **Mistral** (610-222-8009), 2046 Skippack Pike. Dinner daily, Sunday brunch. This special-occasion restaurant in the Hotel Fiesole opened in late 2006. The main dining room is elegant and inviting with a stained-glass ceiling, white tablecloths, and a large fireplace. The northern Italian menu features a wide range of pastas, seafood, and meats, including braised rabbit, buffalo, and free-range chicken. A less-expensive and abbreviated menu is available at the more casual Bella Rossa downstairs. Entrées $26–42.

& ℉ **Roadhouse Grille** (610-584-4231), 4022 Skippack Pike. Lunch and dinner daily, Sunday brunch. Located in a renovated 18th-century home, this handsome restaurant is a local favorite for steaks and seafood. Portions are huge. Lunchtime brings a large business crowd, and the prices reflect it. Reservations recommended. Leave time for a cocktail at the elegant mahogany bar. Lunch $11–15. Dinner entrées: $21–32.

EATING OUT & **Berwyn Pizza** (610-647-6339), 1026 E. Lancaster Avenue, Berwyn. The pizza's very good, but it's the cheesesteak that wins the biggest raves.

& **Hymie's Delicatessen** (610-554-3544), 342 Montgomery Avenue, Merion. Breakfast, lunch, and dinner daily. You won't find much in the way of decor at this always-busy spot along a busy stretch of Montgomery Avenue, but you won't care once the food arrives. As much a diner as a deli, it serves amazing matzo ball soup, thin-sliced pastrami sandwiches with homemade coleslaw, and other deli staples. Breakfast is served all day. Expect a wait on weekends. Dishes $6–16.

Johnnie's Dog House (484-582-0151), 11 Louella Court, Wayne. Lunch and dinner daily. The hot dogs (veggie, beef, or turkey) are grilled and come on toasted buns. The menu covers most East Coast palates, with a Coney Island Chili Dog, a Boston Back Bay dog with baked beans and onions, and even a Philly Freedom Dog with sautéed onions and melted cheddar cheese. Don't forget the gravy fries on the side. Dogs $2–3.

Landis Catering (610-688-9999), 118 W. Lancaster Avenue, Wayne. Lunch Monday through Saturday. Excellent fresh-made Italian hoagies and hamburgers. Sandwiches $4–7.

& **Minella's Diner** (610-687-1575), 320 W. Lancaster Avenue, Wayne. A popular 24-hour diner that serves breakfast all day and night. The huge menu includes everything you'd expect from a good diner: eggs every way, pancakes, burgers, salads, fried flounder, moussaka, and more. Breakfast $5–8; lunch and dinner $10–29.

Phoenixville
♠ **Irish Joe's Café** (610-935-3625), 180 Bridge Street. Breakfast and lunch Tuesday through Friday, breakfast Saturday and Sunday. This small down-home diner was here long before gentrification set in and still has the low prices to prove it; it's known for its ample portions (try the sticky-bun French toast or garden omelet) and brick-size portions of scrapple. Dishes $2–7.

Steel City Coffee House (610-933-4043; www.steelcitycoffee house.com), 203 Bridge Street, Phoenixville. Open daily. Everything you'd want in an independent coffeehouse: a loftlike space, four different special roasts on tap at any given time, and a wide selection of panini, salads, and

scones. Coffee refills are free. For dessert, there are homemade cookies, frozen Snickers bars, and all kinds of ice cream variations. (See also Entertainment.)

BAKERIES & FARM MARKETS & **Hope's Cookies** (215-660-9607), 1125 W, Lancaster Avenue, Rosemont. This local bakery has a thriving business delivering preservative-free cookies to homesick college students. Fun flavors include caramel pecan, lemon cooler, White Russian, and chocolate raspberry.

& **Ardmore Farmers' Market** (610-896-7560), Anderson and Coulter Avenues, Ardmore. Closed Monday. This popular market in Suburban Square includes indoor and outdoor dining areas and 20 vendors selling everything from hoagies and sushi to artisanal cheeses and African spices.

Lancaster County Farmers' Market (610-688-9856), 289 W. Lancaster Avenue, Wayne. Open 6–4 Wednesday, Friday, and Saturday. If you can't make it to Amish country, this large indoor market is the next best thing. It has more than a dozen stalls selling hand-rolled pretzels, fresh turkeys, wood-smoked hams, silk flower arrangements, and all kinds of seasonal produce. It's less frenetic and roomier than other indoor farm markets.

Town Hall Coffee (484-270-0841; www.townhallcoffee.com), 358 Montgomery Avenue, Merion

Station. Some say this handsome café makes the best cup of joe in town; there's a large selection of teas, too. It's in the same block as Hymie's Delicatessen (see Eating Out).

BYO Where to buy wine on the Main Line:

You'll find **Wine & Spirits** stores in Bryn Mawr at 922 W. Lancaster Avenue (610-581-4560); in Wayne at 161 E. Swedesford Road (610-964-6724); and in the Ardmore Plaza Shopping Center at 56 Greenfield Avenue (610-645-5010).

✳ Entertainment

MOVIES ♿ **Colonial Theatre** (610-917-1228; www.thecolonial theatre.com), 227 Bridge Street, Phoenixville. A 1903 theater that was the site of *The Blob*'s last supper in the 1958 sci-fi film starring Steve McQueen. It was restored by a nonprofit group in the 1990s and now shows art and independent films and children's classics. Every July, the theater celebrates its 15 of minutes of fame with a Blobfest (see Special Events).

Narberth Theater (610-667-0115), 129 N. Narberth Avenue, Narberth. This classic Art Deco theater has added an additional screen and stadium seating and shows first-run films.

Anthony Wayne Theater (610-225-0980) 109 W. Lancaster Avenue, Wayne. Another old theater divided into four screens

showing first-run films. It's within walking distance of many shops and restaurants.

Bryn Mawr Film Institute (610-527-9898), 824 W. Lancaster Avenue, Bryn Mawr. Restored 1926 movie palace showing independent, documentary, art, and repertory films.

MUSIC **Steel City Coffee House** (610-933-4043; www.steel citycoffeehouse.com), 203 Bridge Street, Phoenixville. This hip café turns into a happening place to hear live music on Friday and Saturday nights. There is a BYO policy during live-music events.

MilkBoy Acoustic Café (610-645-5269; www.milkboycoffee .com), 2 E. Lancaster Avenue, Ardmore. You'll find poetry readings, free open-mic nights, and a solid lineup of singer-songwriters (members of Wilco and Guster, for example) at this centrally located coffeehouse. Comfy couches, easy parking, and reasonable cover fees ($8–10) add to its charm. It doubles as a Monday through Friday breakfast and lunch spot and may be the only place in the state that makes a respectable vegan scrapple.

THEATER **Forge Theatre** (610-935-1920), 241 First Avenue, Phoenixville. Located in a former funeral home, this company has been staging Broadway and off-Broadway shows for more than 45 years. Ticket prices are absurdly reasonable.

People's Light and Theater Company (610-644-3500; www .peopleslight.org), 39 Conestoga Road, Malvern. This venerable theater group produces eight or nine plays per season, mixing world premieres, contemporary plays, and new approaches to classic texts like *Anne of Green Gables*. The main stage is in a beautifully restored 18th-century barn.

Villanova Theater (610-519-7474; www.theatre.villanova.edu), Lancaster and Ithan Avenues, Villanova. Villanova University's well-regarded theater department stages four shows a year, ranging from classic and contemporary plays to musicals.

NIGHTLIFE Main Line nightlife tends to cater to cash-strapped college students. You'll find plenty of beer and pool halls with happy hour deals.

The Grog (610-527-5870), 863 W. Lancaster Avenue, Bryn Mawr. A popular hangout for students from Bryn Mawr, Haverford, and Villanova, it's an amiable place to relax with a beer and a few friends. Families fill the upstairs nonsmoking dining room in the early evening.

John Harvard's Brew House (610-687-6565), 629 W. Lancaster Avenue, Wayne. Part of an East Coast chain of brewpubs, this is a popular after-work and late-night watering hole for Main Line professionals and college students.

The beer selection and boisterous ambiance outshine the food.

McShea's (610-667-0510), 242 Haverford Avenue, Narberth. A friendly neighborhood pub with a large beer selection and a variety of nightly entertainment, including DJs, open-mic nights, and beer pong games.

Rusty Nail (610-649-6245), 2580 Haverford Road, Ardmore. Specializes in live original music from local bands. There's also satellite TV, as well as pool tables and a late-night pub menu.

✴ Selective Shopping

King of Prussia Court and Plaza (610-265-5727; www.kingof prussiamall.com) 160 N. Gulph Road, King of Prussia. When I was a kid, my friends and I would brag to out-of-towners that this sprawling shopping complex was the biggest mall in the world. Not quite, but it comes awfully close— with a square footage equaling two Louisiana Superdomes and enough marble flooring to cover the entire flight deck of an aircraft carrier. The Plaza was refashioned in the 1990s to match the swankier Court across the parking lot. Today, the two malls are linked by a pedestrian walkway and have more than 400 shops and restaurants, including Bloomingdale's, Nordstrom, Versace, Cartier, Hugo Boss, L.L. Bean, Sephora, and Urban Outfitters. An estimated 25 percent of its visitors are tourists. Serious shoppers could easily spend an entire weekend here.

On or near Lancaster Avenue

Bryn Mawr Hospital Thrift Shop (610-525-4888), 801 County Line Road, Bryn Mawr. Closed Sunday. No thrift-store junkie should miss this sprawling shop stocked with hand-me-downs from some of the area's richest neighborhoods. The main store sells furniture, jewelry, bric-a-brac, and women's clothing on three floors. Across the street are small shops for men's and children's clothing.

Earthworks (610-667-1143), 233 Haverford Avenue, Narberth. Closed Sunday and Monday. A fun-to-browse gallery in Narberth's downtown selling handcrafted ceramics, glass, and other high-end gifts.

Gold Million Records (610-525-4500), 851 W. Lancaster Avenue, Bryn Mawr. It's all about vinyl at this well-regarded music shop—classic rock, blues, glam rock, punk—plus bowls, clocks, and other items made out of recycled record jackets.

Ardmore

&. **Suburban Square** (610-896-7560; www.suburbansquare.com), Anderson and Coulter Avenues, Ardmore. This attractive outdoor mall is perhaps the best place around to immerse oneself in the Main Line lifestyle: shop for dresses at Lily Pulitzer, hand-embroidered napkins at Maleka Fine Linens, and kid-size Ugg

boots at Olly Shoes. Then head over to the adjacent Ardmore Farmers' Market (open Tuesday through Sunday) for Lancaster County meats and fresh produce.

Junior League Thrift Shop (610-896-8828), 25 W. Lancaster Avenue. Closed Sunday. Frequently named by local papers as the best thrift store on the Main Line, this well-maintained store sells furniture, designer clothing, jewelry, toys, and books.

Wayne

Readers' Forum (610-254-9040), 116 N. Wayne Avenue, Wayne. Pleasantly cluttered used bookstore in downtown Wayne with a wide selection and reasonable prices.

&. **Eagle Village Shops** (610-293-2012; www.eaglevillageshops .com), Lancaster Avenue and Eagle Road. A small complex of upscale independent shops, many specializing in home furnishings or women's clothing. It's east of downtown with a large parking lot.

uBead2 (610-688-8842), 105 W. Lancaster Avenue. Closed Sunday. A very cool neighborhood shop selling beads in all shapes, colors, and sizes. Buy your beads to go or design a piece and assemble it at one of the worktables. Bead soirees and workshops are held regularly.

* **Special Events**

May: **Devon Horse Show** (last weekend and first weekend of

June), Horse Show Grounds, Devon—the oldest and largest annual outdoor horse competition in the U.S. features more than 1,200 horses competing for prizes and a county fair with Ferris wheel rides, equestrian-themed crafts, and cotton candy.

June: **Main Line Jazz and Food Festival** (first weekend), Wayne—showcases some of the finest jazz performers in Philly, plus signature dishes from more than 20 Main Line restaurants. Visit www.mainlinejazz.com for information.

July: **Blobfest** (second weekend), Bridge Street, Phoenixville—this small town celebrates its prominent role in the 1958 film with a two-day festival of *The Blob* screenings, scene reenactments, a tinfoil hat contest, and a street festival.

August: **Philadelphia Folk Fest** (third weekend), Old Pool Farm, Upper Salford Township. John Prine, Bonnie Raitt, Arlo Guthrie, and the Decemberists are just a few of the famous artists who have performed at this country music bash, which celebrated its 50th anniversary in 2011. For more info, visit www.pfs.org.

December: **March-in of the Continental Army** (second or third weekend), Valley Forge National Historical Park. Costumed soldiers reenact the Continental Army's arrival in Valley Forge, followed by musket and artillery demonstrations. In mid-June, there's a similar march-out event marking the army's departure.

THE BRANDYWINE VALLEY

An easy drive from Philadelphia and Baltimore via I-95, the Brandywine Valley follows the Brandywine River from southeastern Pennsylvania into northern Delaware. Featuring dozens of excellent restaurants and some of the states' best B&Bs, it's a popular weekend getaway for Philadelphians and Washingtonians, though one could easily spend a week here and find plenty to do and see. This is where the Battle of Brandywine Creek was fought and a young French soldier named Lafayette made his auspicious military debut. It's where the duPont family made its fortunes and built the extraordinary mansions and gardens that now draw millions of visitors. It's where Nelson Conyers (N. C.) Wyeth, one of America's top illustrators, got his start as an artist at Howard Pyle's Brandywine School of Illustration, and where his eccentric son Andrew and grandson Jamie took inspiration for their own acclaimed landscape and portrait paintings. Just over the state line in Delaware are the Hagley Museum and Library, the Nemours Mansion and Gardens, and Winterthur Estate.

The Brandywine Valley was an important paper-milling center in the 18th century, supplying paper to Ben Franklin's print shop in Philadelphia and throughout the colonies. William Penn's influence was prominent and can still be seen today in the many Quaker meetinghouses that dot the valley.

Today, US 1 and US 202 are two main routes that cut through the heart of the Brandywine Valley, each with its share of strip malls and chain hotels. But turn off these thoroughfares and you'll soon find yourself surrounded by rolling farmland, old gristmills, antiques shops, and arguably the best used book store in the country, Baldwin's Book Barn. Closer to the Maryland border west of Kennett Square is mushroom country, where nearly half of the country's mushrooms originate from greenhouses and special buildings that once grew carnations. The industry has seen its share of labor conflicts and residential complaints over the years, but the town vigorously celebrates its heritage each year with a big street party.

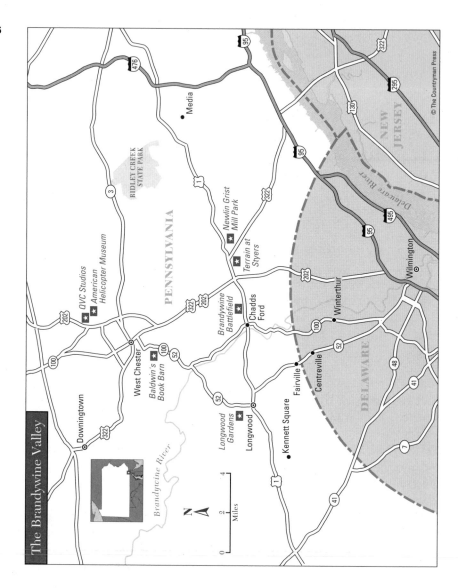

© The Countryman Press

While the Brandywine Valley tends to be geared toward grownup getaways, it has many kid-friendly places, such as Linvilla Orchards on the northern edge, Jimmy John's hot dogs, and children's gardens at Winterthur and Longwood.

GUIDANCE You'll find maps, history exhibits, and information on Philadelphia and surrounding areas at the **Chester County Visitor Center** (610-388-2900; www.brandywinevalley.com), Kennett Square. It's just outside the gates of Longwood Gardens in a Quaker meetinghouse that once served as a stop on the Underground Railroad. In Chadds Ford just south of US 1, the **Brandywine Conference and Visitor Bureau** (610-565-3679; www.brandywinecvb.org) has maps and brochures of Delaware County and other attractions and a helpful staff. In Delaware, the **Greater Wilmington Convention and Visitor Bureau** has two offices, downtown at 100 W. 10th Street, and in the Delaware Travel Plaza along I-95.

GETTING THERE By air: The center of the Brandywine Valley is about a 20- to 30-minute drive from **Philadelphia International Airport** (215-937-6800) via I-95. **Baltimore-Washington International Airport** is about 100 miles away, also via I-95.

By car: I-95, via Philadelphia or Delaware, cuts to the west of the Brandywine; US 202 between West Chester and the Maryland border cuts right through it.

By train: The R3 line of the Southeastern Pennsylvania Transportation Authority, or SEPTA, (215-580-7800; www.septa.org) runs regularly between Philadelphia's 30th Street Station and Media.

KENNETT SQUARE

GETTING AROUND The easiest way to navigate the Brandywine Valley is by car. Try to avoid US 1 and US 202 during rush hour; both are popular truck routes that connect to I-95. US 30, which runs east-west above West Chester, is also a main route into Philadelphia and is best avoided at rush hour.

WHEN TO GO The fall and Christmas seasons are particularly attractive in the Brandywine Valley. Unlike some areas of eastern Pennsylvania, many of its attractions, including Longwood Gardens and Winterthur, stay open year-round. January and February bring a melancholy (but no less beautiful) starkness to the area and mean fewer crowds and lines. Winter is the perfect time to visit the Brandy-wine Valley Museum and pay homage to Andrew Wyeth's landscapes.

MEDICAL EMERGENCY Riddle Memorial Hospital (610-566-9400), 1068 W. Baltimore Pike, Media. Farther west along US 1 is **Jennersville Regional Hospital** (610-869-1000), 1015 W. Baltimore Pike, West Grove.

✳ Towns & Villages

Centreville, Delaware. This small village is at the center of hunt country, between Longwood Gardens and Winterthur on PA 52. Named after the nearby Quaker Friends Center Meeting House around 1750, it was a popular spot for Chester County farmers and cattle ranchers to stop on their way to market at the river port of Wilmington, Delaware. It has several antiques shops, galleries, and cafes, including a favorite local watering hole, Buckley's Tavern.

Chadds Ford takes its name from a small stretch of the Brandywine Creek that was once forded by travelers and John Chads, who started a ferry business nearby to carry passengers when conditions were rough. US 1 passes right through town, making it a popular base for visiting the entire valley. It's home to the Brandywine Battlefield, the Brandywine River Museum, and many antiques shops and B&Bs.

Kennett Square. This hamlet at the west end of the Brandywine Valley calls itself "the mushroom capital of the world." Its pretty downtown includes many mom-and-pop shops and restaurants and is surrounded by rural B&Bs and farms that produce nearly half of the country's mushroom supply.

Media. The county seat of Delaware County, Media has a population of about 6,000 and an attractive main street with good restaurants, shops, an arts theater, Trader Joe's, and a small veterans' museum. It's on the eastern edge of the Brandywine Valley and is connected to the Upper Darby section of Philadelphia by the 101 trolley, which runs down the middle of its main street.

West Chester. A settlement since 1692, this historic town of about 18,000 people has served as the Chester county seat since 1786. It is one of the largest towns in the Brandywine Valley and offers the widest options for dining, nightlife, and shopping. US 30 and 202 are busy thoroughfares that cross through or near the center, but it maintains an attractive and walkable downtown with shops, small cafes, and the area's best nightlife options. It is also home to a 130-year-old state college, West Chester University, and the QVC shopping network.

DOWNTOWN WEST CHESTER IS FULL OF HISTORIC BUILDINGS.

✳ To See

HISTORIC SITES ♿ **Brandywine Battlefield State Historic Park**
(610-459-3342; www.ushistory.org/brandywine), US 1, east of Chadds
Ford. Open Wednesday through Sunday, March through November and
Thursday through Sunday, December through February. The largest
single-day battle of the Revolutionary War took place here on September
11, 1777, marking the first military action for a certain young Frenchman,
the Marquis de Lafayette. Unfamiliar with the terrain, the Americans
were outwitted and ultimately defeated by British troops. Perhaps for this
reason the historic site doesn't get the attention or funding it deserves, but
volunteers are happy to discuss the sequence of events and give you a
sense of what Colonial-era life was like. Watch a 20-minute video in the
small visitor center, then take a driving or walking tour of the property and
two modest farmhouses that served as headquarters for Washington and
Lafayette. Every September, the park hosts a reenactment of the battle.

Chester Courthouse (610-872-0502), 412 Avenue of the States, Chester.
Open 9–4 Monday through Friday. This beautifully restored 1724 courthouse was the official court of Chester County until 1789 when the county
was split and Delaware County was created. It claims to be the oldest continually operating building in the country and features original chairs,

wainscoting, and woodwork. The Delaware County Historical Society offers occasional guided tours of the interior; call ahead for a schedule.

Nemours Mansion and Gardens (302-651-6912; www.nemoursmansion .org), Powder Mill Drive (PA 141) and Alapocas Road, Wilmington, Delaware. $15 adults; reservations recommended. Open Tuesday through Sunday, May through December. Built by Alfred I. duPont in 1910 for his second wife Alicia Maddox duPont, this 102-room French-neoclassical mansion may be the most extravagant east coast property you will ever visit. Its treasures include Marie Antoinette's musical clock, paintings from four centuries, a vintage car collection, iron gates that belonged to Henry VIII and Catherine the Great, and many more nods to the duPont's European roots. Plan to spend at least half a day here—tours begin with exhibits and a film about duPont at the visitor center, then a bus takes you to the mansion for an intimate docent-led tour (groups are limited to 6 people), followed by about 45 minutes to independently roam the vast manicured gardens.

MUSEUMS ⫝̸ ⛬ **Brandywine River Museum** (610-388-2700; www .brandywinerivermuseum.org), Chadds Ford. Open 9:30–4:30 daily. $10 adults, $6 ages 6–12. This former 1800s gristmill on the banks of the Brandywine River houses works by three generations of Wyeths—N. C., Andrew, and Jamie—as well as such renowned illustrators as Howard Pyle, Maxfield Parrish, Reginald Marsh, and Theodor Geisel (Dr. Seuss). Plan to spend an hour in the galleries and another hour wandering the wildflower gardens and browsing the marvelous gift shop; I have visited this museum more often than any other in the Philadelphia area and never tire of its contents. Andrew Wyeth's witty and forthright granddaughter Victoria leads anecdote-filled tours of the galleries in spring and fall. From April through November, for an additional $5 the museum offers one-hour tours of N. C. Wyeth's nearby studio and home, where he raised his very creative children; it's well worth the extra time and money.

⫝̸ ⛬ **Christian C. Sanderson Museum** (610-388-6545; www.sanderson museum.org), 1755 Creek Road, Chadds Ford. Free. Open Saturday and Sunday, 1–4:30 PM, March through November. Another fascinating museum unique to the Brandywine Valley: Christian Sanderson was a local teacher and American history fanatic who happened to be close friends with his Chadds Ford neighbor N. C. Wyeth. Sanderson's wide-ranging collection of letters, paintings, flags, and signs now fills every room of this country house and features original sketches and paintings by N. C. and a hauntingly beautiful portrait of Sanderson by Andrew Wyeth. There's also a book owned by Benjamin Franklin, along with a lock of George Washington's hair, unexploded Civil War munitions, and much more. Pair this with a stop at the nearby Brandywine Battlefield— Sanderson helped it gain recognition as a state historic site.

☂ ✎ ⚐ **American Helicopter Museum and Education Center** (610-436-9600; www.helicoptermuseum.org), 1200 American Boulevard, West Chester. Closed Monday and Tuesday, $10 adults, $6 ages 2 and up. A tribute to the rotor-blade industry and its roots in southeastern Pennsylvania, this QVC neighbor has more than 35 aircraft on display, including the evacuation helicopter from TV's *M*A*S*H* and the V-22 Osprey currently used by the Marine Corps. Kids can climb in and take the controls of some of the aircraft; there's also a toddler area to keep the preschool set occupied. Helicopter rides are sometimes available to the public for $40 a person; call for a schedule.

☂ ✎ **Hagley Museum and Library** (302-658-2400; www.hagley.org), DE 141 between PA 100 and US 202, Wilmington, Delaware. Adults $11, children $4. Open daily. Maybe it's the gunpowder connection, but the Hagley sometimes gets ignored amid the opulence of other duPont estates in the area. In fact, it's a great place for families, and for anyone curious about early American industry and about how the duPonts acquired their immense wealth. E. I. DuPont began producing black gunpowder on the site in 1802. The 230-acre complex along the Brandywine River includes massive stone mills, a waterwheel, and the duPont's first U.S. home. Plan to spend at least half a day, if not longer. There's also a great little organic café on the premises.

✴ To Do

Herr's Snack Factory Tours (800-637-6225; www.herrs.com), 20 Herr Drive, Nottingham. Tours Monday through Thursday 9–noon and 1–3 PM, Friday 9–11 AM. Free, but call ahead to guarantee a spot. This family-owned potato-chip giant began with a 1938 panel truck, three kettles, and a couple of knives; now it processes 500 pounds of potatoes a day. Its free 45-minute tours begin with a film about the company's history, then lead you past front-row views of the potato-chip and pretzel-making process. The best part: fresh out-of the-oven chips to all visitors at the tour's end. The gift shop features every Herr's product imaginable, plus a half-price table.

FOR FAMILIES ✎ **Linvilla Orchards** (610-876-7116), 137 W. Knowlton Road, Media. This 300-acre family farm has seasonal hayrides, a massive wooden playground, and animal feeding areas featuring deer, sheep, goats, and emus. For parents, there are fresh corn, peaches, and blackberries in the summer, apples and pumpkins in the fall, and fresh-baked pies year-round. There always seems to be a weekend festival celebrating whatever the current crop is. Expect big crowds every weekend in October.

✎ **Sugartown Strawberries** (610-647-0711; www.sugartownstrawberries .com), 650 Sugartown Road, Malvern. Pick your own strawberries begin-

QVC

QVC Studios Tour (800-600-9900; www.qvctours.com), 1200 Wilson Drive, West Chester. Tours are offered on the hour daily between 10 and 4; $7.50 adults, $5 kids 6–12. How do those ankle bracelets and skin-care systems pass muster with quality-control experts? When is Isaac Mizrahi most likely to turn up in person? What is host Rick Domeier's favorite movie? Learn these and other facts about the fascinating world of round-of-clock shopping on QVC's popular daily tours. Friendly guides share behind-the-scene anecdotes and blooper videos (everything is live), then lead you past the color-coordinated product warehouse, the audio-visual computer nerve center, and an observation deck overlooking the various studio sets, where you might glimpse Mizrahi (a Philly native), Marie Osmond, or other celebrity guests. No reservations are needed, but the tours are limited to 20 people and often fill up in the summer.

A deluxe three-hour tour is given most Fridays; it's $75 a person, includes lunch in the QVC Commissary, visits to the green room where celebs chill before going on camera, and to the workshop where sets are created. Tickets for some of the shows are available but require advance reservations; check the Web site for more information. Tours include a coupon to use in the well-stocked gift shop, and there's a small convenience store selling coffee, tea, and packaged snacks.

QVC TOURS INCLUDE TIME FOR SHOPPING.

ning in May, or schedule a bird-watching tour with Farmer Bob (a.k.a.
caretaker Robert Lange), who will explain the farm's diverse habitats and
wetlands. There's a pumpkin patch, along with wagon rides and a hay-bale
maze on October weekends.

SCENIC DRIVES For a terrific back-roads drive between West Chester
and Chadds Ford, take Lenape Road (PA 52) south. You'll pass Baldwin's
Book Barn on the right, where Adirondack chairs dot the lawn and a barn
full of written treasures beckons. Continue on 52 as it veers south and
turns into Creek Road, and follow that along the east side of the Brandywine River for another mile. You'll end up at US 1 near two of the area's
best attractions, the Brandywine River Museum and the Christian C.
Sanderson Museum.

WINERIES The Brandywine Valley has several wineries set on picturesque farmland and operating out of century-old buildings and barns. Visit
www.bvwinetrail.org for information on events and a complete listing of
wineries.

Black Walnut Winery (610-857-5566; www.blackwalnutwinery.com),
3000 Lincoln Highway (near the end of the US 30 bypass), Sadsburyville.
The setting, a renovated 200-year-old barn with a deck and patio overlooking a landscaped pond, doesn't get much better than this; tastings are $7
for seven reds or whites. They also have a tasting room in Phoenixville.

Chadds Ford Winery (610-388-6221; www.chaddsford.com), 632 Baltimore Pike (US 1). Open 12–6 daily. One of the first large wineries to open
in Chester County, this scenic estate sells a variety of wines, including
Chambourcin, Syrah, and Pinot Noir, and has evolved into a true destination with daily tastings, cellar tours, wine-education classes, and live concerts and other events in the summer. It's just down the road from the
Brandywine River Museum.

J. Maki Winery (610-286-7754; www.jmakiwinery.com), 200 Grove Road,
Elverson. This lovely 32-acre estate in the far northern reaches of Chester
County produces red and white varietals, plus award-winning champagnes
and dessert ice wines. The tasting room is open daily.

Kruetz Creek Vineyards (610-869-4412), West Grove. Open 11–6 Saturday and Sunday. Jim and Carol Kirkpatrick grow 13 varieties of grapes
on 8 acres of farmland southwest of Kennett Square. Free tastings, plus
there's often live music on weekends throughout the year. They also run a
cheery tasting room in downtown West Chester where you can bring your
own food (BYOF) to go with your bottle or flight.

GARDENS

Two of the biggest attractions in the Brandywine Valley are **Longwood Gardens** in Kennett Square and **Winterthur,** about a 15-minute drive across the Delaware border. Both belonged to members of the duPont family and have lush gardens and grand estates, and both are money and time well spent. They are also very different. Here's the rundown on each one. A tip: don't ever, ever attempt to visit either property on Mother's Day.

🌿 ♿ **Longwood Gardens** (610-388-1000; www.longwoodgardens .com), $18 adults, $8 ages 5–18 (rates are higher at peak holiday times). Established by Pierre S. duPont, the former chairman of General Motors and a big fan of freely running water, Longwood Gardens resembles a formal 20th-century European pleasure garden with its ornate marble fountains and shrubs clipped to perfection. Highlights include a conservatory that shelters 20 indoor gardens and 5,500 types of plants (changed to intimately reflect each season), a flower garden walk that blooms with thousands of tulips in the spring, and a main fountain garden with more than 350 water jets that soar as high as 130 feet. One of its newest additions is a restored 1930s pipe organ, at 10,010 pipes it's the largest of its kind in the world; check the Web site for a concert schedule. For kids, there's an indoor children's garden within the conservatory with bamboo mazes and plenty of water-based activities. The gardens stay open until 10 PM on Tuesday, Friday, and Saturday in the summer, when colorful illuminated fountain

CONSERVATORY AT LONGWOOD GARDENS

WINDSOR CHAIRS AT WINTERTHUR

shows are accompanied by live orchestra music. The elaborate poinsettia display at Christmas draws big crowds, as does the Summer Concert Series, whose performers have included Keb' Mo and Pink Martini.

&. 🐾 Less than 10 miles away is **Winterthur** (302-888-4600; www.winterthur.org), the country estate of collector and horticulturist Henry duPont until 1951. If Longwood is the proper Sorbonne-educated uncle, Winterthur (the "h" is silent) is its slightly nuttier and laid-back second cousin. Whimsical displays of wildflowers, azaleas, daffodils, and magnolia and quince trees surround the estate; inside exhibits include an entire wall of hanging Windsor chairs and a collection of unusual soup tureens. The marquee attraction here is the 175-room house, where the duPonts lived and entertained for more than 20 years, which features their splendid collections of antique American furniture and other artifacts that were made in America between 1640 and 1860. The one-hour tours change throughout the year; a popular one is the "Elegant Entertaining" tour of the grand dining room, sitting rooms, and other public rooms. In December and early January, the "Yuletide" tour includes 18 festively decorated rooms and sells out quickly. Free trams run every few minutes from the visitor center through the gardens to the main house and often include banter from witty drivers. A ticket for only the galleries and gardens is $18, packages that include admission and one or two guided house tours start at $30 per adult.

✳ Outdoor Activities

BOAT EXCURSIONS/RENTALS The Brandywine River tends to be calm and meandering, perfect for self-guided canoeing and kayaking trips. **Northbrook Canoe Company** (610-793-2279; www.northbrookcanoe .com), 1810 Beagle Road in West Chester, rents one-person canoes and kayaks starting at $30 an hour. Inner tubes are also available for $18 an hour or $23 for three hours. Canoeing is also offered at **Brandywine Creek State Park**; call 302-655-5740 for fees and a schedule. **Wilderness Canoes** (302-654-2227) offers two and four-hour canoe or tandem kayak trips down the Brandywine starting at $55 per canoe.

FISHING Ridley Creek State Park in Media and **Newlin Grist Mill Park** are two good spots for trout fishing. Anglers may also fish for smallmouth bass, bluegill, crappie, and trout at **Brandywine Creek State Park.** A fishing license and a trout stamp are required, and can be obtained at any of the park offices (see Green Space).

GOLF Broad Run Golf Club (610-738-4410), 1520 Tattersall Way, West Chester. An 18-hole course with sloped fairways, deep bunkers, and three ponds on 370 acres of countryside.

HIKING Brandywine Creek State Park (302-577-3534), 41 Adams Dam Road, Greenville, Delaware.

HORSEBACK RIDING At Ridley Creek State Park, **Hidden Valley Farms** (610-892-7260) operates a stable that offers private and group lessons. **Gateway Stables** (610-444-1255) in Kennett Square offers year-round guided treks for families and individuals through the woods and fields along the Pennsylvania/Delaware border. Hour-long rides start at $40 a person; pony rides also available.

✳ Green Space

🐾 **Brandywine Creek State Park** (302-577-3534), 41 Adams Dam Road, Wilmington, Delaware. Open daily 8–sunset. Once a dairy farm owned by the duPont family, this 933-acre park has 14 miles of trails, open meadows that encourage picnicking and kite-flying, and plenty of recreational water activities such as fishing and canoeing. A nature center has maps, a gift shop, and an observation deck. Rocky Run is a popular 2-mile trail that winds along the creek and through pine forest and meadows. It begins at Thompson Bridge parking lot.

🐾 **Newlin Grist Mill Park** (610-459-2359), 219 S. Cheyney Road. This small park off US 1 is home to several miles of trails and the oldest operating 18th-century gristmill in the state. The visitor center is located in a

restored 1850s train station. The easy 1.5-mile Water Walk follows the west
banks of Chester Creek past dense woodland, trout ponds, and a 300-year-
old dam to the gristmill, then loops back around to the visitor center.

✦ ✿ **Ridley Creek State Park** (610-892-3200), 1023 Sycamore Mills
Road, Media. This 2,600-acre park has 12 miles of hiking, biking, and
equestrian trails, 14 picnic areas, and fishing platforms. Its crown jewel
is the **Colonial Plantation** (610-566-1725), a working farm restored to
its late 18th-century appearance. On weekends April through November,
there are costumed demonstrations of open-hearth cooking, food preservation, field plowing, and other chores of the era. Open 11–4 Wednesday through Sunday, $6 adults, $4 children. Closed mid-December
through March. Enter from West Chester Pike (PA 3). Be sure to check
out the Belgian horses, Devon milking cows, and other animals that live
on the property; they all represent the types of breeds that were around
in the late 1700s.

✳ Lodging

INNS & MOTELS ⅙ Brandy-
wine River Hotel (610-388-1200;
www.brandywineriverhotel), US 1
and PA 100, Chadds Ford. A
European-style inn along busy US
1 that combines the amenities of a
business hotel with homey bed-
and-breakfast touches like afternoon tea and cookies. The 40
rooms and suites are handsomely
decorated; many have queen or
king beds, convertible sofas, and
Jacuzzi tubs. A fitness center and a
cocktail bar are also on the premises. Rooms and suites $129–189.

🍴 ⅙ **Steak & Mushroom Motel**
(610-444-5085; www.kennettsteak
andmushroom.com), 201 Birch
Street, Kennett Square. Attached
to the Steak & Mushroom restaurant, this small motel opened in
1999 and has 13 clean and basic
rooms with queen beds, televisions, and coffeemakers. Downtown Kennett Square is a few
blocks away. Rooms $90.

BED & BREAKFASTS
⅙ **Fairville Inn** (610-388-5900;
www.fairvilleinn.com), 506 Kennett
Pike (PA 52). A longtime favorite
for romantic weekend getaways,
this pretty three-building complex
is just above the Delaware border
and five minutes from the Winterthur estate. The five rooms in
the 1820s Federal residence have
queen or king beds and private
baths; there's also a carriage house
with four rooms and two large and
quiet suites, as well as a springhouse with four rooms with fireplaces and private decks that face a
rolling meadow. Breakfast in the
dining room is a lavish event: a
buffet of fruit, yogurt, and pastries,
plus a choice of three hot entrées.
No children under 13. Rooms
$170–295, with a two-night mini-
mum on Saturday.

🍴 ♂ **Faunbrook** (610-436-5788;
www.faunbrook.com), 699 Rose-
dale Avenue, West Chester. A

classic B&B near West Chester University that masterfully blends 1880s history and decor with modern comforts such as WiFi, ultra-comfortable beds, and central air. Each of the five rooms is unique and named after the children of the U.S. Congressman who owned the stately property in the late 1800s. Edith's Room on the third floor is a quiet haven of lace curtains and wicker; most of the rooms have unusually large private bathrooms with claw-foot tubs, perfect for a luxurious soak. A wraparound porch is framed by original wrought iron and common rooms include a cozy mahogany-ceilinged den for afternoon wine or tea. Owners Steve and Lori Zytkowicz live on premise and

FAUNBROOK B&B IN WEST CHESTER

serve an elegant breakfast (crème brulee French toast is a specialty) in the dining room with fine china and candlelight. Baldwin's Book Barn is just a mile down the road. Rooms $135–209.

Hamanassett (610-459-3000; www.hamanassett.com), 725 Darlington Road, Media. Owner Ashley Mon, who was raised in New Orleans, infuses this 1856 mansion with Southern charm and her exquisite taste in antique furniture and collectibles. It can be found at the top of a hill of a residential development a few blocks from US 1 near the Brandywine Battlefield. The seven rooms are spacious with queen or king beds, large bathrooms, and top-quality linens. Be sure to check out Mon's antique toy collection and sip sherry amid the books and grand piano in the great room. Breakfast is a gourmet delight here, featuring such items as pesto pinwheel omelettes and homemade crawfish bread. Themed cooking school packages (Brandywine Bounty, Last Dinner on the Titanic) are also available some weekends. There's a two-bedroom carriage house behind the main house, where kids and pets are allowed. Rooms $165–230; carriage house $350–550.

Sweetwater Farm (610-459-4711; 800-793-3892; www.sweet waterfarmbb.com), 50 Sweetwater Road, Glen Mills. This 18th-century Quaker farmhouse on 50 bucolic acres 2 miles off US 1 is now a luxurious bed and breakfast owned by Grace Kelly's nephew, Chris Levine, and his wife, Vicki. With seven handsome guest rooms, five kid- and pet-friendly cottages, a landscaped swimming pool, fitness center, and nature trail, it's geared toward anyone looking for a complete weekend escape with minimal use of the car keys. Horses and sheep roam the grounds. The royal blue master bedroom in the 1815 wing is a guest favorite, with its meadow views and large fireplace; the Dormer Room, a large exposed-brick attic room, served as an infirmary during the Civil War. The farm is a popular site for wedding receptions. A winery, named after Chris's sister, Grace, and 5 acres of vineyards were added in 2009. Rooms $150–230, cottages $195–250.

CAMPGROUNDS KOA of West Chester (610-486-0447; 800-562-1726), 1659 Embreeville Road, Coatesville. Open late March through early November. About 7 miles west of West Chester, this attractive property skirts the Brandywine River and has 28 tent sites, 75 RV sites, and 15 one- and two-room cabins. A large swimming pool, playground, and fishing pond are also on-site. Tent sites start at $35, cabins are $72–86.

✷ Where to Eat

DINING OUT

West Chester

Ⓨ & **Dilworthtown Inn** (610-399-1390), 1390 Old Wilmington

Pike. Open daily for dinner. This restored 18th-century tavern may be the most romantic restaurant in the entire state. It seats 200 on any given night, but its three floors of separate candlelit dining rooms, many with walk-in fireplaces, make for an intimate and unique dining experience. The menu leans toward American with Asian influences, plus standbys such as chateaubriand for two, Australian rack of lamb, and Crab imperial. The wine selection is excellent, with more than 800 vintages. Reservations strongly recommended. Jackets strongly suggested for men. Entrées $24–47.

Ⓨ **Blue Pear Bistro** (610-399-9812), 275 Brintons Bridge Road. Dinner Monday through Saturday. A modern, more casual alternative to the adjacent Dilworthtown Inn (but with the same owners). There are USDA prime cheeseburgers, tenderloin chicken nuggets with truffle-honey mustard, tuna tartare, and other upscale snacks. Dishes $12–28.

Gilmore's (610-432-2800), 133 E. Gay Street. Open for dinner Tuesday through Saturday with seatings on Friday and Saturday at 6 and 8:30 only. A classic French restaurant that lets you bring your own wine? Believe it. Chef owner Peter Gilmore was the chef de cuisine at Philadelphia's Le Bec Fin for 22 years before opening this romantic bistro in downtown West Chester. The menu changes regularly and might include scotch-flavored lobster bisque, veal scaloppini in a Madeira cream sauce, and Caribbean butter fish coated with coconut and almonds. Desserts are just as decadent; try the milk-chocolate mousse or amaretto soufflé. Reservations recommended. BYO. Entrées $25–29.

&. ♟ **Limoncello** (610-436-6230), 9 N. Walnut Street. Lunch and dinner daily. Gourmet pizzas and southern Italian cuisine are the specialty here. The huge menu can be overwhelming, but it's a popular spot for lunch. Appetizers are half price during Monday through Friday happy hour.

♟ **Lincoln Room** (610-696-2102), 28 W. Market Street. Lunch and tea Tuesday through Saturday. West Chester's oldest building serves loose-leaf tea, cucumber sandwiches, and lemon-lavender scones in its cozy basement. The first biography of Abraham Lincoln was published here in 1860, and the tea room embraces the connection with old photos and mementoes of the 16th U.S. president. The signature dessert is croissant bread pudding. Dishes $4–8, tea for two $24.

&. ♟ **Vudu Lounge** (610-696-7435), 322 S. High Street. Lunch Tuesday through Friday, dinner daily. Formerly the High Street Caffe, this local favorite changed its name and decor in 2011 but kept its Cajun Creole menu of jambalaya, etouffee, blackened alligator, and more. It also has a full-service bar and live jazz on weekends.

Nearby

♟ &. **Fellini's Café** (610-892-7616), 106 W. State Street, Media. Lunch and dinner Monday through Friday; dinner Saturday and Sunday. A festive Italian trattoria with Old Country wall murals, live opera music on Monday nights, and a huge selection of pastas. Daily specials might include penne tossed with veal tips and chopped tomatoes, or grilled ahi tuna with lump crabmeat. Entrées $12–20.

♟ **Sovana Bistro** (610-444-5600; www.sovanabistro.com), 656 Unionville Road, Kennett Square. Lunch and dinner Tuesday through Saturday, dinner Sunday. Suave European bistro in the middle of horse country. Don't miss the thin-crust pizzas (broccoli and egg, house-made meatballs with ricotta). Other menu highlights: house-made pappardelle with wild boar Bolognese, and hanger steak with burgundy crema and caramelized onions. The no-reservations policy can mean long waits on weekends. Pizzas $15, dinner entrées $23–35.

♟ **Half Moon** (610-925-4984), 115 W. State Street, Kennett Square. Dinner Monday through Saturday. The rooftop bar and seating area is the draw here in summer; Belgian beers and creative game dishes (kangaroo, alligator, buffalo) are the specialty. The buffalo short-rib sandwich with caramelized onions is a favorite, but there are also many vegetarian options. Lunch $8–13, dinner entrées $16–32.

♠ ⅄ **Taqueria Moroleon** (610-268-3066), 8173 Newport Gap Pike (PA 41), Avondale. Open daily 11 AM–1 AM. Hugely popular Mexican restaurant near the Delaware border. Named after owner Isidro Rodriguez's hometown in Mexico, it somehow manages to appeal to both foodies who praise its citrus-marinated skirt steak tacos, authentic chile rellenos, and rich seafood soup, and Saturday-night diners who just want a strawberry margarita and Tex-Mex fajitas. No one should miss the molcajete Moroleón, a mortar bowl full of sizzling chicken, shrimp, beef, and cumin-scented chorizo in a pool of spicy tomatillo salsa. Be prepared for a wait on weekends, or take a seat at the boisterous bar. Lunch $4–9, dinner $10–17.

⅄ **The Whip Tavern** (610-383-0600), 1383 N. Chatham Road, Coatesville. Daily 11 AM–midnight. Catch a Phillies game while you dig into bangers and mash, Welsh rarebit, or vinegar fries in this true-blood English pub and restaurant. Happy hours feature $2 Bud Lights and lagers.

EATING OUT ♿ **Hank's Place** (610-388-7061), Baltimore Pike at PA 100, Chadds Ford. Breakfast and lunch daily, dinner Tuesday through Saturday. An old-school diner known for its calories-be-damned breakfasts—shiitake mushroom omelets, eggs Benedict topped off with chipped beef, and crispy scrapple are a few favorites.

Lunch and dinner include homemade meatloaf, chicken potpie, and macaroni and cheese with stewed tomatoes. Bonus fact: Andrew Wyeth liked to have breakfast here. Cash only. Dishes $6–$11.

♠ ♿ ⅄ **Kennett Steak & Mushroom** (610-444-5085), 201 Birch Street, Kennett Square. Owned by local mushroom growers Lou Caputo and Herb Guest, this boxy gray building may not look like much from the outside, but it has some of the best mushroom dishes around, plus a wide selection of top-quality steaks. Try the wild mushroom soup or the steak and exotic mushroom egg-roll appetizer before moving onto a rib eye topped with mushroom and onion marmalade. There are free samples of exotic mushrooms on Saturday nights. Lunch $7–14, dinner entrées $14–26.

West Chester
⚓ ♿ **Jimmy John's** (610-459-3083), West Chester Pike (US 202). Open daily for breakfast, lunch, and dinner. This institution on US 202 has been serving "pipin' hot sandwiches" to omnivores since 1940. The specialty is hot dogs, but you can also get burgers, cheesesteaks, and pork roll sandwiches. You can add bacon on anything for an extra 50 cents. Kids will love the electric trains that circle the dining area. A fire in 2010 didn't stifle its spirit; the owners rebuilt and were operating business as usual within a few months. Sandwiches $2–$5.

Ϋ **Kooma** (610-430-8980), 151 Gay Street. A lively bar scene and quality sushi attract a young and hip crowd. The stir-fry dishes are also tasty. Dishes $7–15. Entrées $15–26.

& **Three Little Pigs** (610-918-1272), 131 N. High Street. Open 10–3 Monday through Friday. This small deli serves salads, soup, and a dozen types of gourmet sandwiches including shrimp and crab salad, honey ham and Brie, and corned beef and coleslaw. Service is usually fast and no-nonsense. Dishes $6–7.

Nearby

🍴 & Ϋ **Buckley's Tavern** (302-656-9776), 5812 Kennett Pike, Centreville, Delaware. Open daily for lunch and dinner; Sunday brunch. Patrons of this 19th-century watering hole include employees of Winterthur (it's right down the road), out-of-towners, and the ascot-wearing horsey set. The Southern-influenced menu features everything from wild-mushroom calzone and burgers to shrimp, grits, and seared gaucho steak with sweet potato fries. Sunday brunch entrées, such as smoked salmon quiche and blueberry johnnycakes, are half-price for anyone wearing pajamas. The adjoining tavern is a lively local gathering place. Dishes $10–21.

Talula's Table (610-444-8255), 102 W. State Street, Kennett Square. Open daily 7–7. This gourmet food shop specializes in takeout prepared foods such as exotic mushroom risotto and chicken potpie; you may also eat in at the long table in the back. In the morning there are croissants, lemon ginger scones, sticky buns, and all kinds of coffee and tea drinks. Its Farm Table dinners for 8 to 12 people are renowned throughout the area and require reservations a year in advance.

Sarcone's Deli (215-860-9500), 2100 S. Eagle Road (at Swamp Road), Newtown. Chester County outpost of the venerable South Philadelphia hoagie maker. The rolls are every bit as fresh as the original spot.

CAFES & FARM STANDS

Eclat Chocolate (610-692-5206), 24 S. High Street, West Chester. Truffles, caramels, and signature chocolates from master chocolatier Christopher Curtain. The hand-crafted obsession bars are a treat, mixing dark chocolate with unique ingredients such as crushed Pennsylvania Dutch pretzels or wasabi peas. Samples are usually available.

Neuchatel Chocolates (610-932-2706), 461 Limestone Road, Oxford. The U.S. headquarters of the Swiss chocolatier is located just off US 1 near Lincoln University. Its store sells truffles, butter creams, and its signature Swiss Chips, local Herr's potato chips dipped in rich Swiss chocolate.

Haskell's SIW Vegetables (610-388-7491), 4317 S. Creek Road (PA 100), Chadds Ford. Open daily June through October. Sweet corn, melons, peppers, and dozens of varieties of heirloom tomatoes, all grown across the street at Hill Girt Farm.

The Woodlands (610-444-2192), 1020 Kaolin Road, Kennett Square. Open Monday through Friday 10–4, Saturday 10–3. The retail store of the Phillips Gourmet Mushroom empire is located in a restored 1820s farmhouse about a mile south of PA 1. You'll find every type of mushroom here, from plain white to oyster, plus pickled mushrooms, mushroom-centric cookbooks, and even mushroom freezer pops. There's also a 20-minute film about the process of growing mushrooms, as well as cooking demonstrations in the kitchen and specialty cooking classes. There are no public tours of the mushroom farms, but this is the next best way to learn more about this dominant southeastern Pennsylvania industry.

BYO Where to buy wine in the Brandywine Valley:

Collier's (302-656-3542); 5810 Kennett Pike, Centreville, Delaware, has a large selection of local and international wines, as does **Tim's Liquors** (302-239-5478), 6303 Limestone Road, Hockessin, Delaware. There's also a **Wine & Spirits** store (610-436-1706) at 933 Paoli Pike, West Chester. In Kennett Square, **Country Butcher Fine Food** (610-444-5980) sells wine from local wineries.

✳ Entertainment

MUSIC The Brandywine Valley isn't known for its active night life or live-music scene. The best late-night options are in downtown Media or West Chester along Gay and High Streets, where stores stay open until 9 on the first Friday of every month.

Ⓨ **Brickette Lounge** (610-696-9656), 1339 Pottstown Pike, West Chester. A fun bar and restaurant featuring live country bands like the Double Clutchin' Weasels. There's karaoke on Wednesday and line dancing on Tuesday and Thursday.

& Ⓨ **Iron Hill Brewery** (610-738-9600), 3 W. Gay Street, West Chester. This popular local brewery has live music on Wednesday nights from 9–11.

The Note (484-947-5713; www.thenotewc.com), 142 E. Market Street, West Chester. Live bands, and the occasional midget wrestling show, for a 21 and over crowd, with some all-ages shows. Settle in with a Philly Pale Ale at the long inviting bar, or head to the balcony overlooking the stage. Cover charge $5–15.

Ⓨ **Vudu Café and Lounge** (610-696-7435; www.highstreetcaffe.com), 322 S. High Street, West Chester. Live blues and jazz most nights, and a DJ on Friday. Open jazz jam on Wednesday nights. See also Eating Out.

THEATER Media Theatre (610-891-0100; www.mediatheatre.org),

104 E. State Street. A former vaudeville house that stages five Broadway shows a year and children's plays such as *Snow White* and *Robin Hood*.

✳ Selective Shopping

&. **Terrain at Styers** (877-583-7724; www.shopterrain.com), 914 Baltimore Pike (PA 1), Glen Mills. The founders of Urban Outfitters are behind this unique home decor shop and nursery. It's an oasis of wine-barrel chandeliers, French

BIRDHOUSES FOR SALE AT TERRAIN AT STYERS

BIRDHOUSES FOR SALE AT TERRAIN AT STYERS

birdcages, zinc fountains, teak furniture, and lavender plants in the middle of an ugly stretch of urban development and busy traffic. Leave time for lunch or dinner in the flower-filled greenhouse café.

Chadds Ford
Brandywine River Antiques Market (610-388-2000), 878 Baltimore Pike, Chadds Ford. Closed Monday and Tuesday. Local antiques shoppers like this large multi-vendor warehouse for its reasonable prices and wide selection of pottery, glass, books, and country and Victorian furniture. It's near the busy intersection of US 1 and PA 100 and right in front of the Brandywine River Hotel.

Chadds Ford Gallery (610-459-5510), 1609 Baltimore Pike (US 1). This two-story gallery features a huge selection of prints by N. C., Andrew, and Jamie Wyeth, including signed limited editions. It also holds exhibits by local artists.

Pennsbury-Chadds Ford Antique Mall (610-388-1620), 641 E. Baltimore Pike (US 1). More than 100 dealers selling everything from Civil War artifacts and vintage clothes to antique dolls and Oriental rugs. The upper level is open Thursday through Monday; the lower level, Saturday and Sunday.

R. W. Worth Antiques (610-388-4040), 810 Baltimore Pike. Exquisite (and expensive) furniture and decorative arts from the 18th and 19th century. You might find a

1790 mahogany sideboard, a dozen New York Sheraton chairs made between 1800 and 1820, or portraits of 18th-century men and women.

Kennett Square

Marion's Room (610-444-8312), 107 W. State Street. Framed photographs of Chester County, horse figurines, and locally made hot sauces are some of the items you'll find in this eclectic gift shop. Ask about the monthly wine and cheese tastings.

McLimans (610-444-3876; www .mclimans.com), 940 W. Cypress Street. Two stories of used and antique furniture at reasonable prices. The current inventory can be viewed on the Web site, so you can browse before you go.

The Mushroom Cap (610-444-8484), 114 W. State Street. This small store in downtown Kennett Square is devoted to the town's largest export. You'll find mushroom magnets, charm necklaces, and cookbooks, plus marinated mushrooms, mushroom pate, and fresh-picked shiitake and whites from owner Kathi Lafferty's family farm. There's a great little museum in the back with displays of tools, product labels, a miniature model of a mushroom house, and a video that explains how the crop is produced.

Quilt Sampler (610-444-1887), 719 W. Baltimore Pike, Kennett Square. A consignment shop for local quilters and artisans, this unique store in a red-shuttered

stone house features a changing inventory of antique quilts, pillows, table-top runners, toys, and blankets.

Thomas Macaluso Rare and Fine Books (610-444-1063), 130 S. Union Street, Kennett Square. Closed Monday. Carefully selected used books and first editions, plus antique maps and prints.

West Chester

Baldwin's Book Barn (610-696-0816; www.bookbarn.com), 865 Lenape Road (PA 100). This former dairy barn is now a book lover's utopia with 300,000 used and rare books crammed into five floors of crooked shelves and creaky planked floors. Start in the welcoming front room, where there's a large wood-burning stove and a large collection of antique maps and drawings, then just start wandering. Chairs are thoughtfully placed throughout the place (and Adirondacks are outside on the lawn) for those who feel like curling up with their finds. This is a unique place that is alone worth a trip to the Brandywine Valley.

QVC Outlet (610-889-3872), US 30 and Malin Road (in the Lincoln Park Shopping Center). One of a handful of outlets run by the shopping network. Everything's discounted, but the selection changes daily—one day you might find a treasure trove of 18-karat jewelry; another might feature B. Makowsky bags and Spanx undergarments. There's also a branch in Lancaster's Rockvale Square shopping center.

THE FRONT ROOM OF BALDWIN'S BOOK BARN

✳ Special Events

May: **Point to Point Steeplechase** (first Sunday), Centreville, Delaware. The social event of the season includes a parade of antique carriages, steeplechase racing, and tailgating on the elegant grounds of the Winterthur estate.

September: **Mushroom Festival** (first or second weekend), Kennett Square. The mushroom is the star of this two-day event featuring tours of local farms, a mushroom soup cook-off, an antiques and art show, and food offerings

like pumpkin-mushroom ice cream. Also in September is the **Revolutionary Times at Brandywine** (second weekend), when costumed soldiers reenact the 1777 Battle of Brandywine at the battlefield site.

December: **Candlelight Christmas in Chadds Ford** (first weekend)—the Chadds Ford Historical Society (610-388-7376) sponsors a driving tour of fieldstone farmhouses, Victorian mansions, and other historic buildings decorated in 18th-century style.

Bucks County 3

LOWER BUCKS

CENTRAL BUCKS

UPPER BUCKS

∎ INTRODUCTION

Situated in the southeastern corner of Pennsylvania and less than an hour's drive from Philadelphia, Bucks County has long been associated with old farmhouses, rolling green hillsides, and a peaceful Green Acres way of life. It was one of three original Pennsylvania counties founded by William Penn in 1862 and takes its name not from the deer that still populate its forests and rolling hillsides, but from the Penn family's native village of Buckinghamshire, England. Its place in history was cemented on Christmas Day 1776, when George Washington rallied his troops to cross the Delaware River in lower Bucks County in the middle of a fierce winter storm. The Continental Army then headed downriver and surprised the British soldiers camping out in Trenton, New Jersey, marking a major turning point of the Revolutionary War.

The river dominates the county's east side and separates Bucks County from central New Jersey. A historic 60-mile towpath parallels the river between Bristol to the south and Easton in the Lehigh Valley. Once trod by mule teams pulling cargo-laden boats along the canal, the towpath is used today by walkers, joggers, bicyclists, and cross-country skiers. Ever since Dorothy Parker bought 40 acres in Pipersville and took up gardening in the 1930s, burnt-out city dwellers have been coming to Bucks County, especially the central and northern parts, to decompress and listen to the grass grow. The area has been home to lyricist Oscar Hammerstein II, writers Pearl S. Buck and James A. Michener (who was raised in Doylestown), anthropologist Margaret Mead, and Stan and Jan Berenstain, authors of the popular children's book series. Residential development over the last couple of decades has changed the landscape of Central and Upper Bucks County (for the worse, if you ask any local who predates 1985), but the bucolic feel remains on its backcountry roads and in its quaint stone inns, and keeps visitors coming back again and again.

Just about every B&B here will claim that Washington slept, ate, tippled, soaked his feet, or hatched a battle in the very spot where you are standing. Quite often, they are right. Fortunately, many of the inns have been upgraded since the general's visits with luxuries such as indoor plumbing, 300-thread-count bed linens, and whirlpool tubs. The ones that remain on the rustic side often have their own appeal, like very reasonable rates, and a chance to encounter the many "friendly" ghosts of soldiers and other Revolutionary War-era figures said to haunt the streets of New Hope and its vicinity.

Unlike Washington and his troops, many business owners in Bucks County have no interest in braving a freezing winter along the Delaware and shut down for the better part of January or February. I mention this whenever possible in the listings, but it's a good idea to call ahead during this slow time of year.

Bucks County has a total population of more than 600,000 and tends to be viewed in three parts: Lower Bucks, easily accessible via I-95, is the most urban of the three, and home to Pennsylvania's second-largest casino, a *Sesame Street*-themed amusement park, and the many chain hotels that come with these attractions. Central Bucks has the hip riverfront village of New Hope and the brilliant museums and county-seat bustle of Doylestown. Upper Bucks remains largely rural and sleepy, with family-friendly campgrounds, old-fashioned general stores, and narrow, winding country roads that make perfect Sunday drives, but that you wouldn't ever, ever want to drive under the influence of anything stronger than a cup of tea.

It's tough to cover all three parts of Bucks County in one trip; the rural, two-lane roads that give much of the area its beauty also mean that drives can take two or three times longer than a map or online program suggests. For many visitors, that's part of the charm.

LOWER BUCKS

AREA CODE The entire Lower Bucks region lies within 215.

GUIDANCE **Bucks County Conference and Visitor Bureau** (800-836-2825; www.buckscvb.org), 3207 Street Road, Bensalem. This shiny new center in the southeast corner of Bucks County is a good source of information for the entire region. Their annual visitor guide offers detailed listings of many of the area's attractions, lodging, and eating options.

GETTING THERE By car: I-95, via Philadelphia or Trenton, New Jersey, cuts right through the lower end of Bucks County. The Pennsylvania Turnpike has three exits for Bucks County: exit 343 for PA 611 north (Doylestown), exit 351 for US 1 north (Quakertown), exit 358 for US 13 north.

By train: SEPTA's R3 line (215-580-7800; www.septa.org) runs regularly between Philadelphia's 30th Street Station and Yardley; the R2 stops in Warrington.

By bus: SEPTA bus route 14 to Bensalem and Langhorne.

By air: Lower Bucks County is accessible from two major airports, **Philadelphia International** (215-937-6800) and **New Jersey's Newark International** (800-397-4636).

GETTING AROUND By car: The small towns of Yardley and Newtown are pedestrian-friendly, but a car is your best way of getting around the south end of Bucks County. Major sights such as Pennsbury Manor, Sesame Place, and Washington Crossing are easiest to reach by car.

By foot: Lower Bucks County's many parks offer a variety of hiking trails for all fitness levels (see Green Space). For an urban walking experience, head to Newtown's historic district. Many people like to walk the Delaware Canal towpath between Yardley and Washington Crossing, a 3-mile stretch.

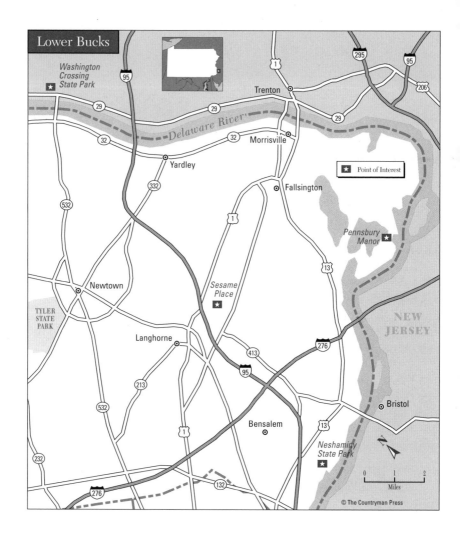

Lower Bucks

Washington Crossing State Park ★

Trenton

Delaware River

Morrisville

Yardley

★ Point of Interest

Fallsington

Pennsbury Manor ★

Newtown

Sesame Place ★

TYLER STATE PARK

NEW JERSEY

Langhorne

Bristol

Bensalem

Neshaminy State Park ★

0   1   2
Miles

© The Countryman Press

WHEN TO GO The fall brings a riot of color to the area's forests and rolling hills, while December means a flood of lights and festivals in places such as New Hope, Peddler's Village, and Byers' Choice. If you plan to be here in early spring, check with local sources about the condition of roads and towns near the Delaware River, which is prone to flooding.

MEDICAL EMERGENCY Frankford Hospital, Bucks County Campus (215-949-5000), 380 N. Oxford Valley Road, Langhorne. The **Bucks County Rescue Squad** (215-788-0444) is a nonprofit ambulance squad serving the Lower Bucks area.

✳ Villages

Bristol. First settled in 1681, Bristol is one of the oldest towns in Bucks County and home to the venerable King George Inn, which claims to be the oldest continuously run inn in the country. The focal point of the town is a waterfront area near Mill and Radcliffe Streets, where you will find the King George, a number of stores and cafés, a theater, and a pretty waterfront promenade.

Newtown. This thriving town was the county seat from 1725 to 1813. Its historic district, intersected by State and Washington Streets, is lined with many preserved Colonial-era residences, taverns, and inns. Newtown sponsors a pedestrian-friendly bash on the first Friday of the month, when many downtown shops and galleries stay open late.

Yardley. Anchored by a restored gristmill, this quaint town south of I-95 has several good restaurants, a man-made pond, and a pretty main street lined with trees and Victorian homes. It was a station for the Underground Railroad during the Civil War and is home to the family-owned Cramer's Bakery and the Yardley Inn. The Delaware River, bordering the town to the east, adds to its beauty.

✳ To See

HISTORIC SITES ♿ **Pennsbury Manor** (215-946-0400; www.pennsbury manor.org), 400 Pennsbury Memorial Road, Morrisville. Open 9–5 Tuesday through Saturday, 12–5 Sunday; $7 adults, $4 ages 6–17. As much as William Penn contributed to this state in name and philosophy, few sites

PENNSBURY, WILLIAM PENN'S COUNTRY HOME

or museums offer a window into his time here. That's why this 43-acre site, to which the Quaker governor and his family retreated to escape the "city life" and political mayhem of Philadelphia, is more than just an English gentleman's 18th-century country estate. The redbrick manor house that Penn designed and built fell into ruin in the early 1700s, but was reconstructed painstakingly by historical architects in the 1930s. It includes an herb garden, one of the state's largest collection of 17th-century furnishings, and views of the Delaware River. On weekends, costumed artisans demonstrate open-hearth cooking, woodworking, sheep shearing, and other trades and crafts of the time. Don't forget to check out Penn's personal sailing barge in a covered garage near the main house. A shiny new visitor center, which unfortunately doesn't match the regality of the estate, opened in 2007. Tours of the house are given several times each day during the summer, and twice a day on weekends in winter. Perhaps because of its remote location, it is often blissfully uncrowded.

Philadelphia Athletics Historical Society (215-323-9901; www .philadelphiaathletics.org), 6 N. York Road, Hatboro. Open 10–3 Monday through Saturday; free. Shoeless Joe Jackson started his Major League Baseball career with the Philadelphia Athletics in 1908. You'll learn about this, along with many more stories about the A's, from the loyal volunteers behind this unassuming storefront just west of the Bucks County line. The back part is filled with original baseball jerseys, World Championship pennants, an original 1909 turnstile from Shibe Park (later re-named Connie

A MUSEUM HONORS THE PHILADELPHIA ATHLETICS BASEBALL TEAM.

Mack Stadium), and many photos of the players and legendary owner and manager Connie Mack. There's a gift shop in front that sells autographed bats and balls, replica World Series programs, souvenir stadium bricks, and much more. It's 2 miles off the Pennsylvania Turnpike and about a 30-minute drive from Philadelphia.

WINERIES Many of Bucks County's wineries started as hobbies or pipe dreams, but have grown into serious producers of Chardonnay, Cabernet, and other drinkable wines, much to the pleased surprise of everyone involved. The historic buildings and peaceful rural settings of the properties are sometimes as enjoyable as the wines themselves. Some wineries are only open for tastings on weekends, while others are open daily. Check Web sites for specific hours or visit www.buckscountywinetrail.com for more information.

& **Buckingham Vineyards** (215-794-7188; www.pawine.com), 1521 PA 413, Buckingham (central Bucks). Open 11–6 Tuesday through Saturday, 12–5 Sunday. One of Pennsylvania's largest and oldest wineries was begun in the 1970s by two University of Pennsylvania graduates. The Forest family still runs the place, conveniently located between New Hope and Doylestown. offering a selection of wines from deep, oak-aged reds to dry whites, as well as self-guided tours. It's a laid-back environment, with self-service tastings and picnic tables that encourage lingering.

& **Crossing Vineyards** (215-493-6500; www.crossingvineyards.com), 1853 Wrightstown Road, between Washington Crossing and Newtown (lower Bucks). The Carroll family began selling wines in 2003 and regularly wins awards for its Viognier and Pinot Noir. Set on a 200-acre estate, the facility has separate barrel and bottling rooms and a tasting room overlooking 15 acres of vineyards. It also serves as a community gathering place, with evening lectures, singles events, and "meet the winemaker" dinners.

& **New Hope Winery** (215-794-2331; www.newhopewinery.com), 6123 Lower York Road. A music destination as much as a winery, this large property added a bar and restaurant in 2010 and hosts accomplished blues guitarists and singer-songwriters such as Joan Osborne and Peter Yarrow. Wine is available for $25 a bottle during concerts.

& ♂ **Rose Bank Winery** (215-860-5899; www.rosebankwinery.com), 258 Durham Road, Newtown (lower Bucks). Even teetotalers will be charmed by this 1790 manor estate north of Newtown. Besides a winery, it's a sheep farm and a popular setting for weddings. Its specialty is a sweet wine made with New Jersey blueberries. Vineyard tours on weekends, weather-permitting.

✐ **Washington Crossing Historic Park** (215-493-4076; www.ushistory .org/washingtoncrossing), 1112 River Road, Washington Crossing. Open 9–5 Tuesday through Saturday, 12–5 Sunday; free. Of all the Washington-slept-here places in Bucks County, this is the place history buffs will most want to witness. It was here that George Washington rallied his troops to cross the Delaware River in the middle of a fierce winter storm on Christmas Day 1776, which resulted in surprising the British soldiers over in Trenton and one of the most significant battles of the Revolutionary War. Even on a gentle summer day, it's easy to stand at the spot where Washington's demoralized troops embarked on their 11-hour journey, gaze across the powerful river, and marvel at the determination it must have taken to pick up those oars. The park is spread out along River Road and home to several picnic areas, easy walking trails, and 13 historic buildings, including **McConkey's Ferry Inn,** the guard outpost where General Washington and his aides ate dinner and made plans prior to the crossing, and the **Thompson-Neely House,** a private home that served as a convalescent hospital in the winter of 1776 and 1777. Start at the visitor center on River Road north of PA 532, where you can watch a short film, pick up maps, and check out the digitally mastered photomural of Emanuel Leutze's famous painting *George Washington Crossing the Delaware* (staffers will grumble that New York's Metropolitan Museum of Art has the real thing). Just outside the visitor center is the stone marker that commemorates the spot where the troops crossed and a 20th-century barn with several replica Durham boats that were used to transport soldiers, horses, and equipment across the river on that famous night. A short drive north on River Road is **Bowman's Hill Tower,** a 125-foot tower that was built in 1931 as a monument to the Rev-

♿ **Sand Castle Winery** (800-722-9463; www.sandcastlewinery.com), 755 River Road, Erwinna (Upper Bucks). The 11,000-square-foot main facility really looks like a sand castle. Ascend the winding road just above the Golden Pheasant Inn and sample Johannesburg Riesling, Chardonnay, Cabernet, and Pinot Noir drawn from the surrounding vineyards. Tours of the barrels and underground wine cellar are available for $5–10. It's worth a stop for the views of the vineyards and Delaware River alone, and the upstairs art gallery, opened in 2010, is a hushed oasis of Bohemian glass

SITE OF WASHINGTON'S CROSSING THE DELAWARE RIVER

olutionary War and offers sweeping views of the Delaware River Valley. It's open May to December, though the hours can be erratic. Guided tours are $5 and include entrance to the tower and tours of McConkey's Ferry Inn and the **Thompson-Neely House.** Also worth a stop is the memorial grave site of 40 to 60 unknown soldiers who died during that bitter winter. It can be accessed via the Delaware Canal towpath east of the Thompson-Neely House. The park is visited most often in December, when dozens of "soldiers" and a carefully selected General Washington cross the river in an annual reenactment of the event. The visitor center was closed for extensive renovations at press time but expected to re-open in late 2012.

and paintings by artists from Slovakia, the homeland of the winery's owners, Joseph and Paul Maxian.

Unami Ridge Winery (215-804-5545), 2144 Kumry Road, Trumbauersville (Upper Bucks). The county's newest winery is also its smallest, located at its northwestern-most tip near Quakertown. It's a charming spot, however, where you can sip fine Chardonnay on a patio overlooking the vineyard. They also produce Scheurebe, Riesling, Cabernet Franc, and Pinot Noir.

UNAMI RIDGE WINERY IN UPPER BUCKS

✳ To Do

FOR FAMILIES ✍ ❧ **Sesame Place** (215-752-7070; www.sesameplace
.com), 100 Sesame Road, Langhorne. Open May through October; $52.99
adults and kids 2 and up; parking $15. Let's face it: most sane adults
would rather get a root canal than come here on a summer weekend and
put up with the long lines and elbow-to-elbow crowds. But if you catch
this 14-acre theme park on a weekday or early in the day when the lines
are manageable and the noise levels bearable, there is fun to be had. It's
the only theme park around featuring Elmo and his Sesame Street pals in
live dance shows, a twice-a-day parade, and 28 different rides and water
attractions that splash, climb, bounce, and twirl. Most attractions are
geared toward ages 2–12. There are also regular breakfasts with Elmo,
lunches with Cookie Monster, and dinners with Big Bird (for an extra fee).

Shady Brook Farm (215-968-1670; www.shadybrookfarm.com), 1 Stony
Hill Road, Yardley. Pick your own peaches, raspberries, and apples at one
of the last remaining working farms in Bucks County. The store and café
sells raw milk, local organic beef, homemade ice cream, and all kinds of
prepared foods. Seasonal events include summer wine fests on Friday
nights, a pumpkin festival at Halloween, and a holiday light show in
December.

GAMBLING ❧ **Parx Casino and Racetrack** (215-639-9000; www.parx
casino.com), 3001 Street Road, Bensalem. Dubbed a "racino" because it

houses both a casino and thoroughbred horse racetrack, this five-story bet- 149
ting parlor 25 miles east of Philadelphia opened in late 2006 after the
Pennsylvania Gaming Board voted to grant permanent casino licenses to
six existing horseracing facilities. It can't compete with Atlantic City's glitz
and high-stakes jackpots, but local crowds fill up the parking lot on weekends and keep the 3,300 slot machines clanging. Electronic gaming tables
(blackjack, poker, and roulette) were added in 2010, and there are weekly
poker tournaments on Tuesday and Saturday. For sustenance, there's an
upscale steak house, a deli, and a branch of the Philly crab house, Chick-
ie's and Pete's. The adjacent racetrack hosts thoroughbred races year-
round, including the $750,000 Pennsylvania Derby over Labor Day
weekend.

✻ Outdoor Activities

GOLF Makefield Highlands Golf Club (215-321-7000; www.makefield
highlands.com), 1418 Woodside Road, Yardley. An 18-hole par-72 course
featuring 7,058 yards of golf from the longest tees.

TENNIS Frosty Hollow Tennis Center (215-493-3646), New Falls
Road, Levittown. Ten indoor public courts.
Bucks County Racquet Club (215-493-5556), Washington Crossing.
Indoor and outdoor courts are open to the public starting at $18 an hour.
Core Creek Tennis Center (215-322-6802), Woodbourne Road, Lang-
horne. Outdoor public courts.

✻ Green Space

✐ 🐾 **Churchville Nature Center** (215-357-4005; www.churchvillenature
center.org), 501 Churchville Lane, Churchville. Open 10–5 Tuesday
through Sunday. Despite its proximity to busy roads and new housing
developments, this 54-acre preserve is an oasis of wild gardens, dense
woodland, and salt marshes with 2 miles of hiking trails and a large picnic
grove. There's also a visitor center, as well as a re-created Lenape Indian
village with traditional wigwams and elm-bark wickiups (the Lenni-
Lenape were the original residents of the Delaware River Valley). Public
tours of the village are available Sunday, April through October. It's about
a 15-minute drive from Bensalem and a 10-minute drive from Newtown.
🐾 **Neshaminy State Park** (215-639-4538), 263 Dunks Ferry Road, Bensalem. Neshaminy Creek meets the Delaware River at this 330-acre park
just south of I-95. The short River Walk Trail has a wonderful view of the
Philadelphia skyline and is a favorite trail for dog-walkers. Pick up a
brochure at the park office for more information on the estuary. There's
also a swimming pool, along with picnic areas.

LOWER BUCKS

✦ ✿ **Tyler State Park** (215-968-2021), 101 Swamp Road, Newtown. Neshaminy Creek winds through this popular 1,700-acre park, which was once the estate of the Tylers, a wealthy farming family that developed one of the finest Ayrshire dairy herds in the county. It has 10 miles of hilly bike trails, seven picnic areas, playgrounds, and walking paths that lead past original stone buildings and the longest covered bridge in Bucks County. Not enough? You can also rent canoes, fish for carp and small-mouth bass, play disc golf, or walk the dog.

✳ Lodging

Lower Bucks has more hotels than anywhere else in the county, though the majority tend to be run-of-the-mill chains catering to I-95 travelers. **Courtyard by Marriott** (215-945-8390), in Langhorne, is the closest hotel to Sesame Place and offers free shuttle service to the park for its guests. There are also some interesting, comfortable sleeping options for intrepid travelers who don't mind staying off the beaten path or sharing a yard with a pot-bellied pig.

BED & BREAKFASTS
♂ **Salem Creekside Inn** (215-384-4084; www.salemcreekside inn.com), 1031 Totem Road, Bensalem. Sleep in a beautifully converted 1697 ferry house next to Neshaminy Creek, then enjoy the modern conveniences of nearby Parx Casino or Sesame Place. The three tidy guest rooms have private baths, flat-screen TVs, and views of the creek or gardens. There's also a third-floor suite with two separate bedrooms that accommodates four. Rooms $125–$150. Suite $225–254.

⊕ **Temperance House** (215-860-9975; www.temperancehouse.com), 5 South Street, Newtown. First opened as an inn in 1772, this red-shingled brick building in the heart of downtown Newtown has served as a gathering place for those fighting colonists' causes and a teetotaling restaurant whose hardest drink was lemonade. Today, "the Temp" is attached to a full-service bar and restaurant (see also Dining Out) and has 11 unique rooms and suites with private baths that are modern and comfortable while retaining the inn's historic feel. Breakfast is included in the rate. Light sleepers might want to avoid the rooms facing State Street. Rooms start at $120, and suites with fireplaces are $150–185.

Bridgetown Mill House (215-752-8996; www.bridgetownmill house.com), 760 Langhorne-Newtown Road (PA 413), Langhorne. One of the few luxury lodging options in lower Bucks County, this former gristmill property has five guest rooms, 8 acres of lawns and gardens, and a first-rate restaurant (see also Dining Out). Kim and Carlos DaCosta bought the place in 1995 and spent three years converting it into a high-end bed and breakfast, preserving the Federal architecture that exemplifies many of Bucks County's historic rural estates. Rooms have four-poster canopy beds, private baths, and TVs, and include breakfast. Guests also have access to the library, solarium, formal dining room, sitting room, brick patio, and 0.25-mile jogging track that winds past Neshaminy Creek. Rooms $155–225.

OTHER LODGING *Cottage at Kabeyun* (215-736-1213; www.buckscountycottage.com), 699 River Road, Yardley. Alfred and Emily Glossbrenner own this white-shingled riverfront cottage about 2 miles south of downtown Yardley. It's perfect for families or couples looking for a home-away-from-home getaway. The 700-square-foot cottage has one master bedroom, one bathroom, a full kitchen, and an office or second bedroom with a twin bed and pop-up trundle. The Glossbrenners, who live next door, are on hand to answer questions and keep the place stocked with towels, fireplace logs, books, and other amenities. Another bonus: access to the Delaware Canal towpath is 0.25-mile away. It sometimes books up for a month at a time, so reserve early if you can. A three-night minimum stay, at $195 a night, is required. The weekly rate is $1,000.

*** Ross Mill Farm** (215-322-1539; www.rossmillfarm.com), 2464 Walton Road, Rushland. Owners Richard and Susan Magidson call their farm north of Newtown the world's only boardinghouse for pet potbellied pigs. But they also let humans stay on the premises in a 17th-century cottage for the bargain price of $120 a night. The rustic cottage sleeps up to six people and has a full kitchen, working fireplace, and 30 surrounding acres that guests are welcome to share with the pigs. It's a great place for families (though note that the upstairs bedroom can be accessed only via spiral staircase), and pets are welcome. Unlike the piggy spa, the cottage doesn't come with pool or daily maid service, though the Magidsons sometimes let guests borrow one of the pigs for the night.

⁜ Where to Eat

DINING OUT *Bridgetown Mill House* (215-752-8996; www.bridgetownmillhouse.com), 760 Langhorne-Newtown Road (PA 413), Langhorne. Lunch Tuesday through Friday, dinner Tuesday through Saturday. This is a special-occasion restaurant worth the splurge; reservations are recommended. The wait staff dress in tuxedoes, tables are set with fine white linens and crystal stemware, and large picture windows framed in oak line the main dining room. The classic continental menu changes every three months;

among the standouts are Prince Edward Island mussels steamed with Guinness stout, leeks, and chorizo, caramelized filet mignon gorgonzola, and pan-roasted scallops in a Caribbean tomato broth. A la carte entrées are $17–30, but a three-course prix-fixe menu is available for $30 on weekdays. There's also a summer tapas menu served on the expansive patio.

Charcoal (215-493-6394; www.charcoalbyob.com), 11 S. Delaware Avenue, Yardley. Breakfast, lunch, and dinner Tuesday through Sunday. Breakfast and lunch at this riverfront café, which was renovated and reopened in 2008 after a devastating flood, means simple diner fare: omelets, turkey burgers, and club sandwiches. Dinner, on the other hand, is bold and modern: five-spice duck breast with kimchi, corned beef tongue in rye jus,

fried chicken with smoked buttermilk biscuits. Expect lots of nightly specials and whimsical gastro-science creations. Reservations are recommended at dinner.

&. ⍓ **King George II Inn** (215-788-5536; www.kginn.com), 102 Radcliffe Street, Bristol. This 17th-century landmark was a stagecoach stop for travelers between New York and Philadelphia. Have a cocktail in the cozy, wood-panelled bar then enjoy acorn squash risotto or slow-roasted prime rib in a dining room with lovely views of the Delaware River. This beloved watering hole has had its ups and downs over the years but happily remains open. You may bring your own wine on Monday nights. Entrées $12–28.

⍓ **Temperance House** (215-860-9975), 5 South Street, Newtown. Bargain Tuesday through Thursday dinner specials (three courses

KING GEORGE II INN ON THE DELAWARE

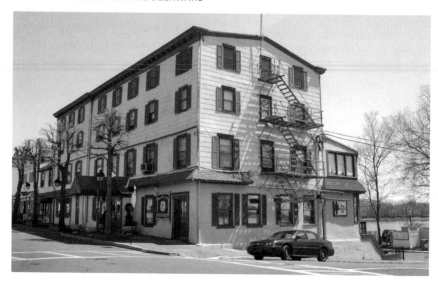

for $18) keep this place buzzing on weekday evenings. The classic American menu includes filet mignon, New York strip steak, Guinness BBQ ribs, and pan-seared scallops and shrimp with sun-dried tomato risotto,; the more casual tavern menu features roast pork sandwiches, crab cakes, and cheesesteak spring rolls. Lunch $8–12. Entrées $14–33.

 ♿ ♂ ⌢ **Washington Crossing Inn** (215-493-3634), PA 32 and PA 532, Washington Crossing. Open daily for lunch, dinner, and late-night snacks. Not long ago, this 18th-century inn around the corner from the site of Washington's historic crossing was known more for its quirkiness—a parrot greeted patrons at the entrance and portraits of Elvis hung on the walls—than its culinary attributes. But the menu has been revamped and modernized in recent years, and it's a good choice if you like pomp and history with your meal. Dinner might be Scottish salmon in a truffle-lemon vinaigrette, or lamb chops with bacon grits and onion and pepper piquillo marmalade, or slow-roasted prime rib (weekends only). Request a table in the inn's anteroom, a step-down former porch featuring murals of Bucks County's covered bridges. Staffers will tell you that General Washington ate one of his last meals here before heading over to Trenton. Lunch $9–17. Entrées $26–44.

♿ ⌢ **Yardley Inn** (215-493-3800), Afton Avenue at River Road, Yard-

ley. Lunch and dinner daily, Sunday brunch. Locals favor this circa-1890 restaurant across from the Delaware River for its classic modern decor, friendly environment, and an upscale menu that includes grilled New Zealand lamb, Long Island duck, and mushroom-crusted salmon. The reasonably priced bar menu features sirloin burgers, salads, and a variety of tasty appetizers, including lobster mac and cheese and crab quesadillas. Reservations are recommended on weekends. Entrées $24–38, bar menu, $6–18.

EATING OUT ♂ ♿ ⌢ **Bowman's Tavern** (215-862-2972), 1600 River Road, New Hope. A good place for a casual meal (crab cakes, hot roast beef sandwiches, Caesar salads, grilled pork chops) between New Hope and Washington Crossing. There's live music in the piano lounge every night; expect big crowds on weekends. Sandwiches and salads $6–9, entrées $15–30.

❀ **Daddypops Diner** (215-675-9717), 232 N. York Road, Hatboro. Open daily 6 AM–2 PM. The nutmeg-spiked flapjacks, crisp home fries, and low prices make up for indifferent service at this old-school diner near the Bucks County line. People drive miles for its house-made scrapple, which was featured on the Food Network's *Diners, Dives, and Drive-ins.*

♿ ⌢ **Isaac Newton's** (215-860-5100), 18 S. State Street, Newtown. The burger, pizza, and salad menu is decent, but the stellar selection of microbrews and Belgian-style beers keep this place buzzing every night. It's in a two-story building in the municipal parking lot behind State Street. Domestic pints are half-price on weeknights 10–midnight. The outside deck is a popular spot on summer evenings.

Jack's Cold Cuts (215-639-2346), 1951 Street Road, Bensalem. This New York–style deli near Philadelphia Park Casino features 80 different varieties of sandwiches (turkey with roasted peppers, hot brisket, roast pork and sauerkraut, and white fish salad, to name a few). The prices are as reasonable as the sandwiches are tasty. Sandwiches: $4–7.

Jules Thin Crust Pizza (215-579-0111; www.julesthincrust .com), 300 Sycamore Street, Newtown. Open daily for lunch and dinner. This BYO is the place to go when you want your pizza with a dash of Gwyneth Paltrow sophistication. The delicate pies are served on wood slabs with toppings such as fig jam, organic artichokes, and arugula. There are also branches in Doylestown and Jenkintown.

♫ ♞ **Nifty Fifties** (215-638-1950), 2555 Street Road, Bensalem. A kids' nirvana of thick milk shakes and mini-golf near both I-95 and the Pennsylvania Turnpike. Adults will like the varied menu (creamed chipped beef omelets at breakfast, crab cakes at lunch), jukebox tunes, and reasonable prices.

BYO Where to buy wine in Lower Bucks:

Wine & Spirits stores are in Yardley at 635 Heacock Road (215-493-3182) and Morrisville at 229 Plaza Boulevard in Pennsbury Plaza (215-736-3127).

CAFÉS & BAKERIES

♫ ♿ **Cramer's Bakery** (215-493-2760), 26 E. Afton Avenue, Yardley. Specialties at this venerable bakery include seven-layer cake, raisin bars, and pumpkin chocolate cookies. They also sell delicious German butter cake, a yeast-based cake with a pudding center that was a popular Philadelphia dessert until people started to realize its calorie count was higher than the state deficit.

Colonial Farms (215-493-1548), 1108 Taylorsville Road (at PA 532), Washington Crossing. Pick up a ham and Brie sandwich or sack of pastries at this gourmet market and bring a picnic to nearby Washington Crossing State Park.

Lochel's Bakery (215-773-9779; www.lochelsbakery.com), 57 S. York Road, Hatboro. Closed Monday. Stop here for a delicious cream-filled donut or cannoli cupcake after a visit to the Philadelphia Athletics Historical Society. The cinnamon buns and French apple pie are also good, and the cakes are design masterpieces of buttercream icing and rosebuds.

Sweet Pea Creams and Confections (215-968-0466), 254 N. Sycamore Street, Newtown.

Frozen yogurt, chocolate-dipped pretzels, cupcakes, and more.

🍴 ♿ **Zebra-Striped Whale** (215-860-4122), 12 S. State Street, Newtown. Named after a children's book written by owner Shari F. Donahue, this inviting café serves micro-roasted coffee, frozen hot chocolate, and custom-made ice cream "whirlwinds" of candy, fruit, or nuts. There's live jazz in the back room on Thursday evenings.

✳ Entertainment

MUSIC ♿ ♟ **Washington Crossing Inn** (215-493-3634), PA 32 and PA 532. The piano bar features live performances (usually on the mellow side) every weekend and some weeknights.

The Newtown Chamber Orchestra (215-968-2005; www.newtownchamberorchestra.org) performs at various sites throughout the area, including Bucks County Community College. Check Web site for details.

360 Lounge at Parx Casino (888-588-PARX; www.parxcasino.com) in Bensalem hosts DJs and live performers such as Sheena Easton and Micky Dolenz. Check Web site for schedules.

THEATER ♿ **Bristol Riverside Theatre** (215-785-0100; www.brtstage.com), 120 Radcliffe Street, Bristol. This restored 300-seat theater hosts professionally staged musicals, dramas, and art exhibits. Fun children's shows, too.

Langhorne Players (215-860-0818; www.langhorneplayers.org) stages five dramas and comedies a season at the Spring Garden Mill at Tyler State Park. Past shows include David Lindsay-Abaire's *Rabbit Hole* and Edward Albee's *Seascape*.

Newtown Theatre (215-968-3859, www.newtowntheatre.com), 120 N. State Street, Newtown. One of the nation's oldest movie theaters screens first-run films, plus four plays and musicals a year staged by the Newtown Arts Co. Lucky for us, the owners installed air-conditioning in 2002 for a gala screening of *Signs*, the M. Night Shyamalan movie that was filmed in and around Newtown.

✳ Selective Shopping

Franklin Mills Mall (215-632-1500), 1455 Franklin Circle, Philadelphia, just west of the Bucks County line, is the king of discount shopping, easily reachable via I-95. It has 200 stores, including Burlington Coat Factory and Last Call by Neiman Marcus. For a small-town experience, Newtown's walkable main street offers many boutiques and art galleries. Head to the Bristol waterfront for antiques and tattoos.

Another Time Antiques (215-788-3131), 301 Mill Street, Bristol. Fun-to-browse shop selling period lamps, vintage jewelry, and a large selection of furniture.

Delaware River Gallery (215-321-3285), 19 E. Afton Avenue,

Yardley. This 25-year-old gallery across from Cramer's Bakery represents local and national artists. On display are original paintings and limited edition prints, ranging from landscapes by Bucks County artists to exotic wildlife art and historical events.

Newtown

Bucks Gallery of Fine Art (215-579-0050), 201 S. State Street. Two floors of artworks by contemporary and traditional Bucks County painters and sculptors.

Dragonfly (215-579-8888), 110 S. State Street. Whimsical gift shop selling handcrafted pottery, mixed-metal jewelry, and garden flags. There's also a great selection of baby gifts.

Newtown Book and Record Exchange (215-968-4914; www .newtownbookandrecord.com), 102 S. State Street. Looking for a Stephen King paperback or 1960s Band of Joy LP? You just may find it at this well-organized storefront where owner Bobbie Lewis has been selling used books, records, and CDs for 30 years.

stown fair grounds—real country agricultural fair, with farm products, livestock judging, horse shows, and barbecue dinners.

October: **Fall Fine Craft Festival** (third weekend), Tyler State Park, Newtown—the Pennsylvania Guild of Craftsmen's biggest outdoor exhibition features more than 180 displays of paintings, sculptures, and other works, plus live music and fine foods.

December: **Reenactment of Washington's Crossing** (Christmas Day), Washington Crossing State Park—Thousands of people gather on the banks of the Delaware to watch costumed volunteers re-create General George Washington's historic boat ride across the icy river. The reenactment begins around 1 PM and finishes across the river in Titusville, New Jersey. Musket-firing ceremonies and speeches are held on both sides of the river. It's the cornerstone event of this park, and much time and consideration goes into selecting the volunteer who portrays General. Washington.

✳ Special Events

August: **Middletown Grange Fair** (third weekend), Wright-

CENTRAL BUCKS

AREA CODE The entire Central Bucks region lies within the 215 area code.

GUIDANCE New Hope Information Center (215-862-5030; www.new hopeinformationcenter.org), 1 Mechanic Street Open daily. Housed in New Hope's first city hall, school, and jailhouse, this is a great source for free walking maps, calendars, gallery schedules, and local newspapers. If you're really smitten with the town, there are New Hope–emblazed mugs, shot glasses, tote bags, and snow globes available for purchase. Across the river, visit the **Lambertville Chamber of Commerce** (609-397-0055; www.lambertville.org), 60 Wilson Street, for maps and other info. **Doylestown Business Alliance** (215-340-9988; www.doylestownalliance.com), 17 W. State Street, offers detailed walking maps and visitor guides.

GETTING THERE By car: I-95, via Philadelphia or Trenton, New Jersey, cuts right through the lower end of Bucks County. To get to points north, take the River Road/PA 32 exit and head toward New Hope. US 202 is also a good way to reach New Hope or Doylestown from the east.

By bus: **Trans-Bridge Lines** (800-962-9135; www.transbridgebus.com) operates daily bus service to Lambertville from New York City and from Newark and JFK airports. The bus stops at Main and Bridge streets in Lambertville, New Jersey.

By train: SEPTA regional R5 line runs between Philadelphia's 30th Street Station and downtown Doylestown.

By air: Bucks County is accessible from two major airports, **Philadelphia International** (215-937-6800) and **New Jersey's Newark International** (800-397-4636). **Lehigh Valley International Airport** in Allentown (888-359-5842) is about an hour's drive away from the central region.

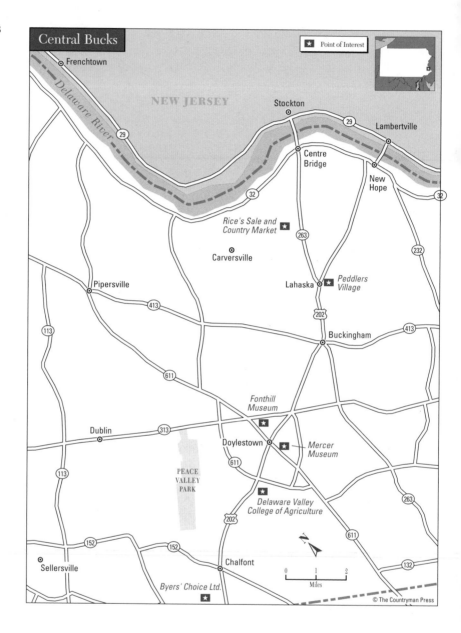

Central Bucks

★ Point of Interest

NEW JERSEY

Frenchtown

Delaware River

Stockton

29

Lambertville

Centre
Bridge

New
Hope

32

32

Rice's Sale and ★
Country Market

263

232

Carversville

Pipersville

Lahaska ★ Peddlers
Village

202

413

113

Buckingham

413

611

Fonthill
Museum ★

Dublin

313

Doylestown ★ Mercer
Museum

611

113

PEACE
VALLEY
PARK

★
Delaware Valley
College of Agriculture

202

263

611

152

152

Chalfont

Sellersville

0   1   2
Miles

132

Byers' Choice Ltd.
★

© The Countryman Press

GETTING AROUND By car: The two-lane roads that link New Hope with Doylestown and other Central Bucks towns are easy to navigate and lined with antiques shops and farm estates. US 202 runs east-west across central Bucks County, passing through the towns of New Hope, Lahaska, Doylestown, and Chalfont. PA 611 is the easiest way to reach Doylestown from Philadelphia and points west.

By foot or bicycle: ✍ ♿ **Delaware Canal State Park** (610-982-5560; www.dcnr.state.pa.us). The Delaware Canal runs parallel to the Delaware River and was used to transport coal and other cargo from inland Pennsylvania to Philadelphia and New York in the 19th century. Its 60-mile towpath makes a fine bicycle or walking route that runs between Bristol and Easton and passes through Washington Crossing, New Hope, and other river towns. Parking is easiest (read: free and unlimited) at **Washington Crossing State Park** (see Lower Bucks) and **Virginia Forrest Recreation Area,** on River Road north of Centre Bridge. Many cyclists like to cross the bridges at Lumberville or Upper Black Eddy over to New Jersey, then take the Jersey-side towpath south back to Lambertville or Washington Crossing. An easy 8-mile loop begins in New Hope and follows the towpath north to Centre Bridge, then crosses over to Stockton, New Jersey, and takes the path south past an 18th-century gristmill to Lambertville and crosses the bridge back into New Hope. Sometimes the bridges are closed due to maintenance or flooding damage, so it's a good idea to check with the state park office before setting out.

MEDICAL EMERGENCY Doylestown Hospital (215-345-2200), 595 W. State Street, Doylestown.

✴ Villages

Doylestown. Driving west on US 202, you will find this bustling county seat, birthplace of James A. Michener and Margaret Mead and home to several good museums. Courthouse and other office workers fill its streets on weekdays, but weekends and evenings bring more of a hip, urban feel to its restaurants and coffeehouses.

Lahaska. This small town between New Hope and Doylestown is most often associated with Peddler's Village, a quaint shopping village that once housed a chicken farm known as Hentown. You'll also find a cluster of outlet stores directly across from Peddler's Village, and several home-grown antiques shops.

Lambertville, New Jersey. This town of about 4,000 is an easy walk or drive from New Hope via a two-lane car and pedestrian bridge. Once called Coryell's Ferry, after the ferry service used by George Washington and his troops, it was renamed Lambertville after the town's postmaster in 1810. Today, its wide streets are lined with Victorian-era homes, a few inns and B&Bs, and many independent shops and restaurants. It's easier to find free parking here than it is in New Hope, and the streets always seem a little quieter on weekends than they do across the river. The Shad Festival in April is one of its biggest events of the year.

New Hope. Situated on a picturesque spot next to the Delaware River, this is perhaps the best known of central Bucks County's tourist destinations.

Gay and straight vacationers like the creative vibe of its downtown, with its hodgepodge of antiques shops, art galleries, open-patio bars, and Washington-slept-here B&Bs. Others find the packed sidewalks and lack of parking intolerable, and prefer to seek out the country flea markets, horse farms, and lush parks that fringe the northern and western parts of town.

✴ To See

MUSEUMS Most of Central Bucks County's museums are within walking distance of one another in Doylestown.

🕈 **Fonthill Museum** (215-348-9461; www.fonthillmuseum.org), 84 S. Pine Street. Open daily for guided tours. Adults $12, $5 ages 5–17; an $18 "Mercer experience" pass gets you into both Fonthill and the Mercer

MY NEW HOPE

When my future husband and I sought a place in eastern Pennsylvania to get married, New Hope seemed like the perfect setting. Walkable streets, quaint inns to accommodate out-of-town guests, and a unique combination of history and artistic whimsy—all anchored by the mesmerizing Delaware River.

Much has changed since we wed, in 2001, at St. Martin of Tours on the hill above town. For one thing, the old stone church is now a community center and police station headquarters. Flooding over the years has wreaked havoc on access roads and caused some longtime businesses to close or relocate.

Yet the things that make New Hope such a popular weekend destination remain exactly as I remember them: the steel truss bridge that links New Hope to the equally picturesque town of Lambertville and makes such a pleasant sunset walk; the modern sculptures fronting 18th-century buildings such as the local library and Parry Mansion; the shops selling mystical potions, Indonesian masks, and sketches of the surrounding countryside; the bed-and-breakfast owners who point out Underground Railroad tunnels beneath their homes one day and deliver cream-cheese-stuffed French toast to your door the next.

A Dunkin' Donuts has taken over the fancy dress shop that long anchored the Bridge and Main Streets intersection. Ney Alley on the canal towpath, once a collection of art galleries and a meeting place

Museum. There's a bit of California's Hearst Castle in this imposing early-20th-century mansion, once the home of Henry C. Mercer, a wealthy Benjamin Franklin–like character. Just about every inch of the 44 rooms is covered with handcrafted, multicolored tiles; there are also 18 fireplaces, 32 stairwells, and 200 windows.

⊤ **Mercer Museum** (215-345-0210; www.mercermuseum.org), 84 S. Pine Street. Open daily. $10 adults, $6 ages 5–17. Henry Mercer believed that the story of human progress and accomplishments was told by the tools and objects that people used, and he set about collecting and preserving those tools with extraordinary perseverance. His exhaustive collection of blacksmith's anvils, ox yokes, apple grinders, whale oil lamps, and thousands of other items are on display on seven rambling stories of a medieval-like castle, which was designated a National Landmark in 1985.

VIEW OF THE DELAWARE RIVER FROM NEW HOPE-LAMBERTVILLE BRIDGE

for Pennsylvania Impressionists like Edward Redfield, is now deserted save for a tattoo parlor. No one is sure what will happen to the beloved Bucks County Playhouse, which closed in 2010.

But it's still the New Hope I fell in love with years ago, a place to wander and discover, or break bread and relax with friends for an hour or two. The river has tested the town's patience in recent years, but it still has the ability to charm and comfort anyone who visits.

A visitor-friendly lobby and entrance area were added in 2011. Exhibits and tours geared toward kids ages three and up are held throughout the year. Though all the Doylestown museums mentioned here are worth a visit, this would be my top choice if I had time to hit only one.

George Nakashima Woodworker (215-862-2272; www.nakashima woodworker.com), 1847 Aquetong Road, New Hope. The renowned Japanese American woodworker passed away in 1990; his daughter Mira still lives and designs her own furniture on the family's rural compound. The 14 buildings, all designed and built by the artist without plans, and grounds are open to the public on Saturday afternoon only. It's a rare chance to see Nakashima's masterpieces arranged in a domestic setting. Group tours for 10 or more are available most Saturday mornings for $20 a person.

Ġ ⏚ **The James A. Michener Museum** (215-340-9800; www.michener museum.org), 138 S. Pine Street. Open Tuesday through Sunday, April through December; closed Tuesday, January through March; $12.50 adults, $6 ages 6–18. Bucks County native son James Michener funded this small-but-notable art museum, which features changing exhibitions of Pennsylvania impressionist painters and other contemporary and historic artists from the area. Don't miss the Japanese-style reading room featuring furniture by renowned woodworker George Nakashima. There's also a small room dedicated to the Pulitzer Prize-winning author, featuring books and records from his personal collection and the typewriter and desk on which he wrote *Sayonara* and *A Floating World.*

✄ **Locktender's House Interpretive Center** (215-862-2021), 145 S. Main Street, New Hope. Open Monday through Friday 10–4. Boats can't go uphill or downhill, so Delaware Canal engineers installed 23 locks to raise and lower them on stretches of level water. Learn how they did this through the center's exhibits, murals, and artifacts.

⏚ **Moravian Pottery and Tile Works** (215-345-6722), 130 Swamp Road, Doylestown. Open daily; $3.50 adults. When he wasn't collecting artifacts or building castles, Henry Mercer designed tiles. Not just any tiles, as you will see on a visit to the Spanish-style building that served as his studio. These tiles were forged in three-dimensional relief and depicted scenes from folktales, the Bible, and Dickens novels. Tours run hourly and include a movie and the chance to observe full-time ceramicists who continue to produce tiles according to Mercer's designs.

National Shrine of Our Lady of Czestochowa (215-345-0600; www .czestochowa.us), 654 Ferry Road. Millions of people, including Pope John Paul II, have visited this sprawling Polish spiritual center since it opened in 1966. The grounds on the outskirts of Doylestown include a modern church with stained-glass panels that tell the history of Christiani-

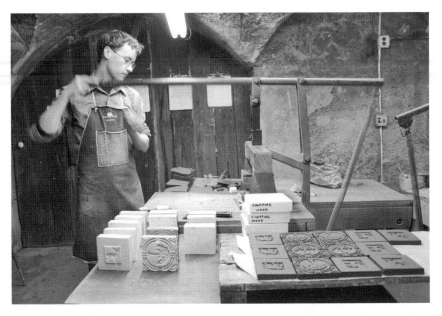

ARTISAN AT MORAVIAN TILE WORKS

ty in Poland and the U.S., a huge cemetery, and a gift shop. Some masses are in Polish. A cafeteria serves kielbasa, pierogi, and other authentic Polish fare on Sundays. Its Polish-American festival each September draws crowds from all over the state (see Special Events).

✳ To Do

BICYCLE RENTALS The mostly flat 60-mile Delaware Canal towpath is popular with all levels of cyclists. **New Hope Cyclery** (215-862-6888), 186 Old York Road, rents every kind of bike and support item. On the Jersey side, try **Cycle Corner of Frenchtown** (908-996-7712), 52 Bridge Street, Frenchtown.

BOAT EXCURSIONS **Coryell's Ferry Historic Boat Rides** (215-862-2050), 22 S. Main Street, New Hope. Captain Robert Gerenser leads half-hour excursions on a Mississippi-style stern paddlewheel pontoon boat. Rides leave roughly every 45 minutes 10–5:30, May through September.

FLY-FISHING The catch in the Delaware River includes shad in April, striped bass in May, and small- and largemouth bass in October. **Gary Mauz** (215-343-1720; www.flyfishingguideservice.com) has been fly-fishing along the Delaware for 25 years and offers half- or full-day excursions, plus lessons. Book early for summer outings.

FOR FAMILIES 🎨 🎠 **Giggleberry Fair** (215-794-8960), Peddler's Village, Doylestown. Open daily. Kids will love this indoor playground, with its wooden-horse carousel, indoor obstacle course, and discovery room for the under-5 set. The place can be quite loud on weekends, when birthday groups show up. A $15 pass gets your child into all the attractions, but there's also an á la carte option.

🎨 🎠 **Bucks County Children's Museum** (215-693-1290; www.bucks kids.org), 500 Union Square, New Hope. Closed Monday; $7 ages 1 and up. This hands-on kids wonderland opened in late 2011. Geared to the 8-and-under set, it features a science-based tree house, simulated balloon ride, and archaeological dig in which kids may unearth replica historical items such as a Civil War bugle or a piece of the boat George Washington used to cross the Delaware. In another nod to the area's roots, there is also an old-fashioned general store, a post office, and a covered bridge.

🎨 **New Hope and Ivyland Railroad** (215-862-2332; www.newhope railroad.com), 32 W. Bridge Street, New Hope. Open daily late May through October, weekends only winter and early spring; $17.50 adults, $13 ages 2–11. Beautifully restored vintage steam- and diesel-powered engines carry passengers between New Hope and Lahaska several times a day; professional uniformed conductors lend an old-school aura to the ride and take you back to the country's locomotive heydays. There are also storytelling theme rides for kids in the summer and murder mystery and wine- and beer-tasting rides for adults on some weekends. Check the Web site for updated schedules.

NEW HOPE'S VINTAGE TRAIN AND STATION

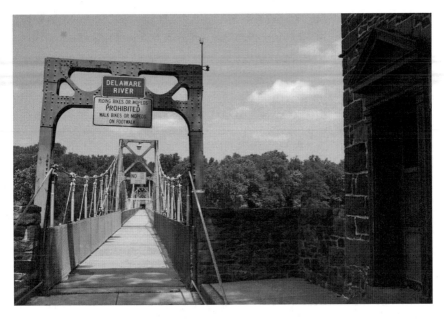

PEDESTRIAN BRIDGE NEAR BLACK BASS HOTEL

GHOST TOURS Adele Gamble (215-343-5564; www.ghosttoursofnew hope.com) leads lantern-lit walking tours through New Hope every Saturday night at 8, June through November, for $10 per person. She assures her charges that all her ghosts are friendly. Tours begin at the corner of Main and Ferry Streets.

SCENIC DRIVES A classic Sunday drive, the **Delaware River Loop** rambles along winding roads that hug the river and pass by dense woodlands, antiques stores, and inns that have hosted presidents and founding fathers. Begin in Pennsylvania near Morrisville and follow PA 29 (River Road) north past Washington Crossing State Park. Stop in New Hope for some shopping or a stroll along the Delaware Canal towpath, then continue 7 miles to Lumberville, where the **Black Bass Hotel** (215-297-5770) serves a lavish brunch in a room overlooking the Delaware. Continue a few more miles north to Upper Black Eddy, where you can cross the truss bridge into Milford, New Jersey, and browse the antiques shops along Bridge Street). Have a delightful seafood dinner at the **Milford Oyster House** (or if it's early hold out for coffee and pastries at the **Lovin' Oven** just south of Frenchtown). From Milford, head south along NJ 519 to NJ 29, which passes through the quaint riverfront towns of Frenchtown and Stockton. At Lambertville, make a right on Bridge Street and cross back into New Hope. Cap the day with a drink or decadent dessert on the river-view deck of **The Landing** (215-862-5711). It can take as little as an hour or an entire afternoon to drive the loop, depending on how much eating and shopping you do along the way.

✴ Green Space

Bowman's Hill Wildflower Preserve (215-862-2924; www.bhwp.org), 1635 River Road, between New Hope and Washington Crossing. Open 8:30–sunset daily; $5 adults, $2 ages 4–14. Established in 1934 to preserve Pennsylvania's native flora and fauna, Bowman's Hill features more than a thousand species of plants and flowers, 26 walking trails, and a bird observatory. Some of the paths are wheelchair- and stroller-accessible. Free guided wildflower walks are held every Tuesday and Sunday at 2 PM April through October.

Carousel Lavender Farm (215-862-2924; www.carouselfarmlavender .com), Mechanicville Road, Mechanicsville (between Lahaska and Carversville). You'll think you've wandered into southern France when you see the fields covered with over 15,000 lavender plants, all organically grown. The marvelous gift shop sells soaps, candles, sachets, and fresh and dried lavender. Also on hand are llamas, Scottish Highland cattle, donkeys, and horses; visitors are welcome to bring a picnic and linger. The fields and shop are open to the public Saturday; group tours are available at other times by appointment for $10 a person.

PEACE VALLEY LAVENDER FARM

♪ & ☙ **Peace Valley Park and Nature Center** (215-345-7860), 170 Chapman Road, Doylestown. A 1,500-acre park with a lake framed by rolling hills, 14 miles of walking trails, and a bird blind that is frequented by cardinals, woodpeckers, finches, and sparrows. The 6-mile paved biking/walking trail around the lake is arguably the prettiest bike path in the county. Stop at the nature center at 170 Chapman Road for maps, birdseed, and information on guided hikes. At the north end of the park is **Peace Valley Lavender Farm** (215-249-8462), where visitors may wander across violet-hued fields and witness how lavender is harvested and dried. Admission is free, but the gift shop sells tough-to-resist soaps, oils, and sachets.

✳ Lodging

INNS & MOTELS ❧ Centre Bridge Inn (215-862-9139; www.centrebridgeinn.com), 2998 N. River Road.

It's not the most luxurious or charming hotel in the area, but the river views from most rooms are fantastic and the weekday rates are reasonable. The suites include separate sitting areas or balconies. Dilly's Corner is across the street and there's a restaurant on the premises; it's about a five-minute drive to New Hope village. Rooms $125–165, suites for two $199–255, including a Continental breakfast.

& **Doylestown Inn** (215-345-6610; www.doylestowninn.com), 18 W. State Street, Doylestown. This elegant century-old inn in the center of town has 11 understated rooms with four-poster beds, jetted tubs, and cable television. Premium rooms are larger with turreted sitting areas and gas fireplaces. The rate includes free parking and a voucher for breakfast at Starbucks across the street. Rooms $155–230.

❧ & ♂ ♈ **Inn at Lambertville Station** (609-397-4400; www.lambertvillestation.com/inn), 11 Bridge Street, Lambertville, New Jersey. This riverfront inn, just over the bridge from New Hope, has 45 antiques-filled rooms with nice views of the Delaware, but the high standard of service really sets it apart. Want to check in early or have breakfast delivered to your room? The staff will do everything they can to accommodate you. There's also an honor bar, a creekside deck off the lobby, and wireless Internet access in every room. It's a popular spot for weekend weddings; guests who book a first-floor room should take note that their hallway serves as the main entrance path to the ballroom. Rooms $125–220; suites $165–300.

☙ **Logan Inn** (215-862-2300; www.loganinn.com), 10 W. Ferry Street, New Hope. This three-story hotel, which fronts Main Street, opened in 1727 and claims to be the longest continually running inn in Bucks County. All 16 rooms were refurbished in 2001 and feature Colonial-style antiques, cable television, and private baths. Rumor has it that Room 6 is haunted by a former owner who lost the inn at a sheriff's sale. The ghost of Aaron Burr, who fled to New Hope after his famous duel with Alexander Hamilton, is also suspected of roaming the premises on occasion. The first floor has a large patio with a bar and is near several other watering holes, so late-night noise, especially on weekends, can be an issue. Standard and premium rooms $120–205; deluxe rooms with sitting areas $145–220.

BED & BREAKFASTS
♂ 😺 ✎ **1870 Wedgwood Inn** (215-862-2570; wedgwoodinn .com), 80 W. Bridge Street, New Hope. Innkeepers Carl and Nadine Glassman expertly oversee three renovated Victorian homes just a few blocks north of Main Street. The main house has front and back sitting porches and attractive rooms with intricate stenciling, brass ceiling fans, antiques, and queen or king beds; some have fireplaces, small private balconies, and sitting areas. Next door, the 1833 Umpleby House has eight handsome rooms and suites (the huge third-floor Loft Suite is a favorite), and across the street is the Aaron Burr House, named for the former VP who fled to New Hope after his infamous duel with Alexander Hamilton. Enjoy breakfast on china and teacups in the Wedgwood's lace-curtained dining room or request it delivered to your room. It's one

ONE OF NEW HOPE'S MANY INNS

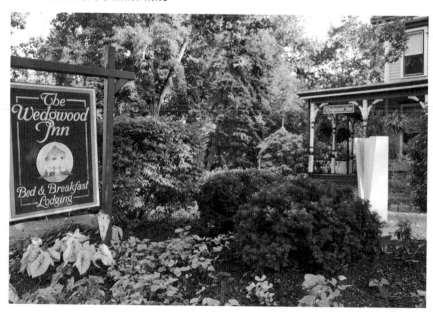

of the few B&Bs in the area to accommodate kids and dogs (in designated rooms). Guests have access to a beautiful hidden yard with a hammock and gazebos and (for a small fee) a private swimming and tennis club 0.5-mile away. Rooms $90–199, suites $159–289, two-night minimum on weekends.

♂ **Ash Mill Farm** (215- 794-5373; www.ashmillfarm.com), 5358 York Road (US 202). Six sheep and two pygmy goats, named Gizmo and Billy Jean, live on this working 11-acre farm between Peddler's Village and Doylestown. The circa-1790 house underwent a major renovation in 2003, and the six rooms are tastefully decorated with Colonial antiques, Andrew Wyeth prints, and flat-screen TVs. The private Shepherd's Cottage fronts the grazing pasture and has an in-room Jacuzzi. Breakfast is served in the home's original dining room next to a huge cooking fireplace. Rooms $145–195.

♂ **Inn at Bowman's Hill** (215-862-8090; www.innatbowmans hill.com), 518 Lurgan Road. The rates are higher than many other area B&Bs, but you'll want for nothing at this secluded retreat a couple miles south of New Hope village, whether it's heated towel racks, multiple-jet showers, or vine-covered pergolas. The manicured grounds include a swimming pool, spa, and large outdoor deck. The traditional English breakfast is made with eggs from the inn's free-range hens. Last-minute specials are sometimes available. Rooms and suites $395–485.

& **Mansion Inn** (215-862-1231; www.themansioninn.com), 9 S. Main Street. George Washington rested on the front lawn here before mounting the Battle of Trenton, according to the plaque outside. Walk inside this 1865 Victorian mansion in the heart of downtown New Hope, and you'll feel like you stepped into a world of hoop skirts and top hats. A polished-wood staircase leads to the comfortable second- and third-floor rooms, which have four-poster feather beds, down comforters, and whirlpool baths. There's also a swimming pool, and a gazebo out back to escape the sidewalk crowds in summer. If you like abandoning your car for the weekend and being in the center of the action, this is the place to stay. Rooms $195–225.

& **Porches on the Towpath** (215-862-3277; www.porches newhope.com), 20 Fisher's Alley. Hidden away at the end of a quiet lane yet within walking distance of town, this two-story Federal house was once the home of "Pop" and Ethel Reading, who ran a popular sandwich shop out of it in the 1930s. Now owned by interior designer John Byers, the 10 rooms (4 of which are located in a restored carriage house) have nice touches such as claw-foot bath-tubs, antique furnishings, and French doors that open to shady porches or patios. A country breakfast is served each morning in the chandelier-lit dining room. Walkers and cyclists will appreciate the easy access to the canal towpath, but many guests prefer relaxing on the hotel's wide, inviting porches. Rooms $105–195; two-night minimum for Saturday stays. There is no Internet access.

✸ Where to Eat

DINING OUT Domani Star (215-230-9100), 57 W. State Street, Doylestown. Lunch Monday through Saturday, dinner daily. Bring your own wine to this boisterous awning-topped bistro down the street from the Doylestown Inn. There is little elbow room and the noise levels can be high, but the cucina Italiana by Chef Chris Oravec is consistently good. Highlights include penne rigate Bolognese, veal scaloppini, and fillet of beef with balsamic vinaigrette. Don't miss the chocolate pudding for dessert. BYO. Entrées $19–30.

Honey (215-489-4200; www.honeyrestaurant.com), 42 Shewell Avenue, Doylestown. The lighting is soft and golden, while the menu is bold and modern at this cozy café run by two William Penn Inn alums, Amy and Joe McAtee. Dinner choices include black tea-glazed spare ribs, porcini-Parmesan risotta cakes, Hudson Valley foie gras sliders with sour-cherry catsup, and veal cheeks braised in coffee-chipotle barbe-

cue; the drink menu showcases Pennsylvania craft beer and honey-infused cocktails. Save room for dessert: the fried apple pie with rosemary-cream cheese ice cream is the bee's knees.

Lambertville, New Jersey
Ψ **Anton's at the Swan** (609-397-1960), 43 S. Main Street. Dinner Tuesday through Sunday. The food is good and thoughtfully prepared, but it's the formal surroundings and exceptional service that you'll remember most about this 1870 hotel-turned-upscale-restaurant. The simple menu includes sautéed halibut, grilled filet of beef, and pan-roasted duck breast with air-dried cherries. The separate bar, with its pressed-tin ceiling, fireplace, and leather couches, is a must stop before or after dinner for a perfect martini.

&. **Hamilton's Grill Room** (609-397-4343), 8 Coryell Street. Broadway set designer and restaurateur Jim Hamilton (and father of star Manhattan Chef Gabriella Hamilton) has been serving fresh seafood in a romantic canal-side setting for years. The menu changes daily but might include chilled pork tonnato, sautéed skate with olive tapenade, or seared salmon fillet with chipotles and rum. BYO. Entrées $25–35.

&. **Ota-Ya** (609-397-9228), 21 Ferry Street. Lunch Tuesday through Friday, dinner Tuesday through Sunday. For years, this was Bucks County's only Japanese restaurant. It's still a local favorite for sushi and outdoor patio dining. BYO. Dishes $17–27.

Manon (609-397-2596),19 N. Union Street. Tiny French bistro that only locals seem to know about. The food (chicken in garlic-cream sauce, mussels in a tomato and herb broth) is consistently praised, and the atmosphere dubbed authentically Provencal. BYO. No credit cards. $35–44.

Siam (609-397-8128), 61 N. Main Street. Sleek Thai restaurant behind a modest storefront with moderate prices. Try the crispy duck or chicken curry. Reservations recommended. BYO. Entrées $12–20.

New Hope/Lahaska

Ⓨ **Earl's Bucks County** (215-794-4020), 2400 Street Road (at US 202), Lahaska. Lunch and dinner Monday through Saturday, dinner and brunch Sunday. The former Earl's Prime is now all about sustainable seafood and celebrating one's inner locavore. It uses locally sourced meats, cheeses, and produce whenever possible. Small plates include salt-roasted beets with goat cheese, Buffalo bison burgers, and oysters with Kelchner's horseradish; entrées might include house-smoked ribs in an apple-cider glaze or local trout with bacon-mustard vinaigrette. A fine place for an early dinner after a shopping excursion to Peddler's Village. On Monday you can bring your own wine without a corkage fee. Dishes $8–15, entrées $18–32.

Ⓨ **Karla's** (717-862-2612). 5 W. Mechanic Street. Karla's open-air dining room is a lovely place to be on a warm summer night. The menu features a nice assortment of burgers, salads, and interesting entrées such as lamb moussaka and seared scallops in a blood-orange emulsion sauce. There's a full bar as well as live jazz some evenings. Lunch $10–14, dinner entrées $15–27.

Ⓨ **The Landing** (215-862-5711), 22 N. Main Street. Lunch and dinner daily. Known for its large deck overlooking the river, the Landing also has good food to match its primo views. Its all-day menu includes a prime rib sandwich with mushroom gravy, peppercorn-crusted tuna, lobster ravioli, and a long list of gourmet salads and appetizers. The extensive wine list changes frequently. In the cooler months, grab a table by the roaring fireplace. Dishes $8–33.

Ⓨ **Marsha Brown** (215-862-7044), 15 S. Main Street. Open for lunch Saturday and Sunday, dinner daily. Ecclesiastical roots meet culinary excellence at this Methodist-church-turned-restaurant in the center of town. The menu specializes in prime beef and seafood, as well as Creole recipes from the New Orleans-raised owner's family stash. Reservations recommended. Entrées $24–44.

Sprig and Vine (215-693-1427), 450 Union Square Drive. This upscale vegetarian restaurant has

NEW HOPE STREET SCENE

been a hit since it opened in the Union Square complex in 2010. Loyalists love the soft jazz, laid-back vibe, and creative menu with dishes such as blackberry-BBQ eggplant, cornmeal-crusted tempeh in maple-mustard sauce, and zucchini and black-eyed pea griddle cakes. Desserts are also excellent. Small plates $5–9, large plates $17–19.

EATING OUT ☿ **Mesquito Grille** (215-230-7427), 128 W. State Street, Doylestown. Open for lunch and dinner daily except Tuesday. This unpretentious bar and restaurant serves the best Buffalo chicken wings outside of New York state, plus steaks, pork spareribs, and barbecue chicken. The esteemed beer menu boasts 150 different bottles and is avail-

able for takeout. There are separate smoking and nonsmoking bars and lots of sports on the wide-screen TVs. Dishes $7–22.

New Hope

❦ ✍ ♿ **El Taco Loco** (215-862-0908), 6 Stockton Avenue. Open daily. One of Bucks County's few Mexican restaurants, this is a pleasant place for a quick burrito or quesadilla. The Mexican BLT is a steal at $3.25. Dishes: $3–9.

♿ ☿ **Mother's Wine Bar and Restaurant** (215-862-5857), 34 N. Main Street. Lunch and dinner daily. This New Hope institution is known for its huge portions and window seats overlooking New Hope's street scene. The large menu includes burgers, smoked salmon risotto, filet mignon, and many vegetarian options. There is live jazz on weekends in the bar. Owners and oenophiles Theresa Rubio and Lenore Picariello host free wine tastings on Wednesday evenings. Dishes $10–24.

Ⲩ **Via Vito Ristorante** (215-862-9936), 26 W. Bridge Street. Lunch and dinner daily. This family-owned restaurant serves big salads and decent cheesesteaks and pastas, but the delicious thin-crust pizza makes it worth a visit. Try the white spinach or sausage. Dine on the shady backyard patio in the summer. Dishes $6–18.

🍴 Ⲩ **Wildflowers** (215-862-2241), 8 W. Mechanic Street. This casual eatery off Bridge Street is always busy, thanks to reasonable prices, a secluded patio, and consistently good food. The secluded patio is a wonderful place to have an unhurried meal with friends. The eclectic 12-page menu includes many Thai, Italian, and Mexican dishes, plus Yankee pot roast, chicken cordon bleu, Polish kielbasa, and cheese fondue. The wait can be long during peak times, but there's a full bar and lounge to make the time go by faster. Dishes $7–18.

CAFÉS & BAKERIES C'est La Vie (215-862-1956), 20 S. Main Street, New Hope. If you're not staying in one of the area's many B&Bs, try this hidden riverfront spot for a morning croissant or cappuccino.

🍴 **Gerenser's Exotic Ice Cream** (215-862-2050), 22 S. Main Street, New Hope. Stephen and Julia Gerenser and their descendents have been scooping out dozens of unique flavors, from German Peach Brandy and Spanish Rum Raisin to cinnamon-infused Jamaican Tree Bark, for more than 55 years.

Bucks County Coffee (215-345-0795), 22 N. Main Street, Doylestown. Pennsylvania's top microroaster began life in a carriage house in Langhorne, and has proliferated to 33 locations. The Doylestown branch has art-covered brick walls, high ceilings, and couches.

Let Them Eat Cupcakes (215-345-7750), 17 E. Oakland Avenue, Doylestown. Chic patisserie near the County Theater. Cupcake flavors change daily (cookies and cream is a favorite) and there's also gelato.

BYO Where to buy wine in Central Bucks:

In New Hope, try the **Wine & Spirits** store (215-862-4650) in Logan Square Shopping Center. Or drive up to the service-friendly **Phillip's Wine Shoppe** (609-397-0587) in Stockton, New Jersey and browse their well-organized selection.

✳ **Entertainment**

MUSIC Ⲩ **John and Peter's** (215-862-5981; www.johnandpeters.com), 96 S. Main Street, New Hope. Bucks County's largest newspaper calls this intimate night club "the musical heart and soul of New Hope." A must stop for music lovers, it has hosted Norah Jones, George Thoroughgood, and countless other artists. Burgers and other bar food are served all day; smoking is allowed.

& Y **Triumph Brewing Company** (215-862-8300; www.triumph brew.com), 400 Union Square, New Hope. This busy microbrewery stays open late with a varying entertainment slate of karaoke, acoustic guitar, and Texas Hold 'Em.

CABARET & Y **Bob Egan's New Hope** (215-862-5225), 6426 Lower York Road in the Ramada Inn. The top place for cabaret and other live performances on the west side of the river.

& ♂ Y **Stockton Inn** (609-397-1250), 274 S. River Road, Stockton, New Jersey. This 300-year-old inn and restaurant just north of Lambertville hosts a popular cabaret night on Monday.

DANCING Y **The Raven** (215-862-2081; www.theravenresort .com), 385 Bridge Street, New Hope. A popular gay night spot any night of the week, this oak-paneled bar and restaurant transforms into a huge dance party Saturday and every other Thursday.

MOVIES County Theater (215-345-6789; www.countytheater.org), 20 E. State Street, Doylestown. Current independent releases screened in a restored 1938 Art Deco theater in the center of

town. There are often weekday screenings of classic films such as *To Kill a Mockingbird* and *Pulp Fiction.*

THEATER & **Bucks County Playhouse** (215-862-9606; www .newhopearts.com), Stockton Street, New Hope. Grace Kelly and Julie Harris made their theatrical debuts here in 1949 and 1964, respectively. At press time, the beloved riverfront gristmill had closed, but there was hope that a buyer would surface and reopen it.

New Hope Arts Center (215-862-9606; www.newhopearts.com), Stockton Street. Bucks County Playhouse's artistic director began staging contemporary plays at this artists' hub in the center of town. It also hosts sculpture exhibits and other community events.

✳ Selective Shopping

New Hope's Main Street is lined with shops, many of which shout "tourist trap" from the tops of their refinished 18th-century eaves. The best discoveries come by exploring the alleys and roads that branch off the main strip, like Mechanic and Union Streets, or stopping at the many antiques shops along York Road (US 202) between New Hope and Buckingham.

Farley's Bookshop (215-862-2452), 44 S. Main Street. An old-fashioned, independent bookshop in the heart of New Hope with more than 70,000 titles and a strong section on local culture and history, this shop is a must visit for anyone who loves to read.

Heart of the Home (215-862-1880), 28 S. Main Street. The perfect place to shop for the person who has everything, this customer-centered shop sells elephant birdhouses, leaf-embossed leather handbags, porcelain teapots, and jewelry.

Integrity Studio (215-534-1500; www.IntegrityStudio.com), 40 W. Bridge Street. Owner Carl Christensen is a photographer and woodcrafter who founded Integrity Studio to present his fine art photography of Bucks County landscapes in his handcrafted frames. He and his wife are active supporters of land conservation and charitable organizations in the region.

Tear Drop Memories (215-862-3401), 12 W. Mechanic Street. Death-related antiques are the specialty here—mourning brooches, vintage casket handles, old funeral-parlor ads, and more.

Love Saves the Day (215-862-1399), 1 S. Main Street. The East Village branch of this vintage toy and clothing shop was featured in the film *Desperately Seeking Susan*, and has developed something of a cult following among teenagers. The New Hope branch is a browser's paradise of feather boas, vintage T-shirts, and Betty Boop lunch boxes.

Lambertville, New Jersey
The People's Store (609-397-9808), 28 N. Union Street. Three floors of antique lamps and furniture, books, art displays, and vintage clothing.

Panoply Books (609-397-1145), 46 N. Union Street. Everything you'd want in a used book store: a diverse, offbeat collection, plus leather chairs and the occasional tribal artwork and silk rug for sale.

The Sojourner (609-397-8849,) 26 Bridge Street. The ever-changing merchandise includes embroidered cottons from China, sterling silver jewelry from Mexico and Italy, and sapphire swirl lamps from Istanbul. You never know what exotic items owners Elsie and Amy Coss might bring back from regular trips abroad. It's also known for its large bead collection.

Elsewhere in Central Bucks
Byers' Choice (215-822-0150; www.byerschoice.com), 4355 County Line Road, Chalfont. Open 10–5 Monday through Saturday, 12–5 Sunday. It's Christmas all year at the headquarters of Byers' Choice, maker of handcrafted caroler figurines that are sold at specialty shops around the country. Here, you can shop for doe-eyed Kindles (elves), Christmas tree cookie molds, and red velvet Santas at the gift emporium and watch the company's 180 artists put the finishing touches on the figurines (each one is unique) at the Christmas Museum.

Cowgirl Chile Co. (215-348-4646), 52 E. State Street, Doylestown. You can watch artists hand-etch the semi-precious metal jewelry at this fun shop. The A–Z charm collection is a favorite.

Doylestown Bookshop (215-230-7610), 16 S. Main Street, Doylestown. A homegrown bookstore with a helpful staff, wide selection, and one of the most comprehensive collections of Berenstain Bears titles around.

Peddler's Village (215-794-4000; www.peddlersvillage.com), US 202 and PA 263, Lahaska. Inspired by the village of Carmel, California, this former chicken farm opened in 1962 with seven shops and one restaurant. It's now home to 70 independent shops selling everything from Lladro figurines and lace lingerie to soy candles and apple dumplings. With its landscaped brick pathways and easy, free parking, it's a low-maintenance alternative to New Hope's busier streets. It plays host to many different events throughout the year, including a Strawberry Festival in May and a scarecrow-making contest in October. Several good dining options, such as Earl's Bucks County and Sweet Lorraine's, make it easy to spend an entire day here. **Skin n' Tonic** (215-794-3966) is an excellent day spa in a charming old house on the complex.

FLEA & FARM MARKETS

Delaware Valley College Farm Market (215-230-7170; www.the marketatdelval.com), 2100 Lower State Road, Doylestown. Open 9–7 daily. An abundance of produce (and vinegars and honey and sausages) straight out of the adjacent 500-acre teaching farm. In the summer, there's homemade ice cream from the college's creamery, as well as wine fests on Friday nights with live music.

Golden Nugget Flea Market (609-397-0811; www.gnmarket .com), 1850 River Road, Lambertville. Open 6–4 Wednesday, Saturday, and Sunday. Roseville pottery, 1950s pinball machines, comic books, and vintage jewelry are some of the items you'll find at this indoor-outdoor market south of downtown Lambertville.

✍ **Rice's Sale and Market** (215-297-5993; www.ricesmarket.com), 6326 Greenhill Road, New Hope. Open 7–1 Tuesday year-round, Saturday, March through December. Bargain hunters and avid collectors won't want to miss this 700-vendor market about 6 miles northwest of downtown New Hope. It began as a livestock auction in 1860 and evolved into an indoor-outdoor extravaganza of fresh produce, woodcrafts, antique furniture, Amish pastries, used CDs, and dried-flower arrangements. Those in the know skip Saturday and show up on Tuesday (the earlier the better), when all the vendors are present and accounted for. There is a small fee for parking.

✳ Special Events

January: **Winter Festival** (last weekend), New Hope and Lambertville, New Jersey—includes ice-carving demonstrations, a chili cook-off, children's theater performances, and a festive parade led by mummers string bands. For more info, visit www .winterfestival.net.

April: **Shad Festival** (last weekend), Lambertville, New Jersey— riverfront bash that includes crafts displays, culinary tents, and live music, all in celebration of the silvery fish's spring appearance in the Delaware River.

May: **Mercer Museum Folk Fest** (second weekend), Doylestown—a hundred skilled artisans demonstrate early American crafts; New Hope Gay Pride Festival (third weekend), street festival that attracts thousands of local and out-of-state visitors.

June: **New Hope Film Festival** (second weekend)—screens features, short films, and documentaries from all over the world, with many of the filmmakers attending the events at New Hope Arts Center.

UPPER BUCKS

Development has found its way to Upper Bucks in recent years, but it remains the least trammeled and traffic-plagued area of the county. It has more covered bridges and state parks than anywhere else in Bucks County, and its two-lane roads make perfect Sunday drives. The region attracts a good deal of nature-seekers from New York and northern New Jersey because of its easy access via I-287 and I-78. Many of its B&Bs are hidden at the end of unpaved roads or within dense woodlands, but they are no less gracious and comfortable than lodgings elsewhere in the county, and tend to be less expensive to boot.

AREA CODE Except for the northernmost corner, which uses 610, Upper Bucks region lies within 215.

GUIDANCE Bucks County Visitor Center (800-836-2825; www .experiencebuckscounty.com), Quakertown Train Station. This branch of the tourism bureau's Bensalem office has maps, visitor guides, and information on the area's attractions, lodging, and eating options.

GETTING THERE By car: From New York and northern New Jersey, take I-287 south to I-78 west. From Philadelphia or points south, take the Northeast Extension of the Pennsylvania Turnpike to the Quakertown exit.

By bus: **Carl Bieber Tourways** (800-243-2374) runs an express bus from New York City's Port Authority to Hellertown, about 25 minutes north of Quakertown.

By air: Upper Bucks County is about an hour's drive from **Philadelphia International** (215-937-6800) and **New Jersey's Newark International** (800-397-4636). **Lehigh Valley International Airport** in Allentown (888-359-5842) is about a 45-minute drive.

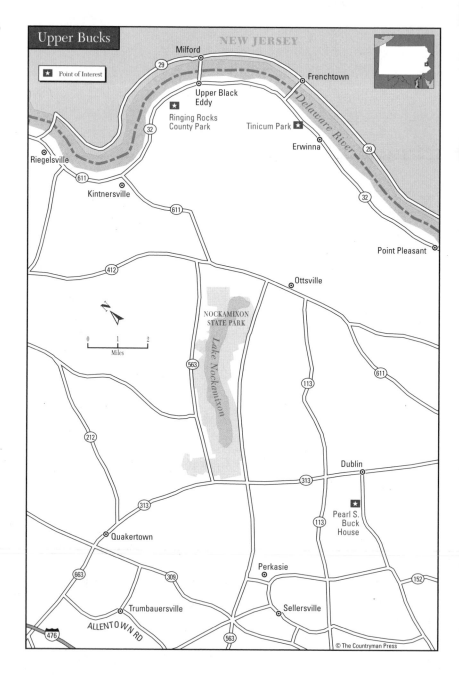

Upper Bucks

NEW JERSEY

★ Point of Interest

Milford

Frenchtown

Upper Black
Eddy

Ringing Rocks
County Park

Tinicum Park ★

Erwinna

Riegelsville

Kintnersville

Point Pleasant

Delaware River

Ottsville

NOCKAMIXON
STATE PARK

Lake Nockamixon

Dublin

Pearl S.
Buck
House

Quakertown

Perkasie

Trumbauersville

Sellersville

ALLENTOWN RD

0   1   2
Miles

© The Countryman Press

MEDICAL EMERGENCY St. Luke's Quakertown Hospital (215-538- 181
4500), 1021 Park Avenue, Quakertown.

UPPER BUCKS

✱ Villages

Lumberville. George Washington most decidedly did not sleep in this tiny Tory-sympathizing river town 7 miles north of New Hope. Named after the lumber mills that operated here in the late 1800s, it is today anchored by a general store, a footbridge that connects it with New Jersey, and the Black Bass Inn, a charming, if faded, 18th-century inn and restaurant still steeped in Tory memorabilia.

Point Pleasant. A few miles north of Lumberville, this river village was a popular fishing spot for the Lenape Indians; later its inns and taverns catered to the rafters and canalmen who transported goods along the Delaware River and Canal. Today it's home to River Country and known for its recreational water activities. You'll also find a general store and shops selling garden accessories and antiques here.

Quakertown. This growing bedroom community serves both the Delaware Valley and the Lehigh Valley to the north. In the 18th century, it was home to a community of Welsh and German farmers and these roots are evident today in the hex signs that decorate barns, and the funnel cakes and chow-chow for sale at the local farmers market. Its quaint downtown, centered around Broad and Main Streets, is a pleasant mix of historic buildings, mom-and-pop stores selling everything from Italian ice to antiques, and even an old-fashioned 5-and-10.

Just as the southern part of Bucks County likes to tout its Washington-slept-here connections, Quakertown and its environs can't help but brag that the Liberty Bell slept there—at least for a night, on its way to its hiding place in the Lehigh Valley during the Revolutionary War.

Riegelsville. A National Historic District in the northern reaches of Upper Bucks, Riegelsville is a sleepy river town overlooking the Delaware River and spanned by a 1904 Roebling bridge with a walkway crossing to New Jersey. Once a booming mill town, it is home to antiques shops, a mid-19th-century inn, and rows of stately stone residences that were built by Riegel Paper Company executives in the late 1880s. For paddlers, Riegelsville has a put-in for easy river access.

✱ To See

HISTORIC SITES ⚘ **Pearl S. Buck House** (215-249-0100; www.psbi .org), 520 Dublin Road. Guided tours Tuesday through Sunday; closed January and February; $8 adults. Pearl Buck used to say this house's solid stone walls and 1835 age symbolized her strength and durability. The

CARVERSVILLE

Once a Lenni-Lenape Indian gathering place, Carversville today is a classic Bucks County hamlet of 18th-century stone homes anchored by an old mill, a storybook stream, and waterfall. A center of commerce in the 1700s, it was home to gristmills and a factory that made roram hats, fur-covered caps worn by Revolutionary-era boys. Today, the town claims toy historian Noel Barrett, a longtime host of PBS's *Antiques Roadshow,* as an enthusiastic resident. Its general store, located in a former livery stable, is the place for local gossip, homemade donuts, and reasonably priced sandwiches and soup—you also may spot Barrett, a regular. Across the way, the **Carversville Inn** (215-297-0900) serves an innovative Cajun-influenced lunch and dinner menu in formal 1813 surroundings. On the last Monday night of the month during the summer, the village runs underappreciated films like *Joe Versus the Volcano* on the side of the general store. To get to Carversville from River Road, head west on Fleecydale Road in Lumberville to the intersection of Aquetong Road. It's a beautiful, though narrow and curvy, ride that follows a tree-shaded stream.

CARVERSVILLE INN

author of The Good Earth and numerous other books lived with her family on this farmstead, known as Green Hills, from 1933 to 1973, and her gravesite sits just off the main driveway. The China-born Buck's love for Asia comes through in many of the rooms, which are decorated with Chinese screens, Chen Chi paintings, and a silk wall hanging given to Buck by the Dalai Lama. There is also a rich collection of Pennsylvania country furniture and a room dedicated to all of Buck's awards, including the Nobel and Pulitzer prizes.

Liberty Hall, 1235 W. Broad Street, Quakertown. The Liberty Bell slept in this 1772 house on September 23, 1777, after being evacuated from Philadelphia to protect it from the approaching British Army. It was on its way to its wartime hiding place of Allentown. A replica of the famous bell (pre-crack) sits out front.

✳ To Do

BOAT RENTALS At Lake Nockamixon, **Nockamixon Boat Rental** (215-538-1340; www.nockamixonboatrental.com) rents canoes, motorboats, rowboats, sailboats, paddleboats, kayaks, and pontoon boats during the summer.

FLYING Sport Aviation Inc. (610-847-8320), Van Sant Airport, 516 Cafferty Road, Erwinna. I know someone who comes here every year on his

PEARL S. BUCK HOUSE

birthday and takes an aerobatic glider ride over Bucks County. It sure beats a cupcake. They also offer rides in biplane barnstormers, plane and glider rentals, and flying classes.

GOLF Fox Hollow Golf Club (215 538-1920), 2020 Trumbauersville Road, Quakertown. Eighteen holes featuring 6,613 yards of golf from the longest tees for a par of 71.

Sylvan Golf Center (215 348-5575), 1208 Swamp Road (PA 313), Fountainville, has a driving range and two miniature golf courses. There's also miniature golf at **Ottsville Golf Center** (610-847-2547), 22 Tohickon Valley Road, Ottsville.

COVERED BRIDGES

With due respect to Robert James Waller, Bucks County would win handily if its covered bridges went head to head with the bridges of Madison County, Wisconsin. It has 11 picturesque bridges dating from 1832 (compared to Madison's 6) and, except for a little graffiti here and there, they are a historic preservationist's dream. A 12th bridge, **Mood's**

COVERED BRIDGE

HORSEBACK RIDING Haycock Stables (215-257-6271; www.haycock stables.com), 1035 Old Bethlehem Road, Perkasie. Trail rides are $30 an hour.

HUNTING About 3,000 acres are open to seasonal hunting and trapping at **Nockamixon State Park.** Common game are deer, pheasant, rabbit, and turkey. Call the Pennsylvania Game Commission (717-787-4250) for more details.

RIVER EXCURSIONS ❧ **Bucks County River Country** (215-297-5000; www.rivercountry.net), 2 Walters Lane, Point Pleasant. Open mid-May through October. This veteran river-outfitting operation offers

on Blooming Glen Road near Perkasie, was destroyed by arsonists in 2004 but was rebuilt and reopened to the public in 2007.

The best way to view the bridges is by driving tour, weather permitting. Here's one that covers five of them in the northwest region of the county between Doylestown and Upper Black Eddy. Begin your tour at Durham Road (PA 413) and Stump Road, just east of Plumsteadville. Head east on Stump Road and make a left on Wismer Road. **Loux Bridge,** a small white structure surrounded by farmhouses and a scenic valley, is 1 mile ahead. After crossing the bridge, turn right onto Dark Hollow Road to Covered Bridge Road and make a right. This runs into the brick-red **Cabin Run Bridge,** which crosses Cabin Run Creek. Return to Dark Hollow Road and head straight past the Stover-Myers Mill to Cafferty Road. Make a left and follow 0.6 mile to **Frankenfield Bridge,** one of the county's longest bridges at 130 feet. Drive across the bridge to Hollow Horn Road and make a right. Continue 1.3 miles to Headquarters Road, make a right and continue 1 mile to Geigel Hill Road. Turn right and soon you will reach the **Erwinna Bridge,** which crosses Lodi Creek. From here, you will want to return to Geigel Hill Road and head west about 0.5 mile to River Road. Make a left and go 1.7 miles to **Uhlerstown Bridge,** the only covered bridge that crosses a canal instead of a creek. This shouldn't take more than two hours total, with time figured in for photographs; be mindful that the bridges can be dangerous to cross in icy weather conditions.

ALLENTOWN ROAD

There aren't many scenic drives that follow an Underground Railroad route *and* present the opportunity to play vintage pinball, eat smoked buffalo tenderloin, and visit a chocolate factory, all within 20 miles. Upper Bucks County is full of scenic drives, but one of my favorite escape-the-city routes begins in upper Montgomery County near the Lansdale exit of the Pennsylvania Turnpike. Allentown Road is a north-south two-lane road with lots of farms, few traffic lights, and several unusual points of interest. Begin just south of the intersection of Valley Forge Road in Lansdale, where **R and J Farm Market** (267-203-8094; 325 Allentown Road) sells crafts, raw honey, jams, and fresh fruits and vegetables from its farm across the road. Continue north a few miles to the **Rising Sun Inn** (215-721-6350; 898 Allentown Road; dinner Thursday through Sunday; lunch Saturday and Sunday), an 18th-century restaurant and bar known for its North American bison dishes (specialties include braised bison-brisket pot roast, buffalo potstickers, and sautéed medallions of bison with brandied mushrooms). After your meal, head upstairs for a peek at the room where the Liberty Bell spent the night on its way from British-occupied Philadelphia to Allentown. From here, it's an easy ride past preserved old homes and rolling countryside to the Bucks County village of Trumbauersville, home to the old-fashioned **Spor's General Store** (215-536-6754; 22 W. Broad Street) and **Ann Hemyng Candies** (118 N. Main Street), a small chocolate factory selling truffles, peanut butter cream cups, and seasonal items like Easter bun-

rentals, plus two- to four-hour guided trips down the Delaware; all-day outings and season passes are also available.

☞ **Delaware River Tubing** (866-938-8823; www.delawarerivertubing .com), 2998 Daniel Bray Highway, Frenchtown, New Jersey, just across the Uhlerstown Bridge. The tubing and rafting rides include a free lunch or dinner at what may be the world's only swim-up hot dog stand.

SCENIC DRIVES About 6 miles north of New Hope off River Road, Cuttalossa Road is a rambling 2-mile drive past wooded hills, fieldstone estates, sheep pastures, and a gushing creek that once powered several mills along its run to the Delaware River. Turn off River Road at the **Cut-**

TRUMBAUERSVILLE'S CHOCOLATE FACTORY

nies. If it's the weekend, head over to **Unami Ridge Winery** (215-804-5445; 2144 Kumry Road), an up-and-coming "hobby gone amok" winery that makes a fine full-bodied Chardonnay. Finally, retrace your steps south to the **Pinball Parlour** in Earlington (215-723-5405; 808 Allentown Road). The two-story garage is packed with pinball machines dating to the 1950s. Remember 1981's Hyperball? That's here, and so is the 1990s favorite The Addams Family. It doesn't open until 7 PM, but should not be missed by anyone who appreciates a little nostalgic fun (unlimited play is $6 an hour).

talossa Inn. After the paved road turns to packed dirt, look for a small mill and pond on the left side of the road. Across the road is the white-shingled former home and studio of Daniel Garber, a Pennsylvania impressionist painter known for his vibrant Bucks landscapes. (It is privately owned and not open to the public.) From here, you can cross a small one-lane bridge to N. Sugan Road, turn left and follow it as it turns into Phillips Mill Road back to River Road.

✳ Green Space

✐ ⅙ ❀ **Lake Nockamixon** (215-529-7300; www.dcnr.state.pa.us), 1542 Mountain View Road, Quakertown. This 5,300-acre park 4 miles east of

LAKE NOCKAMIXON

Quakertown is a scenic and popular recreation spot for locals and nature-loving out-of-towners. Its centerpiece is a 1,450-acre reservoir that allows sailing, boating, windsurfing, and fishing (but no swimming). Surrounding the lake are picnic areas, several miles of biking and hiking trails, 20 miles of equestrian trails, and 10 modern log cabins (see Lodging). In the winter, this is a popular spot for ice-skating, sledding, and cross-country skiing. There's also a great swimming pool overlooking the lake that's open to the public during summer.

Quakertown Swamp is the largest freshwater inland wetland in southeastern Pennsylvania, with more than 500 acres of cattail marshes, ponds, and gnarled tree groves. It's home to the largest breeding colony of great blue herons in eastern Pennsylvania, as well as a variety of songbirds, turtles, frogs, ducks, muskrats, and beavers. Since much of it is on private property, the Bucks County Heritage Conservancy has created a self-guided walking tour that steers visitors to public areas. For a free copy, call 215-345-7020 or download the map online at www.heritageconservancy.org.

✐ 🎄 **Ringing Rocks Park** (215-757-0571), Ringing Rocks Road at Bridgeton Hill Road, Upper Black Eddy. Open 8–sunset daily. This has to be the only park around that encourages its visitors to pack hammers along with their picnic baskets and bird binoculars. That's because smack in the middle of it lies an 8-acre field of large boulders, many of which ring like bells when struck lightly by hammers. According to park history, these are diabase rocks that 175 million years ago were formed by fire and cooled underground, meaning they solidified at super-fast speed. This put the bonds composing the rocks under a great deal of stress and, just like with the tightening of a guitar string, caused them to produce a high-pitched sound when tapped. Not surprisingly, this park is very popular with families, who can be seen trudging toward the boulder field on weekends like Snow White's dwarves going off to work. It's a bit challenging to find, so be sure to bring a good map.

✄ ♿ 🐾 **Ralph Stover State Park** (610-982-5560), 6011 State Park Road, Pipersville. This 47-acre park 2 miles north of Point Pleasant is best known for its sheer rock cliff and stunning views of Tohickon Creek and the dense woodland surrounding it. Experienced rock climbers may scale the 200-foot sheer rock face, but anybody can enjoy the safety-railed view from the top, thanks to a nearby parking area off Tory Road and a generous grant from the late James A. Michener. The park also has a pretty picnic area and a couple of short hiking trails. Whitewater kayaks and canoes may be launched from Tohickon Creek. The trails here link up with nearby Tohickon Valley Park, which is owned by the county.

✄ ♿ 🐾 **Tohickon Valley Park** (215-757-0571), Cafferty Road. Crowds flock to this park in late March and early November, when water flows from Lake Nockamixon to the north flow at a rate of 500 cubic feet per second and the normally staid Tohickon Creek turns into a raging

RINGING ROCKS PARK

whitewater playground. It also has a playground, a trout-fishing stream, and tidy cabins that book up fast in the spring and summer (see also Lodging). Its hiking and biking trails are among the most challenging in Bucks County and connect with Ralph Stover State Park.

✳ Lodging

INNS, BED & BREAKFASTS

Inland

Bucksville House (610-847-8948; www.bucksvillehouse.com), 4501 Durham Road, Kintnersville. Built in 1795, this old-fashioned inn on 4 landscaped acres has five guest rooms and a history of friendly ghosts. Rooms are furnished in 19th-century antiques, Asian rugs, and colorful quilts; several have fireplaces. Guests have access to a deck, screened gazebo, herb gardens, and a fish pond. Rooms $125–$150.

🐸 **Frog Hollow Farm** (610-847-3764; www.froghollowfarmbnb .com), 401 Frogtown Road, Kintnersville. This intimate three-room inn is about 20 miles from Quakerstown. Petie's Room (named after the resident dog) is the showcase room, but I'm partial to the Cathedral Room with its sunlit loft, exposed stone walls, and a bathroom that overlooks the barn and sheep pasture. Sun tea or mulled cider is served on the outdoor deck every afternoon and port is served in the reading room in the evening. Owners Patti and Mitch Adler can also arrange a dinner package at nearby Ferndale Inn or Riegelsville Inn, which includes a chauffeured ride in a restored 1931 Ford Coupe. Rooms $105–160.

&. 🐎 **Stone Ridge Farm** (215-249-9186; www.stoneridge-farm .com), 956 Bypass Road, Dublin. Just down the road from the Pearl S. Buck House, this 10-acre farm used to belong to the Buck family, who raised prize-winning Guernsey cows on it. Now it's a horse farm and eight-room B&B with a swimming pool and what could be the most inviting barn-turned-living room in all of Bucks County. Guests are welcome to bring their horses but should check with owner Jackie Walker before bringing any kids under the age of 12. Horseback riding packages are available. The four "hayloft" rooms have private entrances overlooking horse pastures and are $145–$185 a night. Suites that sleep four are $199–$249.

On River Road

🐟 **1836 Bridgeton House** (610-982-5856; www.bridgetonhouse .com), 1525 River Road, Upper Black Eddy. This riverfront B&B is the perfect antidote for stressed-out city dwellers looking to get away from it all. The only thing old about the place is the 1836 building; everything else, from the staff's attentiveness to the whimsical styles of the rooms, is as modern as it gets. All 12 rooms have private baths, televisions, plank floors, and feather beds. Many have private balconies and fireplaces. Guests may have breakfast in their rooms or next to a cooking fireplace in the dining room. There's also a private dock, along with an outdoor living room that's great for an afternoon of reading or lounging. Rooms are $179–$289, suites start at $329. A detached one-bedroom cottage, known as the Boathouse, is also available for $399–429.

Black Bass Hotel (215-297-9660; www.blackbasshotel.com) 3774 River Road, Lumberville. George Washington most definitely did not sleep in this historic inn (the 1770s innkeeper was loyal to the British crown), but anyone who likes a little luxury with their history lessons will want to spend the night. The nine suites were renovated and glammed up in 2008 with ornate beds, antique furniture, and flat-screen TVs; most have private balconies overlooking the river. Suites $195–225; deluxe suites with private balconies $300–395. Breakfast in the riverfront dining room is included.

🐾 **Golden Pheasant Inn** (610-294-9595; www.goldenpheasant inn.com), 763 River Road, Erwinna. Built as a mule-barge rest stop in the late 1800s, this six-room inn is located right on the Delaware Canal and a short walk from the Sand Castle Winery. It is perhaps best known for its excellent French restaurant (see Dining Out), but its simple upstairs rooms, furnished with antiques and canopy beds, are a good value at $95. Pets and children are allowed in a detached cottage suite for an additional $20 a night. A hearty breakfast is included. Cottage suite $175–225.

CAMPGROUNDS, CABINS, & HOSTELS

🏕 **Lake Nockamixon** (888-727-2277; www .dcnr.state.pa.us), 1542 Mountain View Road, Quakertown. Ten modern cabins that sleep six to eight people can be rented at weekly rates starting at $348.

🏕 **Colonial Woods Family Camping Resort** (610-847-5808; www.colonialwoods.com), 545 Lonely Cottage Drive, Upper Black Eddy. Open mid-April through October. Known as the Four Seasons of campgrounds, this facility has 208 tent and RV hookup sites, plus a swimming pool, playground, laundry facilities, stocked fishing lake, and air-conditioned community lodge. Tent sites $36–46.

🏕 **Tohickon Family Campground** (866-536-2267; www .tohickoncampground.com), 8308 Covered Bridge Drive, Quakertown. Full-service campground with more than 200 tent and hookup sites, a swimming pool, and lots of free kid and adult activities. Tent sites $35–44.

Weisel Youth Hostel (215-536-8749), 7347 Richlandtown Road, Quakertown. This country estate-turned-hostel makes a perfect base for budget travelers who want to take advantage of Lake Nockamixon's recreational activities. There are 25 bunk beds and one dorm-style room for families. Three-day maximum stay. Beds cost $17 for members and Bucks County residents, $20 for anyone else.

✴ Where to Eat

DINING OUT

On River Road

& ⅄ **Bucks Bounty** (215-294-8106), 991 River Road, Upper Black Eddy. Open for lunch and dinner Tuesday through Sunday. You'll find rustic-lodge-meets-Southwest-adobe decor and a simple menu (slow-roasted prime rib, stuffed pork chop, chicken saltimbocca). The tavern room is a popular local gathering place, and there's usually a selection of homemade pies available. Dishes $11–21.

& ⅄ **Golden Pheasant Inn** (610-294-9595; www.goldenpheasant inn.com), 763 River Road, Erwinna. Dinner Tuesday through Saturday, brunch Sunday. Michel Faure, a former chef at Philadelphia's Le Bec Fin, specializes in gourmet French cuisine with a seasonal menu that features trout, venison, pheasant, and frog legs in an array of intensely flavored sauces. The Faures added a modern glass-enclosed dining room, but the original Tavern Room, with its fireplace, antique chandeliers, and hanging copper pots and pans, couldn't be more warm and welcoming. Entrées $22–28.

& ⅄ **Indian Rock Inn** (610-982-9600; www.indianrockinn.com), 2206 River Road. Dinner Wednesday through Sunday, lunch Saturday and Sunday. This 1812 inn is a fine place to stop for a hearty dinner on a chilly winter evening; one dining room boasts a large stone-hearth fireplace, a second has views of the river. The menu includes a creative selection of appetizers and entrées. Try the mozzarella en carroza with garlic-cream sauce or the pecan-crusted salmon. The changing dessert menu sometimes features a raspberry-almond frangipane tart and white-chocolate bread pudding. Lunch and bar menu: $7–10; dinner entrées $18–28.

Nearby

& ⅄ **Ferndale Inn** (610-847-2662), 551 Church Hill Road, at PA 611, Ferndale, 2 miles south of Kintnersville. Dinner Wednesday through Monday. The traditional menu features clams casino, filet mignon with horseradish sauce, scallops in curry cream sauce. Packages available for guests of Frog Hollow B&B (see also Lodging). The wine list includes selections from Sand Castle Winery. Entrées $12–29.

Maize (610-257-2264), 519 Walnut Street, Perkasie. Dinner Tuesday through Saturday. Chef Matthew McPhelin worked at the Rittenhouse Hotel's LaCroix before opening his own BYO bistro near Quakertown. The menu highlights local ingredients and changes daily; entrées might include chicken, okra, and creamed corn in a red pepper sauce or pork ribs with pickled watermelon and arugula.

ঙ ৺ **Milford Oyster House** (908-995-9411; www.milford oysterhouse.com), 92 NJ 519 (Water Street), Milford, New Jersey. Dinner daily, except Tuesday; Sunday brunch. Fresh seafood and attentive service are the specialties of this converted 18th-century stone mill on the New Jersey side of the river across from Upper Black Eddy. Chef Ed Coss whips up many nightly specials plus a regular menu that includes beer-batter shrimp, cashew-crusted tilefish, steak au poivre, and a splendid crab Norfolk. The ever-changing tavern menu features a variety of burgers, fresh-made pizzas, and a raw bar selection. Full bar with a robust wine list and creative cocktails. Entrées $19–33.

EATING OUT ঙ ঙ **Bucks County Seafood** (215-249-1295; www .buckscountyseafoodpa.com), 164 N. Main Street, Dublin. Dine in on fresh conch chowder and rich crab cakes, or take home salmon steaks, red snapper, or scallops to throw on the grill. Crabs are available by the bushel in summer.

ঙ ঙ **Dublin Diner** (215-249-3686) PA 313, Dublin. Open daily. Everything you want in a diner– low prices, gruff waitresses, and a salad bar big enough to satisfy a football team-in-training. For a real Pennsylvania breakfast, try the pork roll with eggs.

ঙ ঙ ঙ **Luberto's Brick Oven Pizza and Trattoria** (215-249-0688), 169 N. Main Street, Dublin. Next door to the Dublin Diner. Heaping portions and good simple Italian food served in unfancy surroundings. Order the prosciutto white pizza or anything that comes with pink vodka sauce. There can be a long wait on weekends. BYO. Dishes $5–15.

OwowCow Creamery (610-847-7070), 4105 Durham Road, Ottsville. Sinfully good ice cream shop near Nockamixon State Park with flavors such as chocolate jalapeno, pecan pie, and rosewater cardamom.

BYO Where to buy wine in Upper Bucks:

In Ottsville, just south of Ferndale, there's a **Wine & Spirits** store at 8794 Easton Road (610-847-2472).

✳ Entertainment

ঙ ঙ ৺ **Sellersville Theatre** ·(215-257-5808; www.st94.com), Main and Temple Streets, Sellersville. Eclectic lineup of entertainment featuring classical ballet and children's theater matinees to Don McLean and the Bacon Brothers.

ঙ ৺ **Washington House** (215-257-3000; www.washingtonhouse .net), 136 N. Main Street, Sellersville (next to the Sellersville Theatre). George Washington may

GRISTIE'S ANTIQUES, RIEGELSVILLE

have slept in this restored 18th-century inn; today, it's known for its lively bar, which features free live music on select weekdays and regular wine and beer tasting events.

✳ Selective Shopping

For a fun old-fashioned shopping experience, head to downtown Quakertown, a mix of antiques shops, bookstores, bakeries, and cafés anchored by **McCoole's Red Lion Inn** (215-538-1776), 4 S. Main Street. **Sine's 5 and 10 Cent Store** (215-536-6102), 236 W. Broad Street sells bulk candy, Christmas knickknacks, and other items; a lunch counter serves creamy milk shakes and home-made soups. **Lion Around Books** (215-529-1645; 302 W. Broad

Street) has a wide selection of new and used books. On the outskirts of town is the **Quakertown Farmers' Market** (215-536-4115), 201 Station Road, a huge indoor-outdoor affair whose motto is "bargains are our business" and where more than 400 vendors sell everything from antique armoires and premium cigars to three-for-$1 toothbrushes.

ANTIQUES Antiques lovers will want to head to the north-east towns of Riegelsville and Kintersville.

Antique Haven (610-749-0230), 1435 Easton Road, Riegelsville. A variety of antiques and col-lectibles, from vintage cocktail shakers and old books to late 19th-century furniture.

Gristie's Antiques (610-847-1966), 9730 Easton Road, Kintnersville. A co-op of about 25 dealers selling antique and vintage furniture in an old gristmill.

✴ Special Events

May: **Arts Alive!** Quakertown (third weekend)—art exhibits, sidewalk sales, strolling performances, and cooking and glass-blowing demonstrations take over Quakertown's center.

July: **Tinicum Art Festival** (second weekend), Tinicum Park—annual two-day party of arts and crafts displays by local artists, live music, a white-elephant barn, and book signings.

Pennsylvania Dutch Country

4

PROFESSIONAL
POTTING SOIL
WE MAKE IT...
WE USE IT...WE RECOMMEND IT

LANCASTER COUNTY/
AMISH COUNTRY

READING & KUTZTOWN

LANCASTER COUNTY/ AMISH COUNTRY

L ancaster County, about 65 miles west of Philadelphia, was settled
in the early 1700s by the Amish, Mennonites, and the Brethren, Anabaptist Christian communities who trace their roots back to 16th-century
Europe. It is home to one of the country's biggest Amish populations. The
Amish are known for their plain dress, pacifism, and avoidance of modern
conveniences such as electricity and cars. Most, however, have accepted,
even embraced, the tourism industry that dominates the area, allowing
visitors to eat dinner in their homes (for a small fee), selling their crafts
and baked goods in commercial shops and out of their homes, and even
leading and narrating buggy rides through the countryside.

The city of Lancaster is the county seat and hub of Lancaster County,
with a population of more than 50,000 and an urban downtown with nifty
attractions such as the Central Market and Fulton Opera House. The
heart of Amish Country, however,
lies east of here in the rural towns
of Bird-in-Hand, Intercourse, and
Paradise. This is where you'll find
fourth-generation Amish farms,
the largest concentrations of craft
and quilt shops, hand-painted root
beer for sale signs, and large commercial operations, from buggy
rides to F/X theaters, that are
squarely aimed at tourists.

ALONG ROUTE 340

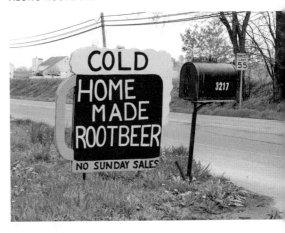

You don't have to spend much
time in Lancaster County to realize
tourism is the dominant industry.
While the area still has an attractive rural backdrop of farms and

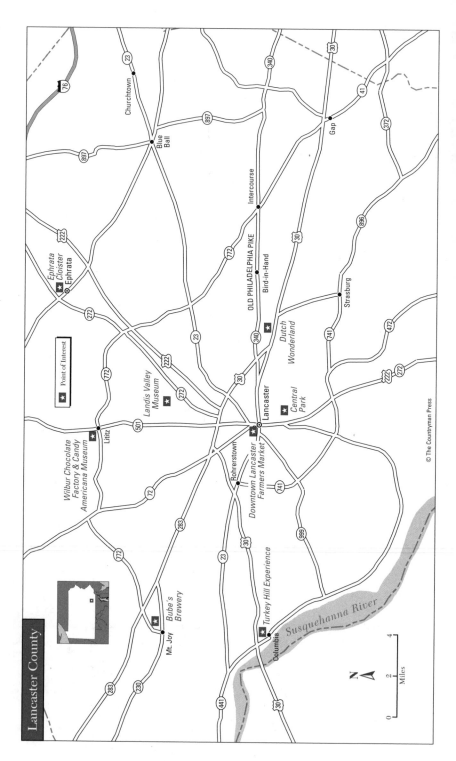

Lancaster County

Point of Interest ★

Ephrata Cloister
Ephrata

Landis Valley Museum

Wilbur Chocolate Factory & Candy Americana Museum
Lititz

Bube's Brewery
Mt. Joy

Churchtown

Blue Ball

Intercourse

OLD PHILADELPHIA PIKE

Bird-in-Hand

Gap

Strasburg

Lancaster

Dutch Wonderland

Central Park

Rohrerstown

Downtown Lancaster Farmers Market

Turkey Hill Experience

Columbia

Susquehanna River

© The Countryman Press

N

Miles
0   2   4

rolling green hills, it is also home to dozens of souvenir shops, all-you-can-eat smorgasbords, and just about every chain motel in existence. I suggest that first-time visitors do some advance research and planning about Amish Country before heading there. If you wind up seeing the area from development-crazy Lincoln Highway (US 30), you may wonder what all the fuss is about and leave before ever sampling some of the state's tastiest soft pretzels or viewing the amazing selections of handcrafted Windsor chairs, farm tables, and quilts.

One of the best ways to enjoy the area is to slow down your pace (don't honk when the horse and buggy trots along in front of you at 12 miles an hour, for instance) and follow the winding back roads as much as possible. It's difficult to get lost, and some of the best views, shops, and ice cream can be found away from the crowds and traffic.

Today, families from New York, Philadelphia, and the Washington, D.C., area come to Lancaster to give their citified kids a chance to milk cows, romp through corn fields, ride in horse-drawn buggies, and climb around old steam engines. Bus tours are big, too, filling the area's family-style restaurants, biblical-themed theaters, and farm markets and auctions. Individuals and couples looking for a quiet getaway of antiques shopping and romantic dinners will also find that here—most notably in the quaint northern towns of Lititz and Ephrata.

AREA CODE Except for the southeastern edge, which uses 610, Lancaster County lies within the 717 area code.

GUIDANCE Mennonite Information Center (717-768-0807), 3551 Old Philadelphia Pike, Intercourse. Open Monday through Saturday 8–5. Near Kitchen Kettle village, it has maps and local tourist information, postcards, books, and fair-trade crafts for sale, plus exhibits and a short film on the faith and lifestyle of the Amish and Mennonites .

Pennsylvania Dutch Country Visitor Center (717-299-8901; 800-723-8824), 501 Greenfield Road, Lancaster. Just off US 30, this large facility has rest rooms, maps and brochures, and a staffed information desk.

Southern Market Center (717-392-1776), 100 S. Queen Street, Lancaster, has free maps and brochures and changing art and history exhibits. It also runs daily downtown walking tours April through October.

Lititz Springs Welcome Center (717-626-8981), 18 N. Broad Street, Lititz. This center, located in a replica of an old railway station, can provide you with details on Lititz and other Lancaster County towns and attractions.

Ephrata Chamber of Commerce (717-738-9010), 16 E. Main Street, Ephrata. Maps, brochures, postcards, and more are available at this old train depot.

GETTING THERE By air: **Lancaster Airport** (717-569-1221), on PA 501 south of Lititz, has limited service. The nearest full-service airports are **Philadelphia International** (215-937-6800), about 65 miles away, and **Harrisburg International,** about 40 miles away.

By car: Three main thoroughfares run through Lancaster County. US 30 runs from Philadelphia's Main Line through the city of Lancaster, then west toward York County. US 222 runs north-south through Lancaster between Reading and the Maryland border. From Hershey, take US 322 east.

By bus: **Capitol Trailways** (800-333-8444) runs bus service to and from Philadelphia.

By train: **Amtrak** trains to Philadelphia and New York run several times a day from the Amtrak station (717-291-5080), 53 McGovern Avenue, Lancaster.

GETTING AROUND Most people drive between destinations within the Lancaster area. You can join the Amish and take a horse-drawn buggy ride around the back roads, but these tend to be leisurely tours that return you to the same place.

Red Rose Transit (717-397-4246; www.redrosetransit.com) runs buses all over Lancaster County. Pick up a schedule and tickets at the downtown visitor center.

MEDICAL EMERGENCY Lancaster General Hospital (717-544-5511), 555 N. Duke Street, Lancaster.

WHEN TO GO The Lancaster area is busy throughout the year, with August and October attracting the largest crowds. Those in the know visit in May and early June, when the weather's usually good and there are fewer crowds. Keep in mind that many shops and restaurants, especially those owned by Amish and Mennonites, are closed on Sunday. It's a great day to see locals out and about on walks or buggy rides or attending hymn sings, but you won't find many commercial activities open, except at large tourist attractions such as the Amish Homestead and Kitchen Kettle.

✳ Towns & Villages

Bird-in-Hand. Despite a population of just 300 residents, Bird-in-Hand is home to several of Lancaster's biggest tourist attractions, including the Plain & Fancy Farm and Restaurant and the Bird-in-Hand Farmers' Market, and several midsize hotels and inns. Most of these are located along busy Old Philadelphia Pike, but it is also surrounded by scenic farmland

and two-lane country roads. It's about 5 miles east of Lancaster city, and takes its name, according to legend, from a debate between two road surveyors about whether they should stay at their present location or push ahead to Lancaster. One of them supposedly responded: "A bird in the hand is worth two in the bush." So they stayed. One of the best things about Bird-in-Hand is its bake shop, a sticky bun and whoopie pie mecca that should not be missed.

Ephrata. Considered a hub of northern Lancaster County, Ephrata (pronounced EH-fra-ta) was founded by Conrad Beissel, the German-born man who also started the town's famous religious cloister. Its name means fruitful in old Hebrew, and it has less of a tourist feel than other towns in the area. Besides the monastery, the town boasts a pedestrian-friendly downtown lined with shops, restaurants, and homes with wide front porches. It is also home to one of the area's largest and best farm markets, the Green Dragon, which features antiques and animal auctions, flea-market finds, Pennsylvania Dutch food, and Donecker's, an upscale shopping complex, restaurant, and inn.

Intercourse. No one seems to know for sure how the town got its name, though it has certainly been the butt of countless jokes and postcards. One guess is that it stems from the town's location at the intersection of two busy roads, which also explains its earlier name, Cross Keys. This is perhaps Lancaster's busiest town and one that is heavily geared to tourists, though its dry goods and fabric stores also attract many local Amish and Mennonites. About 2 miles east of Bird-in-Hand, it's home to Kitchen Kettle shopping village, the People's Place Museum complex, plus dozens of independent quilt and crafts shops. Expect traffic, even gridlock, along this stretch of PA 340 most weekends.

Lititz. Founded as a Moravian community in 1756 and named after a castle in Bohemia, this town of about 9,000 people has one of the most charming main streets you'll ever find. It's about 6 miles north of Lancaster and makes a good base for a visit to Amish Country with many good B&Bs, parks, independent shops, and restaurants. It is also home to one of the oldest pretzel bakeries in the nation, as well as the Wilbur Chocolate Factory and Linden Hall, the country's oldest female boarding school. Many of its attractions and shops are within walking distance of one another.

Mount Joy. Located on Lancaster County's western edge, this town of 8,000 people can also be visited in context with trips to Hershey, Harrisburg, and York. It is home to several well-regarded farm-stay inns and B&Bs, and its revitalized main street has many antiques and gift shops and restaurants. You'll also find Bube's Brewery, a 19th-century brewery-turned-theme-park of sorts, here.

Strasburg. Trains are the main theme in this village south of Lancaster, though it traces its roots back to 17th-century French hunters and traders who named it after the town of Strasbourg in France. Today, it's a small child's dream, with several different train-themed attractions and even a motel that lets you sleep in spiffed-up cabooses. Its anchor is the Strasburg Railroad, which dates to 1832 and is touted as the oldest continually operating public utility in the state. Unless you have a child between the ages of 2 and 7, avoid the town by any means possible when the railroad hosts Thomas the Train events in spring and fall. Strasburg is also home to Sight & Sound Theater complex, a live theater company known for its massive Biblical-themed stage extravaganzas. You'll notice that many of Strasburg addresses list only the street or route name, but it's nearly impossible to get lost here; almost everything is within throwing distance of PA 741 (Gap Road) and PA 896.

✻ To See

HISTORIC SITES ✿ **Ephrata Cloister** (717-733-6600; www.ephrata cloister.org), 632 W. Main Street (US 322), Ephrata. Open daily March through December, closed Monday, January and February; $9 adults, $6 ages 6–17. Founded in 1732 by the German-born Conrad Beissel, this somewhat radical religious community practiced celibacy and asceticism and was known for its calligraphy, a cappella music, and printing and bookbinding skills. Today, you can visit the cluster of preserved medieval-style buildings where its nearly 300 members lived, in a grassy area near downtown Ephrata. You may opt for a self-guided tour, but the guided tours (included in the admission price) include access to more buildings and insights into the austere lifestyle and habitat. Plan to spend about two hours here, and leave time to browse the gift shop.

Hans Herr House (717-464-4438; www.hansherr.org), 1849 Hans Herr Drive, Lancaster. Guided tours 9–4 Monday through Saturday, April through November; $7 adults, $3 ages 5–12. Andrew Wyeth, a descendent of Herr, painted many pictures of this 1719 stone structure, which served as the first Mennonite meetinghouse in America and is considered the oldest structure in the county. The property also includes a blacksmith's shop, and three centuries' worth of farm equipment, orchards, and gardens.

✒ ⊤ **Wilbur Chocolate Company** (717-626-3249), 48 N. Broad Street, Lititz. Open 10–5 Monday through Saturday. This century-old candy maker is one of Lititz's top attractions. It runs a large gift shop and chocolate memorabilia museum in the front of its huge brick factory on PA 501. There's a fabulous display of antique chocolate pots and hundreds of unusual tins and molds. You can also watch candy makers create peanut

WILBUR CHOCOLATE COMPANY

butter meltaways, chocolate-covered strawberries, and other treats in the glass-walled kitchen in back. You may sample Wilbur Buds, the company's signature candy, or buy a box and enjoy them by the creek at adjacent Lititz Springs Park.

& **Wheatland** (717-392-8721; www.wheatland.org), 1120 Marietta Avenue (PA 23), Lancaster. Open 10–4 daily April through October, call for hours other times of year; $8.50 adults, $4 ages 6–12. James Buchanan was the only president to hail from Pennsylvania. When he left the White House, he was widely criticized for failing to prevent the Civil War, but he found solace in this 1828 Federal house and lived there for 20 years until his death in 1868. Costumed guides lead hour-long tours of the home, which contains many of Buchanan's original belongings.

MUSEUMS ❧ & ♂ **Landis Valley Museum** (717-569-0401; www.landis valleymuseum.org), 2451 Kissel Hill Road, Lancaster. Open Monday through Saturday 9–5, Sunday 12–5; $12 adults, $8 ages 6–17. George and Henry Landis started a small museum in north Lancaster to exhibit family heirlooms in the 1920s; the state acquired it in the 1950s and expanded it into a 21-building village that showcases Pennsylvania German culture, folk traditions, decorative arts, and language. The best time to visit is in summer and early fall, when costumed clock makers, tavern keepers, farmers, and others demonstrate their trades throughout the complex. The

Weathervane gift shop sells beautiful handcrafted gifts and books on local history and farming.

Lancaster Heritage Museum (717-299-6440; www.lancaster heritage.com), 5 W. King Street. Open Tuesday, Friday, and Saturday 9–2, first Friday of month until 9 PM; free. It will take you less than an hour to walk through this worthy history and culture museum across from Central Market. Housed in an 18th-century Masonic Lodge Hall, it features displays of folk art, quilts, furniture, and toys produced by generations of Lancaster County craftsman, plus an impressive restored 1933 ceiling mural.

Demuth Museum (717-299-9940; www.demuth.org), 120 E. King Street, Lancaster. Open Tuesday through Sunday, closed January; donations. Lancaster-born Charles Demuth was a master watercolorist known for his uniquely modernist renderings of the area's factories, grain factories, and churches. This wonderful little museum was his childhood home and painting studio. It contains 40 original Demuth works, plus exhibits showcasing the work of artists who influenced him. There is also a lovely outside garden planted with flowers cultivated by the artist's mother, and the adjacent Demuth Tobacco Shop, the oldest operating tobacco shop in the country. You don't have to know Demuth's work to appreciate this quietly beautiful attraction. It's within walking distance of Central Market and the Quilt Museum.

Railroad Museum of Pennsylvania (717-687-8628; www .rrmuseumpa.org), PA 741, Strasburg. Open daily April through October; Tuesday through Sunday, November through March; $10 adults, $8 ages 3–11. The main attraction of this train lover's mecca is the Rolling Stock Hall, home to four railroad tracks and two dozen preserved locomotive and passenger cars dating from 1875 to the 20th century. There are also displays of train tickets, art, uniforms, and tools; kids will love Stewart Junction and its hands-on electric train set-ups; prepare for tantrums when it's time to leave. It is directly across the street from the Strasburg Railroad.

Intercourse

People's Place Quilt Museum (800-828-8218), 3518 Old Philadelphia Pike, Intercourse. Open 9–5 Monday through Saturday. This small second-story exhibit features modern quilts made after the year 2000. It's an oasis of calm from the busy car and pedestrian traffic on PA 340. The downstairs gift shop, the Old Country Store, sells wooden Shaker-style boxes, folk dolls, hand-dyed cotton pillows, and, yes, all types of quilts (see Selective Shopping).

American Military Edged Weaponry Museum (717-768-7185), 3562 Old Philadelphia Pike, Intercourse. Open 10–5 Monday through Saturday, May through November; $3 adults, $1.50 ages 5 and up. Military history buffs will want to check out the comprehensive collection of military knives on display, from swords and sabers to fencing bayonets and Ka-Bars. There are also displays of old recruiting posters and weapons and artifacts from the Spanish-American War, the Vietnam War, and Desert Storm.

✳ To Do

Amish Homestead and Experience (717-768-3600), 3121 Old Philadelphia Pike (PA 340), Bird-in-Hand. Open daily. It's hokey and a bit faded, but this is a good place for those who know little about the Amish to start their visit to Lancaster. There's a an easy-to-digest multimedia show (complete with 3D sound and special effects) about an Amish family struggling with their teenage son's desire to leave the church, as well as guided tours of a replica of a typical Amish homestead. Combo deals are available for $14; if you must do only one, take the house tour—guides are knowledgeable and full of anecdotes about the Amish lifestyle. Be sure to pick up a

PEOPLE'S PLACE QUILT MUSEUM

couple of hot buttered soft pretzels at Sarah Mae's bakery before you leave—they cost $1 and are as rich as French toast.

Julius Sturgis Pretzels (717-626-4354; www.juliussturgis.com), 219 E. Main Street, Lititz. America's first pretzel bakery; 20-minute tours are $3 and end with a hands-on pretzel-twisting demonstration (you get to keep your creation). Expect short waits in the summer.

↑ 𝒆 **Lancaster Science Factory** (717-509-6363; www.thelancaster sciencefactory.org), 454 New Holland Avenue, Lancaster. Closed Monday; $7.50 adults, $6 ages 3–15. The perfect place to take the kids on a rainy Sunday. They can build a truss bridge, learn about acoustics, and partake in dozens of impressively low-tech brain teasers and puzzles that require more thinking than button-pushing. It's next to the Cork Factory Hotel and a five-minute drive from Penn Square.

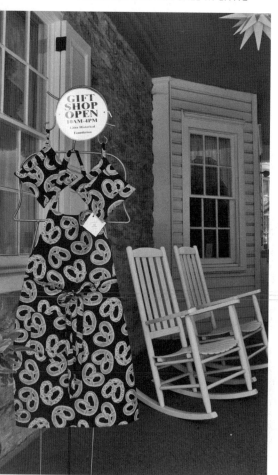

PRETZEL APRON FOR SALE IN LITITZ

FOR FAMILIES 𝒆 ⛄ **Dutch Wonderland** (717-291-1888; www.dutchwonderland.com), 2249 Lincoln Highway east, Lancaster. Open daily mid-June through August, weekends May, September, and early October; $35 adults and kids ages 2 and up, $50 two-day flex passes. Beyond the flamboyant faux castle on US 30 lies a compact and very manageable amusement park targeted to the 12-and-under set. The 35 kid-friendly rides include a kid-powered train cars, double-splash log flume, carousel, bumper cars, and paddleboats. It also has a fun water park (with lounge chairs for parents) and daily medieval-themed stage shows and princess story times. Don't miss the homage to retired rides in the park's north section. Hershey Park's owners bought the property in 2001, and discounted combo deals are available.

DAIRY-THEMED PLAYGROUND NEAR LITITZ

✍ **Strasburg Railroad** (717-687-22; www.strasburgrailroad.com), 301 Gap Road (PA 741), Strasburg. Open daily mid-April through mid-October. Standard coach fare is $14 adults, $7.50 ages 3–11. Take a 45-minute ride on a coal-powered 1860s-era steam locomotive though the rural countryside. Guides describe the railroad's history along the way.

✍ ♿ **National Toy Train Museum** (717-687-8976; www.nttmuseum .org), 300 Paradise Lane, Strasburg. Open Friday through Monday, May through October, weekends in April, November, and December; $6 adults, $3 ages 6–12. Owned and operated by the Train Collectors Association, this is a splendid place to take kids before or after a ride on the nearby Strasburg Railroad. Young and old train lovers will enjoy the displays of locomotives and cars from the 1800s to the present. It's next to the Red Caboose Motel (see Inns & Motels).

✍ **Cherry-Crest Farm Maze** (717-687-6843; www.cherrycrestfarm.com), 150 Cherry Hill Road, Ronks. Closed Sunday; $9–15 .This 175-acre farm near Strasburg has hayrides, obstacle courses, animal feedings, and dozens of other kid-friendly activities, but it is best known for its giant cornfield maze, open Friday and Saturday, May through November.

SCENIC DRIVES Head south on PA 896 through the tiny town of Georgetown. The road is dotted with horse farms and small family farm stands selling fresh corn, tomatoes, and other produce that usually let you pay by the honor system. PA 741 near the village of Gap is also a scenic country drive and quieter alternative to busy PA 30; start at **Twin Brook Winery** (717-442-4915; 5697 Strasburg Road, Gap), continue west to **Fisher Farm Stand,** which boasts some of the best prices around for produce, shoofly pies, jams, and pickles. Then wander next door to the small quilt shop attached to a Mennonite home and browse the hand-stitched beauties.

✷ Outdoor Activities

BASEBALL The **Lancaster Barnstormers** are part of the Atlantic League of Professional Baseball, and play at **Clipper Magazine Stadium** (717-509-4487; lancasterbarnstormers.com), 650 Prince Street, near the heart of downtown. Despite its lack of affiliation with Major League Baseball, the team has a loyal local following and may be the only stadium in the country to sell whoopie pies in its snack bars.

BICYCLING/RENTALS The Lancaster area offers a labyrinth of winding country roads that are ideal for cycling. For a detailed list of trails and suggested rides, visit www.lancasterbikeclub.org. **Bike Line** (717-394-8998; 117 Rohrerstown Road) on Lancaster's west side also has good maps and information on local trails and rents road and mountain bikes starting at $15–35 a day and $25–45 for a weekend.

CORN FOR SALE IN AMISH COUNTRY

BUGGY RIDES The competition is fierce for these horse-drawn backcountry rides, which usually last about 30 minutes and roam the countryside. Most places operate daily, except Sunday, from about 9 to 6 with prices starting at $10 for adults and $5 for kids, plus a tip for the driver (though the ones listed below often have discount coupons available on their Web sites). Trips are usually in an open-air family carriage that seats a dozen or so. Most of the drivers are local Amish or Mennonite men who welcome questions about their culture and lifestyles.

& **Aaron and Jessica's Buggy Rides** (717-768-8828; www.amish buggyrides.com), next to the Amish Experience in Bird-in-Hand, offers four different backcountry tours led by Amish or Mennonite guides. They usually stop at an Amish farm, where you can buy produce and baked goods. Ever tourist-friendly, they're also open most Sundays and allow pets on the ride.

Ed's Buggy Rides (717-687-0360; www.edsbuggyrides.com), PA 896, Strasburg. Across the street from the Sight & Sound Theaters, its guides lead you through the cornfields and back roads of southern Lancaster County.

AAA Buggy Rides (717-687-9962; www.aaabuggyrides.com) operates out of the Red Caboose Motel in Strasburg and Kitchen Kettle Village in Intercourse. It's open Sunday. Hour-long rides are $16 per adult and $8 per child.

FISHING **Evening Rise Flyfishing Outfitters** (717-509-3636), 1953 Fruitville Pike, Lancaster. A good source for supplies and information on local rivers and streams. In winter, you can ice fish on Speedwell Forge near Lititz.

GOLF **Tanglewood Manor Golf Club** (717-786-2500; 866-845-0479), 653 Scotland Road, Quarryville. An 18-hole par-72 course surrounded by rolling hills with two man-made ponds, and putting and chipping practice greens. It's about 5 miles south of Strasburg.

Olde Hickory Golf Course (717-569-9107), 600 Olde Hickory Road, Lancaster. Nine holes to 1,600 yards with a par of 28.

Overlook Golf Course (717-569-9551), 2040 Lititz Pike, Lititz. Opened in 1928, this 18-hole public course measures 6,083 yards and has a par of 70. There's also a driving range.

Tree Top Golf Course (717-665-6262), 1624 Creek Road, Manheim. An 18-hole, par-65 course with rolling terrain, good for novices or accomplished golfers looking for a quick round.

Willow Valley Golf Course (717-464-4448), 2416 Willow Street Pike, Lancaster. Nine-hole, 2,300-yard course on 35 manicured acres. Greens fees start at $14.

HUNTING **Middle Creek Wildlife Management Area** (717-733-1512), 100 Museum Road, Stevens. Public waterfowl hunting is permitted here during open hunting season, and special deer hunts are scheduled periodically; check with the visitor center for specific areas and rules.

TENNIS **D. F. Buchmiller Park** (717-299-8215), 1050 Rockford Road, Lancaster, has several public tennis courts. **Central Park** (717-299-8215), 3 Nature's Way, Lancaster, also has courts.

✳ Green Space

PARKS & REFUGES **Central Park** (717-299-8215), 3 Nature's Way (near PA 222 and 272), Lancaster. This 540-acre park along the Conestoga

SOPHISTICATED LANCASTER

It's Friday night and the lobby bar of the **Lancaster Arts Hotel** is packed with office workers sipping organic cosmopolitans and couples dressed for date night. Overnight guests wait amid mixed-media sculptures and floor-to-ceiling abstract paintings to check into a room in the renovated tobacco warehouse. Next door, the **John J. Jefferies** restaurant serves lamb samosas and grass-fed bison tartare with microgreens to eager diners.

This isn't the image most people get when they think of Lancaster County. Amish-driven horse and buggies, Mennonite farm stands, and home-style buffets still dominate the surrounding land-
scape and serve as the
cornerstone of the tourism
industry. In recent years,
however, the area has
upped its sophistication quo-
tient, adding day spas, boutique hotels, expanded
wineries, and elegant art
galleries.

LANCASTER'S MODERN CORK FACTORY HOTEL

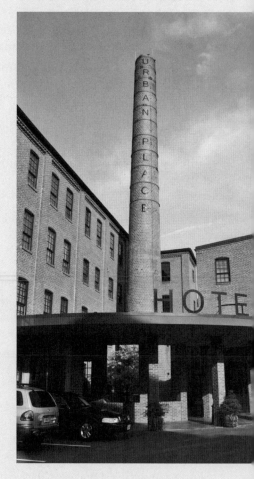

Sometimes you just
might crave a little wine and
cheese with your farm stay
or funnel cake.

Lancaster Arts or the
Cork Factory Hotel (see
Lodging) are good bases for
such a venture: both are
located in gorgeous renovated buildings within easy
reach of the city center.
Nearby at Penn Square, the
Charles Demuth Museum is
a rarely crowded homage to
one of the country's best

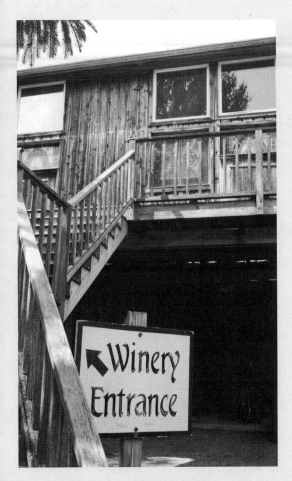

TWIN BROOK WINERY NEAR LANCASTER

watercolorists. **Carr's Restaurant** never fails to provide a romantic dining experience (see Dining Out), while **Fenz Restaurant** (717-735-6999; 398 Harrisburg Pike) is sleek and boisterous and the go-to place for late-night goat-cheese pizza or truffle fries.

If you really want to avoid the horse-and-buggy vibe, the best town to visit is probably Lititz, a few miles north of Lancaster City. Anchored by a girls' boarding school on one side and a lovely park on the other, its main street is a haven of Victorian-era architecture, independent shops, and small museums. A reflexology spa, **Body and Sole** (717-201-7616, 2520 Lititz Pike) is a few miles south of town.

Cap your Sophisticated Lancaster weekend with a visit to the peaceful **Garden of Five Senses** in Central Park (717-299-8215; 3 Nature's Way, Lancaster) or a stop at **Twin Brook Winery** (717-442-4915; 5697 Strasburg Road, Gap), for samples of award-winning Rose and Chardonnay reserve in a bucolic country setting. There will always be time for chow-chow or shoofly pie on your next visit.

River has playgrounds, a skate park, easy biking and walking trails, a photogenic covered bridge, and an environmental center and library. Near the main entrance on Rockford Road, the hilltop Garden of Five Senses invites visitors to use all five senses to appreciate its abundant flowers, shrubs, and waterfalls.

✔ ✤ **Long's Park** US 30 at Harrisburg Pike, Lancaster. A 71-acre park with a spring-fed lake, ducks, picnic pavilions, tennis courts, and a small petting zoo that's open June through September. The playground, which resembles a big wooden castle, is as good as it gets for the younger set— tire swings, turrets, bridges, and lots of giddy children. The park hosts a summer outdoor music series, an arts and crafts festival, and the world's largest chicken barbecue every May (see also Special Events).

✔ ✤ **Lititz Springs Park** (717-626-8981), 15 N. Broad Street. Owned by the Lititz Moravian Congregation, this charming 7-acre park is anchored by a replica of a 19th-century train depot (home to a visitor center) and has two playgrounds, benches, pedestrian paths, and a pretty stream. It's right next to the Wilbur Chocolate Factory and within walking distance of many stores and restaurants.

✔ **Middle Creek Wildlife Management Area** (717-733-1512), 100 Museum Road, Stevens. Run by the state game commission, this 6,254-acre refuge between Lititz and Reading has three picnic areas, a shallow lake for boating and fishing, and 20 miles of year-round hiking trails that traverse the property's varied habitats. Pick up a self-guided driving map at the visitor center off Hopeland Road in Kleinfeltersville, and check out the waterfowl display and hands-on kids' area. Around late February and March, as many as 100,000 migrating snow geese flock to the refuge on their way north to Canada; it's a beautiful sight that draws gawkers from all over the state. Public waterfowl hunting is permitted here during open hunting season, and special deer hunts are scheduled periodically; check with the visitor center for specific areas and rules.

WALKS The flat and straight **Lancaster Junction Recreation Trail** runs just over 2 miles (one way) passing through acres of scenic farmland and following a shaded creek on its northern half. It's also great for biking and horseback riding. To get to the southern trailhead, take PA 283 west of Lancaster City to Spooky Nook Road and turn right on Champ Road. The trailhead is on the left at road's end. For a scenic view of the Susquehanna River, head to **Chickies Rock Park** in Marietta.

✳ Lodging

BED & BREAKFASTS Inn at Twin Linden (717-445-7619; www.innattwinlinden.com), 2092 Main Street, Churchtown. This graceful 19th-century home is about 25 minutes from the tourist heart of Amish Country, but some might consider that a blessing. Housed in a historic mansion with gardens that back up to Mennonite farm fields, it has six rooms and two suites, all with feather beds and luxury linens, many with gas fireplaces and Jacuzzi tubs. The Polo and Churchtown Rooms and both suites face the back gardens and tend to get less street noise. A three-course breakfast is served in a dining room overlooking the back garden; French toast stuffed with pears and Brie is a specialty. They also offer a romantic prix-fixe dinner on Saturday night for their guests and others; cost is $55 per person and you may bring your own wine. Owners Norman and Susan Kuestner know the area well and are full of helpful tips on everything from golf to mud sales. Rooms $130–180, suites $245–275, with a two-night minimum for Saturday stays.

Lovelace Manor (717-399-3275; 866-713-6384), 2236 Marietta Avenue, Lancaster. No children under 12. This beautiful 1882 home is about 5 minutes from Lancaster City and 15 to 20 minutes from outlying towns such as Strasburg and Bird-in-Hand.

Named after the 17th-century poet Richard Lovelace (an ancestor of owner Lark McCarley), it has four spacious rooms decorated in soft beige and brown with private baths, 12-foot-high ceilings, a billiard and games room, and several sitting porches. An outdoor hot tub, wireless access, and 24-hour access to a pantry stocked with soft drinks and snacks are also available. Breakfast is an elegant affair served on china and crystal in the main dining room. Rooms $135–175.

Lititz

❧ **Alden House** (717-627-3363; www.aldenhouse.com), 62 E. Main Street, Lititz. Within walking distance of the shops and restaurants of downtown Lititz, this 1850s Federal home offers lower rates than many other local B&Bs. The six rooms and suites are heavy on antiques, curtains, and floral accents, with queen beds, private baths, and televisions; common areas include three porches and a back garden with a fish pond. Breakfast is a large and lavish affair, featuring fruit, a main entrée (maybe French Acadian crepes or three-egg omelets), breads and muffins, and desserts such as apple cake or lemon pudding. Rooms $99, suites with sitting rooms $139–149.

Swiss Woods (717-627-3358; 800-594-8018; www.swisswoods.com), 500 Blantz Road, Lititz. No children under 12. Surrounded by acres of landscaped gardens and countryside, this seven-room Swiss-themed inn is considered one of the best B&Bs in the north Lancaster area. It's about 3 miles from downtown Lititz and has seven large rooms with private baths, goose down comforters, and natural woodwork. A favorite room is Lake of Geneva, which has a private balcony overlooking the gardens and Speedwell Forge Lake. Breakfasts are very good and might include baked berry French toast or peach cobbler. Rooms $170–205, two-night minimum on weekends.

INNS & HOTELS ✿ ዉ **Amish View Inn** (717-768-1162; www .amishviewinn.com), 3125 Old

PLAIN & FANCY RESTAURANT

Philadelphia Pike (PA 340), Bird-in-Hand. I normally would steer visitors away from hotels on traffic-heavy routes such as 340 and US 30, but this 50-room small hotel is an exception. Opened in 2001, it's adjacent to Plain & Fancy Farm and a good bet for families or anyone who wants to be right in the middle of all the buggy-ride and farm-stand bustle. The spacious rooms have mahogany-frame king beds, DVD players, and refrigerators, and include a huge breakfast of waffles and made-to-order omelets. The north-facing rooms overlook beautiful rolling green pastures. One- and two-bedroom suites have whirlpool tubs and fireplaces. An indoor pool, a Jacuzzi, and a fitness room are also on-site. Check the hotel's Web site for discount coupons. Rooms $114–134. Suites $164–349.

Best Western Eden Resort (717-569-6444; www.edenresort .com), 222 Eden Road, Lancaster. Kid-friendly amenities and a central location near US 222 and PA 272 make this large resort popular with families. The 285 rooms and suites are basic and comfortable with refrigerators, coffeemakers, and flat-panel TVs. Amenities include indoor and outdoor pools, a kids' playground and water splash area, bocce court, and much more. A hot breakfast buffet is included. Rooms $99–195; suites $205–295.

Cork Factory Hotel (717-735-2075; www.corkfactoryhotel.com),

480 New Holland Avenue, Lancaster. Lancaster was once the second-largest cork-producing city in the U.S. One of its largest factories was turned into a luxury hotel in 2008 and is an ideal alternative for folks who prefer modern spaciousness over B&B quaintness or rustic farm stays. The 77 handsome rooms have one or two king beds, exposed brick walls, and enough space to practically accommodate an entire gymnastics team. It's right next to the Lancaster Science Factory and an easy five-minute drive to Penn Square. The rate includes a generous cold breakfast buffet in the Cork n' Cap restaurant with coffee, pastries, cereal, and fruit. Rooms $119–169.

Heritage Hotel (717-898-2431; www.heritagelancaster.com), 500 Centerville Road, Lancaster. This large hotel is right off US 30 and makes a convenient base if you're spending a few days in Amish Country. The 166 traditional rooms are tidy and large with one king or two queen beds. Formerly known as Sherwood Knoll, it changed hands in 2009 and is popular with bus tours and traveling sports teams. There's a small pool (plus a wading pool for kids). It's adjacent to Loxley's, a two-level bar and restaurant that caters to all tastes (from make-your-own pizzas for kids to prime rib and dry martinis for grown-ups. There's live music Wednesday and Saturday. It's also next door to the

Dutch Apple Dinner Theater (see Entertainment). Rooms $99–159.

Lancaster Arts Hotel (717-299-3000 or 877-208-5521; www .lancasterartshotel.com), 300 Harrisburg Pike, Lancaster. Gorgeous local artwork and 79 modern rooms and suites now fill this former tobacco warehouse near the center of downtown. It is one of the city's hippest spots, with a popular lobby bar and a clientele that could be straight out of Manhattan. All rooms have wine refrigerators and iPod docking stations. A Continental breakfast is included and served in the stone-walled dining room or outside on the waterfall-serenaded patio. For dinner, don't miss the highly regarded John J. Jefferies restaurant (see Dining Out). Rooms $160–185, suites $205.

✿ **Red Caboose Motel** (717-687-5000; www.redcaboosemotel.com), 312 Paradise Lane, Strasburg. The "rooms" in this motel next to the National Toy Train Museum are actual 25-ton N-5 cabooses, at least on the outside. The insides have been gutted so they resemble a standard-issue motel room, complete with polyester bed covers and small shower stalls. Still, the complex is a good value for families looking to stay near Strasburg's train attractions. A playground, a petting zoo, a lookout tower, and a picnic area are also on the grounds. In summer, movies are screened on the side of the barn. Rooms $85–139.

RED CABOOSE MOTEL

♪ ⅁ **Harvest Drive Family Inn** (717-768-7186; 800-233-0176; www.harvestdrive.com), 3370 Harvest Drive, Intercourse. Surrounded by corn and alfalfa fields on a quiet road outside Intercourse, this family-owned motel has clean and basic rooms that sleep up to six people. There is a playground and Pennsylvania Dutch-style restaurant on the property. Rates drop considerably January through March. Rooms $49–169, including breakfast.

FARM STAYS More than 30 farms in or near Lancaster County offer "farm stays" to guests for rates of about $60 to 125 a night. They are usually a real treat for kids and a heck of a lot more interesting than staying in a chain motel on US 30. Most include a hearty breakfast (except on Sunday), plus activities such as hayrides and opportunities to help with milking cows and feeding chickens. The rooms tend to be comfortable but basic, often with shared baths. For a more comprehensive list, go to www.afarmstay.com.

Old Fogie Farm (717-426-3992; www.oldfogiefarm.com), 16 Stackstown Road, Marietta. This working farm on the county's western edge stands out for its charming yet modern rooms (with cable and air conditioning) and the down-to-earth attitude of Tom and Biz Fogie ("We're not just a bunch of fluff"). Kids will love the wading pond, tire swing, and friendly yard pig. The Hayloft Family Suite has queen and trundle beds, a full kitchen, claw-foot tub, and deck overlooking the barnyard. Rooms

$99 per couple and $15 per child. Breakfast is extra.

✍ **Rocky Acre** (717-653-4449; www.rockyacre.com), 1020 Pinkerton Road, Mount Joy. You might call this the Four Seasons of farm stays, with its romantic Victorian-style rooms, all of which have air-conditioning and private baths. There is also a two-bedroom apartment that sleeps up to seven and a guest house with a full kitchen and private entrance. Located on a 550-acre dairy farm, it offers delicious multicourse breakfasts and plenty of recreational activities, from pony, train, and tractor rides to guided farm tours and a petting zoo. Owners Eileen and Galen Benner have been in the farm-stay business for more than 40 years. There is a two-night minimum on weekends. Rooms $129–165, apartments and cottage $159–239.

✍ **Stone Haus Farm** (717-653-8444; www.stonehausfarmbnb .com), 360 S. Esbenshade Road, Manheim. Merv and Angie Shenk and their three kids run this 200-year-old stone farmhouse and 100-acre corn, soybean, and celery farm about 5 miles west of Lancaster. The six guest rooms, most of which have shared baths, are nicely decorated with quilts and antique reproductions; some have exposed stone walls and room for extra cots. Kids have access to a game room, playground, picnic area, pedal tractors, and bikes. Rates include a huge breakfast (including Sunday) of eggs, fruit, oatmeal, and baked goods such as shoofly cake and pumpkin muffins. Rooms $69–95.

✍ **Verdant View Farm** (717-687-7353; 888-321-8119; www.verdant view.com), 439 Strasburg Road, Paradise. This 118-acre Mennonite dairy farm is a quick drive or walk from most of Strasburg's train attractions. Kids will love watching the Strasburg train pass through the field behind the Ranck family farmhouse; they may also help milk the cows, feed the swans and geese, fish for bass and bluegills in the pond, and pet the many cats, sheep, and rabbits that call the farm home. Basic rooms in the farmhouse are on the second floor, two have private baths and sleep up to four; a newly renovated first-floor suite includes a master bedroom, private bath, and a small room with bunk beds, perfect for families. Additional lodging is available across the street in a small home on the property. A highlight is the optional breakfast (for an extra $5): a feast, usually led by Don or Ginnie Ranck, of yogurt, applesauce, French toast, eggs, toast, fresh milk, coffee, and good conversation. Rooms $79–107; two-room suites $109–114.

CAMPGROUNDS & CABINS

Flory's Cottages and Camping (717-687-6670; www.florys camping.com), 99 N. Ronks Road. Shaded, level grassy sites with electric, water, sewer, hookups. Tent sites $26–29, with hookups $30–38; cottages $84–234.

Beaver Creek Farm Cabins (717-687-7745), 2 Little Beaver Road (PA 896), Strasburg. Eight 2-bedroom cabins (and one single bedroom) starting at $90 per night and $585 per week.

Loose Caboose Campground (717-442-8429; www.theloose caboosecampground.com), 5130 Strasburg Road (PA 741), Kinzers. Good option for families who plan to spend a lot of time in nearby Strasburg. It's on 26 forested acres with a children's playground, campfire sites, and picnic pavilions. Tent sites $30, with full hookups $35–40.

Spring Gulch Resort Campground (717-354-3100 or 866-864-8524; www.springgulch.com), 475 Lynch Road, New Holland. Huge, highly rated campground with 415 tent sites, cabins, and housing rentals, a day spa, two heated pools, fishing and swimming lakes, and a fitness center. Saturday to Saturday stays required in summer. Its popular Folk Festival the third weekend of May draws big crowds. Tent sites $29–34 primitive, $34–64 with hookup; cottages and houses that sleep 4–10 are $105–177; rates drop in winter, spring, and fall.

SMORGASBORDS

These all-you-can-eat buffets are a staple of Lancaster County. Regular patrons debate passionately over which ones are the best and which ones should be left to stew in their canned sweet potatoes. Many of them are big enough to seat hundreds of diners, making them popular with bus tours. Most offer soup and salad bar, carving stations, many Pennsylvania Dutch dishes, and a wide selection of desserts. Selective or light eaters might want to avoid these buffets and stick with smaller á la carte establishments. For others, here are a few favorite standbys.

& **Shady Maple** (717-354-8222), 129 Toddy Drive, East Earl. Breakfast, lunch, and dinner Tuesday through Saturday. This huge complex along PA 23 began as a farm stand and has expanded into a small city with an 1,100-seat restaurant, grocery store, banquet hall, and stadium-like parking. It gets consistent raves from buffet pros for its homemade fruit breads, wide selection of meats, seafood, vegetables, and hot and cold dessert bar. Lunch buffet $7–10, dinner buffet $14–19.

Dienner's Country Restaurant (717-687-9571), 2855 Lincoln Highway, Ronks. Open daily 7 AM–6 PM, until 8 PM on Friday. Smaller than other smorgasbords, this homey diner is known for its fall-off-the-bone rotis-

✳ Where to Eat

Lancaster County restaurants often specialize in hearty Pennsylvania Dutch foods such as chicken potpie, pepper cabbage, and baked ham. You can also easily arrange to have dinner in an Amish family's home; many inn and B&B owners are happy to help set these up. It typically costs $12 to $15 a person and features a multi-course home-cooked Pennsylvania Dutch meal and genial conversation.

DINING OUT ⵟ **Bube's Brewery** (717-653-2056; www.bubes brewery.com), 102 N. Market Street, Mount Joy. Open daily for lunch and dinner. Alois Bube, a German immigrant, started this small brewery in the 1870s, and later opened a hotel next door. Today, the large complex is as much an indoor theme park as a restaurant and bar, with brewery tours, three different dining areas, a summer biergarten, gift shop, and live music from jazz trios to minstrel performances. Dine on a six-course prix-fixe menu at Alois in the hotel portion or in the Catacombs, where costumed guides lead you on a tour of the cellars before your meal. Lunch and

serie chicken and very low prices (nothing is over $10). It also offers á la carte items such as burgers and daily specials of meatloaf and chicken potpie.

& ⵟ **Miller's** (717-687-6621), 2811 Lincoln Highway east, Ronks. Breakfast, lunch, and dinner daily. This centrally located restaurant caters to bus tours and out-of-towners; it takes reservations and is one of the few smorgasbords to stay open on Sunday and to serve wine and beer. Its huge serve-yourself buffet features items such as top sirloin, baked ham with cider sauce, chicken potpie, and baked cabbage in cream sauce. The large dining room overlooks the countryside. There are free kitchen tours every Wednesday (reservations required). Buffet $10–21.

& **Stolzfus Farm Restaurant** (717-768-8156), PA 772, Intercourse. Lunch and dinner Monday through Saturday, April through October, weekends in April and November. Meals are served family-style (no menu) at long tables and include a typical Pennsylvania Dutch menu of ham loaf, fried chicken, buttered noodles, chow-chow, and pepper cabbage. The sausage and other meats come from the family's adjacent butcher shop. No reservations. Lunch and dinner: $16, $7.50 ages 4–12.

dinner are also available at the more casual Bottling Works on the original brewery site. The menu is as vast as the Lancaster County countryside; the baked tomato soup and grilled cheese with crab-meat are a couple of favorites. The house brews change often, but might include oatmeal stout, brown ale, and Heffweizen. Did I mention that there are ghost tours, too? Bottling Works dishes: $6–27, Alois: $42 prix fixe, Cata-combs: $20–32.

&. Ÿ **Carr's** (717-299-7090; www.carrsrestaurant.com), 50 W. Grant Street, Lancaster. Lunch and din-ner Tuesday through Saturday, Sunday brunch. This upscale restaurant is a great place to sam-ple creative American dishes before a show at the Fulton The-ater. Owner and Chef Tim Carr is a Lancaster area native who uses organic and locally made or raised products, from cheese and mus-tard to free-range chickens, as often as possible. At dinner, try the tuna noodle casserole with applewood bacon, rare tuna and hash browns drizzled with white truffle oil, or veal Oscar layered with Parma ham, fresh mozzarella, and asparagus. The downstairs dining room is inviting with a large mural of a Parisian street scene and view of the restaurant's extensive wine collection. Lunch is a very good value; a favorite is the open-face meatloaf sandwich with hunter's sauce and fries. Reserva-tions recommended. Lunch $9–15, dinner entrées $14–30.

&. Ÿ **General Sutter Inn** (717-626-2115; www.generalsutterinn.com), 14 E. Main Street, Lititz. Open daily; call for hours. The General Sutter has operated con-tinuously since 1764 at the inter-section of PA 501 and 772. Its formal restaurant offers a satisfy-ing dinner menu that includes crisp roast duck, smoked honey-chipotle chicken, and fillet of beef medallions. There's also a less expensive tavern menu of crab cake sandwiches, fish and chips, tenderloin steak wraps, and salads. The outdoor patio is a popular place during the summer. Tavern menu: $8–15. Dinner entrées: $17–28.

John J. Jefferies (717-431-3307; www.johnjjefferies.com), 300 Har-risburg Pike, Lancaster. Just about everything on the menu is locally raised and organic at this hip new eatery in the Lancaster Arts Hotel. The creative menu changes sea-sonally and might include braised bison with tomato, eggplant and onion stew, or pan-roasted halibut with spaghetti squash risotto. Desserts are simple and refresh-ing: strawberry and rhubarb crisp, vanilla crème brulee, warm choco-late lava cake, Reservations rec-ommended. Entrées $18–34.

&. Ÿ **Lily's on Main** (717-738-2711; www.lilysonmain.com), 124 E. Main Street, Ephrata. Lunch Monday through Saturday, dinner daily, brunch Sunday. This modern bistro overlooking Ephrata's down-town is the place to go when you've had enough of smorgasbords and down-home diners. The creative American menu might include raspberry chicken baked in almond bread-crumb crust and topped with melted Brie, lobster macaroni and cheese with roasted tomatoes and asparagus, or sautéed calves liver with sweet red onion preserves. There's also a lighter menu of sandwiches and salads served at both lunch and dinner. It has an extensive wine list with bottles running between $30 and 125. Lunch $8–20; entrées: $17–33.

& ⅋ **Olde Greenfield Inn** (717-393-0668; www.thegreenfield restaurant.com), 595 Greenfield Road, Lancaster. Lunch and dinner Tuesday through Saturday, Sunday brunch. This restored 1790s stone farmhouse is regularly rated among the area's top romantic restaurants by local newspapers

and magazines. Try to reserve a table in the intimate wine cellar. The American menu includes roasted Dijon- and herb-crusted rack of lamb, lemon-thyme chicken, and filet mignon. A bar lounge offers live music on Wednesday and Friday nights. Reservations suggested. Lunch $9–15; dinner entrées $18–28.

EATING OUT & **Café Chocolate** (717-626-0123), 40 Main Street, Lititz. Open daily. Besides a large assortment of desserts made from fair-trade chocolate, this cute café serves salads, crepes, quiche, and savory small dishes such as hickory-smoked chicken and vegan chili. Dishes $4–10.

& **Central Market** (717-291-4723), 23 N. Market Street, Lancaster. Open 6 AM–4 PM Tuesday

CENTRAL MARKET

and Friday, 6 AM–2 PM Saturday. Seating is limited, but the delicious food and wide range of choices make this a terrific lunch spot if you're in the downtown area. Housed in a beautiful brick 1880s building, it is home to dozens of stalls selling everything from chicken corn chowder and Kunzler hot dogs to Greek salads, mission-style burritos, and Italian cannoli. The wonderful Carr's restaurant has a stall, as do S. Clyde Weaver Meats and Maplehofe Dairy. I've never had a bad meal here; the best thing to do is just wander around until your stomach tells you to stop. And consider picking up some cream-line milk and fresh-picked flowers on the way out.

⚐ ♨ **Country Table Restaurant** (717-653-4745; www.country tablerestaurant.com), Bake Shoppe and Deli, 740 E. Main Street, Mount Joy. Closed Sunday. This Western Lancaster County eatery has plenty of fans who say it serves the best Pennsylvania Dutch food in the county. For breakfast, you might find cherry-baked oatmeal, sausage gravy over biscuits with home fries, and waffles with fresh blueberries. The lunch specials, which include soup, salad, and a sandwich such as ham, cheddar, and bacon on rye, are a good value. Dishes $4–13.

✿ ⚐ **Leola Family Restaurant** (717-656-2311), 365 W. Main Street, Leola. This 24-hour diner is a good place to stop for a quick

meal if you're traveling to or from Lancaster on PA 23. It specializes in home-cooked food such as hot turkey sandwiches, pork sauerkraut, and chicken potpie. Dishes $7–13.

✿ ⚐ **Isaac's Deli** (717-687-7699), Shops at Traintown, Gap Road (PA 741), Strasburg. You'll find a reliable selection of salads, soups, flatbread pizzas, and grilled sandwiches at this local kid-friendly chain with a pink flamingo mascot. For a unique twist, try any of the grilled soft-pretzel roll sandwiches. Dishes: $5–8.

✿ ⚐ ♨ **Oregon Dairy Restaurant** (717-661-6804; www.oregon dairy.com), Oregon Pike (at US 222), Lititz. Big portions and hearty Pennsylvania Dutch platters make this a favorite of families. A train running around part of the dining room will keep the kids occupied until the food comes. Every breakfast platter comes with a hockey puck-sized donut and a glass of fresh milk, and there's a well-regarded lunch and dinner buffet on Friday and Saturday. A la carte dinner options include ham loaf, liver and onions, and chicken and waffles. Also on premise is a full-service supermarket, a terrific kids' play area (complete with cow chutes and a milk carton slide), and an ice cream shop with plenty of patio seating. Breakfast $3–9, lunch and dinner $6–11.

BAKERIES & FARM STANDS

Farm stands can be found all over

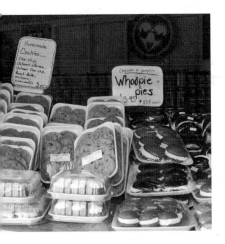

WHOOPIE PIES FOR SALE

Lancaster County on busy highways and rural backcountry roads. They often sell everything from fresh produce and poultry to root beer and homemade potato chips.

Elam and Naomi Fisher sell homemade root beer, whoopie pies, potato chips, and other items from a kiosk on their large farm off PA 340 (3217 Old Philadelphia Pike, Ronks) between Bird-in-Hand and Intercourse. Follow the root beer for sale signs up the long driveway and ring the bell for service.

🦃 ♂ **Bird-in-Hand Bake Shop** (717-656-7947), 542 Gibbons Road, Bird-in-Hand. A terrific Mennonite-owned bakery known for its reasonable prices and whoopie pies, cinnamon raisin bread, and shoofly pies. A playground and petting zoo are outside for the kids.

Farmette Farms, Rothsville Road, Ephrata. Closed Sunday. This roadside Mennonite stand sells peaches, corn, tomatoes, and other seasonal produce at reasonable prices. There are always baked goods on hand, such as raisin bars and peach pie, and the nursery sells potted flowers, plants, and homemade peat moss. There's neither phone nor address, but it is less than a mile west of Main Street.

Fisher's Farm Stand, Strasburg Road, PA 741. Closed Sunday. Mennonite-owned roadside stand selling homemade jams, bread-and-butter pickles, produce, and pies at very fair prices. Next door is a quilt shop (in the basement of a home) with full quilts starting at $395 and children's-themed quilts starting at $155.

♂ ♿ **Intercourse Pretzel Factory** (717-768-3432), 3614 Old Philadelphia Pike (in Cross Keys Village), Intercourse. Closed Sunday. This shop sells soft and hard hand-twisted pretzels; choose from plain, herb, cheddar cheese, and brown butter. Free 12-minute factory tours run at least once an hour, depending on demand.

♂ **Lapp Valley Farm** (717-354-7988), 244 Mentzer Road, New Holland. A Mennonite dairy farm that produces the best homemade ice cream in the region. Try the vanilla. Seriously.

FARM MARKETS 🦃 **Green Dragon Market and Auction** (717-738-1117; www.greendragonmarket.com), 955 N. State Street, Ephrata. Open 9–9 Friday. As the local saying goes: "If you can't buy it at the Green Dragon, it chust ain't fer sale." This venerable old market, about 4 miles north of downtown Ephrata, is a shopper's mecca of 400 growers and vendors selling fresh flowers, produce, wood furniture, handmade clothing and quilts, and more. Its two auction houses specialize in antiques and livestock, and are fun to watch even if you're not buying. When you get hungry, have a Pennsylvania Dutch meal at the five sit-down restaurants or grab a soft pretzel or sausage sandwich at the many snack stands. Plan to spend at least a couple of hours here, if not an entire afternoon.

Bird-in-Hand Farmers' Market (717-393-9674), PA 340 and Maple Avenue, Bird-in-Hand. Open 8:30–5:30 Friday and Saturday year-round, Wednesday through Saturday, July through October, and Wednesday, Friday, and Saturday, April through June, and November. This small market gets a lot of bus-tour traffic because of its prime location on PA 340. Look for the usual assortment of crafts, produce, baked goods, and hand-rolled soft pretzels. It's owned by Good 'N Plenty Restaurant, which is nearby.

Root's Country Market and Auction (717-898-7811), 705 Graystone Road, Manheim. Open 9–9 Tuesday. Just off PA 72 between Lebanon and Lancaster, this always-lively family-run market has 200 vendors selling smoked meats, fresh and dried herbs, doll clothes, hand-painted wooden ducks, and furniture. For instant nourishment, visit the Amish food stalls for soft pretzels, homemade potato chips, and apple dumplings. Locals bide their time until the afternoon produce auction (starting at 1 PM), when there are great deals on seasonal fruits, vegetables, and flowers. An indoor-outdoor flea market with 175 vendors, also open Tuesday, is just across the street.

✳ Entertainment

MUSIC ♿ **Fulton Theatre** (717-397-7425; www.thefulton.org), 12 N. Prince Street, Lancaster. A former roadhouse and vaudeville stage that now hosts symphony, opera, and Broadway shows. Scholars lead free programs and Q&A sessions about the current production one half-hour before showtime.

Ten Thousand Villages (717-721-8400), 740 N. Reading Road, Ephrata. The fair-trade store's café hosts live acoustic music every Friday evening.

THEATER & MOVIES ♿ **American Music Theater** (717-397-7700), 2425 Old Lincoln Highway east (US 30), Lancaster. Live concerts and original Broadway shows.

♿ **Sight & Sound Theatres** (717-687-7800; www.sight-sound .com), PA 896, Strasburg. This Christian theatrical company stages elaborate shows using actors, live animals, special effects, and music on two separate stages, the Millennium Theater and Living Waters. The shows are wildly popular, attracting as many as 900,000 people a year. Evening shows are on weekends at 7 or 7:30. The Christmas shows book up fast.

♧ **Dutch Apple Dinner Theatre** (717-898-1900; www.dutch apple.com), 510 Centerville Road, Lancaster. Traditional Broadway favorites and comedy shows, accompanied by a decent buffet dinner and ice cream bar in a tiered dining room. It's very popular with kids and seniors.

✱ Selective Shopping

Amish and Mennonites have created their own exquisite baskets, quilts, dolls, furniture, toys, wall hangings, and hex designs for centuries. You will find much of it for sale in stores along Old Philadelphia Pike in Intercourse and Bird-in-Hand, as well as PA 772

between Intercourse and Leola. Most shops are closed on Sunday. Two large outlet malls, **Rockvale** (717-293-9595), 35 S. Willowdale Road, and **Tanger** (717-392-7260), 311 Stanley K. Tanger Boulevard, can be found on US 30 in Lancaster near Dutch Wonderland.

CANDLES & CRAFTS Lapp's **Coach Shop** (717-768-8712), 3572 Newport Road, Intercourse. Wide selection of reasonably priced wooden chests, wagons, and toys made by local craftspeople.

Moravian Mission Gift Shop (717-626-9027), 8 Church Square, Lititz. Open 10–4 Thursday, Friday, and Saturday. Tucked behind the archives building on the square, this is the place to find Moravian crafts, books, etched glass, multicolored glass stars, and beeswax candles.

Old Candle Barn (717-768-3231), 3551A Old Philadelphia

MUD SALES

Named for the soggy late-winter ground, mud sales are Amish-run auctions that have been a festive rite of spring in Lancaster County for nearly 50 years. Even if you're not in the market for the goods, which range from outdoor sheds to small crafts and handmade quilts, this is an ideal opportunity to mingle with the Amish at their most relaxed and natural, not to mention feast on hot buttered pretzels and roast pork sandwiches. Mud sales are held in small towns throughout the county, with proceeds going to local volunteer fire companies. They are usually on Saturday in late February through early April and start around 8 or 9 AM. Call 1-800-723-8824 or visit www.padutchcountry.com for information and a current schedule.

Pike, Intercourse. Open daily. Don't be put off by its World War I Quonset hut appearance; this huge shop features an impressive variety of handcrafted candles, potpourri, and crafts. If you're here on a weekday, you can watch the candles being dipped and poured in the downstairs factory. **Weathervane Shop** (717-569-9312), 2451 Kissel Hill Road, Lancaster. The gift shop at the Landis Valley Museum sells pottery, wooden cabinetry, linens, and folk art produced by the museum's own craftspeople.

QUILTS Many back roads have simple signs indicating places where quilts are sold; selection is often more limited than in the shops, but prices are usually lower.

Old Country Store (717-768-7171), 3513 Old Philadelphia Pike, Intercourse. Open daily. This pleasant shop below the People's Place Quilt Museum has a knowledgeable sales staff and a wide selection of contemporary quilts. It also sells quilt fabrics at fair prices.

Quilts and Fabric Shack (717-768-0338), 3127 Old Philadelphia Pike, Bird-in-Hand. Quilts and wall hangings handmade by Amish and Mennonite women. They also carry a large selection of fabrics.

Witmer Quilt Shop (717-656-9526), 1070 W. Main Street, New Holland. Emma Witmer, who took over the family quilting shop from her mother, sells more than 100 patterns out of the second floor of her home. Most of the quilts for sale are contemporary, but she also stocks some antique beauties.

FURNITURE **E. Braun Farm Tables** (717-768-7227; www.braun farmtables.com), 3561 Old Philadelphia Pike, Intercourse. This family-owned company makes gorgeous farm tables, chairs, bed frames, and other furniture using wood salvaged from farm buildings from the late 1800s and 1900s. It also has a shop in Bird-in-Hand at 2688 Old Philadelphia Pike.

SPECIAL SHOPS **Aaron's Books** (717-627-1990; www .aaronsbooksonline.com), 43 S. Broad Street, Lititz. Named after the owners' son, this welcoming family-owned store sells new and used books and fair-trade gifts and note cards; there's also a neat children's play area. It regularly hosts book groups and author readings and is a widely used community resource.

Outback Toys (888-414-4705), 101 W. Lincoln Avenue, Lititz. This might be the best shop for farm-themed toys in the world. The warehouse-sized space, just north of town, is full of kid-size tractors, toy barns, Breyer horses, and all things John Deere. Staff members are knowledgeable and happy to help you find that limited-edition miniature Gleaner combine.

Ephrata
 ♿ **Doneckers** (717-738-9503;
www.doneckers.com), 100 N.
State Street. This upscale shopping complex began as a designer
clothing store in the 1950s and has
expanded over the years into three
stories of art galleries, high-end
furniture showrooms, a restaurant,
and a 40-room inn.

**Ten Thousand Villages and
Oriental Rug Gallery** (717-721-
8400), 240 N. Reading Road (PA
272). Closed Sunday. The original
store of the fair-trade empire (its
headquarters are nearby) has an
ever-changing selection of handcrafted vases, baskets, batiks, stationery, and jewelry; it often holds
big sales to make room for new
merchandise. Save time for a
quinoa salad or espresso in the
cheerful café, which has free WiFi
and live music on Friday nights.

Intercourse
♿ **Intercourse Canning Company** (717-768-0156), 3612 E.
Newport Road. This large shop is
known for Pennsylvania Dutch
delicacies such as chow-chow,
apple butter, and pickled red beet
eggs, and its generous samples.
During the week, you can observe
Amish and Mennonite workers
canning all kinds of fruits and
vegetables.

♭ ♿ **Kitchen Kettle Village**
(717-768-8261), PA 340. Yes, it's
contrived, but this shopping village is a fun one-stop destination
of buggy and tractor rides, kettle
corn stands, live music (on week-

ends), and about 30 shops selling
everything from personalized
teddy bears to hex signs and soft
pretzels. The Jam & Relish
Kitchen is a favorite stop for
chow-chow, jams, jellies, and rel-
ishes; they are generous with samples. You can also get Lapp Valley
Farms ice cream here (see also
Bakeries & Farm Stands).

Zook's Dry Goods (717-768-
8153), 3535 Old Philadelphia
Pike. This Amish variety store sells
everything from board games to
knit sweaters. It is considered one
of the best places around to purchase high-quality quilting fabrics
at reasonable prices.

✺ **Special Events**

May: **Sertoma Club Chicken
Barbecue** (third weekend),
Long's Park, Lancaster—the
world's largest chicken barbecue
(it's even in the Guinness Book of
World Records) turns out more
than 33,000 chicken dinners for a
donation of $7 per person.

August: **Pennsylvania Renaissance Faire** (second weekend,
then weekends through October),
2775 Lebanon Road, Manheim—
one of the county's most popular
events with lots of jousting
knights, costumed wenches, and
terrific interactive street performances. There are 90 shows daily on
12 stages, microbrewed ales on
tap, period food, and a scotch egg-
eating contest, it's impossible not
to have a good time. For more
info, visit www.parenfaire.com.

September: **Ephrata Fair** (fourth weekend), downtown Ephrata—a huge country fair featuring carnival rides, live music, livestock competitions, and a street parade; don't miss the toasted cheeseburgers.

October: **Lititz Chocolate Walk** (first weekend), downtown Lititz—two dozen of the area's chocolatiers offer displays and demonstrations of their work around town.

READING & KUTZTOWN

About 60 miles west of Philadelphia, Reading is the state's fifth-largest city with about 81,000 residents. Once a major manufacturing center for hosiery and hardware, it was also the site of one of the nation's oldest and largest railroads, known as the Philadelphia and Reading. In the early 1970s, abandoned textile mills on the outskirts of town were developed to create one of the country's first outlet malls (it still operates under the name VF Outlet Village).

Despite struggles with crime and suburban flight, downtown Reading has seen a revitalization in recent years, with the opening of GoggleWorks, a hip complex of artists' studios, a large performing arts center, and a solid roster of good restaurants and bars. An interesting footnote: Reading was the actual setting (fictionalized as Mount Judge) in the book *Rabbit Run*, written by John Updike, who grew up in nearby Shillington and worked as a copyboy for the *Reading Eagle* in the early 1950s.

A few miles to the south of Reading just across the Berks County line, you'll find Adamstown, a shopper's paradise of antiques stores and markets. To the city's north are winding country roads dotted with hex-sign barns, historic hotels, and Pennsylvania Dutch diners.

Kutztown, also featured in this chapter, is about 20 miles to the northeast and more rural, with a rich Pennsylvania Dutch heritage. Founded around 1779 as Cootstown, which was later changed to Kutztown, it is home to a pretty and walkable downtown, Kutztown University, and a comprehensive museum on Pennsylvania Dutch culture and traditions. Every June and July, it hosts the Kutztown Folk Festival, a renowned nine-day celebration of all things Pennsylvania Dutch.

GUIDANCE Greater Reading Convention & Visitor Bureau (610-375-4085; 800-443-6610; www.readingberkspa.com) has a visitor center in the GoggleWorks complex at 201 Washington Street. It's open Friday, Saturday, and the second Sunday of the month.

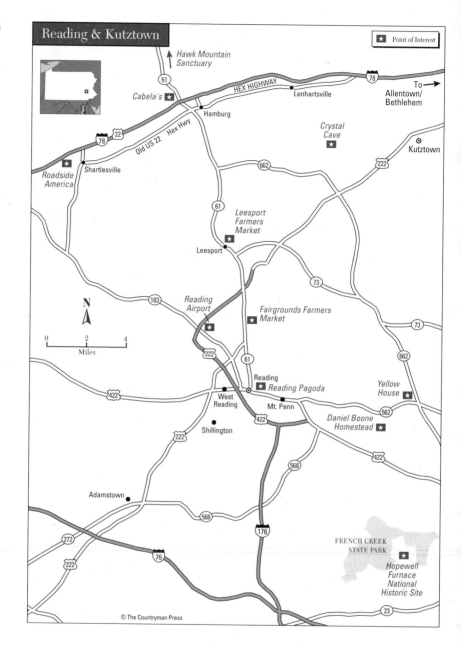

Reading & Kutztown

★ Point of Interest

Hawk Mountain Sanctuary

Cabela's ★

HEX HIGHWAY

Lenhartsville

78

To →
Allentown/
Bethlehem

Hamburg

78   22
Old US 22   Hex Hwy

Crystal
Cave ★

Kutztown

Roadside
America ★

Shartlesville

662

222

61

Leesport
Farmers
Market ★

Leesport

73

N

0   2   4
Miles

183

Reading
Airport ★

Fairgrounds Farmers
Market ★

73

222

61

422

West
Reading

Reading
★ Reading Pagoda

Mt. Penn

662

Yellow
House ★

Daniel Boone
Homestead ★

562

222

Shillington

422

568

422

Adamstown

568

176

272

222

76

FRENCH CREEK
STATE PARK

★

Hopewell
Furnace
National
Historic Site

23

© The Countryman Press

GETTING THERE By air: Major airports serving Reading and Kutztown are **Lehigh Valley International Airport** in Allentown (888-359-5842) and **Philadelphia International** (215-937-6800). **Reading Regional** (610-372-4666) offers limited service.

By car: From Philadelphia and points east, take I-76 to exit 298 (Morgantown–Reading), then follow US 422 west to downtown Reading. To reach Kutztown from Reading, take US 222 to Old US 22 and head east. From Philadelphia, take the Northeast Extension of I-76 (I-476) to I-78/US 22 west.

GETTING AROUND **BARTA** (610-921-0601; www.bartabus.com), offers more than 20 bus routes in and around Reading that begin at the Berks Area Regional Transportation Authority (BARTA) Transportation Center downtown and run to FirstEnergy Stadium, Hamburg, and other towns.

MEDICAL EMERGENCY **Reading Hospital and Medical Center** (610-988-8000), Sixth Avenue and Spruce Street, West Reading. Downtown, there's **St. Joseph's Medical Center Community Campus** on Sixth Street.

WHEN TO GO Most of the antiques and collectors markets are open year-round. The country and hillsides surrounding Reading and Kutztown are ablaze in brown, yellow, and orange in October, adding a visual

OLD PENNSYLVANIA DUTCH SIGN

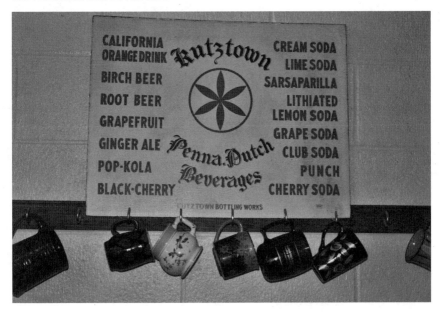

element to visits to the area's flea markets and rural towns. Kutztown is at its best in late June and early July when the Pennsylvania Dutch folk festival is in high gear.

✳ Villages

Adamstown. As a *Washington Post* writer aptly put it in an article about the area: "If it's old and American, chances are it's in Adamstown." This small town at the northeastern edge of Lancaster County describes itself as the Antiques Capital of the U.S.A. Indeed, it probably has more antiques shops and markets than it does residents. (At last count, the population was 1,200.) A mile from the Pennsylvania Turnpike, it's a shopper's paradise of junk stores, high-end antiques shops, consignment malls, and several massive Sunday-only flea markets. There are a few restaurants to fuel up, in between buying and browsing marathons, but little else to amuse those who hate shopping.

Hamburg. Named after the city in Germany and framed by rural countryside and the Blue Mountains to the north, this place epitomizes the American small town. The opening of Cabela's in 2003, and with it several chain hotels and restaurants, changed its look and demographics a bit, but its main street, located on Old US 22 remains frozen in time, with family restaurants that date to the 1800s, a couple of old-fashioned inexpensive hotels, a few antiques shops, and a five-and-dime store.

Shartlesville. Not far from Hamburg, this town urges visitors to "slow down the fast pace of life." Established in the 1800s by German and Swiss trades people, it's a good place to stop for an hour or two if you happen to be visiting Cabela's or making your way to or from Harrisburg and Allentown. You'll find here several Pennsylvania Dutch restaurants, homegrown vegetable stands, and Roadside America, an indoor miniature village and beloved landmark of sorts.

✳ To See

GoggleWorks (610-374-4600; www.goggleworks.org), 201 Washington Street, Reading. Open daily 11–7. Housed in a former safety goggle factory (hence the name) near downtown, this hip arts complex and community hub opened in 2005 as a place that lets artists create and display their work in public; you'll find everything from folk art and photography to lithographs and pottery represented, plus a glass-blowing facility, jewelry studio, dance and music studios, movie theater, and café. Stop at the front desk for a map before setting off to explore. The best time to visit is the second Sunday of the month, when you'll find many of the artists at work in their studios, or the first Friday of the month, when some of the

HEX HIGHWAY

Hex signs are an important part of Pennsylvania Dutch folk art, used to decorate barns and symbolizing good luck and good harvest. This approximately 22-mile drive follows part of the designated Dutch Hex Highway past many old barns and farmhouses decorated with the round and colorful signs, as well as past historic churches, small towns, and rural countryside. Begin in Shartlesville north of Reading and follow Old US 22 east through Shartlesville's frozen-in-time main street. In Hamburg, stop at **Stoudt's Fruit Farm** (610-488-7549) for some apples or nectarines, then continue to Lenhartsville, where you can examine the old hex signs on the **Deitsch Eck Restaurant** (610-562-8520; Old US 22) before dining on pork and sauerkraut or chicken potpie. From here, head north on PA 143 toward Kempton and turn left at Hawk Mountain Road. Continue another 7 miles through scenic farmland to **Hawk Mountain Sanctuary** (610-756-6961; 1700 Hawk Mountain Road), and spend the rest of the afternoon hiking the nature trails or watching raptors fly by at eye level. A complete map of the Dutch Hex Highway is available for download at www.hexsigns.org.

HEX HIGHWAY BARN

galleries host opening receptions for new exhibitions. Parking is ample and free.

♈ & **Boyertown Museum of Historical Vehicles** (610-367-2090), 85 S. Walnut Street; $6 adults; $4 ages 6 and up. The theme is locally made vehicles of all kinds—from Charles Duryea's three-cylinder wagonette to pre-Harley motorcycles to a late 18th-century Kutztown sleigh. There's also a preserved roadside diner/decommissioned train car (the late Fegley's of Reading), which was moved by crane to the museum in 2003. You'll leave with a greater appreciation for the Reading area's important role in auto and wagon manufacturing. There is a good local farmers' market in the museum's parking lot every Saturday from June through October (with plenty of street parking).

♈ **Central Pennsylvania African American Museum** (610-371-8739; www.cpaam.org), 119 N. 10th Street, Reading. Open Wednesday, Friday, Saturday 10:30 AM–4 PM; $4 adults. The Underground Railroad was started not far from here by a Quaker farmer in Columbia, Pennsylvania. Reading's oldest black-owned church traces its history as well as displays all kinds of interesting African American art, antiques, books, and relics of slavery.

GOGGLEWORKS

The Pagoda (610-375-6399; www .pagodaskyline.org), 98 Duryea Drive; $1 suggested donation. The best views in the city can be found atop this seven-story traditional Japanese-style pagoda on Mount Penn. Built in 1906 by a local businessman, it was intended to be a luxury hotel but instead was sold to the City of Reading for $1. Visitors may climb (87 steps) to the observation deck for gorgeous views of the Berks County countryside and to admire the historic bell, cast in Japan in 1739 and shipped to Reading in 1907; a café serves drinks and light meals on Friday, Saturday, and Sunday afternoons. The drive up to the Pagoda is also

HISTORIC READING PAGODA HAS
PANORAMIC VIEWS OF BERKS COUNTY.

impressive; in the 1900s, the steep, winding road was the final test for cars made by the Charles Duryea Power Co. If they didn't make it up to the top, they were sent back to the factory for retooling.

☂ ✎ **Reading Public Museum** (610-371-5850), 500 Museum Road, Reading. Closed Monday; $8 adults, $6 ages 5–17. This multifaceted museum has a planetarium (with Friday-night laser shows, an arboretum, and more than a dozen science, art, and history galleries displaying dinosaur fossils, Pennsylvania German artifacts, taxidermy-mounted animals, and more. The art collection includes works by such notables as Winslow Homer, Benjamin West, Milton Avery, John Singer Sargent, Edgar Degas, and local boy Keith Haring. Pretty Wyomissing Creek runs through the arboretum; plan a visit in the spring to see the cherry blossoms in bloom. On Sunday mornings, live music and breakfast (Bagels, Bach, and Beyond) are in the atrium.

Pennsylvania German Cultural Heritage Center (610-683-4000), 22 Luckinbill Road, on the Kutztown University campus. Open 10–4 weekdays; free. The site of the annual Kutztown Festival, this is also the place to go any time for a crash course in Pennsylvania Dutch history, culture, and traditions. The museum offers thousands of 19th- and 20th-century artifacts, plus ancient farm equipment, a one-room schoolhouse, and reconstructed log homes.

✳ To Do

✎ ✾ **Berks County Heritage Center** (610-374-8839; www.countyof berks.com/parks), 2201 Tulpehocken Road, Wyomissing. A complex on the Union Canal of stone buildings, cemetery, herb garden, and gristmill all dating back to the 1800s. It's also home to the must-see Gruber Wagon Works, a reassembled 1900s-era wagon manufacturer with original

BUTTERFLIES AND BANK BARNS

In 1947, a man named J. I. Rodale started the Soil and Health Foundation on his small farm near Kutztown to promote his theory that healthy soil, not chemical fertilizer, is the basis for growing healthy food. Some call it the birth of the organic farming movement. Today, the 333-acre farm is home to the **Rodale Experimental Farm** (610-683-1400; 611 Siegfriedale Road, Kutztown), a research farm and educational center that is open to the public for self-guided tours and workshops. Surrounded by lush rolling hills and farmland, it's a 30-minute drive (yet a world away) from the publishing giant's Emmaus headquarters. Start in the old stone schoolhouse, where books on gardening and cooking, and locally made honey and jams are for sale. The self-guided walking tour ($5 per map) begins here, too—

CROPS AT RODALE EXPERIMENTAL FARM

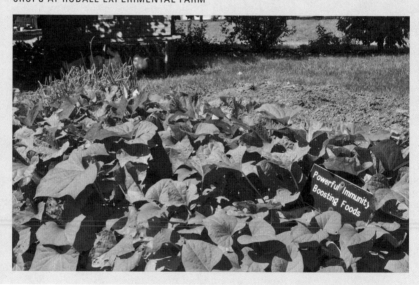

Conestoga wagons and thousands of the original tools used to build them. A National Historic Site, it is one of the few remaining places where you can witness the intricate work that went into making hayflats, wheelbarrows, and other specialty wagons of the era. A fee of $8 gets you a thorough guided tour of both the C. Howard Hiester Canal Center, home to the largest collection of 19th-century canal memorabilia in the country, and the Wagon Works. Don't leave without checking out Wertz's Bridge,

VIEW FROM THE MEADOWS OF RODALE EXPERIMENTAL FARM

wear sturdy walking shoes and be prepared to trudge through thick grass and woodland at times. This is not your average manicured garden tour, but a window into a working sustainable organic farm. You will pass garden beds bursting with cantaloupes and zucchini, compost windrows, bank barns, owl hollows, and patchwork-quilt fields of corn, alfalfa, wheat, and soybeans. In summer, an unfathomable number of bugs and butterflies— plus the occasional herd of cows—will cross your path. The gift shop often sells healthy snacks and drinks, or bring a picnic lunch and have it on one of the picnic tables outside. Plant sales and gardening workshops are held throughout the year and there are guided tours on Saturday for $12 a person; visit www.rodaleinstitute.org for details. Closed Monday.

the longest single-span covered bridge in the state. Cars are not allowed on the bridge, but pedestrians are.

✄ **Hopewell Furnace National Historic Site** (610-582-8773), 2 Mark Bird Lane, Elverson. A huge iron furnace that supplied cannon and shot to the Continental Army and Navy is just one of the highlights of this unsung National Park Service site in the middle of French Creek State Park. The self-guided tour takes you past a barn that now shelters dozens

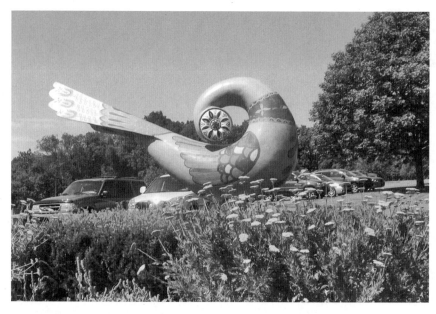

A DISTELFINK ANCHORS THE BERKS COUNTY HERITAGE CENTER

of sheep, boarding houses once occupied by furnace workers, and the ironmaster's circa-1770 mansion. There's also an easy junior ranger program that kids can complete in an hour or two, along with access to the Horseshoe Trail, one of French Creek's best hikes. The best time to visit is weekends, when the furnace is sometimes lit and there are often blacksmithing and forging demonstrations. In September and October, visitors may pick apples from the 250 trees that surround the site for $1 a pound.

HOPEWELL FURNACE NATIONAL HISTORIC SITE

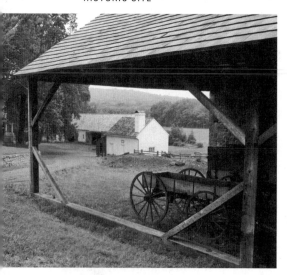

FOR FAMILIES ♦ 🛖 **Crystal Cave** (610-683-6765; www.crystal cavepa.com), 963 Crystal Cave Road, Kutztown. Open daily March through November; $11.50 adults, $7.50 ages 6–12. Few kids from eastern Pennsylvania completed their childhoods without seeing Crystal Cave. It was discovered in 1871 by two Pennsylvania Dutchmen and has been a tourist

YUENGLING BREWERY

About 30 miles northwest of Kutztown sits the hilly former coal-mining town of Pottsville, home to the oldest operating brewery in the United States. D. G. Yuengling & Son has been producing moderately priced beer since 1831 and is now owned by fifth-generation family members. Sometime in the last two decades, someone realized that everyone loves a good brewery tour and opened up the factory and its production lines to the public. The free tours last about an hour and are very hands-on and personal: you can peek inside the giant beer vats, ask questions of the knowledgeable guides, and walk inside the hand-dug caves that were used to store kegs of beer before refrigeration made things easier. In the taproom, visitors are treated to generous samples of the lager they just watched being made (non-alcoholic birch beer is also available). There is a gift shop, of course. This is one of finest free tours around and worth the detour if you are in the Poconos or Reading/ Kutztown area. Tours are free and run Monday through Saturday, April through December and Monday through Friday the rest of the year. Expect big crowds (40 or more people) on Saturdays and most summer days; no reservations. For more information, visit www.yuengling.com or call 570-628-4890.

YUENGLING BREWERY SIGN

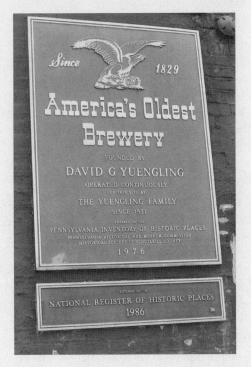

KUTZTOWN'S CRYSTAL CAVE

attraction pretty much ever since. It's not unusual to see a few tour buses in the parking lot, but the entire complex still has a quiet, unhurried vibe. One-hour tours take you 125 feet below where it's 54 degrees year-round and guides point out formations that resemble animals and rooms with names like the Bridal Veil (it was the site of Pennsylvania's first "cave wedding" in 1919). There's also a free geological museum, along with a shady miniature golf course; a moderate nature trail leads to a view of the surrounding valley. It seems to be in the middle of nowhere, but it's only about a 20-minute drive off I-78 or US 222.

✏ **Koziar's Christmas Village** (610-488-1110; www.koziarschristmas village.com), 782 Christmas Village Road, Bernville. Open evenings in November and December; call for days and times; $8 adults, $6 ages 6–12. Koziar's began in 1955 as a family's personal holiday display and has turned into one of the state's top Christmastime attractions. Millions of lights decorate an entire farm; an indoor electric train display, appearances by Santa, and a reasonably priced gift shop selling ornaments and other tis-the-season decorations are also on hand. The view as you drive in over the hill is amazing.

✏ ৬ ↑ **Roadside America** (610-488-6241; www.roadsideamericainc.com), 109 Roadside Drive, Shartlesville. Open daily, except Christmas; $6.75 adults, $3.75 ages 6–11. Road kitsch doesn't get much better than this: a giant statue of a smiling Amish couple greets you near the entrance and inside is a replica of "the American countryside as it might be seen by a giant so huge he could see from coast to coast." This indoor miniature village draws ooohs and aaahs from its many fans (and eye rolls from some locals) but it's a truly unusual experience and worth a stop for anyone who likes a little old-fashioned fun with their road trips. You could easily spend an hour or two examining the tiny bake shops, churches, theaters, gas stations, and some 400 other buildings that make up the display—most kids love the buttons that let them ring church bells, operate steamrollers, and steer trains.

✍ **Daniel Boone Homestead** (610-582-4900; www.danielboonevillage .com), 400 Daniel Boone Road, Birdsboro. Open Tuesday through Saturday 9–5, Sunday 12–5; tours $4 adults, $2 ages 6–17. The famous frontiersman spent his adolescent years on this large farm east of Reading before his father moved the family to North Carolina. Not much data exists on his life back then, but the tour provides a thorough look at life in the 1700s. Set on more than 570 acres, it includes the original log house where Boone was born, a blacksmith shop, smokehouse, and circa-1810 sawmill. You don't have to take the tour to enjoy the property's two picnic areas, lake, and walking trails.

✍ **Wanamaker, Kempton & Southern Railroad** (610-756-6469; www .kemptontrain.com), 42 Community Center Drive, Kempton. Train rides depart four times a day Sunday in May and June, Saturday and Sunday in July, August, and October; $8 adults, $4 ages 3–11. One of the more reasonably priced locomotive joy rides on the Pennsylvania train circuit. Kids

DANIEL BOONE'S FARM

will want to check out the Schuylkill and Lehigh Model Railroad in the decommissioned coach behind the station.

✍ **Terry Hill Water Park** (610-395-0222), 10000 Hamilton Boulevard (PA 222), Breinigsville. Admission $15–20. Fun family water park with seven different themed slides and a lazy river for tubing. Miniature golf is included in the price of admission, and there's a snack bar.

WINERIES

Berks County's wineries are relatively new to the state's tasting trail bandwagon. Many are located in the northern reaches of the county

BASEBALL
READING PHILLIES

Once known as the Reading Pretzels, this Double-A farm team began its long affiliation with the Philadelphia Phillies in 1967. Its home games at FirstEnergy Stadium, which lead the Eastern League in attendance, are a mix of carnival-like entertainment, community spirit, and good old-fashioned baseball. There's a swimming pool behind right field. There are contests and music between innings, hot dogs and funnel cakes, and pre- and post-game concerts. Tickets will set you back no more than $10. Visit www.readingphillies.com for more information.

READING BASEBALL

DUTCH HEX SIGN

surrounded by quiet countryside. They offer pleasant, low-pressure tasting experiences and regular themed weekends like "Wine and Chocolate." For a comprehensive list, visit www.berkscountywine trail.com.

Blair Vineyards (610-683-8463; www.blairvineyards.com), 99 Dietrich Valley Road, Kutztown. Knowledgeable staff (likely a member of the Blair family) and a cozy tasting room framed by views of the Blue Mountains make this a standout. Pinot Noir is a specialty.

Clover Hill Winery (610-395-2468; www.cloverhillwinery.com), 9850 Newton Road, Breinigsville. A veteran vintner by Berks County standards, it produces a variety of vintages including an award-winning Riesling and Cabernet Sauvignon. Its main tasting room is big and modern (some complain that it's too sterile) with windows overlooking vineyards.

Long Trout Winery (570-366-6443; www.longtroutwinery.com), 84 Fork Mountain Road, Auburn. Open Wednesday evening, Saturday, and Sunday. The wine itself is almost an afterthought at this mellow mountain winery, whose motto is WHERE THE WINE IS COOL AND HIPPIE CHICKS RULE. The tasting room is a shrine to the 1960s, and the PG-rated wine labels are a hoot. Tastings are free and generous. There are picnic tables to settle in and enjoy your purchase. There is also disc golf.

Pinnacle Ridge (610-756-4481; www.pinridge.com), 407 Old US 22, Kutztown. Hex signs decorate the renovated bank barn that houses the processing area and tasting room. Sparkling wines are a specialty, and its Veritas and Chambourcin took home a slew of awards at the 2011 Pennsylvania Farm Show.

✳ Outdoor Activities

BICYCLING The 23-mile loop around **Blue Marsh Lake** (610-376-6337), 1268 Palisades Drive, Leesport, was named one of America's top ten bike trails by *Bicycling* magazine in the 1990s. It hasn't changed much since then, with a tight and twisting single track, short uphill climbs, and stellar views. The Union Canal Trail is also a cyclist favorite (see Hiking).

FISHING **Hunsickers Grove** (610-372-8939), 9350 Longswamp Road, Mertztown, has a wheelchair-accessible dock and a pond stocked with fish. It hosts a popular children's fishing rodeo every May.

GOLF **Blackwood Golf Course** (610-385-6200), 510 Red Corner Road, Douglassville. Attractive and relatively undemanding 18-hole course with three tees to 6,403 yards.

Reading Country Club (610-779-1000), 5311 Perkiomen Avenue, Reading. This 18-hole course dates to 1923 and has gently rolling terrain and tree-lined fairways.

HIKING The 4.5-mile **Union Canal Trail** at Tulpehocken Creek Valley Park (610-372-8939; www.co.berks.pa.us/parks) is a perfect way to combine exercise with local history lessons. Start at **Stonecliff Recreation Area** and follow the path past old stone buildings and original locks dating back to the 1820s, when the canal was built. After about 2 miles you'll reach the **Berks County Heritage Center,** home to a sweet little museum about the state's canal history and Wertz's Covered Bridge, the longest surviving single-span covered bridge in Pennsylvania. The trail ends at near the parking area for Blue Marsh Lake. Maps are available at the Heritage Center (See To Do).

SIGN IN FRENCH CREEK STATE PARK

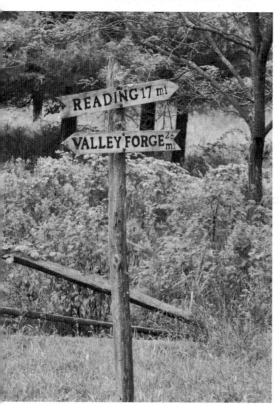

HORSEBACK RIDING French **Creek State Park** (see also Green Space) has 8 miles of equestrian trails. The clearly marked Horseshoe Trail, which begins in Valley Forge, skirts the park's two lakes and continues to the Appalachian Trail near Harrisburg.

Up near Hawk Mountain, **Kindred Spirits Farm** (610-756-3469), 614 Hawk Mountain Road, offers lessons starting at $30 an hour and guided trail rides through wooded valleys and countryside for $25 a person. It's open April through December (closed Sunday and Monday).

✴ Green Space

Blue Marsh Lake (610-376-6337), 1268 Palisades Drive, Leesport. Recreational hotspot north of Reading with good swimming, fishing, and boating opportunities. In summer, there are ranger-led hikes, bat programs, and stargazing events. Nature trails run near the water's edge (the Foxtrot Trail can be accessed from the swimming beach), while mountain bikers like Skinners Loop. There's a $3 entry fee to enter; more info is available at the visitor center.

🐾 🐾 **French Creek State Park** (610-582-9680), 843 Park Road, Elverson. Set amid picturesque farmland straddling Berks and Chester counties, this 7,340-acre tree-filled park offers two lakes—Hopewell and Scotts Run—plus picnic areas, two disc courses, a campground, and 30 miles of hiking trails. You can fish for trout and bass, and ride nonmotorized boats in the lakes. Swimming isn't allowed, but there's a large public pool near Hopewell Lake. This is also a popular spot for orienteering, with a self-guiding course that lets you locate markers in the park with the aid of a map and compass. Maps and other information are available at the park office. In the center of the park sits the lovely **Hopewell Furnace National Historic Site** (see To Do).

✴ Lodging

BED & BREAKFASTS Overlook Mansion (610-371-9173; www .overlookmansionbedandbreakfast .com), 620 Centre Ave, Reading. Daphne Miller and Paul Strause are the friendly owners of this Second-Empire mansion across from Centre Park in north Reading. The three large high-ceilinged rooms have queen beds, televisions, wireless access, and refrigerators. Have breakfast delivered to your room or eat outside on the porch overlooking a garden. Miller, a reliable source of information on the area, also hosts theme weekends and events such as chocolate socials and ghostly walking tours through the nearby Charles Evans Cemetery. Rooms $149–179.

Nearby
🐾 **Adamstown Inns & Cottages** (800-594-4808; www.adamstown .com), 62 W. Main Street, Adamstown. A good place to base an antiquing visit to Adamstown, this complex of two separate inns (Adamstown and Amethyst) is within walking distance of most of the town's shops and flea markets. The rate includes a continental breakfast, served in the dining room of the Amethyst. Two nearby two-story homes (where pets and kids are allowed) are also available for rent. Rooms $119–219. Cottages $199–495.

🍴 ♿ **Land Haven** (610-845-3257; www.landhavenbandb.com), 1194 Huff's Church Road, Barto. This comfortable B&B was once an 1870s general store, and owners Ed and Donna Land take care to honor its history. The five rooms are named after the original proprietors and have queen or king beds, private baths or showers, and a lovely mix of whimsical and antique decor. It also has an antiques store, a large library of old cookbooks (7,000, plus!), and special events such as cooking classes and live singer-songwriter concerts. It's about 18 miles from Reading. Rooms $90–125.

☞ ♿ **Hawk Mountain Bed and Breakfast** (610-756-4224; www.hawkmountainbb.com), 221 Stone Valley Road, Kempton. This lodge, tucked in the scenic Stoney Run Valley and about 8 miles from the hawk sanctuary, has a large swimming pool and eight attractive rooms with queen beds, TVs, and private entrances and baths. Two deluxe rooms have fireplaces and Jacuzzi tubs. A full country breakfast of pancakes or waffles, sausage, and fruit comes with the rate, as do complimentary beverages (including Yuengling lager). Standard rooms $145; deluxe $195, two-night minimum in September and October.

Main Street Inn (610-683-0401; www.kutztownmainstreetinn.com), 401 W. Main Street, Kutztown. Refurbished Victorian home one block from Kutztown University and six blocks from Renninger's Market. Attention to detail is owner Pam Corrado's specialty, from round-the-clock kitchen

snacks and wine, to exquisitely old-fashioned rooms with clawfoot bathtubs and gas fireplaces. No children under 12. Rooms $125–160.

Pamela's Forget-Me-Not (610-756-3398; www.pamelasforgetme not.com), 33 Hawk Mountain Road, Kempton. The closest accommodations to Hawk Mountain Sanctuary with four private romantic rooms in a country Victorian home. The Carriage House loft features a large deck, Jacuzzi, and sleeps up to six people, while the Honeymoon Cottage has a gas fireplace, two-person Jacuzzi, and deck. The eponymous owner Pamela Gyory is a gracious host and happy to share tips about the area (she got engaged on Hawk Mountain). A full breakfast (crepes with organic fruit and maple syrup are a specialty) is delivered to the outer rooms or served in the dining room or the wraparound porch. Rooms and suites $99–169.

MOTELS AND CAMPGROUNDS
Blue Rocks Family Campground (610-756-6366; www.blue rockscampground.com), 341 Sousley Road, Lenhartsville. The closest camping option to Hawk Mountain Sanctuary with swimming pools, a fishing pond, lots of kids' activities, and hiking trails that access the Appalachian Trail. The highlight of the property is a glacier deposit that spans 15 miles and dates back 350 million years. Tent sites $25–35; basic cabins $45–65.

⚓ **Country Inn Motel** (610-777-2579; www.countryinnmotel.com), 330 E. Wyomissing Avenue, Mohnton. A clean, unpretentious motel that's a good value, especially for families. The one-bedroom suites have microwaves, cable television with HBO, free WiFi, and private entrances. Two-bedroom suites have kitchenettes. The location between Reading and Adamstown is convenient to the Vanity Fair outlets and Maple Grove Raceway. Suites $49–69.

✈ ➻ 🎯 **French Creek State Park** (610-582-9680), 843 Park Road, Elverson. You'll find 201 wooded tent sites, 50 with electric hookups, near the east entrance of the state park. There are also several cabins and yurts, and cottages that sleep five, with a two-night minimum in summer and fall. (See also Green Space.)

✳ **Where to Eat**

DINING OUT

Reading

Ⴘ ➻ **Anthony's Trattoria** (610-370-2822; www.anthonystrattoria.com), 900 Byram Street. Family-run Italian eatery in a residential neighborhood east of downtown. The menu is almost as long as a Mario Puzo novel: There's everything from wood-fired pizza with artichokes and homemade ravioli to entrées such as veal saltimbocca and Chateaubriand for two. The strip-mall exterior gives way to a soft-lit burgundy-walled dining room and top-shelf service.

There's a full bar that has lounge singers on weekends.

⚓ **Hong Thanh** (610-374-0434), 22 N. 6th Street. Well-regarded Vietnamese-Chinese BYO across from the county courthouse. Lunch Wednesday through Friday, dinner Wednesday through Sunday. Specialties include sautéed filet mignon over watercress, crab and white asparagus soup, and chicken, pork, or beef stew with lemongrass, curry, and coconut. There's homemade coconut or ginger ice cream for dessert. Expect crowds on the weekend.

➻ Ⴘ **Judy's on Cherry** (610-374-8511), 332 Cherry Street, Reading. Lunch and dinner Tuesday through Friday, dinner Tuesday through Saturday. A Mediterranean-style downtown café serving simple yet creative dishes such as fig and prosciutto pizza, cedar-planked salmon, and tomato-basil chicken. Next door is the Speckled Hen Pub (see Nightlife). Lunch $10–15; dinner entrées $15–25.

Nearby

Blue Orchid Inn (610-682-6700), 1565 State Street, Mertztown. Creative entrées include barbecued duck breast with wild rice pancakes, and steamed Indian catfish curry, in a rural farmhouse setting southeast of Kutztown. It's on the expensive side, but its customer base is large and loyal. Entrées $26–36.

Ⴘ ⚘ **Gracie's 21st Century Café** (610-323-4004), 1534 Manatawny Road, Pine Forge. Dinner

HAWK MOUNTAIN SANCTUARY

🦉 🦅 ♿ Hawk Mountain Sanctuary (610-756-6961), 1700 Hawk Mountain Road, Kempton. Open dawn to dusk daily; sturdy shoes are recommended. One of the top bird-watching sites in North America, Hawk Mountain is also a quiet refuge of hiking trails, thick forest, and panoramic views. During fall migration, an average of 20,000 hawks, eagles, and falcons from 18 different species pass by daily, often at eye level, as they travel down the Appalachian corridor. The largest migration takes place between mid-August and December, though mid-September and October are considered the peak times and also usually mean spectacular leaf-peeping opportunities. First-timers will want to stop at the visitor center for trail maps, guides, and tickets ($5–7 if you're not a member). It also has an awesome display of hand-carved and painted model raptors. South Lookout, with rewarding views of mountains and valleys, is 200 yards from the visitor center and can be accessed by wheelchair or stroller. Most hikers and birders opt for the mile-long North Lookout trail, which leads to a boulder-strewn jetty that yields the clearest views of southern-bound birds. From

HAWK MOUNTAIN SANCTUARY

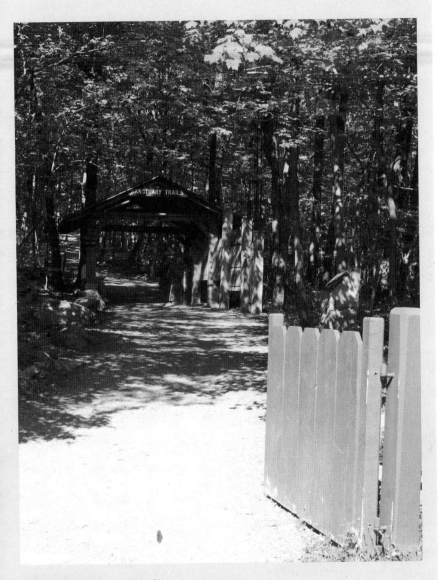

HAWK MOUNTAIN SANCTUARY

here, you can access the Appalachian trail by continuing another 2.5 miles on the rugged, ridge-top Skyline Trail. If you're coming in from the east side, consider stopping at **Wanamaker General Store** (610-756-6609; 8888 Kings Highway, Kempton) for sandwiches to bring on the hike. There's not much commerce around the sanctuary itself, and let's hope it stays that way.

Wednesday through Saturday. It's doubtful you will find another restaurant like this in Pennsylvania or quite possibly anywhere. Owner and Chef Gracie Skiadas bought a decaying early-1800s building in the middle of nowhere more than 20 years ago and turned it into a hip Santa Fe– meets-1776 hangout. The entrée prices are high for this area, but the good food and ambiance make it a perfect special-occasion place. The global fusion menu features a huge vegetarian section and might include fried blue-corn ravioli, wild black bass stuffed with shrimp, and pan-seared salmon prosciutto; don't miss the leg- endary Jamaican curried-crab bisque or the "Ole Hippy" carrot cake for dessert. Extensive wine list. Entrées: $15–38.

👤 ☥ **Yellow House Hotel** (610- 689-9410), 6743 Boyertown Pike, Douglassville. Lunch and dinner Monday through Saturday; brunch and dinner Sunday. Once a stage- coach stop and general store for travelers between Reading and Philadelphia, this country inn has three attractive dining rooms and a separate bar. The traditional menu offers many steak, chicken, and seafood entrées, as well as lighter fare such as burgers, stir fries, and salads. Specialties include barbecued spare ribs with red cabbage slaw and duck with dried cherry-orange marmalade sauce. Entrées $18–28.

☥ **American House Hotel** (610- 562-4683), 2 N. Fourth Street,

Hamburg. Dinner Wednesday through Sunday, breakfast Satur- day and Sunday. It's no bargain, but this restored old hotel is the best place for fine cuisine in the area. The dining room has tin ceil- ings, old-style chandeliers, and a full tavern downstairs. Highlights of the diverse menu include chick- en stuffed with Boursin cheese, crab and asparagus, roasted pork chop with apple compote, and citrus-almond salmon. Entrées $20–30.

EATING OUT

Reading

☥ **Jimmie Kramer's Peanut Bar** (610-376-8500), 322 Penn Street. Lunch and dinner Monday through Saturday. This downtown Reading institution serves hot and cold sandwiches, salads, fried seafood platters, and a small num- ber of entrées such as filet mignon and lemon Parmesan flounder. There is also a kids' menu. Join the regulars at the long nonsmok- ing bar or sit at a table and feel the crushed peanut shells under your feet. Dishes $7–13; entrées $18–25. 🍸

☥ 👤 **Ugly Oyster** (610-373-6791), 21 S. Fifth Street. Lunch and din- ner Monday through Saturday. This red-walled Irish pub near the downtown convention center has a *Cheers*-like bar, a wide selection of beers and single malt scotch, and very good food. There's a small selection of steak and seafood entrées at dinner, and a

JIMMIE KRAMER'S PEANUT BAR

lunch and tavern menu (available all day) of crab cake sandwiches, cheesesteaks, salads, a raw bar, and excellent soups. There's live Irish music every Thursday. Dishes $8–25.

Kutztown

Y Basin Street Hotel (610-683-7900), 42 E. Main Street. Open 11 AM–2 AM daily. A popular college hangout, this circa-1897 tavern and restaurant features hearty sandwiches with names such as Professor (sautéed veggies with mozzarella and tomato sauce) and Golden Bear (hot roast beef). There are also salads, fried appetizers, and reasonably priced entrées such as London broil and crab cakes. Dishes $7–17.

☘ Brenda's Eatery (610-683-8873), 15382 Kutztown Road (US 222). Breakfast and lunch daily. Dinner, Thursday and Friday. Look for the Hex signs out front and the adjacent Agway store as you're traveling east out of Kutztown. This unpretentious café serves pork roll and egg sandwiches at breakfast (it opens at 5 AM), and open-face turkey sandwiches, corn fritters, burgers, and delicious homemade soups at lunch. I had a good meal here after a trip to the Rodale Experimental Farm, which is five minutes away.

Nearby

☘ ♪ Deitsch Eck (610-562-8520), Old US 22, Lenhartsville. Lunch and dinner Wednesday through Sunday. Hex signs welcome you to this highly regarded Pennsylvania Dutch restaurant just east of Hamburg on Old US 22. The

PENNSYLVANIA DUTCH EATERY NEAR KUTZTOWN

service couldn't be friendlier and the prices couldn't be more reasonable. Choose from dozens of sandwiches, from burgers to hot roast beef, or a long list of platters such as smoked pork chops, meatloaf, and grilled ham steak. Dishes $2.50–11.

Haag's Hotel (610-488-6692; www.haagshotel.com), 3rd and Main Streets, Shartlesville. Closed Monday and Wednesday. Fuel up on pepper cabbage, potato filling, and other Pennsylvania Dutch specialties after a stop at Roadside America or Cabela's. The $8 breakfast buffet of bacon, eggs, pancakes, scrapple, and shoofly pie will keep you going for hours, if not days. They also rent basic but clean rooms above the restaurant for $40–50 a night.

🍴 ♿ ♪ **Jukebox Café** (610-369-7272), 535 S. Reading Avenue (PA 562), Boyertown. Breakfast and lunch daily. A 1950s-style diner (with a real jukebox and black-and-white tile floors) known for its many vegetarian entrées and liberal use of fresh local produce. Try the vegetarian eggs Benedict (made with portobello mushrooms and sun-dried tomatoes) or the Boardwalk wrap with Italian sausage, eggs, cheese, and salsa. Homemade soups might be corn on the cob or crab bisque. Good food and low prices keep the tables full most days, so there might be a wait. Cash only. Dishes $3–9.

Saville's Diner (610-369-1433), 830 E. Philadelphia Avenue, Boyertown. Classic diner with low prices, large portions, and tasty calorie-laden desserts. If you show up on a day when shrimp soup is on the menu, consider yourself lucky; it's divine.

Wanamakers General Store (610-756-6609), 8888 Kings Highway, Kempton. Its sandwiches, wraps, and seasonal homemade soups are perfect for a picnic at Hawk Mountain Sanctuary, 7 miles down the road. Save time to browse the locally made crafts and wooden toys for sale in the retail store. Dishes $5–7.

FARM MARKETS Fairgrounds Farmers' Market (610-929-3429), N. Fifth Street at US 222, Reading. Open Thursday through Saturday; hours vary. The rather plain building near the Fairgrounds Mall hides a bonanza of tidy stalls selling fresh local produce, smoked meats, free-range chicken eggs, **Longacres Farm** ice cream, and Amish baked goods such as cinnamon buns and cherry-top doughnuts. It's an ideal spot for a cheap, delicious lunch: Cajun crab cakes and jambalaya, Polish sausage sandwiches, piping hot pizza by the slice. **Monte Lauro Italian Gourmet** is a favorite for hoagies and lunch specials like zucchini risotto, and anyone who loves a bargain should seek out the bakery selling mini-doughnuts for $1 a dozen. Go early if you can; it's wildly popular at lunchtime.

Leesport Farmers' Market (610-926-1307; www.leesport

market.com), 312 Gernant's Road, Leesport. Open 8 AM–9 PM Wednesday. North of Reading 8 miles, this indoor-outdoor market features a livestock auction plus a large selection of fresh local produce, baked goods, clothes, antiques, and garden items. There's even a barber shop. It also hosts huge crafts fairs and flea markets several times a year.

Stoudt's Wonderful Good Market (717-484-2757), Reading Road, Adamstown. Open Thursday through Saturday. A new foodie haven within Stoudt's antiques mall: There's artisan cheese made from local cow's milk, as well as fresh breads, plus a gourmet coffee roaster, and a random assortment of other edibles. Prices are reasonable, and it's an easy walk across the street to the shops of Stoudtburg Village.

Zern's Farmers' Market & Auction (610-367-2461; www.zerns .com), 1100 E. Philadelphia Avenue, Gilbertsville. Open Friday 2–10 PM, Saturday 11 AM–10 PM. You could easily spend a day at this large 90-year-old indoor market, which embraces its old-fashioned Pennsylvania Dutch roots and unpretentious cinderblock look. About 400 merchants sell everything from vintage clothes and outdoor furniture to old books and tube socks. It's widely known for its livestock and bid-board (silent) antiques auctions. The number of food stalls has shrunk in recent years, but you'll still find stalls selling soft

FOOD MARKET AND ANTIQUES SHOP IN ADAMSTOWN

pretzels, hoagies, crab cakes, and ice cream. Pro-wrestling matches were added in 2007, creating even better people-watching opportunities.

DESSERTS AND SNACKS

Haute Chocolate Café (610-373-4455), 711 Penn Avenue, West Reading. Closed Sunday. This sleek brown-and-orange café near VF Outlet Village should appeal to everyone from small kids to ladies who lunch. There are 15 types of hot chocolate (from Thai ginger to Venezuelan white), milk shakes made with Swiss cocoa ice cream, bourbon-pecan cake truffles, ice cream, tea, and a chocolate dipping fountain. The chocolate cupcake filled with salted caramel is life-changing.

Longacres Old-Fashioned Dairy Bar (610-845-7551; www .longacresicecream.com), 1445 PA 100, Barto. Open daily, but hours are cut back in fall and winter. The ice cream and milk shakes are freshly made in the adjacent dairy at this family-run ice cream parlor near Zern's Farmers' Market. The setting is old school: leather booths, wood paneling, and a list of flavors as long as your arm, from cherry vanilla to coconut custard and pumpkin. My father was almost brought to tears when he first tasted the butter brickle (vanilla mixed with crushed Heath bars). Expect crowds on summer weekends.

The Shoppes of Premise Maid (610-395-3221; www.premisemaid .com), 10860 Hamilton Boulevard

(US 222), Breinigsville. Open daily. Look for the giant toy soldiers improbably guarding a Tudor-style building in the middle of lush, rolling farmland. Enjoy huge helpings of hand-dipped ice cream before or after a visit to Crystal Cave or Rodale Experimental Farm. Expect lines in the summer, but they move quickly. Sit indoors (they are generous with the air-conditioning), or eat in the Disney-esque courtyard surrounded by trees and wrought-iron tables. Separate areas also sell premium chocolates and pastries (torte cakes are a specialty). All goods are made on premise, hence the name.

Tom Sturgis Pretzel Factory Store (610-775-0335), 2267 Lancaster Pike (at US 222), Shilling-ton. Open Monday through Saturday, 8:30–5:30. There are no tours here, but you'll find pretzel bargains (and generous samples) by the barrelful. Chocolate-covered, cheese, and jalapeno are just a few of the flavors available—plus gift baskets at prices lower than the average grocery store. Don't leave without a photo of the kids in front of the giant pretzel out front. The factory in back has been producing pretzels for more than a century.

✳ Entertainment

MOVIES & THEATER
GoggleWorks Film Theatre (610-374-4600; www.goggleworks .org), 201 Washington Street, Reading. A 131-seat modern venue showing art and independent films

POSING IN FRONT OF TOM STURGIS PRETZEL FACTORY

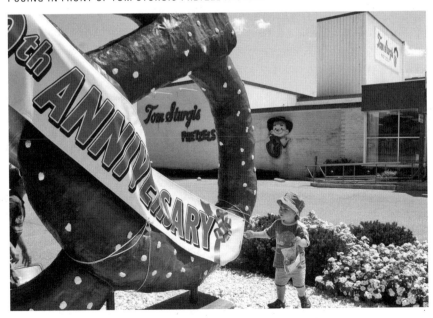

in the evenings and Wednesday afternoons.

♿ Sovereign Center and Reading Eagle Theater (610-898-7200; www.sovereigncenter.com), 700 Penn Street, Reading. This large downtown venue hosts everything from Reading Royals hockey games and indoor football to Broadway shows and Marilyn Manson concerts.

Strand Theater (610-683-8775; www.kutztownstrand.com), 32 N. White Oak Street, Kutztown. Historic old theater with two screens showing first-run movies.

NIGHTLIFE ♈ **Speckled Hen Pub** (610-685-8511), Fourth and Cherry Streets, Reading. Adjacent to Judy's on Cherry restaurant, this comfortable neighborhood pub has tavern food, happy hour specials, and a nice selection of microbrews and ales on tap. Karaoke is on Thursday; live music is on Friday, when it stays open until 1 AM.

Shorty's Bar (610-683-9600), 272 W. Main Street, Kutztown. Closed Sunday. Also known as the Kutztown Tavern, this popular bar and nightclub has pool tables, plasma TVs, and a DJ on weekends. Try the house-made lager.

✳ Selective Shopping

ANTIQUES Adamstown, between Reading and Lancaster, might have more antiques shops and flea markets than Lancaster Coun-

ty has cows. Many of them line PA 272 and offer reasonable prices that experts say are tough to beat anywhere else on the East Coast. Pick up a free map and shopping guide to the area at just about any shop. For a more complete listing of shops, visit www.antiquescapital.com.

Renninger's Antiques and Collectors Market (717-336-2177; www.renningers.com), 2500 N. Reading Road. Open 7:30–4 Sunday. The granddaddy of antiques marts with more than 300 indoor and 200 outdoor vendors selling everything from farm tables to Chippendale desks to comic books and costume jewelry. Expect to see more Windsor chairs than you will ever see again in your lifetime. There are also plenty of food vendors selling everything from cream donuts to soft pretzels. The outdoor section opens at 5 AM, weather permitting; bring a flashlight. Locals know that the produce stands sell some of the sweetest summer corn around. Renninger's also operates markets on some weekends in Kutztown (check Web site for a schedule).

Stoudt's Black Angus Antiques Mall (717-484-2757), 2800 N. Reading Road. Open 7:30–4 Sunday. Just down the street from Renninger's, this 400-vendor market is known for upscale offerings such as 19th-century Normandy farm tables, fine china and porcelain, rare books, gas chandeliers, and more. It shares a roof with

Wonderful Good Market, a foodie haven of artisan cheese, breads, and micro-roasted coffee.

Adams Antiques (717-355-3166; www.adamsantiques.com), 2400 N. Reading Road. Open Monday through Saturday 10–5, Sunday 8–5. A fun to browse antiques mall featuring 85 booths selling vintage dollhouses, toys, beer steins, lawn ornaments, old postcards, and more. There's an outdoor set-up on weekends as well.

Country French Collection (717-484-0200), 2887 N. Reading Road. Open 1–4 Sunday and by appointment. Housed in an 18th-century stone barn full of exquisite (and expensive) armoires, chairs, farm tables, and copper cookware from France and England.

Merritt's Antiques (610-689-9541; www.merritts.com), 1860 Weavertown Road, Douglassville. A large warehouse full of hard-to-find antiques, clocks, and quirky treasures such as horsehead hitching posts, mechanical banks, tin signs, weathervanes, and more.

Fleetwood Antiques (610-207-2322; www.fleetwoodantiques), US 222, Fleetwood. There's a big market for life-size resin farm animals in Pennsylvania, and many of them are made and sold here. Furniture and accessories from the former antiques complex are also for sale in a nearby barn.

Stoudtburg Village (www.stoudt burgvillage.com), Stoudtburg Road (at Reading Road), Adamstown. Local antiques-and-beer king Ed Stoudt came up with the idea for a faux European village after many visits to the motherland. Shopkeepers live above their stores and coffeehouses in a somewhat self-contained arrangement. It's not exactly thriving with stores and shoppers, but it's an interesting place to spend an hour. One of the highlights is the Toy Robot Museum and Store; $1.50 gets you access to thousands of vintage robot toys and often a conversation with the knowledgeable owner.

OUTLETS & ☂ **VF Outlet Center** (800-772-8336), 801 Hill Avenue, West Reading. Open daily. In the pre-outlet-mall era of the 1970s, this old manufacturing complex was known as Vanity Fair, anchored by the lingerie giant, and it was the best place around to get discounted pajamas and Lee jeans. It abbreviated its name and underwent a renovation in the 1990s, and now includes such brands as Bass, Black and Decker, Tommy Hilfiger, Jones New York, and Pepperidge Farm. You can still find heavily discounted lingerie, jeans, and swimsuits at the VF Outlet store on the complex. The mom-and-pop shops and cafés that line nearby Penn Avenue are also worth a look while you're in the area.

SPECIAL SHOPS & ☂ **Cabela's** (610-929-7000), 100 Cabela Drive (off I-78), Hamburg. Open daily. As much theme park as retail store, this outpost of the Nebraska-based outdoor adventure catalog has a café, a walk-through aquarium, and a mini-mountain full of taxidermied animals. Prices are comparable to the catalog's; there's also a bargain cave in the back. It's an easy destination to bundle with a trip to Hawk Mountain Sanctuary or Crystal Cave.

Country Seat (610-756-6124; www.countryseat.com), 1013 Old Philly Pike, Kempton. Closed Sunday; check Web site for schedule on other days. Master weaver Donna Longenecker sells all kinds of supplies for basket- and seat-weaving—wire handles, wooden bases, pine needles, Shaker tape, braided seagrass—plus woven ornaments, jewelry, silk scarves, and gourd art. It's a great place to buy a unique gift or just learn about a fascinating but dying craft. She also teaches weaving classes, from beginner to advanced, once a month.

Five and Divine (610-670-9700; www.fiveanddivine.com), 27 E. Penn Avenue, Wernersville. Closed Monday Vintage piggy banks, hand-painted glassware, recycled glass bowls, baby toys, and other unique gifts.

Dixon's Muzzleloading Shop (610-756-6271), 9952 Kunkels Mill Road, Kempton. Muzzleloaders are firearms that are loaded from the front. This is one of the largest muzzleloading supply shops in the country, and owner Chuck Dixon is an expert at their manufacture and repair.

✳ Special Events

March: **Berks Jazz Fest** (last week), Reading. Ten days of master classes, workshops and performances by top jazz and blues musicians at venues throughout Reading. Past performers have included Al Jarreau, the Dave Brubeck Quartet, Journey's Steve Smith. Info: www.berksjazzfest.com.

June/July: **Kutztown Folk Festival** (last weekend/first weekend), Kutztown University—the state's biggest Pennsylvania Dutch-themed party. Nine days of square dancing, agricultural demonstrations, hex-sign painting, chair caning, folk arts-and-crafts fair, hay mazes, pony rides, and the country's largest quilt sale. Food options include funnel cakes, corn fritters, apple dumplings, ham and chicken dinners, and a 1,200-pound ox roasted on a spit. Info: www.kutztownfestival.com.

August: **Goschenhoppen Festival** (second weekend), Perkiomenville. Preserved German homestead showcases 18th- and 19th-century Pennsylvania Dutch life with furniture-making and tin-smithing demonstrations, hand-churned ice cream and homemade summer sausage, and baking in a restored outdoor oven. It's smaller and lesser known than the Kutztown Folk Festival, but just as interesting and a little easier to manage. For information, visit www.goschenhoppen.org.

Lower Susquehanna River Valley

5

HARRISBURG & HERSHEY

GETTYSBURG

YORK COUNTY

HARRISBURG & HERSHEY

L ess than 15 miles apart from one another, Hershey and Harrisburg are close in distance but quite different in mood and offerings. Harrisburg is the state capital with grand old buildings, historical museums, expense-account steakhouses, and commanding views of the Susquehanna River. Once an important crossroads for Native Americans traveling to and from the Potomac and upper Susquehanna region, it is named for a later settler, John Harris. During the American Civil War, Harrisburg was a training center for the Union Army and developed into a major rail center and link between the Atlantic coast and the Midwest. Today, it's a city of about 49,500 with a reputation for shutting down on weekends and when the state legislature is out of session. But there is more going on than first meets the eye. The city boasts many beautiful parks, most notably down-town's City Island, historic sites such as Fort Hunter, good restaurants, and the best nightlife outside of Philadelphia and Baltimore. One could plan a visit based around a visit to the State Museum of Pennsylvania alone.

Meanwhile, chocolate, theme-park rides, and a man named Milton permeate the small town of Hershey. Mr. Hershey died in 1945 after spending decades building his successful candy empire, but his spirit lives on in this Willie Wonka–like realm of resort hotels, gardens, trolley rides, hot-chocolate lattes, and street lamps shaped like Hershey's Kisses. Recent worthwhile additions to the area include the humongous Antique Auto Museum of America and the Hershey Museum's Chocolate Lab, a hands-on classroom that lets kids and adults play and create. You will have a chance to sample chocolate again and again during your visit: upon check-in at many hotels, in the chocolate fondue wraps at the Hotel Hershey's elite spa, and as a gentle scent wafting throughout the town, especially around the main factory on Chocolate Avenue.

AREA CODE Harrisburg and Hershey are within the 717 area code.

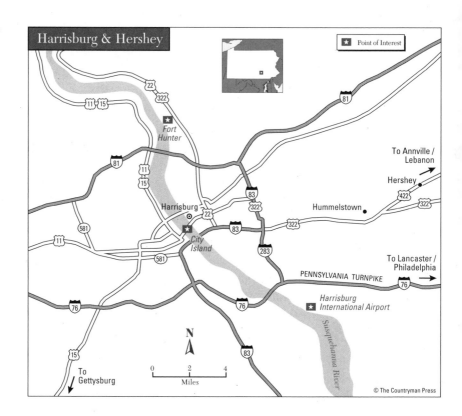

Harrisburg & Hershey

Point of Interest

Fort Hunter

To Annville / Lebanon

Hershey

Harrisburg

Hummelstown

City Island

To Lancaster / Philadelphia

PENNSYLVANIA TURNPIKE

Harrisburg International Airport

To Gettysburg

N

0   2   4
Miles

Susquehanna River

© The Countryman Press

GUIDANCE Contact the **Harrisburg-Hershey-Carlisle Tourism and Convention Bureau** (717-231-7788; 800-955-0969; www.visithhc.com), 415 Market Street, Harrisburg, for maps and a visitor guide. A **Welcome Center** is open weekdays from 8:30–4:30 in the east wing of the Capitol. In Hershey, **Chocolate World** and the **Hershey Lodge** have brochures and maps of the area.

GETTING THERE By air: **Harrisburg International Airport** (717-948-3900; 1-888-235-9442) is about 50 miles northeast of Gettysburg. **Philadelphia International** (215-937-6800) is about a two-hour drive.

By car: From Philadelphia, take the Pennsylvania Turnpike to exit 266 (Lebanon-Lancaster), then US 322 west to Hershey. For Harrisburg, Pennsylvania Turnpike to exit 247, then I-83 south to Second Street.

By bus: **Greyhound** (800-231-2222) offers service between Harrisburg and dozens of major cities, operating out of a terminal at 411 Market Street, Harrisburg.

GETTING AROUND For Harrisburg, **Capital Area Transit** (717-238-8304; www.cattransit.com) offers bus service throughout the city.

The Hershey Trolley (717-533-3000; $12.95 adults, $7.95 ages 3–11) is a great way for first-time visitors to learn the town's layout and history before heading to the park and other attractions. Guides are witty and generous with candy samples. Tours depart regularly in front of Chocolate World.

MEDICAL EMERGENCY Harrisburg Hospital (717-782-3591), 111 S. Front Street, Harrisburg.

Milton S. Hershey Medical Center (717-531-8521), 500 University Drive, Hershey.

WHEN TO GO Hershey Park is a seasonal attraction open May through Labor Day and some weekends in the fall. If you're looking for a bargain and don't mind skipping the theme park, plan to go anytime off-season and you will find that many area hotel rates drop significantly. There are still plenty of attractions that stay open year-round, including Hershey Gardens, ZooAmerica, and in Harrisburg the State and Civil War museums. To see Harrisburg at its busiest, plan your visit for a weekday when the legislature is in session. January is also a great time to visit the state capital; the fabulous Farm Show kicks into gear toward the end of the month, and its huge indoor complex keeps you protected from inclement weather.

HARRISBURG'S RIVER BRIDGES

✳ Villages

Annville. A few miles east of Hershey, Annville has a classic American main street with a historic theater, old-fashioned ice cream shop and general store, and beautifully preserved old homes. It's also home to Lebanon Valley College.

Hummelstown. Before the chocolate industry came along, this small town between Harrisburg and Hershey was the driving economic force in the area: supplying brownstone for buildings from Philadelphia to Chicago. Today, you will find charming tree-lined streets anchored by a square with antiques shops, preserved old homes, and restaurants, including the wonderful Warwick Hotel. It is also home to Indian Echo Caverns, limestone caves that once served as a shelter for Native Americans, and the historic Middletown and Hummelstown Railroad. Its historical society operates a museum that has an extensive collection of Indian arrowheads collected between 1914 and 1940 by Philander Ward Hartwell, the town's newspaper editor.

✳ To See

MUSEUMS

Harrisburg

🐾 ♿ ☂ **State Museum of Pennsylvania** (717-787-4780; www.state museumpa.org), 300 North Street. Closed Monday and Tuesday; $5

COFFEE AND CONVERSATION AT ANNVILLE'S GENERAL STORE

A STATUE OF WILLIAM PENN ANCHORS THE STATE MUSEUM OF PENNSYLVANIA.

adults, $3 ages 1–12; planetarium shows $2. There aren't many places that house a 12,000-year-old reconstructed mastodon, a planetarium, a re-created Susquehannock Indian village, and a Civil War museum, all under the same roof. Next to the Capitol building, this rarely crowded attraction has four floors of exhibits and activities on Pennsylvania's role in history, geology, pop culture, industrial and technological innovations, and war. Highlights of the huge collection include the original Penn Charter of 1691, a set of golf clubs owned by Arnold Palmer, a 1910 cast-iron turnstile from Philadelphia's Shibe Park, and portraits of famous Pennsylvanians such as Marian Anderson and Joe Paterno. There's a hands-on play area for the under-5 set in the basement. The gift shop has a huge inventory of Pennsylvania-themed merchandise, from books on the Pittsburgh Steelers and Philadelphia Phillies to the usual assortment of coffee mugs and magnets.

&. ↑ **National Civil War Museum** (717-260-1861; www.nationalcivil warmuseum.org), 1 Lincoln Circle at Reservoir Park. Open daily April through August; Wednesday through Sunday, September through March; $10 adults. This large hilltop museum on the eastern edge of Harrisburg opened in 2001 with the goal of telling the entire story of the American Civil War "without bias to Union or Confederate causes." Critics complain that it doesn't include nearly enough about the famous battle that happened just down the road in Gettysburg. Its dozen galleries are divided by theme, and include slavery and battle artifacts, electronic battle maps, surgery demonstrations, and interactive displays

NATIONAL CIVIL WAR MUSEUM

that are interspersed with artifacts such as Robert E. Lee's pocket Bible and Ulysses S. Grant's sword belt. It's not geared toward young children.

✐ ⚲ **Whitaker Center for Science and the Arts** (717-214-2787; www .whitakercenter.org), 222 Market Street. Open daily. Science center: $15 adults; $12.50 children; other prices vary. This 130,000-square-foot complex is home to a kid-friendly science museum, an IMAX theater, and a musical performance stage that has hosted string quartets and heavy metal bands. Call ahead or check Web site for performance and 3D movie schedules.

Hershey

Antique Automobile Club of America Museum (717-566-7100; aaca museum.org), 161 Museum Drive; $10 adults, $7 ages 4–12. A must for car buffs or anyone who appreciates a thoughtful, well-organized American history lesson. There are Ford Model Ts, mopeds, and Jeeps; vehicles dating from 1865 through the 1990s (a recent acquisition was Betty White's custom-made 1977 Cadillac Seville), and the country's largest collection of buses, including the Lakeland bus from *Forrest Gump*. Don't miss the detailed dioramas that put the car culture of different eras in context, and the restored 1941 diner airlifted to Hershey from Wichita, Kansas. There's also a hands-on kids' activity area.

Hershey Derry Township Historical Society (717-520-0748; www .hersheyhistory.org), 40 Northeast Drive; $2 suggested donation. Closed

WELCOME TO HERSHEY, PA.

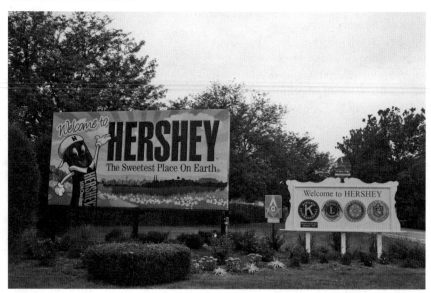

Tuesday and Thursday. Hershey wasn't always about chocolate; this old stone barn has exhibits on the early quarry industry, sports memorabilia, and Native American life. Of course, there's a room devoted to the man behind the chocolate bar.

&. ↑ **Hershey Museum** (717-534-3439; www.hersheymuseum.org), 63 W. Hersheypark Drive. Open daily; admission $10, or $17.50 for admission to the museum and Chocolate Lab. Renovated and expanded in 2008, this museum tells the history of Milton Hershey's boyhood, marketing genius, and philanthropy. The kid-friendly interactive exhibits include a re-creation of Hershey's first shop in Philadelphia, old promotional campaigns, and machines and panels that demonstrate the chocolate-making process (including one for wrapping Hershey's Kisses). The popular Chocolate Lab (for ages 4 and up) lets participants mold, dip, design, and taste their own chocolate creations; arrive early to sign up for a same-day class; space is limited.

HISTORIC SITES & GARDENS ♂ & **Hershey Gardens** (717-534-3492; www.hersheygardens.org), 170 Hotel Road, Hershey. Open daily year-round; $10 adults, $6 ages 3–15, free to guests of any Hershey resort. You'll find Japanese, rock, and herb gardens, a fun children's garden and butterfly house, and more than 7,000 roses in bloom June through August on this lovely 23-acre property. In the spring, 45,000 tulips blanket the seasonal display garden.

& ↑ **Pennsylvania State Capitol** (800-868-7672), North and Commonwealth Streets, Harrisburg. No visit to the Harrisburg area is complete without a visit to this domed downtown building, which was modeled after St. Peter's Basilica in Rome. Free guided tours include stops at the main rotunda and supreme court chambers and run every half hour on weekdays between 8:30 and 4. No reservations necessary.

COVERED BRIDGE AT FORT HUNTER

♂ **Fort Hunter** (717-599-5751; www.forthunter.org), 5300 N. Front Street, Harrisburg. Open daily. Built in 1756 at the beginning of the French and Indian War, this was one of a string of small forts constructed by the British along the Susquehanna River. Today, it's a beautiful place to spend an afternoon with picnic pavilions, a playground, the pedestrian-only

⚕ **Hershey Park and Chocolate World** (717-534-3900; 800-437-7439; www.hersheypa.com/attractions), 100 W. Hersheypark Drive. Open daily mid-May through Labor Day, and some weekends through October; hours vary; $56 adults, $35 ages 3–8, $54–72 for two-day flex passes, $78–100 for three-day passes. Built in 1907 by Milton S. Hershey as picnic grounds for the employees of his candy company, this family-friendly amusement park now encompasses more than 100 acres with dozens of rides and attractions. There are 11 roller coasters that will soak, lift, terrify, and just plain thrill you; **Skyrush,** a megacoaster with winged seating, was slated to open in summer 2012. Kiddie rides include a **Dino-Go-Round** and mini-pirate ship. Don't miss the **Kissing Tower,** which rises above the nearby stacks of the candy factory and gives way to a 360-degree view of the town and surrounding valley. In summer, **East Coast Waterworks,** a mammoth water-play structure features four slides, a roller coaster, and multistory jungle gym. Modeled after Wildwood, New Jersey, and other Atlantic shore boardwalks, it also offers a pier for strolling, hermit crab sales, corn-dog carts, water balloon races, and a sandcastle area for toddlers. You will get wet, so bring a change of clothes if you plan to hit this area of the park.

A cost-saving tip: Many local businesses offer discount park tickets, and one of the best places to get them is at **Giant Food** (717-312-0725; 1250 Cocoa Avenue; open daily), where one-day tickets include a free parking pass if you buy two adult tickets. Another good value is the preview plan: arrive after 7:30 PM when the park closes at 10 or 11, buy a ticket for the following day, and your admission for the evening is free.

Everhart Covered Bridge, and a Federal-style mansion (built on the site of the old fort). Even on weekdays, you'll probably encounter locals enjoying the river views from strategically placed benches. Tours of the mansion are $3–5, or just pick up an informative walking tour brochure and wander the grounds.

✲ To Do

FOR FAMILIES ☯ ⚕ **ZooAmerica** (717-534-3860), 100 W. Hersheypark Drive. Open daily except Thanksgiving, Christmas, and January 1; $10 adults, $8 ages 3–8; free parking. This small yet engaging zoo is home to

HERSHEY PARK

Within walking distance of the park and open year-round is **Chocolate World** (717-534-4900). Loyalists miss the old (read: less high-tech) factory-tour rides that ended in the 1980s, but the complex is still a great place to start your chocolate sojourn, with plenty of seats, sustenance, and a staffed information booth. Take the free ride through a simulated Hershey factory, let the kids wrap their own Hershey's Kisses, then browse what is possibly the best and largest chocolate-themed gift shop around. There's also a big and loud 3D show featuring singing and dancing candy bars. The first two hours of parking are free.

more than 200 species of animals from North America (black bears, wild turkeys, reindeer, black-footed ferrets) and can be covered in two hours or less. You can enter the zoo via a bridge from Hershey Park (entrance is free for season pass-holders). Watch for special events, like Park in the Dark, which lets visitors bring flashlights to check out the animals after hours.

✍ ⛯ **Indian Echo Caverns** (717-566-8131; www.indianechocaverns.com), 368 Middletown Road, Hummelstown. Open daily except holidays; $13 adults, $7 ages 3–11. Open for tours since 1929, this small but popular attraction makes a nice side trip for those wanting a break from the chocolate-covered world of Hershey. The *New York Times* calls it "the undisputed king of the state's show caves." The 45-minute guided tours include up-close views of stalactites, stalagmites, cave coral, and more (it requires a long walk up and down steep steps to get there). During the summer, kids can pan for gemstones in a replica sluice near the gift shop.

🌣 **M&H Railroad** (717-944-4435; www.mhrailroad.com), 136 Brown Street, Middletown. Open May through October; call ahead for days and times; $12 adults, $7 ages 2–11. Kids will love this 11-mile vintage 1920s coach ride along pretty Swatara Creek; the conductor shares historical anecdotes and leads a sing-along on the way back. There's also a boarding platform at Indian Echo Caverns.

🌣 **City Island.** One of Harrisburg's best-known attractions, this 60-acre island in the middle of the Susquehanna River is an easy walk from downtown via Walnut Street Bridge or you can drive onto the island via Market or Front Streets and pay to park in designated lots. It offers a long list of seasonal and year-round activities for locals and visitors: boat, train and carriage rides, minor league baseball games, seasonal swimming, minigolf, shopping, and eating. At **City Island Beach** (717-238-9012) on the north end, you can sunbathe and swim every day but Wednesday mid-June through Labor Day. *The Pride of the Susquehanna* (717-234-6500; $7 adults, $3 children) is an authentic stern paddlewheel riverboat that offers 45-minute rides June through August. Take the kids to **City Island**

PRIDE OF THE SUSQUEHANNA, CITY ISLAND

Railroad (717-232-2332), a scaled version of a Civil War–era steam train that offers rides around the island for $3. Nearby, an antique carousel offers $2 rides. Cap the day with a visit to the concession stands and small souvenir shops at **RiverSide Village Park** (open mid-May through Labor Day). For more things to do here, see Outdoor Activities.

BREWERY TOURS Troëg's Hamsburg Brewing Co. (717-232-1297; www.troegs.com), 800 Paxton Street. This small brewery near the waterfront was launched in 1997 by two brothers from Mechanicsburg and produces seven different handcrafted beers. It offers free brewery tours and tastings every Saturday at 1:30, 2, and 2:30 PM. Reserve a space by phone or online.

✳ Outdoor Activities

AUTO RACING Williams Grove Raceway (717-697-5000; www.williams grove.com), PA 15 South, Mechanicsburg. Open Friday and Saturday March through October. Half-mile track southwest of Harrisburg that has been in operation since 1939.

BASEBALL Baseball in Harrisburg goes back as far as 1907 when the local team played in the class D tri-state league. Today, the **Harrisburg Senators,** a farm team of the Washington Nationals, play at the 2008-renovated Metro Bank Park (717-231-4444; www.senatorsbaseball.com) on City Island.

BICYCLING/RENTALS Susquehanna Outfitters (717-234-7879) rents bicycles on the west side of City Island's north parking lot. Open daily in summer, weekends in April, May, September, and October.

BOAT EXCURSIONS/RENTALS Susquehanna River Trail (www .susquehannarivertrail.org) is a 51-mile river trail with 25 access points between Harrisburg and Sunbury to the north. **Blue Mountain Outfitters** (717-957-2413), US 11 and 15, Marysville, rents canoes and kayaks starting at $45 a day.

GOLF Iron Valley Golf Club (717-279-7409), 201 Iron Valley Drive, Lebanon. Built on an abandoned iron mine, this challenging course offers 18 holes with significant elevation changes (11 of them are carved out of a mountain). **Royal Oaks Golf Club** (717-274-2212), 3350 W. Oak Street, Lebanon. This former cattle ranch has 18 holes featuring 6,730 yards of golf from the longest tees for a par of 71.

SUSQUEHANNA RIVER

HUNTING Fort Indiantown Gap (717-861-2733; 1 Garrison Road, Annville), a National Guard training center, is open for hunting from the first Saturday after Labor Day through February, and late April through May. All hunters must pay a $30 access fee and attend a safety briefing. For more information, visit www.ftig.state.pa.us.

SKIING Ski Roundtop (717-432-9631; www.skiroundtop.com), 925 Roundtop Road, Lewisberry. About 20 miles south of Harrisburg, this resort has 16 ski trails (some winding), plus snowboarding, tubing, and year-round paintball.

✳ Green Space

Reservoir Park (717-255-3020), Walnut Street between 18th and 21st Streets. Built in 1872, this 85-acre park is home to the National Civil War Museum (see also Museums), a restored 1898 mansion that houses several art galleries, a large playground, and a band shell that hosts summer concerts and an annual Shakespeare Fest. The Capital Area Greenbelt passes through here (see also Walks).

Italian Lake (717-255-3020), Third and Division Streets. This 10-acre city park is a popular local gathering place and features formal gardens in the Italian Renaissance style, a Japanese harmony bridge, and two scenic man-made lakes. A paved walking path winds around the larger of the two lakes. Outdoor concerts are held here Sunday evenings in July and August.

Wildwood Lake Sanctuary and Nature Center (717-221-0292; www
.wildwoodlake.org), 100 Wildwood Way. Grounds open daily dawn to
dusk. Nestled in what looks like an industrial section of the city, this lake
is home to all sorts of wildlife. Birding is popular along the paved pathway
that circles the lake. There are several easy hiking trails and boardwalks
that wind through marshes and bogs; bikes are permitted on some trails.
Stop by the nature center for a detailed map.

WALKS Capital Area Greenbelt (717-921-4733; www.caga.org). This
20-mile trail laces its way around the city like a necklace and can be used
for walking, biking, or skating. Start at the **Five Senses Garden** (717-
564-0488) off PA 441 behind the Harrisburg East Mall.

✳ Lodging

HOTELS, LODGES, & MOTELS
Rates usually drop considerably in
the Hershey area during the off-
season of late fall, winter, and early
spring. Many chains, including
Days Inn, Howard Johnson, and
Hampton Inn, line Chocolate
Avenue east of the park.

Hershey
Chocolatetown Motel (717-533-
2330; www.chocolatetownmotel
.com), 1806 E. Chocolate Avenue.
Rooms $54–110, $89–140 in summer. Clean and basic rooms in a
central location near the park.
Don't expect luxury, but the prices
are among the lowest in town,
especially after Labor Day.

& ♂ **Hotel Hershey** (717-533-
2171; www.hersheypa.com
/accommodations), 100 Hotel
Road. It was a bold endeavor to
build a luxury Mediterranean-style
hotel during the Depression, but
that's exactly what Milton Hershey
did when he returned home from
a trip to Europe in the 1930s. It
remains one of Pennsylvania's top

special-occasion hotels, a grand
lodge complete with 232 rooms
and 25 suites, palatial gardens,
indoor and outdoor pools, and
commanding views of the Conewa-
go Valley. Guest rooms have a
sophisticated Victorian feel and
feature original art work, luxury
linens, and chocolate soaps and
bath foam. There are 20 suites,
including the lavish Catherine
Hershey Suite, which sleeps up to
eight and features a garden theme,
three bathrooms, two bedrooms,
living and dining room, and a private balcony. Nearby is Hershey
Gardens, to which hotel guests are
admitted free. You don't have to be
a hotel guest to take a free tour
(offered daily at 10 AM) of the
premises or indulge in a chocolate
fondue wrap or massage at the
Chocolate Spa. Rooms $319–399;
suites $624–1,700.

♂ & ♂ **Hershey Motor Lodge**
(717-533-3311; www.hersheypa
.com/accommodations). Part of the
Hershey Resorts umbrella, this
sprawling complex of more than

A DAY OF CHOCOLATE

I don't include many spas in this guide, but the **Chocolate Spa** at the Hotel Hershey (717-520-5888; 877-772-9988; www.chocolatespa.com/) stands out for its stellar service and unique cocoa-themed treatments. Opened in 2001 amid an elegant marble-floored setting overlooking the hotel's formal gardens, it offers such indulgences as chocolate hydrotherapy, chocolate-oil massages, and cocoa butter scrubs. A Cuban theme was later added in a nod to Milton Hershey's ties to the island's sugar industry, featuring mojito sugar scrubs and green coffee body wraps. For a truly indulgent day, start with a hot-chocolate latte at the hotel's Cocoa Beanery. Follow this with a whipped cocoa bath ($50 for 25 minutes of soaking) or a chocolate fondue wrap, a gentle body brushing and rinse (for $125) that will leave you smelling sweetly, but not overwhelmingly, of cocoa. (For the more traditional spa-goer, there's also a roster of massage, facial, and mani-pedi treatments.) Spend the rest of the afternoon lounging in the spa's quiet areas (guests who partake of any treatment may stay at long as they like at the spa and nearby fitness center). Cap your day with a chocolate soufflé served with malted milk-ball gelato in the hotel's Circular Dining Room.

HOTEL HERSHEY

660 rooms may seem daunting on arrival, but it offers efficient and friendly service, spacious rooms, and a convenient location near Hershey Park and other attractions. It does a huge meetings and conventions business. Rooms are decorated in chocolate tones and have refrigerators, TVs, wireless access, and chocolate-scented toiletries; an indoor and an outdoor pool and four restaurants are also on-site. Rates include passes to Hershey Gardens, Hershey Museum, discounted Hershey Park tickets, and shuttle service to the park. Rooms $199–279; suites and cottages $508–787.

🍴 🛏 ♿ **Simmons Motel** (717-533-9177; www.simmonsmotel.com), 355 W. Chocolate Avenue. This family-owned motel has 23 rooms and 12 large suites with kitchens and is within walking distance of many attractions, including the park, museum, and Chocolate World. Rooms are clean and attractive with desks, TVs, and one or two double beds; try to get one in the back away from busy Chocolate Avenue. There are also several apartments with full kitchens that sleep up to seven people, for $110–285 a night. Coffee, juice, and local maps are available in the small lobby. Rooms $125–165, two-room suite $120–175. Summer rates are higher.

🍴 ♿ **Annville Inn** (717-867-1991; www.annvilleinn.com), 4515 Hill Church Road, Annville. Looking for solace after a day of roller coaster rides? Consider this five-room B&B 6 miles east of Hershey. Meticulously cared for by innkeeper Rosalie George, it has five well-appointed rooms, some with Jacuzzi tubs, fireplaces, and private entrances. Other amenities include a large landscaped pool, game room, and screening room with stadium-style seating. Rooms $129–249.

Harrisburg
Comfort Inn Waterfront (717-233-1611; www.comfortinnriver front.com), 525 S. Front Street. This family-friendly hotel overlooking the Susquehanna is within walking distance of the Capitol building and Metro Bank Park. Its 115 rooms have mini-fridges and microwaves; a swimming pool and a small gym are also available. Rooms start at $99, including breakfast.

BED & BREAKFASTS 🍴 ♿ **Inn at Westwynd Farm** (717-533-6764; www.westwyndfarminn .com), 1620 Sand Beach Road, Hummelstown. This picturesque B&B is located on a 32-acre working horse farm 5 miles west of Hershey. The main house has nine cozy rooms (six with private baths and luxurious linens, some with Jacuzzi tubs and fireplaces), two living rooms, and an inviting wraparound porch with a view of the countryside. A spacious carriage house with sleeping loft is a good option for families. Owners Frank and Carolyn Troxell started a horse training and boarding operation in the 1980s and added the inn portion in 2002; goats, alpacas, cats, and dogs also live on the property, and benches provide front-row views of the property's riding rings. Breakfast (maybe pumpkin waffles or eggs baked in ham) is served on the sun porch or dining room; Fresh-baked snacks, drinks, and candy are available day and night. Rooms $109–159, two-night minimum on weekends.

&. 𝒮 **Canna Country Inn** (717-938-6077; www.cannainnbandb .com), 393 Valley Road, Etters. About 8 miles southeast of Harrisburg, this seven-room B&B is housed in a converted 18th-century barn surrounded by 3 acres of gardens and a picnic grove with hammocks and fire pits. Rooms have king or queen beds, DVD players, and wireless access; some have private entrances and whirlpool tubs. The 600-square-foot common living room invites lounging, with a fireplace and window seat overlooking the grounds. Breakfasts are huge and made to order. Skiers from nearby Roundtop fill the inn during winter; ask about lift discounts. Rooms $109–169, suites $169–225.

CAMPGROUNDS 𝒮 **Elizabethtown/Hershey KOA** (717-367-7718), 1980 Turnpike Road, Elizabethtown. About a 15-minute drive from Hershey off PA 743 with more than 200 tent and hookup sites, a swimming pool, and lots of activities. Tent sites $45–55; cabins $75–105.

𝒮 **Hershey Highmeadow Campground** (717-534-8999; www.hersheycamping.com), 1200 Matlack Road, Hummelstown. There are 300 tent sites (few with shade), 22 rustic log cabins, swimming pools, and a complimentary seasonal shuttle to Hershey Park, about five minutes away. Tent sites $41–55; cabins $94–138; rates drop after Labor Day.

✷ Where to Eat

DINING OUT

Hershey
Devon Seafood Grill (717-508-5460; www.devonseafood.com), 27 W. Chocolate Avenue. Lunch daily; dinner Monday through Saturday; brunch Sunday. Small upscale chain located in the Hershey Press building—the ever-changing menu might include fresh Long Island Sound oysters, chipotle-grilled shrimp enchiladas, San Francisco-style cioppino, or bone-in rib eye with a side of lemon-asparagus risotto. Save room for the fabulous three-layer Hershey's chocolate velvet cake. Lunch $9–21; dinner $20–37.

Y **Circular Dining Room** (717-534-8800), Hotel Hershey. Open for breakfast and dinner Monday through Saturday, lunch Friday and Saturday, Sunday brunch. The area's most elegant (and priciest) restaurant boasts wonderful views of the hotel's immaculate gardens and reflecting pools and a menu that offers a sophisticated twist on the ubiquitous chocolate theme.

The dinner menu might include cocoa-dusted scallops or more traditional offerings, such as grilled fillet of beef with corn custard, and Berkshire pork tenderloin with grits, charred zucchini, and baby leeks. Brunch is an extravaganza of cold seafood, carving and omelet stations, and dozens of fabulous chocolate desserts. Reservations recommended. Breakfast and lunch $16–23; dinner entrées $30–39; brunch $40.

& ⵙ **Fire Alley** (717-533-3200; www.firealley.net), 1144 Cocoa Avenue (PA 743), in the Cocoaplex shopping complex. Lunch and dinner Tuesday through Sunday. It's a couple miles from the park, but good food and pleasant ambiance make it worth the drive. Choose from a long list of appetizers, salads, and sandwiches. Entrées range from creative (chicken wrapped in bacon and drizzled with a root beer glaze) to traditional (filet mignon, crab cakes). Lunch and appetizers $7–14; dinner entrées $14–28.

Harrisburg

& ⵙ **Bricco** (717-724-0222; www.briccopa.com), 31 S. Third Street. Lunch and dinner Monday through Saturday, dinner Sunday. The quote from Marcel Proust on the Web site is the first indication that you're in for a special dining experience. Bricco manages to stand out among the city's many fine-dining options by marrying local Pennsylvania produce with creative French and Tuscan-style cooking. Hand-tossed pizza comes

with Kennett Square mushrooms, caramelized onions, and burrata. Roasted lobster and crab is served with root beer pork belly, fennel, apples, and vanilla-bourbon sauce. Dessert might feature cherry cheesecake in lemon jus or basil-tapioca with rhubarb foam. A truly memorable dining experience. Lunch $10–16, dinner entrées $16–39.

& ⵙ **Sammy's** (717-221-0192; www.sammysitalian restaurant .com), 502 N. Third Street. Lunch and dinner Monday through Friday, dinner Saturday. A two-story BYO bistro near the Capitol with a traditional Italian menu; try the shrimp scampi or eggplant rollatini stuffed with ricotta. The $6.95 all-you-can-eat lunch buffet is a great deal. Reservations recommended on weekends. Lunch: $7–14; dinner entrées $14–24.

EATING OUT Broad Street Market (717-236-7923), 1233 N. 3rd Street (at Verbeke), Harrisburg. Open 7 AM–2 PM Wednesday (with limited vendors), 7 AM–5 PM Thursday and Friday, and 7 AM–5 PM Saturday. A good spot for lunch near the Capitol building and State Museum. This market has been around since the Civil War and fills three city blocks. Its stalls are more varied than most food markets in the area: Offerings include fried and smoked chicken, crepes, subs, and hand-rolled pretzels. Next door in the stone building, expect sushi, Indian curry dishes, sweet potato pie, and Haitian Creole cuisine.

Local bands or singer-songwriters perform in the courtyard most Saturdays.

🐚 **Brownstone Café** (717-944-3301), 1 N. Union Street, Middletown. Breakfast, lunch, and dinner daily. Terrific and unpretentious eatery in an old brownstone building near the M&H Railroad station. Prices are very reasonable; for breakfast, try the hashbrown casserole or generous stack of pancakes. The hot ham and cheese on a pretzel roll is a lunchtime favorite; platters include ham loaf and stuffed cabbage. Dishes $4–10.

Roxy's Café (717-232-9292), 274 North Street (at Third), Harrisburg. Breakfast and lunch daily. Friendly eatery near the Capitol, with hearty sandwiches, beer-battered onion rings, and salads. It's a popular local breakfast spot; don't be surprised if you see the mayor drop in. Dishes $2–8.

What If Café (717-238-1155), 3424 N. Sixth Street, Harrisburg. Lunch and dinner Monday through Saturday. The rooms at this popular BYO eatery are bright and stylish, and the diverse menu includes Angus beef burgers, steamed clams, Panko-crusted chicken over pasta, and veal Marsala. There's also a branch in Hershey. Lunch $7–12; dinner $12–26.

🐚 **Wolfe's Diner** (717-432-2101), 625 N. US 15, Dillsburg. Everything you'd want in an old-fashioned diner: low prices, a menu full of comfort food, and a tidy decor of stainless steel and linoleum. This makes a good stop for travelers between Harrisburg and Gettysburg. Breakfast specials start at $1.25 for eggs, hotcakes, and bacon.

Hershey and Nearby

🍸 **Fenicci's** (717-533-7159), 102 W. Chocolate Avenue. Open Monday through Friday for lunch and dinner; dinner only, Saturday and Sunday. The original home of the H.B. Reese Candy Co. (and the birthplace of Reese's Peanut Butter Cups), this dimly lit tavern has a wide selection of pastas, steaks, and seafood, but the pizzas draw the biggest raves. Toppings include shrimp scampi and buffalo chicken, and bruschetta. It has live music and stays open late on weekends. Dishes $14–28; pizzas $11–15.

Hershey Pantry (717-533-7505; www.hersheypantry.com), 801 E. Chocolate Avenue. Open daily 6:30 AM–9 PM. It's not the best value in town, but the meals (especially breakfast) are reliably good at this cozy spot just east of Hershey Park. Try the cinnamon bread French toast or egg sandwich on a pretzel roll for breakfast. For lunch, there's a nice selection of salads and sandwiches, and dinner entrées include fish tacos, chicken Carbonara, coconut shrimp, and filet mignon. Portions are ample, and kids are welcome. There's even an afternoon tea of scones, soup, tea sandwiches, and rich desserts from the in-house bakery for $17. Breakfast $5–10, lunch $8–10, dinner $12–26.

Lebanon Farmers' Market (717-274-3663; www.lebanon farmersmarket.com), 35 8th Street, Lebanon. Open Thursday and Friday 8–7, Saturday 8–3. Grab a fresh-from-the-oven soft pretzel or a Lebanon bologna sandwich and take it upstairs to a dining room overlooking the entire market. Two of my favorite stops are S. Clyde Weaver, for sweet Lebanon bologna and salt and vinegar potato chips, and Candy Rama, which sells caramels, fudge, and every type of wrapped sweet imaginable. There's even a

sushi place on the second floor for the meat-averse.

♉ **Warwick Hotel** (717-566-9124; www.thewarwickhotel.com), 12 W. Main Street, Hummelstown. Open Monday through Saturday for breakfast, lunch, and dinner; dinner only, Sunday. Locals call it the Wick, and it's a favorite gathering spot, with several dining rooms, an outdoor patio, full bar, and lots of old-fashioned charm. The 12-page menu features all kinds of burgers, sandwiches, salads, pastas, steaks, and seafood. Dishes $9–25.

ICE CREAM AND COFFEE
Kettering Corner (717-867-2004; www.ketteringcornerannville.com), 104 W. Main Street, Annville. Favorite local gathering spot

BIRDS' EYE VIEW OF LEBANON FARM MARKET

known for hand-dipped Hershey's ice cream and homemade waffle cones. It also serves hot dogs, panini, and bagels—all good. The sidewalk patio is an ideal place to read the newspaper and people-watch.

Mazzoli Ice Cream (717-533-2252; www.mazzoliicecream.com), 72 W. Governor Road, Hershey. Open daily in spring and summer; call for other times. Milton Hershey's personal dairy chef, Fred Mazzoli, started this gourmet ice cream business in 1956. Located in a residential neighborhood off US 322, it still makes and sells spumoni, gelato, Italian ice, and fruit-based sorbets. Don't miss the fabulous tortoni, a French custard made with toasted coconut, almond flavoring, and wine bisque.

MJ's Coffeehouse (717-867-3545), 36 E. Main Street, Annville. This would be a good place to eat even if it weren't adjacent to a first-run movie theater. It shares a doorway with the Allen Theater, so you can grab a turkey sandwich and enjoy it with the movie, or hang out in the laid-back, art-filled dining room. There's also free WiFi, and there's live jazz on Friday, Saturday, and the first Thursday of the month.

Sirro's Italian Ice (717-274-9080), 7 S. 8th Street, Lebanon. Belly up to the counter for a banana split, milk shake, or specialty Italian ice at this old-school soda shop near the Lebanon Farmers' Market.

✴ Entertainment

MUSIC Many Harrisburg bars feature live music on Thursday, Friday, and Saturday nights. Pick up copies of *Fly* magazine or *Pennsylvania Musician* available for free around town, or check out the Web sites www.flymagazine .net and www.pamusician.net. They highlight what's going on music-wise each week in the Harrisburg area and beyond.

♈ **Appalachian Brewing Company** (717-221-1080), 50 Cameron Street, Harrisburg. This cavernous microbrewery hosts top-notch acoustic acts and open-mic nights in the Abbey Bar. There's usually no cover, and there's free pool on Sunday and Tuesday. Brewery tours are given Saturday at 1 PM.

Giant Center (717-534-3911; www.giantcenter.com), 550 W. Hersheypark Drive, hosts Hershey Bears hockey games, Disney on Ice shows, and pop-music concerts.

Harrisburg Comedy Zone (717-920-5653; www.harrisburgcomedy zone.com), 110 Limekiln Road, New Cumberland. Open-mic nights, improv, and performances by local personalities like Raymond the Amish Comic.

♈ **Winner's Circle Saloon** (717-469-0661), 604 Station Road, Harrisburg. This "eatin, drinkin, and dancin place" in the Grantville Holiday Inn features live country bands Wednesday through Saturday and line-dancing lessons on Tuesday and Thursday.

THEATER & FILM ㄴ Hershey Theater (717-534-3405; www.hersheytheater.com), 15 E. Caracas Avenue, Hershey. This renovated and gorgeous 1933 building hosts everything from Broadway musicals and Paula Deen Live to classic films and Yo Gabba Gabba! shows. Tours are given on Friday (year-round) and Sunday (summer only) for $7 a person. Call for times.

Allen Theatre and Coffeehouse (717-867-4766), 36 Main Street, Annville. A beautiful restored Art Deco theater showing first-run films. The owner introduces most of the screenings, and local college students and aspiring musicians provide prescreen entertainment. The adjacent café, MJ's, serves sandwiches, pastries, and good coffee, and there's live music most weekends.

Haars Drive-In (717-432-3011), 185 Logan Road, Dillsburg. Open April through September. This 1950s-style drive-in off US 15 shows first-run movies on weekends.

✳ Selective Shopping

Shopping in downtown Harrisburg centers around the **Shops at Strawberry Square** (717-255-1020), 11 N. Third Street, home to more than 40 shops, galleries, and restaurants, and a popular children's theater. Just off I-83 at Paxton Street, **Harrisburg East Mall** (717-564-0980) is another main shopping area, anchored by Macy's, Bass Pro Shops, and Boscov's.

Old Sled Works Antiques and Craft Market (717-834-9333; www.sledworks.com), 722 N. Market Street, Duncannon. Open Wednesday through Sunday 10–5. You'll find 125 vendors selling toys, cookbooks, jewelry, baskets, and all kinds of furniture at this indoor market. Be sure to check out the old sleds on display (a nod to the building's former use) and the vintage penny arcade. An antique forest-fire lookout tower (no climbing) anchors the riverfront property.

West Shore Farmers' Market and Shoppes (717-737-9881; www.westshorefarmersmarket.com), 900 Market Street, Lemoyne. Market open Tuesday, Friday, Saturday, shops open Tuesday through Saturday. Indoor market with prepared foods, butcher, and produce stalls downstairs and crafts, used books, and clothes for sale upstairs. **Kepler Seafood** is renowned for its lump crabmeat and smoked salmon cream cheese. Fewer vendors show up on Tuesdays.

Hummelstown

ㄴ **Olde Factory** (717-566-5685), 139 S. Hanover Street. Three floors of antiques, folk art, quilts, and unusual crafts located in a former dress factory.

ㄴ **Rhoads Pharmacy** (717-566-2525), 17 W. Main Street. This old-fashioned multiservice store sells candles, beer steins, Boyds Bears, and other collectibles in addition to the usual drugstore inventory.

✳ Special Events

January: **Pennsylvania Farm Show** (second and third weeks), 2300 N. Cameron Street, Harrisburg—the largest indoor agricultural event in America includes features more than a million square feet of farm equipment displays, cooking demos, animal beauty contests, and some of the best cuisine the state has to offer. A must-see is the life-size butter sculpture designed in a different likeness each year. Food highlights include potato doughnuts from the state potato cooperative, honey ice cream from the beekeepers association, apple dumplings, chicken corn soup, deep-fried mushrooms, and every variation of beef and pork sandwich you can think of. Admission is free, but parking will cost you.

GETTYSBURG

One of Pennsylvania's top tourist attractions, the small town of Gettysburg sits between Harrisburg and the Maryland border, surrounded by the battlefield that made it famous. It was a tiny isolated farming community before the Union and Confederate armies arrived in 1863 and fought one of the bloodiest battles of the Civil War, with more than 50,000 casualties. Four months later at the dedication of the Soldiers Cemetery, President Abraham Lincoln delivered the *Gettysburg Address,* considered one of the greatest speeches in American history, rededicating the nation to the war effort and to the ideal that no soldier here had died in vain. The war would continue for two more years.

Today's Gettysburg, without a doubt, remains steeped in its Civil War history. It is difficult to find a prewar building that didn't serve as a shelter for wounded soldiers or isn't full of bullet holes, or an attic that wasn't taken over by sharpshooters. Its main streets are lined with souvenir shops, hotels and B&Bs, all types of restaurants, and sightseeing attractions that range from fading kitsch to garish. Buses, RVs, and motorcycles crawl along the battlefield's one-way roads at any given time of day. Yet despite the crowds and touristy vibe, a visit to Gettysburg remains a soul-stirring experience. The force of the battle and the spirits of the dead soldiers stay with you at just about every turn and long after you've left town.

One of the most enjoyable things about Gettysburg is the people. Whether they grew up here, or elected to retire, bought a

GRAVESTONES AT GETTYSBURG
NATIONAL CEMETERY

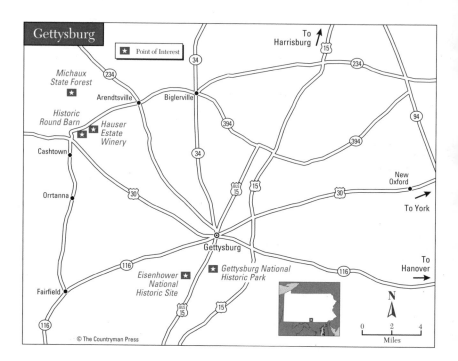

bullet-pocked B&B, or became a guide after years of playing tourist, their fascination with the town's history is earnest and very contagious. Talk to them; they are often happy to share their stories and knowledge.

Another thing to keep in mind is that the area is a pleasant place to spend a few days even if you or your companions don't care much about cannonades and infantry positions. Adams County is a mecca of apple, peach, and pear orchards that is awash in harvest celebrations and gorgeous foliage in the fall. Nearby villages such as New Oxford and East Berlin have antiques shops and quaint inns; to the west, Michaux State Forest offers plenty of biking and hiking opportunities.

AREA CODE The Gettysburg area lies within the 717 area code.

GUIDANCE Gettysburg Convention and Visitor Bureau (717-334-6274; 800-337-5015), 35 Carlisle Street, located in the town's original railway station near Lincoln Square, has maps, brochures, and a central location. It also has a staffed desk at the military park's new visitor center.

GETTING THERE By air: **Harrisburg International Airport** (717-948-3900) is about 50 miles northeast of Gettysburg. **Baltimore-Washington International** (301-859-7111) is about 80 miles away.

By car: Gettysburg is about four and a half hours from New York City, about 90 minutes from Baltimore, and two hours from Philadelphia. From the Pennsylvania Turnpike, take exit 17 to US 15 south.

GETTING AROUND Lincoln Square, where US 30 and 15 meet, is the center of downtown Gettysburg. Carlisle, Baltimore, Washington, and York Streets are main thoroughfares off or near the square.

Freedom Transit Trolley (717-334-6296) runs on three lines from 8 AM–10 PM throughout town, with a hub near Lincoln Square. The tourist-friendly Lincoln Line stops at many major attractions, including the new park visitor center and the American Civil War Museum. A one-way token costs $1, or $3 for a day pass. It's a great way to circumvent parking hassles, especially during the busy summer months. Hours are limited from December through March.

Self-guided historic walking tours begin at the **Lincoln Railroad Station,** 35 Carlisle Street. Pick up a map at the visitor center in the station.

PARKING Parking in Gettysburg can be a challenge. There is a two-hour limit on most of the metered downtown spaces. A small parking garage is located downtown behind Gallery 30 on Racehorse Alley. A handful of metered parking spaces are located here also.

Limited free parking is available in some of the side streets and alleys behind the shops.

LINCOLN SQUARE

A tip: If you opt for on-street parking, bring a roll of dimes. While it may seem easier to pitch three quarters into the meter for an hour's worth of parking, six dimes for the hour ends up being cheaper at the end of the day.

MEDICAL EMERGENCY Gettysburg Hospital (717- 334-2121), 147 Gettys Street, at Washington Street, a few blocks north of the park's visitor center.

WHEN TO GO September is a good time to go if you're looking to find fewer people and decent weather—the summer crowds have left and leaf peeping season and Halloween are a few weeks away. Though hotels often fill up, another quiet time to visit the battlefield is the first week of July, when most people are attending the reenactment outside of town.

Spring brings wildflowers and thawed monuments, but it also means busloads of school groups.

✳ Villages

Biglerville. North of Gettysburg 6 miles, this rural town along PA 34 is home to a country store, a museum that chronicles and celebrates the history of the apple in Pennsylvania, and a couple of casual restaurants. Best of all, it's surrounded by good produce stands. There's no real downtown, but it's a good place to stock up on apples and other fruit on your way north out of town. Just down the road is Arendtsville, home to the popular apple harvest and apple blossom festivals.

Cashtown. West of Gettysburg 8 miles, Cashtown dates back to 1797 and stems from the business practices of the village's first innkeeper, Peter Marck, who insisted on cash payments for the goods he sold and the highway tolls he collected. In June 1863, Confederate leaders met at the Cashtown Inn to discuss their course of action. Still in existence, the inn operates as a restaurant and B&B and is one of the few main commercial establishments in town.

Fairfield. During the Gettysburg Campaign in the American Civil War, the Battle of Fairfield played an important role in securing the Hagerstown Road, enabling Robert E. Lee's army to retreat through Fairfield toward the Potomac River. Lee and his officers stopped to eat at the Fairfield Inn, which still operates as a small hotel.

New Oxford. Anchored by an attractive town square (actually a circle) with brick sidewalks and tree-lined streets, this town of neat Victorian and Colonial homes north of Gettysburg is home to dozens of quaint shops, as well as a few B&Bs and restaurants. Every June, it's the site of a huge antiques and crafts show.

HISTORIC SITES Soldiers National Cemetery, 97 Taneytown Road. Open daily dawn to dusk. Created after the war and dedicated on November 19, 1863, this solemn graveyard is the site of President Lincoln's *Gettysburg Address* and a reminder that the Battle of Gettysburg was a horrific and fatal event for many. Today, American veterans of all the major wars are buried here. Take a guided walking tour or wander through on your own. Be sure to pause to read the passages from Theodore O'Hara's stirring poem, *Bivouac for the Dead,* located on stone tablets throughout the grounds.

☂ **David Wills House** (717-334-2499; www.davidwillshouse.org), 8 Lincoln Square; $6.50 adults. This is where you go to learn how the town coped in the aftermath of the battle. It was here that President Lincoln stayed on his post-war visit to Gettysburg and here that he completed the *Gettysburg Address* the night before he delivered it. The home's five rooms include original furnishings and photographs belonging to the Wills family (David Wills was a prominent local judge) and exhibits on the crafting of Lincoln's most famous speech. The National Park Service took it over in 2004 and it opened as a museum in 2009.

SIGN AT GETTYSBURG NATIONAL CEMETERY

Eisenhower National Historic Site (717-338-9114; www.nps.gov /eise), 250 Eisenhower Farm Drive; $7.50 adults, $6 ages 13–16, $3.50 ages 6–12. Allow at least two hours for this worthwhile tour of Ike and Mamie Eisenhower's dairy farm and weekend retreat from Washington. Adjacent to the battlefield but a separate entity, it was the only home the Eisenhowers owned and remains much as it was when they retired here in 1967, right down to their TV-dinner trays and pink monogrammed towels. Guides start your tour with a short introduction in the formal living room (which has hosted Winston Churchill and other

GRAIN SILO AT EISENHOWER NATIONAL HISTORIC SITE

VIPs); afterward, visitors are free to stroll the house and grounds. Kids 7 and up can partake in a Junior Secret Service Agent program and see black Angus cows that roam the farm. You must buy tickets at the park's visitor center and take a shuttle bus to the farm. Buy your tickets early during the busy summer months; they sometimes sell out.

☂ **General Lee's Headquarters** (717-334-3141; www.civilwarhead quarters.com), 401 Buford Avenue. Open 9–5 mid-March through November; $3 adults. Located near McPherson Ridge, this tiny stone house was the home of Gettysburg resident Mary Thompson and the impromptu headquarters of Confederate General Robert E. Lee. It has a surprisingly large collection of Union and Confederate artifacts, uniforms, and newspaper clippings.

LEE'S HEADQUARTERS

Gettysburg Diorama (717-334-6408; www.gettysburgdiorama .com), 241 Steinwehr Avenue; $5.50 adults, $3 kids. This 800-foot miniature re-creation of the 1863

battle moved from Artillery Ridge Campground to the centrally located Gettysburg History Center in 2010. It's a good prop to help kids understand the logistics of the battle or just to see before setting out to tour the actual battlefield.

OUTSIDE THE NEW GETTYSBURG VISITORS CENTER

MUSEUMS T Shriver House Museum (717-337-2800), 308 Baltimore Street. Open daily April through November, weekends only March; closed January and February. Adults $7.95; kids 12 and under $6. If I had time to hit just one Civil War attraction besides the battlefield, this restored 1860 house would be it. It offers a rare glimpse into civilian life back then, thanks largely to the Shriver family's neighbor, Tillie Pierce, who kept a detailed diary of their experiences. The 30-minute tour, led by a costumed guide, includes a look at the bullet-riddled attic that was taken over by Confederate sharpshooters and the basement saloon of George Washington Shriver, who died before he could open it. The museum hosts a reenactment of Confederate soldiers occupying the home, which occurs annually during the anniversary weekend of the Battle at Gettysburg.

T **Rupp House History Center** (717-334-7292; www.gettysburgfoundation .org), 451 Baltimore Street. Open daily June through August, weekends only April, May, September, and October. Free. Another favorite Civil War attraction in the heart of downtown and a good place to stop before heading to the battlefield. It operated as a tannery during the battle, then later as a B&B until the nonprofit Friends of the National Parks of Gettysburg bought it in 2001 and turned the first floor into three rooms of interactive exhibits that use sight, sound, touch, and smell to show what life was like for civilians and soldiers of the time. You can build your own monument, carry the pack of a Civil War soldier, and take part in scavenger hunts and computer games, all designed to make the scope of the Civil War easy for anyone to digest.

T **Jennie Wade House** (717-334-4100; www.jennie-wade-house.com), 548 Baltimore Street; $7.50 adults; $3.50 ages 6–12. Jennie Wade was the only civilian killed during the Battle of Gettysburg, and it happened in this unassuming brick home near the Dobbin House. A stray bullet struck the 20-year-old while she was baking biscuits for Union soldiers.

Gettysburg National Military Park (717-334-1124; www.nps.gov/gett). Park open 6 AM–10 PM daily April through October, until 7 PM November through March. Visitor center open daily 8 AM–6 PM April through October, until 5 PM November through March.

The Battle of Gettysburg was a crucial and devastating turning point in the Civil War. It ended General Robert E. Lee's most ambitious invasion of the North and was one of the war's bloodiest battles. Managed by the National Park Service since 1933, the battlefield where it all happened is the town's marquee attraction and should not be missed, no matter how short your stay.

In 2008, a bold and expanded new **Visitor Center** opened just outside the battlefield boundaries at 1195 Baltimore Pike, 0.6 mile away from the old Taneytown Road center. Modeled after a 19th-century barn, it is an excellent place to start your tour. You'll find a bookstore, large dining area, a 20-minute film narrated by Morgan Freeman, and a museum with a dozen galleries devoted to each day of the 1863 battle. There's also the 377-foot **Gettysburg *Cyclorama,*** Paul Phillipoteaux's iconic 1884 painting of the battle that was restored to its original format and painstakingly moved to the new center in 2008. Unlike many other national parks, there is no cost or Golden Eagle pass required to visit the battlefield or visitor center, but there is a charge for the film, museum, and *Cyclorama* ($10.50 adults, $6.50 ages 6–18). Tickets may be purchased online or at the visitor center. You may also buy tickets for the **David Wills** house here.

From the visitor center, many people choose to drive around the battlefield with the help of a self-guided map. Allow two to three hours or up to an entire day to cover all the monuments and key cannonade sites. Here are several other ways to view the battlefield:

By guided walking tour. They cover only a fraction of the field, but these free walks by knowledgeable guides are one of the best deals around. Mid-June through mid-August, the National Park Service offers more than 15 different themed walks across sections of the battlefield, lasting from 30 minutes to three hours. There is no need for reservations; just show up at the visitor center and join one. The walks are also offered occasionally in spring and fall.

By car with a licensed battlefield guide. This is a favorite choice of battlefield veterans. For $55 for one to six people, a rigorously trained

GETTYSBURG BATTLEFIELD

Civil War buff will drive your car around the battlefield for two hours and vividly recount the battle with facts and anecdotes. Guides are available daily at the park's visitor center on a first-come, first-served basis. During busy times of the year, the tours often sell out before noon. Reservations may be made up to seven days in advance, but it will cost an extra $15. Call 877-874-2478 for more information.

By car with audiocassette. At a cost of $10–15, you can buy or rent a cassette or CD from the visitor center, the Civil War Museum, and many shops around town (B&Bs also often keep some on hand for guests) and follow along as the voice guides you past important monuments and highlights of the battle.

By bus with a tour guide. These tours operate six times a day in summer (less often in spring and fall) and leave from the visitor center. A licensed battlefield guide leads the two-hour rides past all major monuments. $28 adults, $17 ages 6–12.

Other options for touring the battlefield include by guided horse or bicycle, or by hiking several trails that wind through the battlefield (see Outdoor Activities).

The self-guided tour begins in the kitchen where Wade was struck, and recounts the scene through a talking mannequin dressed like the Confederate soldier. It's a popular stop for ghost lovers.

☂ **Battle Theater** (717-334-6100), 571 Steinwehr Avenue; $6.95 adults. Call ahead to find out when local actor James A. Getty's spot-on portrayal of Abraham Lincoln is on the schedule. On other days, the theater runs a 30-minute multimedia show on the Battle of Gettysburg.

𝒮 ☂ **Lincoln Train Museum** (717-334-5678), 571 Steinwehr Avenue. Closed December, January, and February; $7.50 adults, $3.50 ages 4–11. A narrow hallway lined with shadow boxes tells the story of the railroad's importance in Gettysburg, then gives way to a room filled with a jaw-dropping display of more than a thousand miniature trains and real train whistles. Admission includes a 15-minute simulated train ride that reenacts Lincoln's famous 1863 trip from Washington, D.C., to Gettysburg.

☂ **American Civil War Museum** (717-334-6245; www.gettysburgmuseum .com), 297 Steinwehr Avenue. Open daily March through December, weekends in January and February; $5.50 adults; $2.50 ages 6–12. It's a bit shopworn, but the five hallways of life-size dioramas offer an easy-to-follow approach to the war's precursors and strategies behind the three-day battle. The gift shop has one of the best selections of Civil War books around.

✸ To Do

FOR FAMILIES 𝒮 **Explore and More Children's Museum** (717-337-1951; exploreandmore.com), 20 E. High Street. Closed Wednesday; $4 adults; $6 ages 2–14. When the kids are melting down at the prospect of another battlefield tour, take them here. The preschool teachers who created this play space for the under-8 set managed to squeeze in plenty of history lessons amid the train tables and building blocks. Kids can dress up as Civil War–era shopkeepers in the 1860s room, wash clothes on scrubbing boards, and step inside a giant bubble. It's housed in an 1860s brick home a few blocks from the square. Down side: there's not much for adults to do, except supervise the kids.

𝒮 **Land of Little Horses** (717-334-7259; www.landoflittlehorses.com), 125 Glenwood Drive. Open daily April through August; weekends only September and October; $12 adults and children 2 and older. This farm park north of town stages several daily performances by trained Falabella miniature horses from Argentina in an enclosed arena. Kids of all ages will love the clever shows, which also star a posse of Jack Russell terriers, plus miniature donkeys, cows, and sheep. Call ahead for show times and a schedule of special events, such as petting time with the animals and hands-on activities such as goat milking and horse grooming.

APPLES AND WINE

The ever-efficient Shakers believed the circle to be the most perfect shape because "the devil couldn't trap you in the corner." With this in mind, farmers built dozens of round barns in the late 18th and early 19th century. Only a few remain in the country today, and one of them is 8 miles outside Gettysburg. The **Historic Round Barn** and **Farm Market** (717-334-1984; 298 Cashtown Road, Biglerville) makes a nice respite from the in-town traffic and battlefield tours. The ground-floor farm market sells seasonal apples and peaches at fair prices, plus a wide selection of jams, soup mixes, and other giftable items. Be sure to climb the stairs to the second floor to gape at the huge spoked ceiling—built without machines by a local family in 1914. There's also a small petting farm with goats and donkeys, and there are seasonal events such as haunted barn tours on Friday and Saturday through October.

Just down the road from the barn is **Hauser Estate Winery** (717-334-4888; 410 Cashtown Road), whose magnificent hilltop views alone are worth a visit. Besides red and white wines, the Hauser Estate also makes several kinds of tasty hard ciders (a nod to the property's apple orchard history). Tastings are $2 per flight (or $1 per taste for premiums), and there are regular events such as weekday happy hours and live concerts.

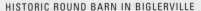

HISTORIC ROUND BARN IN BIGLERVILLE

SCENIC DRIVE The countryside surrounding the town of Gettysburg is lush with apple orchards, vineyards, and family farms. It's worth setting aside a few hours to explore it during your visit. One option is to take US 30 west (Cashtown Road) to the **Historic Round Barn** and **Farm Market** in Biglerville, followed by a stop at the scenic tasting room of **Hauser Estate Winery.**

✳ Outdoor Activities

BICYCLING Bikes are permitted on all paved roads within the battlefield; it's a great way to combine exercise with history lessons.

GettysBikes (717-752-7752; www.gettsybike.com), rents bikes for $10 an hour or $30 per day (cash only). It also offers three-hour battlefield tours led by licensed guides. Reservations recommended.

Gettysburg Bike and Fitness (717-334-7791), 307 York Street, rents bikes for $10 an hour or $30 a day. Reserve ahead on weekends. Closed Sunday.

GOLF Carroll Valley Golf Course (717-642-8282; www.libertymountain resort.com). A clear stream fronts a third of the 18 holes at this championship par-71 course.

The Links at Gettysburg (717-359-8000; www.thelinksatgettysburg.com), 601 Mason Dixon Road. Rated one of the top 10 public courses in Pennsylvania by *Golfweek,* this 18-hole course plays 6,979 yards from the tips, with a 73.9 rating and 140 slope.

Mulligan MacDuffer Adventure Golf (717-337-1518), 1360 Baltimore Street, has 36 holes of mini-golf spread over two courses.

Quail Valley Golf Course (717-359-8453), 901 Teeter Road, Littlestown, has 18 holes to 7,042 yards from the longest tees, with a par of 72 and a slope rating of 123.

HORSEBACK RIDING Artillery Ridge Campground (717-334-1288; 610 Taneytown Road) offers one- and two-hour guided tours by horseback of the battlefield starting at $40 a person. It's especially nice in spring when the dogwood and redbud are blooming or during fall foliage season.

SKIING Liberty Mountain Ski Resort (717-642-8282; www.skiliberty .com), 78 Country Club Trail, Carroll Valley. Ski trails, terrain parks, and snow tubing during the winter. It's about 10 miles south of Gettysburg.

✳ Green Space

Pine Grove Furnace State Park (717-486-7174), 1100 Pine Grove Road, Gardners. Once the site of an iron furnace that made Revolutionary

War-era kettles, stoves, and munitions, this 696-acre state park north of Gettysburg is now home to two man-made lakes (Laurel and Fuller), primitive camp sites, picnic areas, and several miles of easy hiking trails. Swimming and fishing are allowed in both lakes; limited boating is allowed on Laurel. You can also access the Appalachian Trail here. Stop at the visitor center on Pine Grove Road for a map and info on overnight parking.

Strawberry Hill Nature Center and Preserve (717-642-5840; www .strawberryhill.org), 1537 Mount Hope Road, Fairfield. This 609-acre preserve about 8 miles west of town has three ponds, 10 miles of easy to moderate trails, picnic tables, and a nature center with hands-on wildlife and plant displays. Wildflowers cover the grounds in spring; great blue herons, great horned owls, wild turkeys, and other birds have been spotted here year-round.

✳ Lodging

Expect to pay state and local room taxes of 9 percent on top of regular hotel rates.

HOTELS ქ Historic Gettysburg Hotel (717-337-2000; www.hotel gettysburg.com), 1 Lincoln Square. You can't beat the prime location or the guest list of this historic 1797 hotel: Carl Sandburg, Ulysses S. Grant, and Henry Ford are some of the VIPs who have stayed here. Now a Best Western, it has the efficient vibe of a business hotel with family-friendly amenities such as an outdoor pool and babysitting services. Many of the rooms and suites have Jacuzzis and fireplaces; the ones that face the square can be noisy. The Town Trolley stops out front. Rooms $145–220.

ქ **James Gettys Hotel** (888-900-5275; www.jamesgettyshotel.com), 27 Chambersburg Street. This upscale 11-room inn is named after the town's founder and operated as a hotel before and after the 1863 battle. Centrally located a block west of Lincoln Square, it was restored to 1920s-style splendor in the 1990s and is known for its attention to detail. All rooms have full or queen beds and private baths, and feature Egyptian cotton linens and luxury toiletries. Expect some traffic noise in the front-facing rooms. A breakfast of pastries and orange juice is delivered daily to each room. Ask about special rates and packages if you're staying off-season. Rooms $140–185; the Majestic suite is $250.

The Lodges at Gettysburg (877-607-2442 or 717-642-2500; www .gettysburgaccommodations.com), 685 Camp Gettysburg Road. Spacious new luxury cabins dot a quiet hillside southwest of town. It's a peaceful place to escape to after a day of sightseeing, and the view of the battlefield from many of the rooms is unmatched. Flat-screen TVs, WiFi, and iPod docking stations are just a few of the hi-tech amenities. The property also includes a pretty lake and covered bridge. The rate includes a breakfast of pastries, fruit, juice, and coffee. Studios with one or two queen or king beds are $125–165; two-bedroom suites with a full kitchen and living area start at $300.

Comfort Suites (717-334-6715; www.gettysburgcomfortsuites.com), 945 Baltimore Pike. The closest hotel to the park's new visitor center opened in 2009 with 70 suites with mini-fridges, flat-screen TVs, and living areas. Some of the rooms overlook a private cemetery. Amenities include Continental breakfast and an indoor pool.

🐾 🐾 1863 Inn of Gettysburg (717-334-6211; www.1863innof gettysburg.com), 516 Baltimore Street. If you want to stay in the thick of tourist action, this former Holiday Inn is a good choice. It's a mile from the visitor center and within walking distance of the Jennie Wade House and many other attractions. The clean and attractive rooms have two double beds or one queen or king bed with Jacuzzi tubs, and all have exterior entrances; request one in the back for the quietest experience. Pets are allowed in most rooms for an extra fee. Rooms $168–215, includes breakfast.

BED & BREAKFASTS

Baladerry Inn (717-337-1342; www.baladerryinn.com), 40 Hospital Road. This elegant inn on 4 acres at the southeast edge of the battlefield will appeal to visitors looking for a peaceful escape at the end of a day of sightseeing. There are 10 attractive rooms, 5 in the main house and 5 in a separate carriage house (including a large suite that sleeps four). Elaborate breakfasts are served in a large dining area next to a wood fireplace. Owner Suzanne Lonky will share stories about the inn's history of ghost sightings if you ask. Rooms $124–172; two-room suite $208–238.

🐾 Battlefield Bed and Breakfast Inn (717-334-8804; www .gettysburgbattlefield.com), 2264 Emmitsburg Road. Civil War buffs love this comfortable 1809 farmhouse at the southern edge of the park. The eight rooms and suites are attractive and comfortable and the surrounding 30 acres bucolic, but it might be the daily history-themed breakfasts that make this a true standout. Mornings begin at 8 with an animated lecture by a Civil War expert, and are followed by a lavish breakfast of fresh fruit and frittatas, French toast, or crepes. Homemade cookies are served in the afternoon. Kids and dogs are allowed, with some restrictions. There are also ghost stories on Friday nights and a kid-friendly menagerie of goats, sheep, horses, and donkeys on premise. Rates $175–235.

Brickhouse Inn (717-338-9337; www.brickhouseinn.com), 452 Baltimore Street. This charming three-story Victorian inn has 13 rooms and suites, a manicured garden with a koi pond, and a downtown location within walking distance of the military park's visitor center. Five of the rooms are located next door in the Welty House, a restored 1830 home that stood in the battle's firing line and still bears the scars. All rooms have queen beds, original wood floors, and satellite TV; a multi-course breakfast that may include shoofly pie is served on the patio during warm weather. The Kentucky Suite, with its private porch, skylight, and claw-foot tub, is a favorite; value seekers will want to book the cozy Virginia Room. No children under 10. Rooms $99–189.

✿ **Doubleday Inn** (717-334-9119; www.doubledayinn.com), 104 Doubleday Avenue. This quiet house near Gettysburg College is located in a small neighborhood on the actual battlefield at Oak Ridge. Owners Todd and Christine Thomas were veteran Gettysburg tourists before buying the place in 2006 and are happy to share their insider knowledge of the area with guests. Many of the comfortable rooms have splendid views of the battlefield, and breakfasts are ample and delicious (caramel French toast is a specialty). A licensed battlefield guide runs a Q&A from the living room on most Wednesday and Saturday evenings. No children under 13. Rooms $135–195.

⅚ **Farnsworth House Inn** (717-334-8838; www.farnsworthhouse inn.com), 401 Baltimore Street. Named after a brigadier general, this Victorian inn revels in its status as one of the most haunted inns in America, hosting regular candlelight walks and other ghost-related events. Confederate sharpshooters took shelter here during the battle; the south wall is riddled with bullet holes, and one of the men is believed to have shot Jennie Wade (see Museums). Despite its central location, inside is relatively quiet with common areas that include a trellised back garden and enclosed second-story porch; there's also a restaurant and tavern on premises (see Dining Out). Each of the nine rooms has a private bath and antique furnishings; some have TVs and Jacuzzis. Rooms in the main house are on the small side and more susceptible to street noise than the ones off the back garden. No kids under 16. Rooms $145–175, including breakfast served by costumed employees, with a two-night minimum on weekends.

Nearby
Fairfield Inn (717-642-5410 or 334-8868; www.thefairfieldinn .com), 15 W. Main Street, Fairfield. Veteran Gettysburg B&B owners Sal and Joan Chandon bought this 18th-century inn in 2002 and spent the next few years restoring the six rooms and common areas. A 2007 episode of HGTV's *If Walls Could Talk* chronicled its rich history as a field hospital for Confederate soldiers and a stop on the Underground Railroad. The antiques-filled rooms have private baths with whirlpool or claw-foot tubs;

there's also a suite that sleeps four on the third floor, with a private balcony. The Squires Miller tavern is one of the coziest places you will ever raise a glass; there's also a full restaurant; ask about special deals for inn guests. Rooms $130–150; suite $225.

MOTELS & COTTAGES

&. ⚘ **Quality Inn** (717-334-3141; www.gettysburgusa.com), 401 Buford Avenue. There are probably more chain motels in and around Gettysburg than there are walls with bullet holes in them, but this one stands out for its family-friendly amenities, reasonable rates, and central location next to General Lee's Headquarters. It has 41 standard rooms that ring a large swimming pool and 7 large suites that sleep four to six. Rates include admission to Lee's Headquarters and continental breakfast. Rooms $79–124, suites $129–200.

⚘ **Cricket House** (717-891-0607; www.crickethouseatgettysburg .com), 162 E. Middle Street. The quiet neighborhood and gorgeous interior of this two-story carriage house are almost enough to make you want to skip the sightseeing and hang out here for your entire stay. Owner Deb Wills Gemmell has created a wonderful retreat that also happens to be within walking distance of many downtown restaurants and attractions; she is also happy to share her considerable knowledge and tips about the area. The house includes two bedrooms, a living

room with a double futon, full kitchen, three TVs, and a washer/ dryer. There's even a covered Jacuzzi in the enclosed back garden. $175–195 daily.

CAMPGROUNDS Artillery Ridge Camping Resort (717-334-1288; www.artilleryridge.com), 610 Taneytown Road. Open daily April through October, weekends in November. This campground and equestrian center near the southern edge of the battlefield has more than 40 tent sites and several air-conditioned one-room cabins that sleep up to four. It's also home to the Gettysburg Battlefield Diorama, a popular attraction on its own. Tents $35–45; cabins $65–85.

Granite Hill Camping Resort (717-642-8749; www.granitehill campingresort.com), 3340 Fairfield Road. Open April through November. The site of an annual bluegrass festival and Gettysburg's annual bike week, this scenic property about 8 miles south of town has 300 sites for tents and RVs, plus 5 two-room cabins and a small B&B inn with four rooms ($125 a night). It also has a swimming pool, fishing pond, tennis courts, four playgrounds, and a packed activity schedule. Tent sites $33–43; cabins $70–80.

Round Top Campground (717-334-9565; www.roundtopcamp .com), 180 Knight Road. One of the few campgrounds open year-round, it has 200 sites with full hookups and 60 sites with water and electricity. The campground also rents basic air-conditioned cabins and cottages. It also has a swimming pool, mini-golf course, and tennis court. Tents $25–55; cabins $62–72; cottages $89–165.

✳ Where to Eat

DINING OUT ⟨♿⟩ ⟨Ⲩ⟩ **Dobbin House** (717-334-2100; www.dobbinhouse.com), 89 Steinwehr Avenue. Dinner daily. The dining rooms can get quite loud, especially when bus tours descend upon the place, but this painstakingly restored Colonial-era house has its charms. Its owner, Reverend Alexander Dobbin, built the house in the 1770s and its original stone walls and other nifty details remain; the basement was once a station for runaway slaves. Today, waiters dress in period breeches, bonnets, and petticoats, and some authentic 18th-century dishes such as Hunter's chicken and William Penn's broiled pork tenderloin in an "outſtanding raſpberry sauce" are on the menu. For a more casual and intimate experience, head downstairs to the Springhouse Tavern, where the meals are lighter (and cheaper) and the stone walls, roaring fireplaces, and well-stocked bar invite lingering. Reservations are recommended for the restaurant. Tavern dishes $6–20; dinner entrées $20–36.

⟨♿⟩ ⟨Ⲩ⟩ **Farnsworth House** (717-334-8838; www.farnsworthhouseinn.com), 401 Baltimore Street. Breakfast and dinner daily. Expect to be surrounded by Civil War–era paintings, photographs, and antiques when you dine in the candlelit rooms of one of Gettysburg's legendary haunted homes. The house specialty is game pie, a rich casserole of turkey, pheasant,

DOBBIN HOUSE

and duck. Other menu highlights: peanut soup, Yankee pot roast, and sweet potato pudding; children may be placated with macaroni and cheese or chicken tenders. This unique Gettysburg experience should not be missed. A tavern menu is available in the outdoor garden. Dinner entrées $16–27.

&. Ÿ **Herr Tavern and Publick House** (717-334-4332; www .herrtavern.com), 900 Chambersburg Road. Open for lunch Wednesday through Saturday, dinner daily. This historic prewar building has been a tavern, an Underground Railroad stop, and a temporary Confederate hospital; today, it's a small inn and restaurant known for its superb food and service. The lunch menu includes salads, sandwiches, and a few hot entrées such as Parmesan chicken

and shrimp and scallop risotto. A specialty (served weekends only) is prime rib marinated in herbs and slow roasted in applewood bacon; also delicious is the pickled watermelon and tomato gazpacho, and oyster mushroom ravioli with goat cheese and pine nuts. Its high-ceilinged dining rooms overlook Herrs Ridge, where Union General John Buford's cavalry camped the night before the Battle of Gettysburg. Reservations recommended. Extensive wine list. Lunch $9–14, dinner entrées $24–33.

Nearby

Ÿ **Cashtown Inn** (717-334-9722; www.cashtowninnn.com), 1325 Old US 30, Cashtown. Open for lunch and dinner Tuesday through Saturday. This small 18th-century inn west of town provides a nice

---

HAUNTED GETTYSBURG

With more than 50,000 casualties, it's no surprise that ghosts and spirits have been sighted and felt all over Gettysburg. From May through November, you'll stumble upon more than a dozen nightly ghost tours offered in or around downtown. Most run twice nightly and last between one and two hours; kids under age seven are often free. Keep in mind that the tours that center around Baltimore Street can get traffic and pedestrian noise. For storytelling at its most macabre, try the Farnsworth House's **Civil War Mourning Theater** (717-334-8838; www .farnsworthhouseinn.com). **Ghosts of Gettysburg** (717-337-0445; www .ghostsofgettysburg.com) offers several popular walking and bus tours that are based on Mark Nesbitt's best-selling book series *Ghosts of Gettysburg.* The Seminary Ridge and Carlisle Street walking tours are favorites.

escape, either overnight or for a couple of hours, from the downtown Gettysburg crowds. It served as headquarters for the Confederate General A. P. Hill and was featured in the film, *Gettysburg.* Jack and Maria Paladino took over in 2006 and spruced up the dining rooms, tavern, and parlor; they also operate a B&B upstairs. The innovative American menu includes salt-and-pepper-crusted New York strip, pecan chicken in a maple-cream sauce, crab cakes with sesame-rice pilaf and baby spinach, pork medallions with butternut-squash risotto, and an applewood bacon and onion-cider sauce. Reservations are recommended for dinner. Lunch $7–10; dinner entrées $20–26.

EATING OUT ♿ ⛾ **Spiritfields** (717-334-9449), 619 Baltimore Street. Open daily for lunch and dinner. This charismatic Irish pub near the Jennie Wade House is known for its brisket dishes and tasty sangria. Dishes $7–22.

♿ **Dunlap's Restaurant and Bakery** (717-334-4816; www.dunlapsrestaurant.com), 90 Buford Avenue. Open daily for breakfast, lunch, and dinner. This family-owned diner near the north end of the battlefield is the perfect place for an inexpensive sit-down meal. Its wide-ranging menu includes filet mignon, honey-dipped fried chicken, and Maryland crab cakes; they also have daily specials like prime rib, and a Friday night fish fry for $8. For breakfast, there are omelets,

hotcakes, and six different kinds of Danish. Save room for dessert. Breakfast $2–5, lunch and dinner $4–15.

♠ **Ernie's Texas Lunch** (717-334-1970), 58 Chambersburg Street. Breakfast, lunch, and dinner daily. This always-crowded spot off Lincoln Square serves the best hot dogs in town. Try the lunch special of two chili cheese dogs or two hamburgers and a soda for $5.

Lincoln Diner (717-334-3900), 32 Carlisle Street. This 24-hour diner near the center of town is popular for breakfast and has an

THE LINCOLN DINER AT DUSK

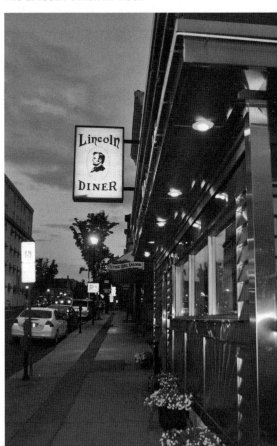

everything-but-the-kitchen-sink menu and wonderful baked desserts. Cash only. Dishes $2–15.

🍴 **Montezuma Mexican Restaurant** (717-334-7750), 225 Buford Avenue (US 30). You'll find tasty fajitas, carnitas, and chile rellenos in this unassuming building west of town. The $4.95 weekday lunch special is a great deal.

♿ **General Pickett's Buffets** (717-334-7580; www.general picketsbuffets.com), 571 Steinwehr Avenue. Lunch and dinner daily. Located next to the field where Confederate General George Pickett led his infamous doomed charge, this all-you-can-eat buffet elicits mixed reactions from those who have tried it. Its central location in the basement of the Battle Theater makes it very popular with bus tours; some say the food suffers as a result. It's tough to beat the price, though— $11 ($7 at lunch) for a huge soup and salad bar, hot entrées such as roast beef, fried catfish, and baked chicken, and desserts.

The Pike (717-334-9227; thepike restaurant.com), 985 Baltimore Pike. The closest restaurant to the park's main entrance caters to big appetites and frugal wallets. Monday means all-you-can-eat spaghetti for $6.25, Thursday is 40-cent wing night, you get the picture. Sports is on the TV and beer specials are plentiful. There's an inexpensive breakfast buffet Monday through Saturday and brunch Sunday. Entrées $8–20.

Pub on the Square (717-334-7100; www.the-pub.com), 20–22 Lincoln Square. One of the few places in town that serves dinner until 10 PM (11 PM Friday and Saturday). If the dining room overlooking the square is packed, head to the friendly tin-ceilinged pub next door and order off the main menu. There are huge sandwiches, salads, steak and pasta entrées, and tasty appetizers like soft pretzel nuggets with dipping sauce. You can't go wrong with most items, but the Ritz cracker-crusted Mahi Mahi and sweet-potato waffle fries come highly recommended. Dishes $14–26.

CAFÉS & BAKERIES Ragged Edge (717-334-4464; www.ragged edgehs.com), 110 Chambersburg Street. This hip art-filled coffeehouse has indoor and outdoor seating, a light breakfast and lunch menu, and a stay-as-long-as-you-like vibe. It's open until 10 PM on Friday and Saturday, until 8 PM the rest of the week. Dishes $4–7.

Cannonball Malt Shop (717-334-9695), 11 York Street. The small but comfortable, old-fashioned shop on Lincoln Square offers superb ice cream, malts, and handmade phosphate sodas, plus a selection of burgers and sandwiches. Dishes $2–5.

Hunt's Café (717-334-4787), 61 Steinwehr Avenue. This small eatery and souvenir shop is known for its hand-cut Battlefield Fries (a twist on the Jersey Shore's Boardwalk Fries), cheesesteaks, and hand-dipped ice cream. Dishes $2–8.

✷ Entertainment

Much of Gettysburg's entertainment revolves around the battlefield; one of the most popular evening activities is the ghost tour (See Haunted Gettysburg). Several convivial watering holes, including the **Pub on the Square** (717-334-7100; 20 Lincoln Square) and **Blue Parrot Bistro** (717-337-3739; 35 Chambersburg Street), stay open late on weekends.

THEATER & FILM ♿ **Majestic Theater Performing Arts and Cultural Center** (717-337-8200; www.gettysburgmajestic.org), 29 Carlisle Street. Built in 1925, this gorgeous 850-seat theater was restored in 2005 and hosts live performances of everything from musical groups to plays and quiz shows. It also has a two-screen cinema showing art films.

♿ **Gettysburg Gateway Complex** (717-334-5577; gateway gettysburg.com), US 30 and US 15, shows first-run films, plus the 30-minute film *Fields of Freedom,* based on the discovered diaries of two soldiers, one Union and one Confederate. Call for show times.

✷ Selective Shopping

All stores are downtown Gettysburg unless otherwise noted. Many of the shops stay open later in the summer. The **Outlet Shoppes at Gettysburg** (717-

337-0091; 1863 Gettysburg Village Drive), a large complex whose stores include Bass, Naturalizer, Gap, Harry and David, and Tommy Hilfiger, is conveniently located down the road from the park's new visitor center. It also has a 10-screen movie theater.

CIVIL WAR GOODS Abraham's Lady (717-338-1798), 25 Steinwehr Avenue. Browse for Civil War–era dresses, corsets, and ankle boots. There's also a nice selection of 1860s-style jewelry, hair nets, and men's civilian vests. Dressmakers are usually on hand to do custom fits.

Stoneham's Armory (717-337-2347), 5 Steinwehr Avenue. This small shop is known for its collection of reproduction and replica guns.

Horse Soldier (717-334-0347), 777 Baltimore Street. Home to one of the largest collections of military antiques around, with items dating from the Revolutionary War through World War II. The emphasis, of course, is on the Civil War, and the shop guarantees that all its inventory, from firearms to discharge papers, is genuine. It also offers a genealogical research service that will help search for an ancestor's war records.

Regimental Quartermaster and Jeweler's Daughter (717-338-1864; 717-338-0770), 49 Steinwehr Avenue. These two shops share a roof and, as the name implies, target Civil War buffs of both genders. On one side, there are bayonets and scabbards, carpet bags, first-aid kits, and an impressive selection of civilian and soldier hats; on the other, you'll find a huge collection of reproduction Victorian jewelry, from earrings and necklaces to pocket watches and hair ornaments.

GIFT SHOPS AND GALLERIES

Antiques, Apples, and Art (717-339-0017; www.170nthesquare.com), 17 Lincoln Square. Just as the name implies, this multivendor shop captures three of Gettysburg's staples: Civil War–era antiques, apple-related items to celebrate the nearby orchards, and local crafts.

Gallery 30 (717-334-0335; www.gallery30.com), 30 York Street. A thoughtful selection of current books shares space with hand-carved duck decoys, unique jewelry, and paintings and sculpture by local artists.

✳ Special Events

May: **Apple Blossom Festival** (first weekend), South Mountain Fairgrounds, Arendtsville—some locals prefer this lesser-known event to the popular harvest festival in September.

July: **Annual Civil War Battle Reenactment** (first weekend), Table Rock Road, north of town.

Costumed volunteers commemorate the famous battle with faux rifles and swords at this three-day ticketed spectator event. For more information, go to www.gettysburgreenactment.com. A week later motorcycles from all over the country roar into town for **Gettysburg Bike Week** (800-374-7540; www.gettysburgbikeweek.com), three days of live music, fireworks, tattoo contests, and a "chrome parade."

August: **Civil War Music Muster** (last weekend), Gettysburg National Military Park—brass bands, fife and drum groups, and individuals bring to life the band and parlor music of the Civil War period.

October: **National Apple Harvest Festival** (first two weekends), Arendtsville—a popular country gathering of food, music, crafts, and pony rides that seems to get bigger each year. The food alone (pumpkin funnel cake, caramel apples, sweet potato fries) is worth the trip.

November: **Remembrance Day** (third weekend)—this solemn event begins with a parade of living history and reenactment groups through town to the battlefield, is followed by the placement of candles at each Civil War grave, and ends with a recitation of Lincoln's *Gettysburg Address*.

YORK COUNTY

Y ork County likes to call itself the snack capital of the world. Spend some time here and you will find this to be a reasonable conclusion. Potato chips, candy, ice cream, and pretzels are all made in the small towns and rural countryside that make up this county of more than 200,000. So are Pfaltzgraff pottery, Bluett Bros. violins, and the bulk of Harley-Davidson's Touring and Softail motorcycles.

Situated between Gettysburg and Amish Country, the region often gets squeezed out by its two more famous neighbors. The pace is a little slower here, the prices a little lower—it feels more like a 9-to-5 kind of place than a tourism destination. This is not to say that the region lacks history or amenities. You will find real farmers' markets, homey B&Bs, and free hands-on tours of Harley-Davidson, Utz Potato Chips, and a dozen other factories and farms. You will leave with a strengthened respect for chocolate-covered pretzels and high-butterfat ice cream.

The small city of York, which anchors the county, was founded in 1741 and named for the English city of the same name. It served as the temporary capital of the Continental Congress during the Revolutionary War. The Articles of Confederation were drafted here in 1777. Several original 18th-century buildings are open for tours downtown, which also features many other Colonial-era buildings, Gothic Revival churches, and wide sidewalks.

About 20 miles to the west sits Hanover, the county's second-largest city and the site of a small but significant Civil War battle. Though small hotels, big-box stores, and franchise food operations are prevalent along the main drag, its town center remains attractive, anchored by a large square and surrounded by historic well-kept homes and churches.

Surrounding York and Hanover are miles of rolling countryside, several golf courses, and small towns with mom-and-pop antiques shops, farm stands, and ice cream stands.

AREA CODE All towns in York County fall under the 717 area code.

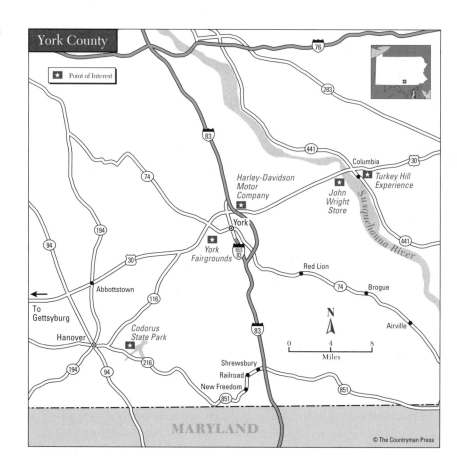

GUIDANCE **York County Convention & Visitor Bureau** (717-852-9675; 1-888-858-9675; www.yorkcountypa.org) has a large welcome center at 149 W. Market Street next to the Plough Tavern. It also operates a small one at the **Harley-Davidson plant** (717-852-6006; 1425 Eden Road) just off US 30. In Hanover, stop by the **Guthrie Memorial Library** (717-632-5183; 301 Carlisle Street) for maps and brochures.

GETTING THERE By air: **Harrisburg International Airport** (888-235-9442) is 30 miles north of downtown York.

By car: US 30 south from Lancaster; I-83 from Harrisburg and Maryland.

By bus: **Greyhound** (800-231-2222) and **Rabbit Transit** (717-846-7743) offer regular service between York and Harrisburg. **Capitol Trailways** has service through Lancaster to Philadelphia and New York.

GETTING AROUND Downtown York is walkable, especially the area around Market and George Streets, but you will need a car to get to most of the factories, including Harley-Davidson and Hope Acres. **Rabbit Transit** operates bus routes in the city and surrounding area.

WHEN TO GO Fall is particularly scenic in this rural part of the state, but most of the factories and museums here are open for tours year-round. Keep in mind that many of the factories aren't air-conditioned, and some, like Susquehanna Glass, close down when temperatures surpass 90 degrees.

MEDICAL EMERGENCY York Hospital (717-851-3500), 1001 S. George Street. About 30 miles to the southwest is **Hanover Hospital** (717-637-3711), 300 Highland Avenue, Hanover.

✳ Villages

Railroad. This tiny town of 300 people near the Maryland border is home to the Jackson House B&B, a popular crab shack, and not much else. It takes its name from the century-old North Central Railroad that passes through town on its way to and from Baltimore and York.

Red Lion. About 5 miles outside York, Red Lion is a quaint town of antiques shops, a B&B, and a few restaurants, and serves as a sort of gateway to the rural countryside east of York. Founded in 1880, it is named after one of its first taverns and was once a major manufacturer of cigars (to this day, the town raises a giant cigar on New Year's Eve, instead of the traditional ball). Also found near Red Lion is Family Heirloom Weavers, a small weaving factory that specializes in Civil War–era clothes.

Wrightsville. Named for one of the area's early settlers, John Wright, this sleepy town on the Susquehanna River is a pleasant place to stop if you're on your way to York from Lancaster or Philadelphia. It was once home to one of the longest covered bridges in the country, which unfortunately was burned during the Civil War to stop the eastern advance of Lee's army. A diorama, housed in a former barber shop, tells the story of the bridge and Wrightsville's role in the Civil War. Today, John Wright cast-iron products are made here and sold in a nearby warehouse. The Susquehanna Glass factory is right across the river in Columbia.

✳ To See

MUSEUMS & HISTORIC SITES Colonial Complex (717-845-2951; www.yorkheritage.org), 157 W. Market Street, York. Open Tuesday through Saturday, April through mid-December; $10 adults, $5 ages 12 and up. This complex of historic buildings includes a 19th-century log cabin, a tavern, and a replica of the Colonial courthouse where the Continental Congress met in 1777 and 1778. Don't miss the half-timbered Plough Tavern, where a plan to overthrow General Washington was derailed in 1778 by the visiting Marquis de Lafayette. A statue of Lafayette, wine glass raised in a toast to Washington, stands in his honor outside the tavern. Call ahead for tour schedules.

✿ ✐ **Indian Steps Museum** (717-862-3948; www.indiansteps.org), 205 Indian Steps Road, Airville (south of Brogue). Open Thursday through Sunday, mid-April through mid-October; free. Eccentric local attorney John Vandersloot built this home on the Susquehanna River for the main purpose of displaying his huge collection of Indian artifacts. More than 10,000 artifacts are embedded in the masonry walls to form Indian patterns, birds, animals, and reptiles. A favorite stop is the kiva, a reproduction of a circular room used by the Hopi Indians for religious assemblies. A second-floor gallery traces the evolution of early Indians who lived by or passed along the nearby Susquehanna River. Outside, there's plenty of open space for kids to run around.

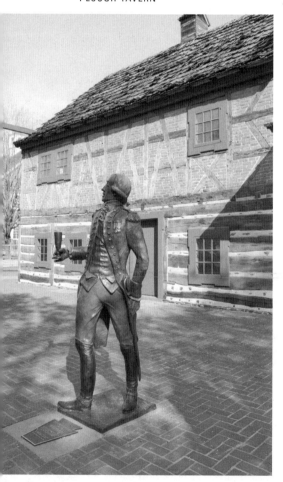

PLOUGH TAVERN

↑ ♿ **U.S.A. Weightlifting Hall of Fame** (717-767-6481), 3300 Board Road, York. Closed Sunday. Look for the giant photo-friendly weightlifter on top of the building as proof you've arrived at **York Barbell Co.** Bob Hoffman, known as the Father of Modern Weightlifting, founded the business in 1932 and it still makes iron dumbbells, kettle bells, and other products in its factory. The first-floor museum is full of vintage barbells and virile statues of Hoffman and other professional bodybuilders. It does a thorough job of tracing the sport's history, from its role in the Olympic games to the accomplishments of famous strongmen such as Charles Atlas, Warren Lincoln Travis, and George Jowett.

✳ To Do

FACTORY TOURS All tours are free unless otherwise noted. Most require advance reservations; it's always a good idea to call ahead as sometimes tours are canceled due to manufacturing schedules or weather.

Bluett Bros. Violins (717-854-9064; www.bluettbros-violins.com), 122 Hill Street, York. Tours Monday and Tuesday, noon–3 PM; $5 per person; no children under 10. Learn how master luthier Mark Bluett makes violins, mandolins, cellos, and other stringed instruments in his exquisitely old-fashioned shop.

Family Heirloom-Weavers (717-246-2431; www.familyheirloomweavers .com), 775 Meadowview Drive, Red Lion. Tours Monday through Friday; reservations required. This family-run weaving factory specializes in Civil War–era clothing and other historically accurate items; it made all the Confederate uniforms for the film *Cold Mountain* and has supplied historic homes belonging to Abraham Lincoln, Mark Twain, and Walt Whitman with ingrain carpets that were popular at the time. Free weekday tours of the small factory, given by founder David Kline, are available and include an up-close look at 40 power-driven looms dating from 1890 to 1980. Leave time to check out the unique gift shop next door; I have a set of woven cotton placemats that have held up beautifully over the years.

Martin's Potato Chips (800-272-4477; www.martinschips.com), 5847 Lincoln Highway (US 30), Thomasville. Tours Tuesday at 9, 10, and 11 AM by reservation only. No tours in April. This family-run chip factory is on the road between York and Gettysburg. The 45-minute guided tours provide an up-close look at the peeling, cutting, and frying process. A small shop sells just about every flavor and type—from kettle-cooked jalapeno to BBQ waffle chips.

Susquehanna Glass (717-684-2155; www.theglassfactory.com), 731 Avenue H, Columbia. Tours Tuesday and Thursday at 10:30 and 1, May through September, and Wednesday and Thursday at 11 and 1, October through April. Reservations required. This century-old glassmaker, located just off US 30 between Lancaster and York, performs etching, silkscreening, and other intricate services for Pottery Barn, Williams-Sonoma, and many other large home-decor companies. A tour lasts about 30 minutes. The gift shop features three floors of heavily discounted glassware, crystal, and crafts.

York County Resource Recovery (717-845-1066; www.ycswa.org), 2700 Blackbridge Road, York. Tours Monday through Friday; call ahead two weeks for reservation. See how tons of solid wastes are converted daily into ash and electricity at this 130-acre facility north of town. Hard-hat tours begin with an orientation talk, and include visits to the tipping floor, where trucks deposit trash into a huge storage pit, and the turbine generator room, where steam produced by the heat of burning garbage is used to produce electricity. It's one of York County's newest tours—fascinating, if not aromatic. No children under 6 are allowed.

Hanover

Revonah Pretzel (717-630-2883), 507 Baltimore Street. This bakery specializes in hand-crafted sourdough pretzels; free 20-minute tours of its

Harley-Davidson Vehicle Operations (414-343-7850; 877-883-1450; www .harley-davidson.com), 1425 Eden Road, York. Tours are first-come, first-served and run 9–2 Monday through Friday; Monday through Saturday in the summer. Children under 12 aren't allowed on the tour. One of four Harley-Davidson plants to give tours (the others are in Wisconsin and Missouri), this plant just off US 30 is home to the company's largest manufacturing facility, covering more than 200 acres and 1.5 million square feet.

The hour-long tours take you right onto the factory floor, where the bikes are being formed, welded, machined, polished, and painted, then to the end of the line, where you can watch them inching along the line by color code on their way to Japan, Australia, and other destinations. The bikers who come from all over to take the tour are just as interesting as the assembly line; their passion for chrome is infectious. Not surprisingly, the gift shop sells plenty of Harley-emblazoned gear, from shot glasses and T-shirts to helmets and heated hand grips.

HARLEY-DAVIDSON COMPANY

small factory are given Tuesday through Thursday from 8–1. Reservations recommended. Don't leave without trying a fresh-baked soft pretzel, or pick up a bag of hard pretzels with flavors such as pumpernickel and onion, honey whole wheat, and roasted garlic.

♥ ▼ **Snyder's of Hanover** (1-800-233-7125), 1350 York Street. Tours 10, 11, and noon Tuesday, Wednesday, and Thursday. Reservations required. You'll see some of the largest pretzel ovens in the world churning out 40 pretzels a second on this hour-long tour that covers the production process of pretzels and potato chips from start to finish. Leave time to shop at the outlet store, where the tours start, which offers great bulk deals on many Snyder's products, plus hard-to-find products like caramel-dipped pretzels.

♥ ▼ **Utz Potato Chips** (717-637-6644), 900 High Street. Tours 8–4 Monday through Thursday. No reservations. Bill and Salie Utz started their company in 1925 in a small summer house behind their Hanover home. Now run by fourth-generation family members, it's still going strong and continues to offer self-guided tours that use videos and audio presentations to describe the process of making hand-cooked chips, flavored chips, and other products.

FOR FAMILIES **Painted Spring Alpaca Farm** (717-225-3941; www .paintedspring.com), 280 Roth Church Road, Spring Grove. Tours are free, but by appointment only. Owners Beth and Neal Lutz breed these gentle creatures on their peaceful farm between York and Abbottstown. A retail shop sells alpaca yarn and fleece and hand-woven and knit items by local artisans. Check the Web site for open house and shearing events, which usually feature spinning and weaving demonstrations and plenty of hands-on contact with the animals.

Perrydell Farms (717-741-3485), 90 Indian Rock Dam Road, York. Kids will enjoy the free self-guided tour of this working dairy farm just south of town. Pick up a map in the retail store, then watch cows being milked (afternoons only), pet the calves, and see fresh milk being bottled. Afterward, return to the store for hand-dipped ice cream or the tastiest chocolate milk in town.

Sweet Willows Creamery (717-718-9219; www.sweetwillows.com), 2812 E. Prospect Road, York. Closed Monday. Brent Lebouitz takes ice cream ingredients to new levels in his homey café: the ever-changing flavors might include midnight cappuccino crunch, Nutella, no-sugar-added strawberry, or Tahitian vanilla Grapenuts. There are also sandwiches, bottomless sodas, and a banana split that could feed an entire preschool class. Anyone can ask for a brief, free tour of the property. More informative guided tours (in which you witness an actual batch of ice cream being

TURKEY HILL EXPERIENCE

Milk a mechanical cow. Free dive into a rainbow ball pit. Create your own ice cream flavor, then make a commercial about it. It's not free like many of York's factory tours, but this new attraction in a former silk mill is as much interactive indoor playground as it is examination of the general ice-cream making process (the Turkey Hill dairy farm is actually a few miles away). A nice touch is the plentiful samples of ice cream and iced tea. There's also a free exhibit on the ground floor about the area's dairy industry and river communities. The large Creamery café sells hard-to-find and seasonal flavors such as whoopie pie and Eagles Touchdown Sundae. **Turkey Hill Experience** (888-986-8784; www.turkey hillexperience.com), 301 Linden Street, Columbia. $11.50 adults, $9.50 ages 5–12.

MILKING MECHANICAL COWS AT TURKEY HILL EXPERIENCE

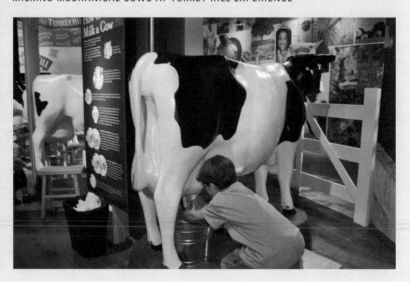

made) are available for groups of 10 or more; $4.95 per person; reservations required.

WINERIES Naylor Wine Cellars (717-993-3370; www.naylorwine.com), 4069 Vineyard Road, Stewartstown. Free tours daily; reservations required. Full-service winery in a rural country setting about 15 miles south of York near the Maryland border.

BICYCLING/RENTALS Serenity Station (717-428-9575; 11 Church Street, Seven Valleys), a stop along the 21-mile **Heritage Rail Trail** (see also Green Space), has a bike shop that rents single bikes, child trailers, and tandems starting at $7.50 an hour. **Gung Ho Bikes** (717-852-9553; www.gunghobikes.com) at 1815 Susquehanna Trail (at US 30) and **Whistle Stop Bike Shop** (800-801-2255) in New Freedom also rent bikes.

BOAT EXCURSIONS/RENTALS Appalachian Outdoor School (717-632-7484; www.appalachianoutdoorschool.com) rents canoes, kayaks, and pontoon and motor boats at the marina at Codorus State Park daily, Memorial Day through Labor Day (see also Green Space).

In Wrightsville, **Shank's Mare Outfitters** (717-252-1616; 2092 Long Level Road) gives kayak lessons and rents single, double, and triple kayaks for trips along the Susquehanna River for $20–40 an hour.

FISHING Lake Marburg in Codorus State Park (see also Green Space) is a warm-water fishery stocked with yellow perch, bluegill, northern pike, crappie, largemouth bass, and catfish. A state fishing license is required; visit www.fish.state.pa.us for more information.

GOLF Heritage Hills Golf Course (717-755-0123), 2700 Mount Rose Avenue, York. Nestled in the rural countryside less than a mile from downtown, this 18-hole course has wide fairways, well-maintained large greens, and a par of 71. A driving range and a mini-golf course are also on-site.

❋ Green Space

⌀ ❅ **Heritage Rail Trail County Park** (717-840-7440; www.yorkcounty parks.org). Established in 1992, this 176-acre park has an excellent 21-mile hiking and biking trail that follows the path of a historic railroad between the Mason-Dixon line and downtown York near the Colonial Courthouse at 25 W. Market Street. It's also popular with horseback riders and cross-country skiers. The trail has many places to stop and rest or explore, including two history museums (New Freedom and Hanover), and a spa/restaurant (Serenity Station) that offers massages, facials, snacks, and live entertainment on weekends. Download a map from the Web site before you go, or pick one up at one of the station stops.

⎕ ⌀ ❅ **Codorus State Park** (717-637-2816), 2600 Smith Station Road, Hanover. The 3,300-acre park is 3 miles southeast of Hanover and about an hour's drive from York. Its top attraction is the 1,275-acre Lake Marburg, which has 26 miles of shoreline and offers boating, sailing, and fishing opportunities. It also has a public swimming pool, disc golf course, and several miles of hiking, biking, and equestrian trails. There's also a campground with 190 tent and RV sites, most with electricity hookups, plus a few cottages and yurts.

✳ Lodging

HOTELS ♿ Yorktowne Hotel

(717-848-1111; www.yorktowne
.com), 48 E. Market Street, York.
F. Scott and Zelda would be right
at home mingling under the brass
and crystal chandeliers in the high-
ceilinged lobby of this 11-story
1920s-era hotel. The Fitzgeralds
never stayed here, but Bill Clinton,
Johnny Cash, and B. B. King did.
It's also popular with business travelers and anyone performing at the
nearby Strand-Capitol Theatre. All
rooms and suites are spacious and
handsomely decorated and come
with king beds, sitting areas, writing desks, and coffeemakers.
There are two restaurants on site,
plus a small fitness center and
laundry room. You can walk to the
city's historic sites and central market from here; though the neighborhood tends to be deserted at
night. Rooms and suites $119–169.

**Heritage Hills Golf Resort and
Conference Center** (717-755-
0123; www.hhgr.com), 2700 Mount
Rose Avenue, York. This large
resort on 150 acres east of downtown attracts many golfers and
families with its all-inclusive package deals. The 128 rooms and
suites were renovated in 2008 and
have luxury beds, flat-screen TVs,
granite-top desks, mini-fridges,
and microwaves. There are also
four restaurants, a fitness center, a

spa, a mini golf course, a summer
kids' camp, and a winter snow-
tubing operation. Rooms $169–249.

BED & BREAKFASTS

🏵 **Jackson House** (717-227-2022;
www.jacksonhousebandb.com), 6
E. Main Street, Railroad. George
and Jean Becker made this small
B&B next to the Heritage Rail
Trail hugely popular with bicyclists
and motorcyclists. They retired in
2007, but left the place in the very
hospitable hands of Pam Nicholson
and Bob Wilhelm. The front of the
1859 red-shingled building abuts a
busy Main Street intersection; the
back features terraced gardens, a
patio, and a hot tub. There are two
small rooms with private baths, two
large suites with private entrances
and sitting areas (the Bordello
Suite shows off a collection of vintage nude pinups from the 1930s
and 1940s), and a separate one-
room cottage. A lavish breakfast of
eggs, coffee cake, fresh fruit, and
more is served in the elegant
stone-walled dining room. Rates
$109–169.

Lady Linden (717-843-2929;
wwwladylindenbedandbreakfast
.com.), 505 Linden Avenue, York.
This 1887 Queen Anne Victorian
home wins raves for its quiet residential location, 19th-century
charm, and generous four-course

YORKTOWNE HOTEL

breakfasts. Owners Jim and Jean Leaman are sticklers for historic detail and have decorated the rooms in period style with feather beds, writing desks, and oriental rugs; the Grecian has its own private sitting porch. Other nice touches are a refrigerator stocked with spring water and wraparound porch with garden. Rooms $129.

Red Lion Bed and Breakfast (717-244-4739 or 888-288-1701; www.redlionbandb.com), 101 S. Franklin Street, Red Lion. A lovely turn-of-the-20th-century brick

home just off the small town's main drag. Bedrooms are comfortable and simply decorated with antiques and hardwood floors; some have shared baths. Common rooms include a sun porch and well-stocked library. Rates $78–105.

Hanover
The Beechmont (717-632-3013; www.thebeechmont.com), 315 Broadway. A couple blocks off Hanover's main square, this stately inn has nine elegant rooms with private baths and a small back garden anchored by a 140-year-old magnolia tree. The yellow-hued Birch Room, which overlooks the garden, is a favorite. I also like the small and bright Walnut Room, which is decorated in blues and greens with an antique rope bed. Breakfast is a lavish affair of fruit smoothies, sticky buns, and a main course that might feature spiced pancakes, buttermilk pie, or an herbed cheese tart. Cookies and other goodies are served in the evening, and there is wireless access throughout the house. Owners Kathryn and Tom White are well-versed in the area and will make dinner reservations or steer you to their favorite shops, eateries, and attractions. Rooms $119–169.

Sheppard Mansion (717-633-8975; www.sheppardmansion.com), 117 Frederick Street. The guest rooms in this Doric-columned neoclassical mansion are as pleasing as the meals at its renowned farm-to-table restaurant. The three rooms and three suites have antique furniture, flat-screen TVs, free WiFi, and marble bathrooms; the Ayres Suite is especially extravagant with a crystal chandelier, fireplace, and private bath with claw-foot tub. This is a good choice for Gettysburg visitors who want to combine their battlefield tours with a little gourmet luxury (it's about 20 minutes away). A full breakfast (croissant French toast and fresh fruit, for example) is $10 extra per person. Rooms $140–240, two-night minimum on some weekends.

✳ Where to Eat

DINING OUT

York

&. ⵏ **Left Bank** (717-843-8010), 120 N. George Street. Lunch and dinner Tuesday through Friday, dinner only Saturday. One of York's finest restaurants, serving creative American cuisine, such as cioppino in Old Bay-seasoned tomato broth, house-smoked Korubata pork belly, and a deconstructed Philly cheesesteak. Eat in the formal dining room or the smoking-allowed bistro. Desserts are grand; try the frozen s'mores tower. Reservations recommended. Lunch: $9–23; dinner entrées: $18–34.

&. ⵏ **Roosevelt Tavern** (717-854-7725), 50 N. Penn Street, York. Lunch and dinner daily. This casual downtown establishment has an extensive menu of steaks, seafood,

chicken, and salads. Crab cakes are a specialty. A choice of tasty sides such as corn pudding and sweet potatoes drenched in honey butter comes with every entrée. There's live jazz or blues in the bar Wednesday and Friday nights. Lunch $9–16. Entrées $20–$32.

Hanover

&. ✐ **Bay City Seafood** (717-637-1217), 110 Eisenhower Drive. This local favorite offers a wide selection of steaks, seafood, and lobster in a casual fisherman-themed environment. Try the crab cakes any way, or the crab pretzel, a huge baked soft pretzel smothered with melted cheese and crabmeat. Lunch $5–9; dinner entrées $12–34.

Sheppard Mansion (717-633-8975; www.sheppardmansion .com), 117 Frederick Street. Dinner Wednesday through Saturday. Chef Andrew Little takes Pennsylvania Dutch haute cuisine to exciting new levels at his elegant restaurant in the center of town. Scrapple, crushed pretzels, and chow-chow are staple ingredients, as are fresh vegetables and meats from local farms or the inn's own garden. Reservations are recommended, but walk-ins are welcome. Entrées $23–26, weekend tasting menu $75 (with wine $130).

Nearby
Lulu's Grille and Spirits (717-259-9535), 20 W. King Street, Abbottstown. The ground-floor restaurant of the Altland House

B&B serves high-end comfort food such as chicken and waffles, crab cakes with house-made tartar, and meat loaf with red-skinned mashed potatoes. An early bird menu is served from 4–6 PM. Entrées $12–29.

EATING OUT ♿ ✇ **Captain Bob's Crabs** (717-235-1166), 1 Main Street, Railroad. Dinner daily March through December. This casual outdoor eatery is known for its steamed Maryland crabs, but it also has clam strips, halibut, salmon cakes, Maine lobster tail, and other fresh seafood dishes. The all-you-can-eat crab fests on Tuesday, Wednesday, and Thursday draw big crowds. Thursday is live Christian music night. Dishes $8–24.

♿ ⚗ ✇ **Central Family Restaurant** (717-845-4478), 400 N. George Street, York. Breakfast, lunch, and dinner daily. This down-home diner is up with the chickens and makes up in good food what it lacks in decor. Breakfast includes omelets, hot cakes, and creamed chipped beef on toast. For lunch or dinner, there are burgers, crab melts, fried chicken, hand-cut steaks, and homemade meatloaf. Dishes $4–16.

Red Brick Bakery and Tea Room (717-332-7427), 55 N. Main Street, Red Lion. Open Wednesday through Saturday. The best place in town for peaches and cream scones, cheesecake, or a light lunch. High tea is available by reservation. Lunch $3–5.

Hanover

⚗ **Famous Hot Weiner** (717-637-1282), 101 Broadway. This small diner serves everything from eggs to hamburgers, but it's best known for its hot dogs with mustard, chili sauce, and chopped onions. There's also a branch in North Hanover. Dishes $2–5.

Reader's Café (717-630-2524), 125 Broadway. Open 9–5 daily, until 10 PM Friday and Saturday. The handwritten menu usually includes soup, coffee drinks, and

FAMOUS HOT WEINER

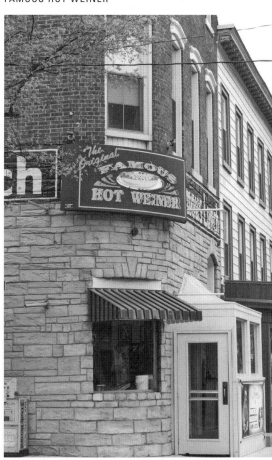

several tasty sandwiches. Best of all, you get to eat surrounded by neatly arranged books and magazines (all for sale, of course). There's often live music or open-mic night in the evening. Dishes: $3–6.

ICE CREAM & FARMERS' MARKETS & Central Market

(717-848-2243), 34 W. Philadelphia Street, York. Open 6–2 Tuesday, Thursday, and Saturday. Saturday is the best day to visit this historic downtown market for local produce, fresh-cut flowers, and homemade peanut butter donuts. It's also good for a quick lunch. Try the Greek salads at

HAVE FUN AT TURKEY HILL EXPERIENCE.

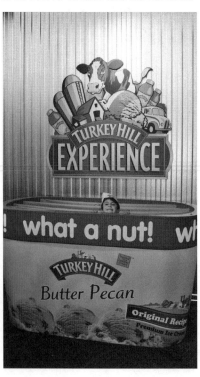

Tina's or the seasoned potato wedges at Bair's Fried Chicken. There are a few tables and a public piano in the center.

Lock 2 Café (717-252-1616), 2098 Long Level Road, Wrightsville. Enjoy Turkey Hill ice cream and a riverfront view from their beautiful porch overlooking the Susquehanna. Homemade soup and baked goods are usually on the menu, and there is live music on the porch most Friday evenings from May through October.

New Eastern Market (717-755-5811), 201 Memory Lane, York. Open Friday 7–7. Apple fritters flecked with raisins, Bair's fried chicken, and a robust selection of meats and produce are some of the highlights of this indoor market in East York. The adjacent Cindy's restaurant is a popular local breakfast and lunch spot.

Perrydell Farms (717-741-3485), 90 Indian Acres Farm, York. Open daily. This small working farm south of downtown sells delicious chocolate milk and hand-dipped ice cream. Self-guided tours are available. (See also For Families.)

✳ Entertainment

THEATER & Strand-Capitol Performing Arts Center

(717-846-1111; www.strandcapitol.org), 50 N. George Street. This restored Italian Renaissance–style theater was once a vaudeville house and now features musicals, dance performances, film festivals, and other events.

York Little Standouts Theater (717-854-5715; www.ylt.org), 27 S. Belmont Street, York. Crowd-pleasing musicals, dramas, and original children's plays.

✳ Selective Shopping

& Markets at Shrewsbury (717-235-6611), 12025 Susquehanna Trail, Glen Rock. Open Thursday through Saturday. Shop for hand-crafted Amish furniture, crafts, and quilts, then sample the wide selection of food offerings at this large indoor-outdoor market just off I-83 near the Maryland border. Sticky buns, soft pretzels, roast beef sandwiches, and local produce are just a few of the highlights.

Sunrise Soap Company (717-843-7627; www.sunrisesoapco .com), 29 N. Beaver Street, York. The scents of sandalwood vanilla or banana coconut might greet you at the door at this quaint little downtown shop. Owner Chris Clarke makes her own soaps, shampoos, facial scrubs, and other bath products with olive oil, shea and cocoa butters, and other natural products. You can watch the soaps being made in the back of the store, or call ahead to schedule a free tour.

York Emporium (717-846-2866 www.theyorkemporium.com), 343 W. Market Street, York. Open Wednesday through Sunday. An extraordinarily good used-book store near the downtown visitor center with more than 250,000 titles in just about every category

you can think of, from Gettysburg to flower arranging. Reasonable prices, too. It also carries comics, videos and DVDs, and music, from CDs to eight-track tapes. There's free parking in the back.

& John Wright Store (717-252-2519), 234 N. Front Street, Wrightsville. Perched on the west bank of the Susquehanna River, this century-old warehouse sells garden products, Vera Bradley bags, jewelry, and more. Don't miss the upstairs displays of discounted cast-iron bakeware, doorknobs, trivets, and other products made nearby at the family-run factory. A restaurant with a full bar and patio overlooking the river serves wood-fired pizza, crab cakes, and burgers most days starting at 3 or 4 PM. Call ahead for hours.

JOHN WRIGHT STORE ON THE SUSQUEHANNA RIVER

✳ Special Events

September: **York Fair** (second week), York Fairgrounds, 334 Carlisle Avenue—one of America's oldest town fairs, this 10-day event has the usual rides, games, and country food stands, but is best known for attracting nationally known performers such as Willie Nelson, Gretchen Wilson, and Lynyrd Skynyrd. Harley-Davidson Open House (last weekend), 425 Eden Road—three days of extended plant tours, demo rides, and a Saturday night parade through downtown York.

June: **Made in America** (third weekend), throughout York County—dozens of area factories, including ones that don't usually offer public tours, open their doors during this three-day event. For more information, visit www.factorytours.org.

Northeastern Pennsylvania

6

THE LEHIGH VALLEY

POCONO MOUNTAINS SOUTH

POCONO MOUNTAINS NORTH

THE LEHIGH VALLEY

The Lehigh Valley is Pennsylvania's third most populous area behind Pittsburgh and Philadelphia, and is known historically for its production of steel and anthracite coal. For nearly 150 years, it was dominated by Bethlehem Steel, one of the world's largest steel manufacturers and shipbuilders, which closed in 2003 and has now reopened as a large casino, hotel, and retail complex. Though the area has plenty to offer vacationers, including a large theme park and picture-postcard historic districts, it sometimes gets overshadowed by its neighbors, the Pocono Mountains to the north and Bucks County to the south.

Today, Allentown, Bethlehem, and Easton are the valley's largest towns. Allentown, the state's third-largest city, is home to Dorney Park and Wildwater Kingdom, a large art museum, and a revitalization effort that has helped bring a new minor-league baseball stadium and a high-tech transportation museum to the area.

Before steel came to Bethlehem, it was known as a haven for religious freedom. The area was settled by Moravian brethren, a denomination of German Protestant settlers who arrived here in 1740. The city was named a year later when Moravian patron Count Nicholas Ludwig von Zinzendorf visited the settlement's first house on Christmas Eve and bestowed the name "Bethlehem" on the community. It's also home to Lehigh University, founded by the railroad pioneer Asa Packer.

The town of Easton sits in the far east side of the Lehigh Valley near the New Jersey border. Anchored by a large historic square and the nearby Lehigh Canal, it is home to prestigious Lafayette College, the Crayola Factory, many good restaurants, and a waterfront park offering canal boat rides and picnic tables.

AREA CODE The entire Lehigh Valley falls within the 610 area code.

GUIDANCE Lehigh Valley Convention and Visitor Bureau (610-882-9200; www.lehighvalleypa.org), 840 Hamilton Street, Allentown. Open

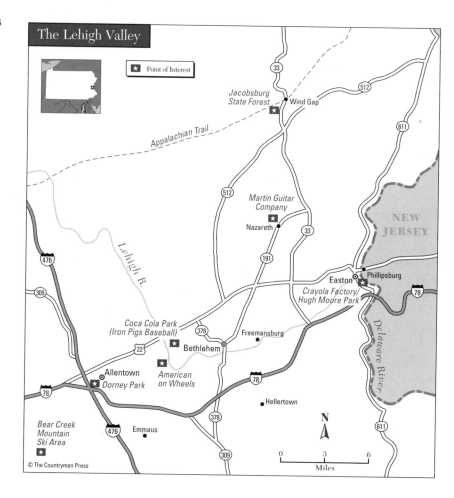

The Lehigh Valley

★ Point of Interest

Jacobsburg State Forest ★ Wind Gap

Appalachian Trail

Martin Guitar Company ★ Nazareth

NEW JERSEY

Easton Phillipsburg

Crayola Factory/ Hugh Moore Park

Coca Cola Park (Iron Pigs Baseball)

Freemansburg

Bethlehem

Allentown

Dorney Park

American on Wheels

Hellertown

Bear Creek Mountain Ski Area

Emmaus

Delaware River

Lehigh R.

N

0   3   6
Miles

© The Countryman Press

10–6 Monday through Saturday. A small welcome center and a gift shop are in **Bethlehem's historic district** (610-691-6055; www.bethlehempa .org), 505 Main Street. Guides lead walking tours from here every Saturday, April through December, for $12 a person. The city also sponsors daily walking tours along the Lehigh River about the rise and fall of Bethlehem Steel; they start at the SteelStacks facility.

GETTING THERE By air: Lehigh Valley is about an hour's drive from two major airports: **Philadelphia International** (215-937-6800) and New Jersey's **Newark International** (800-397-4636). **Lehigh Valley International Airport** (888-359-5842), between Allentown and Bethlehem, offers limited service.

By car: The Lehigh Valley can be reached from the north or south via the Pennsylvania Turnpike. I-78 crosses it from east to west, with exits for Easton, Bethlehem, and Allentown.

GETTING AROUND The Lehigh Valley is quite spread out, so you'll need a car. That said, Bethlehem, Emmaus, and Easton all have attractive walking districts with shops, restaurants, and preserved historic buildings and churches.

MEDICAL EMERGENCY **Lehigh Valley Hospital** (610-402-2273), at Cedar Crest Road and I-78, Allentown. **St. Luke's Hospital** (610-954-4000), 801 Ostrum Street, Bethlehem. **Easton Hospital** (610-250-4000), 250 S. 21st Street, Easton.

WHEN TO GO What better time to visit a place called Bethlehem than December? The town truly rises to the occasion with daily concerts, walking tours, carriage rides, and Christkindlmart, a huge month-long crafts bazaar. Summer is also a good time to be here; top attractions such as Dorney Park and Crayola Factory are open daily, the canal boat rides are open for business, and the farm markets are brimming with local peaches and tomatoes.

✷ Towns & Villages

Emmaus. Founded as a closed community of the Moravian church in the 1700s, Emmaus couldn't be any quainter or more picturesque. Its quaint

SHOPS IN DOWNTOWN EMMAUS

SANDS CASINO

Bling came to the southern Lehigh Valley in May 2009 with the opening of a Las Vegas-style casino and hotel on former Bethlehem Steel property. The **Sands Casino Resort** (877-726-3777; www.pasands.com), 77 Sands Boulevard (PA 412 south), ranks among the state's top money-makers with 3,000 slot machines and more than 100 table games, plus a hotel, shopping mall, food

SANDS CASINO ON FORMER BETHLEHEM STEEL LAND

court, and several restaurants, including the very popular **Emeril's Chop House.** Expect plenty of tour-bus crowds from New York City and Philadelphia. There's free live music (bands, DJs) most nights in the **Molten Lounge,** which also draws big crowds. A 3,000-seat entertainment complex, with the capacity to host big events such as trade shows and rock concerts, is also in the works and expected to open by summer 2012.

SANDS CASINO

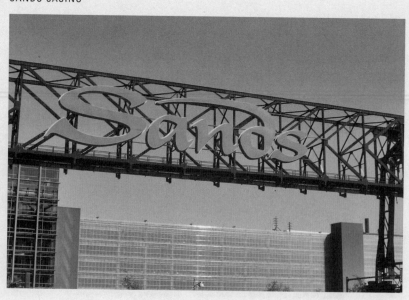

downtown area has historic buildings, hip cafes, and mom-and-pop shops.
About 6 miles west of Allentown, it was named one of the top 100 Best
Places to Live in the U.S. in 2007 by *Money* magazine. It is the headquarters of Rodale Press, publisher of *Prevention* magazine and many other
health and gardening magazines and books.

Nazareth. This town joins Bethlehem and Emmaus as towns in the
Lehigh Valley named after famous Biblical places. Also settled by Mora-
vians, it is about 4 miles north of Bethlehem, with a pretty tree-lined main
street of shops and cafes anchored by a circular plaza. It is home to the C.
F. Martin Guitar Company, known for its quality acoustic guitars, as well
as several cement companies that lie on the outskirts of town.

✳ To See

MUSEUMS

Allentown

🐾 ♿ ☂ **Liberty Bell Museum** (610-435-4232; www.libertybellmuseum
.org), 622 Hamilton Street. Open 12–4 Monday through Saturday, May
through November; Wednesday through Saturday, February through
April; free. The Old Zion Reformed Church served as a hiding place for
the Liberty Bell and 11 other church bells while the British occupied
Philadelphia in 1777 and 1778 (it was feared the Brits would melt the
bells for musket and cannon balls). Today, in the church basement you'll
find a full-size replica of the famous bell (which rings, unlike the real
one), a multimedia light-and-sound show depicting scenes from the Revolutionary War, and a small exhibit of Colonial artifacts and paintings.

♿ ☂ **Allentown Art Museum** (610-432-4333; www.allentownart
museum.org), 31 N. Fifth Street, Allentown. This small facility added
nearly 8,000 square feet and a new entrance and café in 2011. Its collection includes European Renaissance works and American art by Robert
Motherwell, Gilbert Stuart, and local artists. Don't miss the Frank Lloyd
Wright–designed library, which was dismantled from his Prairie-style
Northome in Minnesota and reassembled here in 1973. Fun and unique
special exhibits, too.

♿ **America on Wheels** (610-432-4200; www.americanwheels.org), 5 N.
Front Street; $7 adults, $3 ages 6–12. Closed Monday. This long-in-the-
making museum chronicles the history of over-the-road transportation in
the United States. Its impressive collection includes historic Mack trucks
(the Mack plant is nearby), bicycles and Segways, and cars powered by
hydrogen, electricity, steam, and gasoline (including an 1891 Nadig). Also
on display: one of four replicas of PeeWee Herman's Schwinn and the
lawnmower that won the 2007 US Lawn Mower Racing trophy (top speed:

65 mph). The Hubcap Café serves milk shakes, egg creams, hot dogs, and other soda-fountain staples. Parents of car-crazy youngsters may want to combine a morning visit here with an afternoon stop at the Crayola Factory, about 16 miles to the east.

✳ To Do

& ⸙ **C. F. Martin Guitar Company and Museum** (610-759-2837), 510 Sycamore Street, Nazareth. This family-owned guitar maker has been producing high-quality acoustic guitars since the early 1800s. Johnny Cash, Paul McCartney, Eric Clapton, and Gene Autry are a few artists who have owned them. You don't have to be a serious musician to enjoy the free tours, offered weekdays at 11 AM and 2:30 PM, of its small plant north of Bethlehem. Led by enthusiastic guides, they last about an hour and walk you through the many steps involved in making a guitar. You can stand next to workers as they bend, shape, fit, sandpaper, lacquer, and inspect; as they convert rough fine woods into a brand new instrument. There's also a well-executed display of vintage Martin guitars (including Ricky Nelson's leather-covered one and clips of Elvis Presley playing his Martin in the 1950s) off the lobby and a gift shop that sells new and used Martin guitars, books, T-shirts, and other guitar-related items.

FOR FAMILIES ⸕ & ⸙ **Crayola Factory** (610-515-8000), 30 Centre Square, Easton. Open. 9:30–5 Monday through Saturday, 11–5 Sunday; closed Monday, September through May; $9.75 adults and kids over 2.

MARTIN GUITAR COMPANY

Binney and Smith, the local company that makes Crayola crayons, opened this hands-on discovery center in 1996 after the demand for factory tours became overwhelming. It's more of an activity center aimed at kids 4–12 than a lesson on how crayons are manufactured, but kids will love the coloring stations, drawing on the giant glass walls, and making their own stationery at the printmaking exhibit. Plus, they distribute free crayons and markers here like the town of Hershey hands out chocolate kisses. Weekends can get quite crowded; also keep in mind that school groups flood the place weekdays in late April and May. The price of admission includes entry into the third-floor National Canal Museum (610-559-6613), a terrific museum about America's towpath canals. Kids age 2 and up will love the model canals that let

CRAYOLA FACTORY

them guide their own boats through locks and planes, while adults will find plenty of interesting lore in the railroad and engineering exhibits.

✎ **Dorney Park and Wildwater Kingdom** (610-395-3724; www.dorney park.com), 3830 Dorney Park Road, Allentown. Open daily late May through August; Friday through Sunday, September and October; $46 adults, $28 seniors and kids under 48 inches; two-day consecutive passes are $64 adults, and $35 kids. Discounted tickets are available at local Acme stores. Part of the Cedar Fair chain, Dorney Park has about a dozen thrill rides and roller coasters (including the Steel Force "hypercoaster" and the floorless Hydra: Revenge), plus family-friendly rides such as Tilt-a-Whirl, an antique carousel, and Camp Snoopy. Wildwater Kingdom, a water park with 22 slides, tubing rivers, wave pools, and a kids' area, is included in the price of admission. Waits for rides can be long on summer weekends. An interesting factoid: Dorney Park was the amusement park featured in the 1988 John Waters film *Hairspray.*

DaVinci Science Center (484-664-1002; www.davinci-center.org), 3145 Hamilton Boulevard Bypass, Allentown. Open daily; $11.95 adults, $8.95 ages 4–12. Kids can take a gyroscope ride, control a robotic dinosaur, and learn about earthquakes, smog, and nanotechnology at this sleek science lab. A preschool area includes an indoor greenhouse and Little Learner's Lab. A tip: School field trips are rare on Monday, making for a less crowded experience.

✎ **Lost River Caverns** (610-838-8767; www.lostcave.com), 726 Durham Street, Hellertown. Open daily; $11 adults, $7 ages 3–12. These limestone caves are at the northern edge of Bucks County about 20 miles south of Allentown. Five cavern chambers, discovered in 1883, have an abundance of stalactites, stalagmites, and other crystal formations; guided tours take 30 to 40 minutes. The adjacent no-admission museum has rare fossils, minerals, and gems as well as a large collection of antique weapons.

✳ Outdoor Activities

BASEBALL In 2008, the Lehigh Valley welcomed its first major league-affiliated baseball team since 1960. The Triple-A team, called the **Iron Pigs** in a nod to the area's steelmaking days, is affiliated with the Philadelphia Phillies and plays at the 8,100-seat Coca-Cola Park on Allentown's east side. For information, visit www.ironpigsbaseball.com.

BOAT EXCURSIONS Canal boat rides, narrated by costumed crew members, run regularly throughout the summer and weekends in September from **Hugh Moore Park** (see also Green Space). Cost is $7 adults, $5 ages 3–15.

DIVING Dutch Springs Park (610-759-2270; dutchsprings.com), 4733 Hanoverville Road, Bethlehem. This former quarry is one of the largest freshwater diving facilities in the country, with an average visibility of 20 to 30 feet. It offers SCUBA diving daily April through October for $36 a day and overnight tent camping on Friday and Saturday nights for $10 per person. Ocean kayaks and paddleboats are also available for rental.

FOOTBALL The **Lehigh Valley Steelhawks** joined the Indoor Football League in 2011; home games are played at Lehigh University's Stabler Arena. For more info, visit www.lvsteelhawks.com or call 610-292-3100.

GOLF Bethlehem Golf Club (610-691-9393), 400 Illicks Mill Road, Bethlehem. Built in 1965, this 18-hole municipal course has a mix of flat and hilly terrain and stretches to nearly 7,000 yards. An executive 9-hole course, a driving range, and mini-golf are available.

Center Valley Golf Club (610-791-5580), 3300 Center Valley Parkway, Center Valley. This 18-hole par-72 course near I-78 and PA 309 is in excellent condition with five tees ranging from 4,932 to 6,973 yards.

HUNTING Hunting of squirrels, pheasants, rabbits, and white-tailed deer is permitted on about 900 acres of **Jacobsburg State Park** (see also Green Space). Hunters are expected to follow the rules and regulations of the state game commission (www.www.pgc.state.pa.us).

SKIING Bear Creek Ski & Recreation Area (610-682-7100; www.ski bearcreek.com), 101 Doe Mountain Lane, Macungie. Geared toward novice and intermediate skiers, it has 17 slopes and a half-pipe and snow tubing park. There's a full-service resort at its base.

Blue Mountain Ski Area (610-826-7700; www.skibluemt.com), 1660 Blue Mountain Drive, Palmerton. About 17 miles north of Allentown with 110 acres of skiing terrain and 30 slopes. There's also a half-pipe and snow tubing area.

✳ Green Space

✐ **Hugh Moore Historical Park** (610-559-6613; www.canals.org), Lehigh Drive, Easton. Named after the founder of the Dixie Cup Company, this city-owned park parallels several miles of the Lehigh River and has picnic areas, flat biking trails, and mule-drawn canal boat rides in the summer. A canal boat ticket ($11 adults, $8 children) includes admission to the Emrick Technology Center and its exhibits on the Lehigh Valley's industrial heritage. The park is about an eight-minute drive via Fourth Street from the National Canal Museum (see To See).

HISTORIC LOCKTENDERS HOUSE IN WALNUTPORT

☙ **Jacobsburg Environmental Education Center** (610-746-2801), 835 Jacobsburg Road, Bushkill Township. This 1,200-acre state park near Nazareth is located on a historic site that once housed two 18th-century rifle factories and an iron furnace and forge. Bounded by Bushkill Creek, it has 18 miles of well-maintained hiking and biking trails. Maps are available at the kiosk in the main parking lot on Belfast Road. The pedestrian-only Henry's Woods Trail, also accessible from here, is a 1.5-mile shaded loop that follows the creek downstream past hemlock and oak forest.

☙ **Sand Island** (610-865-7079), 56 River Street, Bethlehem. This 2-mile-long city park on the Lehigh River is near downtown and has tennis and basketball courts, a playground, a boat ramp, and a small cultural center. You'll also find access to the Lehigh Canal and towpath, a popular biking and running trail that follows the canal west to Allentown or east to Freemansburg and then on to Easton. The island can be accessed via car by a small bridge next to an old railroad station just under the Hill to Hill Bridge (I-378).

✳ Lodging

HOTELS & INNS **Bear Creek Mountain Resort** (866-754-2822; www.bcmountainresort.com), 101 Doe Mountain Lane, Macungie. Located in the far western reaches of the Lehigh Valley, this full-service resort attracts skiers and snow tubers in winter and hikers or couples in search of an uncomplicated getaway in summer. Its modern rooms are spacious and comfortable, though the layout is large and maze like. A 5-acre fishing pond stocked with trout, two tennis courts, and a luxury spa are on-site. It's surrounded by quiet farmland, but chances are you won't want to leave once you check in.

Glasbern (610-285-4723; www.glasbern.com), 2141 Pack House Road, Fogelsville. Romance meets businesslike efficiency at this family-farm-turned-country inn on 100 acres a few miles outside Allentown. Seven separately renovated buildings, once used to run the farm, now house 35 large rooms or suites, many with fireplaces and whirlpool tubs. A fitness center, spa, and outdoor heated pool are available. Its fine restaurant is open to the public (see also Dining Out). Rates are on the high side, but most folks looking for a luxury getaway find their expectations are met or exceeded here.

Grand Eastonian Suites Hotel (610-258-6350; www.grandeastonian suiteshotel.com), 140 Northhampton Street, Easton. Anchoring Easton's main square, this gorgeous turn-of-the-20th-century building was restored to its original grandeur in 2004 and, after a brief stint as condos, turned into a hotel in late 2008. It features one-, two-, and three-bedroom modern suites with full kitchens, all furnished in sleek beiges and whites. An indoor pool and fitness room, plus free high-speed Internet, and flat-screen TVs are on-site. It's popular with relocating business folks, but families will want to ask about their package deals with the Crayola Factory, which is within walking distance. Pets are allowed. Suites $125–350.

ᵩ **Radisson Hotel Bethlehem** (610-625-5000; 800-607-2384), 437 Main Street. What this busy urban hotel lacks in warmth it makes up for in rich historical background. Centrally located in the downtown, it was built in 1922 on the site of the area's first house, where a wealthy Moravian patron named Count Nicholas Ludwig von Zinzendorf christened the town Bethlehem. After major renovations, the hotel reopened as a Radisson in 1999 and has 127 rooms and suites with business hotel amenities such as a free airport shuttle, fitness center, and wireless Internet access. Even if you don't stay here, be sure to check out the grand old lobby and the seven George Gray murals that have hung in the hotel since 1937 and chronicle the town's history from religious settlement to industrial center. Rooms and suites $179–399.

BED & BREAKFASTS

ᵩ ᵩ ᵩ **Lafayette Inn** (610-253-4500; 800-509-6990; www.lafayette inn.com), 525 W. Monroe Street, Easton. Perched high on a hill overlooking the valley, this inn near Lafayette College is one of your best and friendliest options for lodging in the Easton area.

Owners Paolo and Laura Di Liello were electrical engineers before joining the hospitality business; they live on premises with their Siberian husky, Lena. All 18 rooms and suites are tastefully furnished with antiques, desks, TVs, and private baths. Deluxe rooms are $175 and can accommodate up to four people; standard rooms are $125 and sleep two. The inn attracts a mix of business travelers, Lafayette College visitors, and general tourists. Breakfast (usually made-to-order omelets and waffles during the week and a feast of homemade granola, fruit, cereals, and stratas or French toast on weekends) is served on individual tables in the sunroom. Kids and pets (in some rooms) are welcome. Rooms $125–175; suites $225.

Morningstar Inn (610-867-2300; www.morningstarinn.com), 72 E. Market Street, Bethlehem. Located in a pretty historic neighborhood within walking distance of Bethlehem's top restaurants and shops, this stately B&B has five elegant rooms with high ceilings, queen-size beds, private baths, and antique furniture. Amenities include free WiFi, an old-fashioned billiard room, and use of the heated outdoor pool. Rooms $150–215, includes a full breakfast.

Sayre Mansion (610-882-2100; www.sayremansion.com), 250 Wyandotte Street, Bethlehem. This Gothic Revival home once belonged to Robert Sayre, founder of the Lehigh Railroad. It's in a central location about a 5-minute drive or 25-minute walk to historic Bethlehem. The 18 spacious and attractive rooms have desks, flat-panel TVs, wing chairs, fireplaces, and luxurious feather beds. Four-course breakfasts are served in the elegant dining room, or you may opt to have it delivered to your room. Home-baked cookies are served in the afternoons, and port is available in the evening. The separate Carriage House has two large suites and a loft. Rooms $160–190; suites $235–325.

✳ Where to Eat

DINING OUT � Apollo Grill (610-865-9600), 85 W. Broad Street, Bethlehem. Lunch and dinner Tuesday through Saturday. Busy bistro near the historic district specializing in innovative tapas such as shrimp limoncello, lobster tacos, beef short-rib lettuce wraps, and duck spring rolls. There's also a selection of sandwiches (blackened prime rib, Southwest chicken) and simple pastas. It is always hopping, so reservations are recommended. Tapas and sandwiches $9–15. Entrées $12–23.

Bay Leaf (610-433-4211), 935 Hamilton Street, Allentown. Lunch and dinner Monday through Friday, dinner Saturday. A reliable upscale dining option at the center of downtown. The lengthy French- and Asian-influenced menu includes seared pepper-crust tuna, lemongrass shrimp with spiced car-

rot sauce, fillet tips with oyster and bearnaise sauce, and many curry dishes. Lunch: $8–10; entrées: $18–26.

Glasbern (610-285-4723; www .glasbern.com), 2141 Pack House Road, Fogelsville. Dinner daily; two seatings at 5:30 and 8:30. This romantic restaurant showcases meats and produce raised and grown on its adjacent farm. Dinners Sunday through Friday are á la carte and might include wild mushroom risotto, tomato soup, roasted Gulf shrimp with apples, bacon, and melted onions, and seared sirloin steak with creamed peppers, onions, and asparagus. The dining room is exquisite and welcoming, with stone walls, vaulted rafters, and a fireplace. A prix-fixe four-course dinner for $55 per person is served on Saturday. Reservations required. Entrées $26–30.

The Farmhouse (610-967-6225; www.thefarmhouse.com), 1449 Chestnut Street, Emmaus. Dinner Tuesday through Saturday; Sunday brunch. This local favorite embraced the farm-to-table concept long before the rest of the world caught on. Open 20 years, it serves innovative dishes, such as pickled golden beet salad, natural lamb burgers, and coconut cream pork satay, in an exquisitely preserved 19th-century farmhouse. Leave time for lingering over a vintage ale or rosemary-infused margarita in the classic English pub. Burgers and small dishes $7–17, entrées $25–38.

Savory Grille (610-845-2010), 2934 Seisholtzville Road, Macungie. Dinner Wednesday through Saturday; lunch and dinner Sunday. Husband and wife Chefs Dorothy and Shawn Doyle serve simple yet creative fare in a historic former hotel south of Bear Creek Resort. The menu might feature chipotle-glazed pork belly with pancetta and Parmesan. Reservations recommended at dinner. Full bar. Entrées $24–42.

Easton

 Υ **Pearly Baker's Ale House** (610-253-9949), 11 Centre Square. Lunch, dinner, and late-night menu daily, closed Monday. Locals love to steer newcomers to this popular eatery and tavern on the square. Menu highlights include pear and Brie salad, a long list of burgers (from venison to veggie), and French-influenced entrées such as coq au vin, steak frites, and locally sourced duck cassoulet. Dine outside overlooking the square in the summer or under the dining room's grand chandelier any other time. There's live music on weekends. Lunch and sandwiches: $7–12; entrées: $14–29.

Sette Luna (610-253-8888), 219 Ferry Street. Lunch and dinner daily, Sunday brunch. Small and bustling bistro near Easton's main square serving wood-burning-oven pizzas, homemade pastas, and excellent salads. The Sunday jazz brunch features homemade tomato juice, open-faced frittatas, and

Salmon Hollandaise. Wine and beer. Pizzas: $10–15; entrées $13–24.

EATING OUT **Billy's Downtown Diner** (610-867-0105), 10 E. Broad Street, Bethlehem. Open 7–6 Monday through Friday, 7–2 Saturday and Sunday. Local celebrity Chef Billy Kounoupis and his wife, Yanna, took over this former newsstand in 2000 and transformed it into a friendly and upscale noshing place. Breakfast menu includes specialty omelets such as smoked salmon or crispy bacon, stuffed French toast, and creamed chipped beef. For lunch, there's a long list of sandwiches, melts, and other diner items such as gravy boat fries, pierogi, and mozzarella sticks. Dishes $3–9.

Pete's Hot Dog Shop (610-866-6622), 400 Broadway, Bethlehem. Breakfast, lunch, and dinner daily. The hot dogs are made to order, and the service is friendly and quick at this casual eatery, with crisp pierogi (three for $2.25), locally made A-Treat soda for 85 cents, and omelets for breakfast. Nothing on the menu is over $6.

Allentown

Wert's Café (610-439-0951; www.wertscafe.com), 515 N. 18th Street. Closed Sunday. There are 15 types of Burgers with Personality on the menu of this family-owned restaurant near the Allentown Fairgrounds, but the one that gets well-deserved top billing is the Wert's Burger. It comes stuffed with mushrooms and onions and has something of a cult following. There are also crispy eggplant fries, batter-dipped pickles, onion rings (the stringy kind), homemade soups, and entrées such as chopped sirloin and country ham. Rounding things out are a full bar, and locally made White Birch beer on tap. Check the Web site for special deals like Monday's package of burger, onion rings, and chocolate cake. Sandwiches $6–10; entrées $12–20.

Yocco's Hot Dogs (610-433-1950), 625 W. Liberty Street. Don't be put off by the gritty white facade and sometimes indifferent service. Founded by the uncle of native son Lee Iacocca, Yocco's makes hot dogs that people drive miles for; the pierogi are tasty, too. There are also branches in Emmaus, Fogelsville, and at 2128 Hamilton Street in Allentown.

Easton
Josie's New York Deli (610-252-5081), 14 Centre Square, Easton. A worthy lunch option over the McDonald's inside the nearby Crayola Factory—the sandwiches are fresh, large, and cheap. People drive miles for the tasty chicken salad. The line to order can be long, but it moves fast. Sandwiches $3–5.

Emmaus
✿ **Trivet Diner** (610-965-2838), 4102 Chestnut Street. Open daily 5 AM–9 PM. Huge portions, low

VENDORS AT ALLENTOWN FAIRGROUNDS MARKET

DOWNTOWN BETHLEHEM

prices, homemade pies, and authentic Pennsylvania Dutch cooking. Early birds should check out the pre-9 AM breakfast specials.

ICE CREAM/DESSERT Baked (610-966-6100), 228 Main Street. Hippest place in town for vegan pumpkin muffins, pear ginger scones, iced organic green tea, and La Colombe coffee, There's also a small selection of sandwiches and soup.

Emmaus Bakery (610-965-2170), 415 Chestnut Street. You'll find handmade cinnamon swirl donuts, apple fritters, and light-as-air glazed donuts at this old-fashioned family bakery.

Purple Cow Creamery (610-252-5544), 14 S. Bank Street, Easton. Tucked in an alley around the corner from the Crayola Factory, this brick-walled ice cream parlor serves Italian ice, milk shakes, real hot fudge sundaes, and delicious ice cream. Choose from tiramisu, toasted coconut, Black Forest cake, cotton candy, and other fun flavors.

Rewired Gallery and Café (610-317-8010), 520 Main Street, Bethlehem. Open daily. Unlike many cafés that also call themselves art galleries, this one is the real thing, with an entire adjacent room dedicated to original works in painting, sculpture, photography, and glass.

The café serves soups and sandwiches, but it's the cakes, scones, and coffee drinks (and free WiFi, of course) that seem to get the most attention.

FARMS AND FARMERS' MARKETS Easton Farmers' Market (www.eastonfarmers market.com), Centre Square (next to the Crayola Factory). Open 9–1 Saturday, May through November. The oldest continuous open-air farmers' market in the country. Shop for grass-fed beef and pork, organic yogurt, Welsh tea cakes, and all sorts of fruits and vegetables. Homemade baby food, fair-trade coffee, tasty prepared foods, and locally made crafts and jellies are also available.

Emmaus Farmers' Market (www.emmausmarket.com), 235 Main Street (in the Keystone Nazareth Bank & Trust parking lot). Sunday 10–2, May through November. More than 20 vendors

CHICKEN POT PIES AT ALLENTOWN FAIRGROUNDS MARKET

sell seasonal local produce, fresh bison, goat's milk cheese, and pastries, at this highly regarded outdoor market.

Fairgrounds Farmers' Market (610-435-7469), 17th and Chew Streets, Allentown. Open 8–6 Thursday through Saturday. You can get a haircut, shop for fondue forks and Avon products, hear Pennsylvania Dutch spoken, and eat some of the finest local specialties around at this large multifaceted indoor market. It is widely known for its meat selection: there's everything from ring bologna and Habersatt scrapple to Italian Braciole and stuffed pork chops ready for the oven. Other favorites include **Dan's Bar-B-Que** for chicken pies and ribs, **Gdynia Polish Market** for hand-shaped pierogi and kielbasa, **Heckenberger's Seafood** for fresh reasonably priced salmon and lobster tails, and the **Kiffle Kitchen** for fruit-filled cookies. It gets more crowded as the day goes on, but there is plenty of free parking. Some vendors only take cash.

✳ Entertainment

 ♿ **SteelStacks** (610-332-1300; www.steelstacks.org), 101 Founders Way, Bethlehem. Another clever use of abandoned Bethlehem Steel property, this huge arts and cultural complex opened in 2011 with multiple entertainment options. The cornerstone is **ArtsQuest Center,** which includes several different venues for live music, plays, films, improv comedy shows, and children's theater. The sleek **Levitt Pavillion** hosts free outdoor summer concerts with blast furnaces serving as the backdrop. Visit the Web site for a current calendar of events.

&. **Symphony Hall** (610-351-7990), 23 N. Sixth Street, Allentown. Home to the Allentown Symphony, the 1,200-seat concert hall also stages non-orchestral music and theatrical performances for adults and kids throughout the year.

&. **State Theater** (610-252-3132; www.statetheatre.org), 453 Northampton Street, Easton. Renovated in the 1990s, this historic theater hosts concerts by nationally known performers, circuses, and off-Broadway hits like *Late Night Catechism*.

&. **Boyd Theatre** (610-866-1521; www.theboyd.com), 30 W. Broad Street, Bethlehem. This great old theater opened in 1921 and has been owned by the same local family since 1970. Its single screen shows first-run films.

Pines Dinner Theatre (610-433-2333, www.pinesdinnertheatre .com), 448 N. 17th Street, Allentown. Crowd-pleasing musicals and multi-course comfort food.

✳ Selective Shopping

For a low-key mix of shops, cafes, and architecture, head to downtown Emmaus. Its pedestrian-friendly streets have a handful of

antiques and home-decor shops, upscale consignment stores, historic churches, and bakeries. For a complete list of stores and a map, visit www.emmausmainstreet.com.

Blind Willow Bookshop (610-965-0500; www.blindwillow bookshop.com), 412 Chestnut Street, Emmaus. Look for the hand-painted hex sign out front, then explore the small but thoughtful selection of used books, with especially robust sections on Pennsylvania, philosophy, and art. The shop also hosts art exhibits, poetry readings, and film screenings.

Elephant's Trunk Consignment Shop (610-967-6621; www.etrunk .org), 348 Main Street, Emmaus. Closed Sunday. Gently used furniture, jewelry, and artwork are tastefully displayed in the town's original library building.

La Belle Cuisine-Fine Cookware (610-928-0070), 447 Chestnut Street, Emmaus. Closed Monday. Browse for copper colanders, mini-cheesecake pans, truffle shavers, and other hard-to-find culinary gadgets in a circa-1865 home.

Nearby
Moravian Bookshop (610-866-5481), 428 Main Street, Bethlehem. Open daily except some holidays. Established in 1745 by the Moravian church, this charming retail complex near the Hotel Bethlehem claims to be the world's oldest bookseller. Besides a wide selection of books on the

Moravian church and Lehigh Valley history, it also offers bestsellers and children's books, candles, pottery, and exquisite ornaments and gifts featuring the symbolic Moravian star. There's even a deli in back, meaning you could lose yourself for an entire afternoon in here.

✳ Special Events

May: **Bethlehem Bach Festival** (first two weekends)—the all-volunteer Bach Choir of Bethlehem ardently and lovingly performs works of the legendary composer during this century-old

MORAVIAN BOOK SHOP

event. For more information, visit www.bach.org.

May through August: **Pennsylvania Shakespeare Festival,** DeSales University, Center Valley—the state's official summer celebration of the Bard and other master dramatists attracts a talented pool of actors from New York and Philadelphia. For details, visit www.pashakespeare.org.

August: **MusikFest** (first week), around Bethlehem—more than 300 musical acts, from polka bands to rock legends, perform at this popular 10-day event that brings more than a million people to indoor and outdoor venues around Bethlehem. Tickets for individual concerts are in the $20–50 range. For details, go to www.musikfest.org.

Great Allentown Fair (late August/early September) started as a small agricultural event in 1852 and has evolved into a three-day celebration with petting zoos, rides, and plenty of food and live entertainment (Journey, Keith Urban, and Lady Antebellum are a few recent headliners).

November/December: **Christkindlmart**, Bethlehem (late November through December)—modeled after Germany's open-air Christmas markets, this fabulous holiday bazaar features handmade crafts, live holiday music, ice sculpting, and more. Related events include trolley and carriage rides, walking tours, and holiday concerts. For details, go to www.christmascity.org.

THE POCONO MOUNTAINS

A couple of decades ago, the Pocono Mountains region was widely regarded as an over-the-top honeymoon destination for couples who liked ceilings painted with cherubs and bathtubs shaped like champagne flutes. A few affordable rustic family lodges attracted vacationing city folk from New York and Philadelphia for a week or two in the summer. Candle shops were plentiful.

A handful of couples-only resorts still exist today, but the area has come a long, long way since then, and has turned itself into a major vacation destination for families and couples of all tastes. Golfers can take their pick of three dozen courses. Outdoor adventure types flock to the Lehigh Gorge area, where stellar whitewater rafting and mountain-biking opportunities abound; there's even dogsledding for those who may want to try a new outdoor adventure sport. Families favor the water parks and affordable camping and cabin rental options. And couples can choose from a long list of upscale B&Bs and country inns that are more likely to have antique brass beds than the mirrored headboards of yore.

Though they are geologically a southwestern extension of the Catskill Mountains, the Pocono Mountains aren't really a mountain chain at all. They are a combination of deep forests, rolling hills, sparkling lakes, and limitless outdoor pastimes. The entire Pocono Mountains region encompasses more than 2,400 square miles and four counties: Carbon, Monroe, Pike, and Wayne. It is home to eight state and two national parks, 170 miles of rivers, 35 golf courses, 63 ski trails, summer camps, and more resorts than anywhere else in the state. The towns of Jim Thorpe, Blakeslee, Marshalls Creek, Stroudsburg, Milford, Hawley, and Honesdale are a part of the Pocono Mountains region; the towns of Wilkes-Barre or Scranton are not, though they are within easy driving distance.

To make it more easily digestible, I have divided the region into two sections: the south region, which includes the Delaware Water Gap, Jim Thorpe, and the region's largest number of resorts, and the north region of Pike and Wayne Counties, which is less than 90 miles from New York

City and known for its quaint towns, unique museums, and Green Acres-meets-Manhattan vibe.

Perhaps because it harks back to the region's heart-shaped-tub days, tourism officials and current business owners tend to frown upon referring to the region by its nickname, the Poconos. I try to adhere to that in this guide, but I apologize in advance if I fall off the wagon occasionally and call it the Poconos. I spent many adolescent summers here, and the area's unpretentious beauty holds a special place in my heart.

POCONO MOUNTAINS SOUTH

AREA CODE The entire southern Pocono Mountain region lies within 570.

GUIDANCE The **Pennsylvania Welcome Center** (570-234-1180), just off I-80 near Delaware Water Gap, is a full-service rest facility with picnic tables, vending machines, maps, and information about attractions throughout the state, as well as the latest road and weather conditions. It's staffed daily 7 AM–7 PM. In Stroudsburg, the **Pocono Mountains Vacation Bureau** (570-421-5791; www.800poconos.com), 1004 Main Street, Stroudsburg, is a good spot for area maps and attractions; they will also send you materials by mail upon request. In **Jim Thorpe,** stop by the visitor center in the old railway station for maps and information on current activities.

GETTING THERE By air: **Philadelphia International** (215-937-6800) and **Newark** are the closest major airports, each more than two hours away. **Lehigh Valley International** (888-359-5842) is about a 45-minute drive from Stroudsburg.

By car: From Philadelphia, I-476 to Lehighton or Blakeslee for the western region. For Stroudsburg and Delaware Water Gap, pick up US 22 in Allentown, then follow PA 33 north. From New York or New Jersey, take I-80 west to Stroudsburg and points beyond.

By bus: **Martz Trailways** (570-421-3040; www.martztrailways.com) runs buses from New York City and Scranton to stations in Delaware Water Gap, Mount Pocono, and Marshalls Creek. **Greyhound** also has service to Scranton and Philadelphia from Delaware Water Gap.

GETTING AROUND Unless you have the Olympian stamina of Jim Thorpe, you'll need a car to get around the region. It can take as long as an hour to drive from Lehigh Gorge to Delaware Water Gap. The main

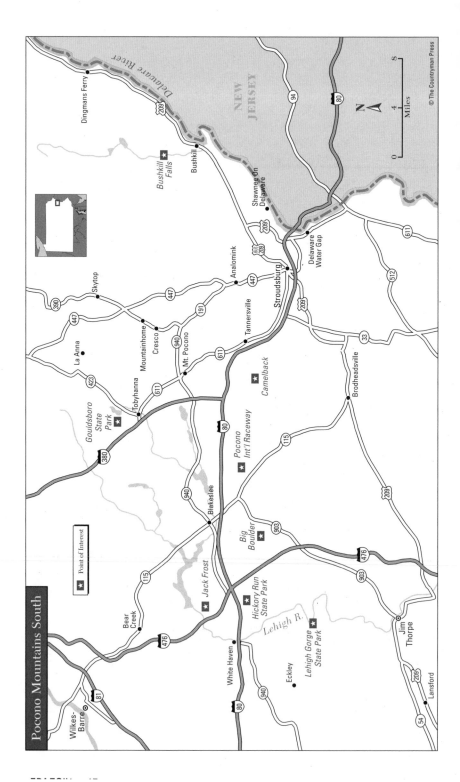

Pocono Mountains South

★ Point of Interest

Delaware River

NEW JERSEY

N

0   4   8
Miles

© The Countryman Press

Dingmans Ferry

Bushkill Falls
Bushkill

Shawnee On Delaware

Delaware Water Gap

Skytop

Analomink

Stroudsburg

La Anna

Mountainhome
Cresco

Tannersville

Mt. Pocono

Tobyhanna

Camelback

Gouldsboro State Park

Brodheadsville

Pocono Int'l Raceway

Blakeslee

Big Boulder

Bear Creek

Jack Frost

White Haven

Hickory Run State Park

Lehigh R.

Lehigh Gorge State Park

Eckley

Jim Thorpe

Lansford

Wilkes-Barre

209
94
80
390
447
447
423
191
940
611
611
80
380
115
940
903
476
115
476
903
940
80
81
54
209
209
33
512
611
209

streets of Stroudsburg and Jim Thorpe are pleasant for walking, with plenty of shops, restaurants, and historic architecture. Be sure to bring a good map and request very clear directions to your destinations, especially places without numbered addresses.

MEDICAL EMERGENCY Pocono Medical Center (570-421-4000), 206 E. Brown Street, East Stroudsburg.

WHEN TO GO Summer is the most popular time to visit the Pocono Mountains, and the time when the lakes and rivers are warmest and most attractions are open and in full swing. The fall, however, is my favorite time to visit. The leaves are turning brilliant shades of gold and orange, the air is crisp, and you can't drive a mile without bumping into a pumpkin or harvest fest. Late March through June (and to a lesser extent in September and October) is the best period for white-water rafting here because of scheduled dam releases along the Lehigh River.

✳ Villages

Delaware Water Gap. Not to be confused with the natural wonder of the same name, this sleepy town of 800 residents was once a thriving resort serving the many people visiting the nearby gorge, including Teddy Roosevelt. Some of its once-grand buildings and hotels are fading and in need of repair, but it still has several worthwhile attractions, such as the jazz performances at the Deer Head Inn, a few art galleries, and a terrific BYO restaurant. The Appalachian Trail crosses right through its main street (PA 611).

Mount Pocono. Home to many of the all-inclusive resorts and souvenir candle shops that first put the Pocono Mountains on the map, this central borough probably best epitomizes the Poconos as a honeymoon capitol. It has been heavily developed in recent years and has a Wal-Mart, freestanding casino, and several grocery stores and strip malls. Busy PA 940 cuts through its center, but there are still numerous forested country roads to its north that lead past old general stores, rustic inns, and bait and tackle shops. It's also home to the old-fashioned Casino Theater and Memorytown, a kitschy destination complex comprised of a tavern, picnic area, game room, and a lake with a faux covered bridge and paddleboats.

Mountainhome. You could call this aptly named town the gateway to the central Poconos. You'll pass through it on your way to such destinations as Canadensis, Skytop, La Anna, and Buck Hill Falls. It's not a walkable kind of place, but it has several cafés, shops, and attractions such as the Pocono Playhouse and Callie's Candy Factory.

Shawnee. Golf. Ski. Swim. Kayak. Those are your main options in this small community next to the Delaware River. Its dominant resident is the Shawnee ski resort, but you will also find a well-regarded theater, several good B&Bs, and the lovely and regal Shawnee Inn and Golf Resort, once owned by Fred Waring and patronized by Arnold Palmer, Jackie Gleason, and other celebrities.

✷ To See

MUSEUMS Antoine Dutot Museum and Gallery (570-476-4240; www.dutotmuseum.com), Main Street (PA 611), Delaware Water Gap. Open Saturday and Sunday 1–5, May through October; $2 donation. This 1850s-era school houses an art gallery, preserved classroom, and history exhibits that cover the area's early development by French plantation owner Antoine Dutot to its current role as a faded resort town.

&. **Pocono Indian Museum** (570-588-9338; www.poconoindianmuseum .com), US 209, Bushkill. Open daily; $5 adults, $2.50 ages 6–16. Located in a white-columned mansion, this unsung, if dated, six-room museum is obviously a labor of love for its employees. Instead of just pinning up their collection of ancient artifacts, many of which were found in the Delaware River area, they present them in context with mannequins and other ways that let you see how they worked within the Lenape lifestyle. You will also find a 1843 Cree Indian scalp from the Dakotas and a full-size wigwam among the displays. The gift shop is huge and fun to browse.

SHAWNEE GENERAL STORE

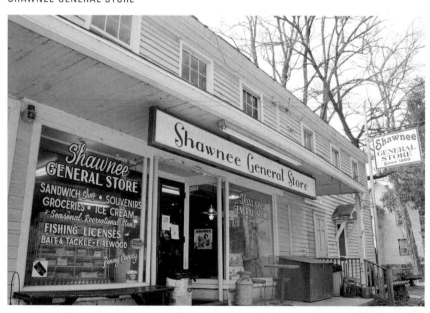

FOR FAMILIES ⚐ 🐾 **Bushkill Falls** (570-588-6682; www.visitbushkill falls.com), US 209 and Bushkill Falls Road, Bushkill. Open daily April through October; $11 adults, $6 ages 4–10. This series of eight scenic waterfalls has long been a popular destination for families. Charles E. Peters started charging visitors a dime to see the falls in 1904. His descendants still run the place. Over the years, they have added a gift shop, Native American museum, small lake with paddleboats, and playground, but it all remains relatively rustic. The "hiking trails" that lead to the falls are actually well-maintained walkways flanked by locust-wood guard rails. You can take an easy path to reach the main falls, or spend as long as two hours hiking to the upper canyons and glens. Families with young kids might want to bring a back carrier. The place gets packed on summer weekends. Don't miss the Bushkill Story cabin, a small house displaying early marketing materials, photographs, souvenirs (like a Bushkill Falls handheld pinball game), and brochures.

🍭 **Callie's Candy Kitchen** (570-595-2280), PA 390, Mountainhome. A visit to this multiroom candy shop is a rite of passage for every school-age kid in the area. Harry Callie, who started the business in 1952, still does regular candymaking demonstrations combined with merry lectures on how he got into the candy business. As you browse the store, you'll find that Callie's isn't afraid to dip anything in chocolate, including whole s'mores, crackers, whipped marshmallows, Oreos, and even cream cheese.

🍭 **Callie's Pretzel Factory** (570-595-3257), PA 191/390, Cresco. Also owned by the Callies, and about 3 miles south of the candy store, this place is a must-stop for pretzel lovers. Show up right around opening hour of 10 AM and you can watch the day's batches being made by a huge machine in the back. Choose from garlic pretzels, pretzels stuffed with apples or cheddar cheese, hot dogs wrapped in pretzels, and even funnel-cake pretzels. For some reason, there's also a gift shop for lefthanders in the back.

⚐ **Camel Beach Water Park** (570-629-1661; camelbeach.com), Tannersville. Open late May through Labor Day; $35 adults, $25 ages 3–11; season passes also available. Every summer, Camelback Ski Area transforms into a wild and wacky water park with a giant wave pool, a tubing "river," and 22 slides with names such as Vortex, Riptide, and Triple Venom. It's popular with teenagers, but there are a few sedate activities such as chairlift rides, mini-golf, and a shallow pool for tots. A tip: Bring your own food and eat in the picnic area outside before or after your visit; the food options inside the park are overpriced and mediocre.

⚐ **Lehigh Gorge Scenic Railroad** (570-325-8485; www.lgsry.com), 1 Susquehanna Street, Jim Thorpe, $12–18 adults, $9–10 ages 3–12. If you don't want to bike the Lehigh Gorge Rail Trail, this is a way to witness some of the same gorgeous scenery. Vintage coaches leave the downtown station for a 16-mile ride along the Lehigh River. Wave to the hikers, cyclists, and rafters, while conductors describe the area's wildlife and plants and history of the anthracite coal industry. The ride is especially beautiful in October when the leaves change color.

GAMBLING The state's first freestanding slots parlor, **Mount Airy Casino Resort** (877-682-4791; www.mountairycasino.com), opened in late fall 2007 on the grounds of a former honeymooners' lodge. It features more than 2,400 slot machines, plus blackjack, craps, and roulette, and is one of

JIM THORPE

Located along the Lehigh River at the southwestern edge of the Pocono Mountains region, Jim Thorpe is a former railroad and coal-shipping town that was known as Mauch Chunk until 1955. That's when the famous Native American athlete died and his struggling widow struck a deal to have his remains buried there and the town renamed for the famous Olympian. Though Thorpe never set foot here, a large monument stands in his honor near a sign declaring the town THE SWITZERLAND OF AMERICA. Today, Jim Thorpe is one of those destinations that more than lives up to the expectations based on postcards or word of mouth. Anchored by a thriving little downtown, it is surrounded by miles of pristine

JIM THORPE'S GRAVE ON THE OUTSKIRTS OF TOWN

the few casinos to offer a non-smoking gambling area. A hotel, spa, and
nightclub are adjacent.

SCENIC DRIVES **Buck Hill Falls,** north of Mountainhome, is home to
the region's first golf course and some of the prettiest stone houses you'll
ever see. Escape the tourist scene around Mount Pocono and head north
on PA 191 for a peaceful 30-minute drive. On the way, you'll pass forested
lands and meadows and a handful of antiques and gift shops and old general stores. Bear left onto Bush Mountain Road in Mountainhome, then
drive several miles to Buck Hill Road and make a right. Once you get
here, there's not much to do except gawk at the stately mansions and

forest, rivers, and a free and easy spirit. Just about every outdoor adventure and cycling magazine has ranked it as one of the top biking destinations in the state, if not the country; it is also a popular spot for paintball,
hiking, and white-water rafting.

The nonathlete will also find things to do here. The opulent **Asa Packer
Mansion** (home of the founder of the Lehigh Valley Railroad) sits on a hilltop overlooking the town and is open for tours daily from June through
October (570-325-3229; www.asapackermansion.com). The **Old Jail
Museum** (570-325-5259) on West Broadway was built in 1871 and offers
fascinating tours of original cells and tales about the Molly Maguires, a
secret society of anthracite miners who used terrorism to force mine owners to improve working conditions (seven were accused and hanged here).
Call ahead for hours.

One can also easily spend a couple of hours poking around the frozen-
in-time downtown, gawking at the varied styles of architecture and visiting
the hip cafes, art galleries, and small shops. The **Mauch Chunk Opera
House** (570-325-4439; 41 W. Broadway), built in 1881, still hosts theatrical
and music performances, films, and art exhibits. For kids, there's a model
train display in the **Hooven Building** next to the train depot, along with rides
on the **Lehigh Gorge Scenic Railway** (570-325-8485; www.lgsry.com).
Sleeping options include the venerable **Inn at Jim Thorpe** and a handful of
B&Bs and nearby campgrounds (see also Lodging). I can't say enough
good things about this town. Go.

natural stone bridges or have a lemonade at the semiprivate **Buck Hills Tennis Club**. Before heading back, you can continue north a few miles on PA 191 to **Holley Ross Pottery** in the tiny village of LaAnna.

✳ Outdoor Activities

AUTO RACING Pocono Raceway (570-646-2300; 800-722-3929; www .poconoraceway.com), Long Pond. Many NASCAR racers consider this 2.5-mile tri-oval speedway to be one of the toughest tracks in the country. Located on a former spinach farm, it draws more than 100,000 fans twice a year to its annual cup races. (See also Special Events.) It also has stock car racing and driving school programs.

Mahoning Valley Raceway (570-386-4900; www.mahoningspeedway.com), PA 443, Lehighton. Open Saturday evenings March through October. Non-stop action rules at this quarter-mile track, which runs modified and late-model stock cars and vintage Camaros and Monte Carlos. Family-friendly features include bring-your-own-picnic baskets, a no-alcohol policy, and free admission for kids under 10. Admission: $12–20.

BICYCLING Once described by *Bicycling* magazine as Durango East, Jim Thorpe is for riders of all abilities. You'll find several good places to rent bikes in town, including **Blue Mountain Sports** (570-325-4421; www.bikejimthorpe.com) across from the train depot; they also rent kayaks, rowboats, and canoes. (See also White-Water Rafting.)

By far the most popular trail around—and arguably one of the top bike rides in the country—is **Lehigh Gorge Rail-Trail**, a 26-mile converted railroad bed between White Haven and Jim Thorpe. Several bike shops offer shuttle service to the northern entrance at White Haven, which takes you past waterfalls, sheer rock walls, and gorgeous scenic overlooks before dropping into Jim Thorpe. **Whitewater Rafting Adventures** (800-876-0285; www.adventurerafting.com/biking) and **Pocono Biking** (800-944-8392; www.poconobiking.com) offer bike rentals and shuttle service, and half- and full-day guided trips.

CANOEING & KAYAKING Kittatinny Canoes (800-356-2852), 102 Kittatinny Court, Dingmans Ferry. Guided canoe and kayak trips at five different points of the Delaware River. Rates start at about $40 per person for two and a half hours. They also do tubing trips.

DOGSLEDDING Learn how to steer a sled pulled by Siberian and Alaskan huskies across snow-covered hills and paths (actually golf courses). The newest sport to arrive in northeast Pennsylvania teaches the exhilarating art of mushing between December and February. **Arctic**

Paws Dog Sled Tours offers hour-long sessions at the Inn at Pocono Manor (www.arcticpawsdogsledtours.com) between December and February, while **Skytop Lodge** (See Lodging) added dogsledding to its all-inclusive winter sports activities.

FISHING **Paradise Trout Preserve** (570-629-0422), PA 191, Paradise, near Cresco. Home to the state's first fish hatchery, the property also has a pond stocked with brown, brook, and rainbow trout. No fishing license is required, though registration costs $2.50 a person (kids under 12 are free). Good fishing spots that require a license include **Tobyhanna Lake** in Tobyhanna State Park, a favorite for bass, brook trout, catfish, and perch. **Hickory Run State Park** has two stocked trout streams and you'll find bass and trout in the nearby **Lehigh River.** In Jim Thorpe, you can fish for bass, pickerel, and trout in **Mauch Chunk Lake.**

GOLF **Split Rock Golf Club** (570-722-9901), Lake Harmony. This public 27-hole course at Split Rock Lodge has midsized greens, nice views, and a par of 72.

Taminent Golf Club (570-588-6652), Bushkill Falls Road, Taminent. Designed by Robert Trent Jones, this 18-hole mountaintop course has tree-lined fairways, undulating greens, and majestic views.

HIKING A popular portion of the **Joseph McDade Recreational Trail** in the Delaware Water Gap National Recreation Area begins at the Hialeah Picnic Area north of Shawnee and follows the river for 5 scenic and flat miles north to Turn Farm. Along the way, you'll pass **Smithfield Beach,** which offers roped-off swimming in the summer, and stellar vistas of the river and mountain ridges. Biking and cross-country skiing is also allowed on this flat well-maintained trail.

HORSEBACK RIDING **Carson's Riding Stables** (570-839-9841), PA 611, Cresco. This 60-acre facility near Mount Pocono offers hourly trail rides for all levels of riders.

SKIING **Camelback** (570-629-1661; www.skicamelback.com), Camelback Road, Tannersville. This is the largest ski area in the region, with 33 trails, most of them easy and intermediate, two terrain parks, and a half-pipe area. Three lodges serve food at the base of the mountain; there's also a restaurant at the top.

Jack Frost (570-443-8425; www.jackfrostbigboulder.com), PA 940, Blakeslee. Known for its challenging terrain, this has 27 trails, nine lifts, a cross-country ski trail, and a popular snow tubing area. It shares some facilities with nearby Big Boulder, known for its beginner trails and programs, allowing you to ski both areas on the same day on one ticket.

Shawnee Mountain (570-421-7231; www.shawneemt.com), Hollow Road, Shawnee. This family-friendly resort is at the southernmost point of

DELAWARE WATER GAP

You don't need to be a geologist to appreciate this natural wonder. Millions of years ago, this area was a level plain; it is believed that over time moving water wore down and pushed through a weak spot in the mountain ridge to form a breathtaking gorge that separates two mountains, **Minsi** and **Tammany**. For a generation after the Civil War, the Delaware Water Gap was one of the top tourist destinations in existence (before the emergence of names such as Catskill, Disney, and Niagara). Today, it's a popular day trip for Pennsylvania and New Jersey residents, as well as outdoors types who come to kayak and canoe the river or hike the Appalachian Trail. The gorge is located at the southern edge of the **Delaware Water Gap National Recreation Area** (570-588-2451; www.nps .gov/dema), a national park that stretches along either side of the Delaware River from Delaware Water Gap north to Milford.

DELAWARE WATER GAP

the Poconos region, with 23 trails, a terrain park, and half-pipe area. A cozy lodge overlooks the bunny slope.

WHITE-WATER RAFTING The **Lehigh River** offers Class III white-water rafting and many outfitters in the area run regular trips during the

The gap itself can be viewed from several parking overlooks around the town of Delaware Water Gap, including Point of Gap, off PA 611, where there's plenty of parking. There are nice views of the carved stone side of Mount Tammany (some say it looks like the profile of the Lenape Indian chief for whom the mountain is named). Another good place to stop is **Kittatinny Point Visitor Center,** just off I-80 across the state border in New Jersey, where you can pick up maps and speak to helpful park rangers. If you have the time and are in decent

VIEW OF MOUNT TAMMANY

shape, consider hiking up Mount Tammany for gorgeous views of the entire gap and surrounding towns. From the New Jersey side, at the Dunnfield Creek parking area in Worthington State Forest, you can access a section of the Appalachian Trail that runs right over the top of Kittatinny Ridge to Sunfish Pond, a beautiful glacial lake surrounded by woods.

If you're short on time or aren't into hiking up a mountain, another good way to learn about the history of the area is via narrated trolley ride. **Water Gap Trolley** (570-476-9766; PA 611; $9.50 adults, $4 ages 3–11) runs tours daily, four or five times a day from March through November. Guides are informative and funny, and the hour-long trip includes stops at several over-looks and historic buildings and tales about local celebrities such as Fred Waring, Jackie Gleason, and Mr. Greenjeans (of Captain Kangaroo fame).

summer and during spring and fall dam release weekends. (See also Lehigh Gorge State Park.) Many also offer kayaking packages and bike rentals and shuttles.

Pocono Whitewater Rafting (800-944-8392; 570-325-3655), 1519 PA 903, also known as **Lehigh Gorge Outpost,** runs rafting trips for all levels, plus offers kayaking, paintball, bike rentals, and shuttles to Lehigh Gorge. **Jim Thorpe River Adventures** (800-424-7238; www.jtraft.com) 1 Adventure Lane, off PA 903, offers guided rafting trips and bike rentals.

✷ Green Space

Big Pocono State Park (570-894-8336), Camelback Road, Tannersville. You can see much of northeastern Pennsylvania and stretches of New Jersey and New York from the summit of this 1,300-acre park, which is also home to Camelback Mountain. It has 7 miles of hiking trails, three picnic areas, and limited hunting grounds. The summit can be reached by foot or car up a steep and winding paved road.

Gouldsboro and Tobyhanna State Parks (570-894-8336). These two family-friendly parks are adjacent and anchored by two large lakes with swimming and boating opportunities and 19 miles of hiking trails for all levels. A park office at Tobyhanna just off PA 423 has maps and other information. The entrance to Gouldsboro is off PA 507.

Lehigh Gorge State Park (570-443-0400), White Haven. This 4,500-acre park follows the Lehigh River from Francis E. Walter Dam in White Haven down to Jim Thorpe in the south. It is dominated by its eponymous gorge, sheer rock walls, rock outcroppings, and dozens of waterfalls. It offers hunting, fishing, and plenty of scenic vistas, but its biggest draw is its white-water rafting and mountain-biking opportunities (see also Outdoor Activities). The Lehigh Gorge Trail, which follows 26 miles of abandoned railroad grade along the river, is beloved by mountain bikers for its scenery, tree canopies, and slight downhill north-to-south grade; horseback riders and hikers may also use it. It can be accessed via White Haven, Tannery Rapid, Rockport, and Glen Onoko, where an iron railroad bridge was renovated in 2009 to provide welcome access into downtown Jim Thorpe. Many bike shops offer a shuttle ride that drops you at White Haven in the north and lets you take the trail downhill all the way back to Jim Thorpe. The upper portion of Lehigh Gorge links with **Hickory Run State Park** (570-443-0400), a 15,500-acre park with plenty of recreational features such as a lake, swimming pool, playground, snack bar, visitor center, and dozens of hiking and snowmobile trails.

✳ Lodging

RESORTS ✐ ⅃ Great Wolf Lodge

(800-768-9653; www.great wolf.com/poconos), 1 Great Wolf Drive, Scotrun. If you're a parent or grandparent of a child under age 12, chances are you've heard of this massive resort and water park. One of 12 Great Wolf Lodges around the country, it has 401 large suites, two restaurants, and lots and lots of kid-friendly activities, the highlight being a Costco-sized water park with 11 slides, six pools, and a four-story tree house. They also considerately operate a spa for parents who need a break from the splashing action. Prices drop considerably on weekdays after Labor Day. Another money-saving tip: bring your own food and snacks (all rooms have fridges), as the dining options (pizza, all-you-can-eat buffets) are nothing to write home about. They also have package deals that include passes to nearby attractions like Camelbeach. Standard suites start at $239.

✐ ⅃ ♂ **Skytop Lodge** (570-595-7401; 800-617-2389; www.skytop.com), PA 390, Skytop, 3 miles north of Canadensis. Built in the 1920s as a members-only hunting lodge, this secluded mountaintop resort ranks among the best all-inclusive destinations in the area. Sprawled on 5,500 acres of woods, streams, meadows, lakes, and waterfalls, it has an air of country elegance and more activities than you can possibly imagine: tennis, swimming, nighttime deer watching, stargazing, downhill skiing, fly-fishing, golf, massages, lawn bowling, and even high tea. You can stay in the original stone lodge, in a nearby modern 20-room inn, or in spacious cottages overlooking the stream, lodge, or golf course;

POCONOS RESORT SIGN

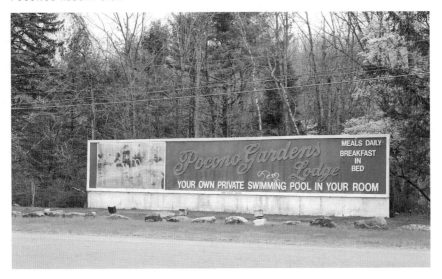

meals are served in the lodge's grandiose dining room, a separate lake-view restaurant, or an English pub. Rates (including three meals): $376–720; there is usually a two-night minimum on weekends.

INNS & GUESTHOUSES

🐚 **Deer Head Inn** (570-424-2000; www.deerheadinn.com), 5 Main Street, Delaware Water Gap. Most people associate the Deer Head with terrific live jazz and don't realize there are eight comfortable rooms and suites for rent upstairs. All the rooms were overhauled in 2007 and have private baths, crown molding, high ceilings, and top-of-the-line mattresses and linens; the suites have sitting areas as well. Ask about packages that include jazz and dinner for two (see also Entertainment). They start at $189 a night and are a very good value if you

like jazz. Rooms and suites $90–150 (weekdays), $120–180 (weekends, includes breakfast).

🐚 ♿ **Inn at Jim Thorpe** (570-325-2599; www.innjt.com), 24 Broadway, Jim Thorpe. This historic hotel is in the heart of downtown, and has beautiful wrought-iron balconies from which to take in all the action. The 34 rooms and 9 suites are decorated in understated Victorian style and have private baths and wireless Internet access; some have fireplaces and Jacuzzi tubs. Rates include a $7 voucher for the adjacent Broadway Grille. They also offer biking and rafting packages that include all equipment and bike shuttles to Lehigh Gorge. Rooms $93–183.

♿ 🐕 **Stroudsmoor Country Inn** (570-421-6431; www.stroudsmoor .com), Stroudsmoor Road,

DEER HEAD INN

Stroudsburg. This would be my pick for the best place to stay near Stroudsburg. Just five minutes from town, it's surrounded by woodlands and feels like a quiet country getaway. The main house has 15 small and attractive rooms and junior suites; newer suites with balconies overlooking the forest are just across the way; there are also small cottages with front porches overlooking an outdoor pool. The rates include a full breakfast at the inn's restaurant. This is a popular spot for destination weddings and sometimes it hosts several over a single weekend. Rooms and junior suites: $89–175; suites $280–800.

BED & BREAKFASTS

Bischwind (570-472-3820; www .bischwind.com), 1 Coach Road, Bear Creek. Located just outside Wilkes-Barre and about a 20-minute drive from many western Pocono Mountains attractions, this eight-room hunting-lodge-turned-B&B is a must for history buffs. A giant carved wooden bear greets you near the entrance in honor of one-time guest Theodore Roosevelt. Handsome and ornate is the best way to describe the living and dining areas, which are decorated with stuffed deer heads, rich red leather chairs, large fireplaces, and wood floors. The rooms have the same grand feel as the common areas, but come with modern upgrades such as TVs, whirlpool tubs, and wireless Internet access; the two-room Teddy Roosevelt Suite is a favorite. Bear Creek is a

stone's throw from the inn and there is an exquisitely peaceful hour-long hiking trail that loops around the lake. Other nice touches include an outdoor swimming pool and a lavish breakfast of poached salmon or filet mignon, sautéed potatoes, eggs, and cheesecake (though guests may opt for a lighter continental breakfast). Rooms $135–245.

Gatehouse Country Inn (570-420-4553; www.gatehousecountry inn.com), P.O. Box 264, River Road, Shawnee. Originally built circa 1900 as a stable and carriage house, the Gatehouse was turned into a summer home by bandleader and Pennsylvania native Fred Waring in the 1950s. Gordon and Cindy Way opened it as a B&B in 2001 with 3 second-floor rooms with private baths and sitting areas. The upstairs game room, where Waring is believed to have entertained friends such as Jackie Gleason and Dwight Eisenhower, features comfy chairs, games, and the original pool table. Guests also have access to a back courtyard flanked by an old-fashioned ice house, which the Ways have turned into a small antiques store. No children under 12. Rooms $160–215.

Hill Home Forge (570-325-0216; www.hillhomeforge.com), 10 Flagstaff Road, Jim Thorpe. Artists Nic and Eileen East run this mountain retreat about 2.5 miles west of town. The three rooms are spacious, quiet and tastefully decorated. The Woodland Suite is large enough for three adults and one child. East teaches stained glass-making classes, or you can just enjoy a tour of his workshop. Breakfast is especially good; apple-stuffed French toast is a specialty. Rooms $140–165; check the Web site for last-minute specials.

Rendon House (570-325-5515; www.rendonhouse.com), 80 Broadway, Jim Thorpe. Owner Pam Rendon runs this centrally located B&B with efficiency and a historian's wisdom. The three large rooms have queen or king-size beds and are tastefully decorated with antiques; the rate includes a delicious three-course breakfast. Other nice touches include a common refrigerator stocked with cold water and Yuengling and a terraced back garden overlooking a lush hillside. Weekday rates are among the lowest around. Rooms $95–125.

Stony Brook Inn (570-424-1100; 888-424-5240; www.stonybrook inn.com), PO Box 240, River Road, Shawnee. Pete and Roseann Ferguson are the gregarious owners of this cozy 1850s inn next to the Shawnee Playhouse. The four themed rooms (Country Bear, Rose, Oak, and the Bridal Suite) have private baths, TVs, and nice individual touches such as claw-foot tubs or Victorian chaise longues. There's also a swimming pool with large patio out back. The Delaware River and access to the McDade Trail are two blocks away. Rooms $110–170.

CAMPGROUNDS & COTTAGES 🐾 🏕 Delaware Water Gap KOA

(570-223-8000; 800-562-0375; www.delawarewater gapkoa.com), 233 Hollow Road, East Stroudsburg. Located just north of Shawnee a few miles off River Road, this year-round camp-ground has over 140 tent sites, primitive and with hookups, plus five cabins and dozens of RV sites. Activities include miniature train rides, mini-golf, volleyball, horse-shoes, and hayrides. Tent sites $36–45; cabins $72–90.

Mauch Chunk Lake County Park (570-325-3669), Jim Thorpe. Open mid-April through October. About 4 miles from downtown, this county park has more than 100 primitive tent sites and 12 two-room cabins with electricity. Many people love it for its access to 4-acre Mauch Chunk Lake and the Switchback Railroad Rail Trail, which crosses through the park. Tent sites: $17–32, cabins $47–68.

🏕 🐾 **Martinville Streamside Cottages** (570-595-2489; www .martinsvillestreamsidecottages .com), PA 390 north, Canadensis. This cluster of cottages has been in the Martin family since the early 1930s. It's ideal for families with children, with a swimming pool, and a pond with a slide and watercraft; a lovely stream runs right through the property. The eight rustic cottages sleep four to eight and have wraparound decks, full kitchens, and modern living rooms with fireplaces and TVs. Two suites above the main lodge have king beds, futons, gas fireplaces, and small refrigerators. Water comes from a local stream; it's a good idea to bring your own for cooking and drinking purposes. Cottages $195–450. Suites $125. Weekday and off-season rates are usually lower.

♦ **Dingmans Campground** (570-828-1551), 1006 US 209, Dingmans Ferry. Its primo riverfront location is what most campers love best about this rustic property about 10 miles north of Delaware Water Gap. Choose from 133 sites; the ones on the river go fast. Primitive tent sites: $25–28, with a two-night minimum weekends.

✴ Where to Eat

DINING OUT ♦ **Antelao Restaurant** (570-426-7226; www.anteleorestaurant.com), 84 Main Street, Delaware Water Gap. Dinner Thursday through Sunday. There are no bad tables in this welcoming bistro owned by Elvi and Michael De Lotto, who ran a popular bakery before opening their own restaurant in a Victorian home near the Delaware Water Gap. Named after a mountain in the Dolomite mountain range in Italy, the restaurant emphasizes seasonal produce: In summer, there might be roasted garlic flan with grilled eggplant, scaloppini of pork tenderloin with red peppers and gnocchi, and shrimp and basil sauté. Leave room for tiramisu. Reservations strongly recommend-

ed; no parties over six. BYO. Entrées $17–27.

Moya (570-325-8957; jimthorpemoya.com), Race Street, Jim Thorpe. Closed Tuesday and Wednesday in fall and winter. Local B&B owners will (rightly) steer you toward this elegant restaurant at the center of town. Chef Heriberto Yunda infuses the cuisine with influences from his native Ecuador such as corn and feta salad, pork tenderloin with balsamic-vinegar chutney, and shrimp with red curry, ginger, and coconut. His wife, Stephanie Yerme, is an artist whose colorful paintings brighten the walls. Beer and wine. Entrées $20–26.

& ⅋ **Blakeslee Inn** (570-646-1100), PA 940, Blakeslee. Dinner Wednesday through Saturday; brunch Sunday. Renovated in 2002, this upscale restaurant is a local favorite. Menu highlights include roasted figs stuffed with gorgonzola and pistachios, pan-seared scallops in lemon-blackberry syrup, and grilled beef tenderloin in a cabernet veal reduction. Extensive wine list. Reservations and proper attire recommended. Entrées $25–32.

& ⅋ **Tokyo Tea House** (570-839-8880), PA 940, Pocono Summit. Lunch and dinner daily, except Tuesday. This small strip-mall restaurant is arguably the best place for quality sushi in the Poconos. The teriyaki and tempura dishes are good, too. Lunch $8–12; dinner entrées $10–25.

EATING OUT & **Barley Creek Brewing Company** (570-839-9678), Sullivan Trail and Camelback Road, Tannersville. Lunch and dinner daily. Part Ye Olde Pub and part timbered ski lodge, this microbrewery near Camelback Ski Area is known for its handmade ales and tasty pub grub. Try the fish and chips or special Reuben of the day. If you happen to be here for lunch, you can join the free brewery tours that begin at 12:30 every day. Sandwiches and appetizers $9–16; entrées $10–24.

& ʏ **The Gem and Keystone** (570-424-0990), River Road, Shawnee. The menu complements the local handcrafted beers on tap: cheddar ale dip with soft pretzels, baby back ribs, hand-cut rib-eye steak, fish and chips, vegetarian or beef chili. Many of the ingredients are locally sourced. In summer, you can dine on a deck overlooking a pretty stream. Weekday happy hours offer beer discounts and $5 appetizer specials. Lunch $8–15; dinner $18–40.

& ʏ **Jubilee Restaurant** (570-646-2377), PA 940, Pocono Pines. Breakfast, lunch, and dinner daily. A local favorite known for its large portions, juicy burgers, and friendly service. Breakfasts are legendary; try the chef's free-for-all Pocono Sampler or any of the omelets. After your meal, you can join in games of billiards, darts, and TV sports-watching in the adjacent pub. Breakfast and lunch: $5–10; dinner: $13–23.

Village Farmer and Bakery (570-476-9440; www.villagefarmer .com), 52 Broad Street, Delaware Water Gap. Open daily at 8 AM. This bakery doesn't have an address on its business card; it just describes its location as between the town's two traffic lights. It's tough to miss—just look for the giant red-lettered sign that says APPLE PIE AND A HOT DOG FOR JUST $1.49. If that sweet deal doesn't interest you, try any of the donuts, cookies, brownies, or other desserts that were made that day. They also sell whole pies— apple is the specialty, but they usually have at least a dozen other kinds.

Jim Thorpe
Bear Appetit (570-732-4700), 29 Broadway. Open daily 6 AM–10 PM (until 9 PM Sunday). New York-style deli without the Manhattan prices. Stop here for a hearty breakfast before a day of hiking or cycling. Dishes $2–9.

Broadway Grille & Pub (570-732-4343), 24 Broadway. Owned by the adjacent Inn at Jim Thorpe, this central eatery is known for its daily specials (Wednesday is pancake day), weekday happy hours, and expansive menu of appetizers, burgers, and pasta, steak, and seafood entrées. There's breakfast, too. Lunch and small dishes $7–12, dinner entrées $13–29.

BYO Where to buy wine in the southern Pocono Mountains region:

You'll find **Wine & Spirits** stores in the **Pocono Village Mall** (570-839-9586), 87 PA 940, Mount Pocono; in the **Blakeslee Corners Shopping Plaza** (570-646-8069), PA 115/940; and in downtown **Stroudsburg** (570-424-3943), 761 Main Street.

✳ Entertainment

MUSIC ⅋ **Deer Head Inn** (570-424-2000; www.deerheadinn.com), 5 Main Street, Delaware Water Gap. Dinner and live performances Wednesday through Sunday. Enjoy terrific live jazz and blues in one of the oldest jazz bars in the country. Covers vary from none to $15 a person.

⅋ **Sarah Street Grill** (570-424-9120), 550 Quaker Alley, Stroudsburg. One of the best places around to hear live original music. Wednesday open-mic nights are popular. For sports fans, there are 17 TVs, plus a pool table and very good sushi bar that's open daily 4–10 PM.

⅋ **Penn's Peak** (610-826-9000; 866-605-7325; www.pennspeak .com), 325 Maury Road, Jim Thorpe. This large venue attracts a mix of country and western bands, tribute bands, and such veteran acts as Willie Nelson and Gordon Lightfoot. A dance floor, a restaurant, and two bars are on premises, as well as a deck with views that stretch for 50 miles.

MOVIES **Grand Cinema** (570-420-9885), 88 S. Courtland Street, East Stroudsburg. This century-

year old theater was restored in the late 1990s and features four screens showing art and independent films. An adjacent café serves specialty coffees and snacks.

Casino Theatre and Village Malt Shoppe (570-839-7831), 110 Pocono Boulevard (PA 611), Mount Pocono. Landmark two-screen theater shows first-run films and also has mini-golf, an arcade, and an ice cream parlor. It's a favorite evening destination for summer vacationers from all over the area.

THEATER ⅊ **Shawnee Playhouse** (570-421-5093; www.the shawneeplayhouse.com), River Road, Shawnee. This small 200-seat theater stages two musicals in the summer, plus Shakespeare plays, kids' shows, and the *Nutcracker Ballet* and *Messiah* sing-along in December.

✳ Selective Shopping

Crossing Premium Outlets (570-629-4650), PA 611 (at I-80) Tannersville. This eight-building complex features more than 100 factory outlet stores (from Timberland and Reebok to Ann Taylor and Banana Republic) and draws huge weekend crowds.

Carroll & Carroll Booksellers (570-420-1516), 740 Main Street, Stroudsburg. Well-stocked and friendly used-book store with many first and rare editions.

Holley Ross Pottery (570-676-3248), PA 191, LaAnna. Open daily May through mid-December. Surrounded by a pretty nature park above Cresco, this factory outlet sells Fiesta dinnerware, Robinson Ransbottom pottery, and other home-decor items at steep discounts. They also make their own ceramic vases, centerpieces, and candle holders, and tours of the operation are given weekdays at 11. Picnic tables and nature trails are on the property, making it very easy to pass an afternoon here.

Olde Engine Works Marketplace (570-421-4340), 62 N. 3rd Street, Stroudsburg. Open daily. This 1902 brick machine shop once made steam-powered winches used to pull nets from shrimp boats; today it's an antiques and collectibles co-op with 125 vendors. The ever-changing inventory ranges from circa-1900 toy pianos and Depression-era glass to industrial-age spools and modern furniture.

Pocono Bazaar Flea Market (570-223-8640), US 209, Marshalls Creek. Open 9–5 Saturday and Sunday. A people-watcher's paradise with hundreds of indoor and outdoor stands selling antiques, produce and baked goods, miracle gadgets, rock 'n' roll T-shirts, housewares, Webkinz, and more. There has been speculation for years that the market would close to make room for development, but as of this writing, there were no such plans in the works.

Water Gap Gallery (570-424-5002), Main Street, Delaware Water Gap. This small gallery across from the Deer Head Inn sells handcrafted pottery, wind chimes, silver jewelry, hand-painted glass, and a great selection of jazz CDs by local artists.

✳ Special Events

June: **Pocono 500 Nextel Cup Race** (first weekend), Pocono Raceway—a hugely popular event that draws NASCAR superstars to compete, plus 100,000 fans who come to watch them. There's a similar race in late July.

September: **Pocono Garlic Festival** (Labor Day weekend), Shawnee Mountain Ski Area—this creative and fun event celebrates the region's love affair with the pungent bulb. Expect plenty of garlic-laced food, crafts, and entertainment by the Garlic-Eating Tuba Troubadours. Also in September is the Celebration of the Arts Jazz Festival (weekend after Labor Day), a nationally recognized four-day event that unites jazz musicians, chefs, and artists on outdoor stages throughout Delaware Water Gap.

October: **Stroudsburg Halloween Parade** (last weekend), Stroudsburg—Costumed kids, adults, and even dogs take over Main Street beginning at noon and march to Courthouse Square for more fun and games.

POCONO MOUNTAINS NORTH

GUIDANCE For a town map and other information on Milford and its outlying areas, visit the **Pike County Tourism Bureau** (570-296-8700), 209 E. Harford Street, Milford. In Honesdale, the **Wayne County Visitor Center** (570-253-1960; 32 Commercial Street) has local maps and information; it's also the place to buy tickets for the adjacent Stourbridge Railway Excursions. For information on Lake Wallenpaupack, stop by the **Hawley-Lake Wallenpaupack Visitor Center** (570-226-3191) just below the dam overlook on US 6/PA 507, or visit www.hawley wallenpaupackcc.com.

GETTING THERE By air: **Newark International** (800-397-4636) is about an hour's drive from Milford. Alternatives include **Scranton/Wilkes-Barre Airport** in Avoca (877-235-9287) and **Lehigh Valley International** in Allentown (888-359-5842).

By car: From the Pennsylvania Turnpike: I-81 to I-84 east. From New York: I-80 west to exit 34B (Sparta); then follow PA 15/US 206 north to Milford. Follow US 6 west to Hawley and Honesdale.

By train: **Metro-North** line from Manhattan to Port Jervis, New Jersey, across the river from Milford.

By bus: **Short Line** (800-631-8405; www.coachusa.com) runs daily bus service between New York's Port Authority and Milford, Hawley, and Honesdale.

GETTING AROUND While Hawley, Honesdale, and Milford are all pleasant walking towns, you'll need a car to get around up here.

MEDICAL EMERGENCY Wayne County Memorial Hospital (570-253-8100), US 6, Honesdale. **Community Medical Center** (570-969-8000), 1800 Mulberry Street, Scranton.

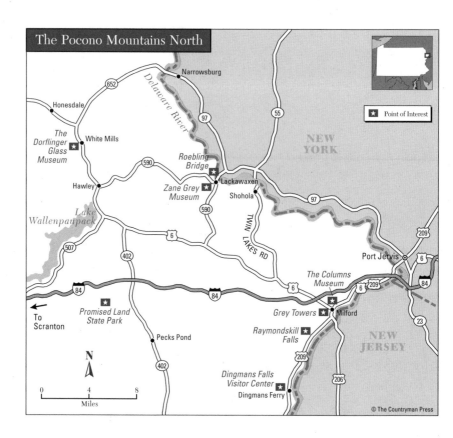

The Pocono Mountains North

Narrowsburg
652
Honesdale
Delaware River
97
55
Point of Interest
NEW YORK
The Dorflinger Glass Museum
White Mills
590
Roebling Bridge
Hawley
Zane Grey Museum
Lackawaxen
Shohola
590
97
Lake Wallenpaupack
6
TWIN LAKES RD
209
507
402
Port Jervis
6
The Columns Museum
6 209
84
84
84
To Scranton
Promised Land State Park
Grey Towers
Milford
23
Pecks Pond
Raymondskill Falls
NEW JERSEY
N
402
Dingmans Falls Visitor Center
209
206
0   4   8
Dingmans Ferry
Miles
© The Countryman Press

WHEN TO GO If you don't ski, summer and fall are the best times to visit the northern Pocono Mountains. Many outdoor (and some indoor) attractions don't even open their doors until Memorial Day and stay open through October.

✳ Villages

Hawley. Named for the first president of the Pennsylvania Coal Company, this town of 1,300 was a thriving center for anthracite coal distribution in the mid-1800s. The coal and lumber industries were replaced by fine cut-glass and silk and textile mills in the 1920s.

Also changing Hawley's identity in the 1920s was the Pennsylvania Power and Light Company's decision to dam a nearby creek to create hydroelectric power. This created Lake Wallenpaupack, the state's third largest man-made lake. The town became known as a recreational destination for families from Pennsylvania, New Jersey, and New York, a reputation it still has today. Hawley is home to one of the state's top family resorts, Woodloch Pines, as well as many well-regarded antiques shops, and several upscale inns and mom-and-pop lakefront motels.

Honesdale. Like Hawley, its neighbor to the north, Honesdale was named for a railroad VIP: Philip Hone, president of the Delaware and Hudson Canal Company and former mayor of New York. It is the largest municipality in Wayne County and home to the Stourbridge Lion, the first steam locomotive to run on rails in the U.S.; rides on a full-scale replica run on a regular basis from the original station. Honesdale doesn't have many hotels or inns, but it makes a pleasant day trip from Hawley or Scranton. Its main street is a treasure trove of Victorian architecture and antiques shops. Detour to Church Street and you'll find many lovely historic churches that date to 1860. On its outskirts are a commercial district and the Dorflinger Glass Museum and Wildlife Sanctuary.

Lackawaxen. This quiet village is named after the river that flows through it. It was once a major center for bluestone quarrying and is home to Roebling Bridge, the oldest existing wire suspension bridge in the country. Zane Grey lived here between 1905 and 1918 and wrote several novels from his home overlooking the river, now a museum run by the National Park Service. It's also a great place to spot eagles in January and February; there is an observation platform next to Roebling Bridge.

Milford. This sophisticated hamlet has a prime location along the Delaware River where Pennsylvania, New York, and New Jersey intersect.

OLD LUMBERYARD ANTIQUES

A few years ago, *New York* magazine dubbed it the New Hamptons, stemming from the influx of New Yorkers who have bought second homes here or use its upscale hotels and country inns for frequent getaways. Settled in 1796 and used as a setting in some of the earliest silent movies starring

SCRANTON AND WILKES-BARRE

About 30 minutes apart, these are the two of the largest cities around, though they are not considered part of the Pocono Mountains. Both towns served as industrial centers for Pennsylvania's anthracite coal mining industry and offer live theater, art galleries, shopping, and nightlife options.

Scranton, with a population of 77,000, is the bigger of the two and about a 45-minute drive from Hawley in the northern Pocono Mountains. Its baseball team, the **Scranton/Wilkes-Barre Yankees,** is a Triple-A affiliate of the New York team; you can catch a game at **Lackawanna County Stadium** (570-969-2255), 235 Montage Mountain Road, Moosic. In recent years, Scranton has become famous as the main setting of *The Office,* the highly-rated TV show starring Steve Carrell. Steamtown Mall, Lake Scranton, and Farley's restaurant are a few of the existing sites that have been mentioned on the NBC comedy. Two of the city's marquee attractions are the **Lackawanna County Coal Mine Tour** (see the Coal Mining sidebar) and **Steamtown National Historic Site** (570-340-5200; www.nps.gov/stea) 150 S. Washington Avenue), a huge and fascinating complex of authentic standard-gauge steam locomotives, freight and passenger cars, and historic exhibits located on an old railway yard; ask about their regular train excursions. Across the parking lot from Steamtown is the **Electric City Trolley Museum** (570-963-6590; www.ectma.org), home to a kid-friendly collection of authentic streetcars, hands-on displays that let you steer model trolleys and ring up fares, and exhibits that chronicle the history of the early electric trolley industry. Both Steamtown and the Trolley Museum are an easy walk to Steamtown Mall's shops and restaurants. For information on the Scranton area, contact the **Lackawanna County Convention and Visitor Bureau** (800-229-3526; www.visitnepa.org).

Between Scranton and Wilkes-Barre is the quaint town of **Old Forge,** which rightly bills itself as the Pizza Capital of the World. Old-

Mary Pickford and Lillian Gish, Milford has art galleries, antiques shops, preserved Victorian-era homes, upscale restaurants and cafes, and a bucolic get-away-from-it-all setting. You will also find Grey Towers, a French chateau-style estate that belonged to a leader of the U.S. conservation

fashioned Italian gravy joints line the sleepy main street. A favorite is **Arcaro and Genell** (570-457-5555; 433 S. Main Street), whose rectangular pizza has been featured in *USA Today.* It really is that good.

Thirty minutes south of Scranton, **Wilkes-Barre** is home to five colleges, a population of 43,000, and more than 200 historic buildings, including a 1909 Beaux Arts courthouse that is the city's pride and joy. You'll also find **Mohegan Sun at Pocono Downs** (570-831-2100; www

WILKES-BARRE COURTHOUSE

.poconodowns.com; 1280 PA 315), one of a handful of racino complexes featuring slot machines and harness racing; the **Frederick Stegmaier Mansion** (570-823-9372; www.stegmaiermansion.com), an ornate 1870s mansion that rents rooms and suites for $135–200 a night; and The **Tubs Nature Area,** a peaceful Walden-like nature park centered around a stream and seven tub-shaped glacial potholes. For more information about the area, contact the **Luzerne County Convention and Visitor Bureau** (888-905-2872; www.tournepa.com).

movement, and a fascinating little museum, the Columns, which houses a piece of American history: the flag that cushioned Abraham Lincoln's head after he was shot at the Ford Theatre.

✷ To See

🍃 **Grey Towers National Historic Site** (570-296-9630; www.fs.fed.us /na/gt), 151 Grey Towers Drive, Milford. Grounds open daily; tours daily 11–4 Memorial Day through October; $6 adults, $3 ages 12–17. Gifford Pinchot, a former governor of Pennsylvania and the founder and first chief of the U.S. Forest Service, used this stunning French chateau-style home a mile outside of town as a summer retreat. If you have the time, join one of the hour-long tours of this fascinating home that showcases Pinchot's quirky and conservation-conscious ways. Fun items on display include artifacts collected in his travels, such as a pair of terra-cotta camels from China's Tang Dynasty, and the family's infamous Finger Bowl dining-room table, which had a pool in the center and required guests to pass the salt by floating it downstream by wooden bowl. The tour isn't for small children, but they will enjoy the broad sloping grounds, which include paved paths and a moat full of koi fish.

GREY TOWERS

The Columns (570-296-8126), 608 Broad Street, Milford. Open April through November; call for hours; $3 adults. The marquee exhibit in this grand old building is the Lincoln flag, a bloodstained American flag that was used to cradle the president's head after he was shot at Ford's Theatre. It found its way to Milford via the daughter of the stage manager who took the flag home that tragic night. She inherited it before moving to the area in 1888, then passed it on to her son, who donated it the county historical society. Members of the Pike County Historical Society have built an interesting little museum around the bloody flag, with exhibits on local history, a vintage clothing collection that includes two fedoras

THE COLUMNS

owned by William Jennings Bryan, and a Hiawatha stagecoach from the mid-1800s.

Zane Grey Museum (570-685-4871), 135 Scenic Drive, Lackawaxen. Open Friday through Sunday in summer and weekends through mid-October; free. The prolific Western author wrote his first novel, *The Heritage of the Desert,* as well as *Riders of the Purple Sage* in this decidedly Eastern riverfront retreat near Roebling Bridge. It was turned into a museum in the 1970s and purchased by the National Park Service in 1989; Grey and his wife, Dollie, are buried nearby. Rangers lead 20-minute tours through Grey's old study, which includes original manuscripts and the Morris chair where he did much of his writing. There's also a gift shop that sells a wide selection of his writings. Every July, the museum holds a Zane Grey festival that celebrates the writer's link to the area.

ZANE GREY MUSEUM

❀ **Dorflinger Glass Museum** (570-253-1185; www.dorflinger.org), Long Ridge Road, White Mills. Open Wednesday through Sunday mid-May through early November; $3 adults, $1.50 ages 6–18. In the late 1800s and early 1900s, the factory that operated here produced some of the finest glass in the world and counted two presidents (Lincoln and Wilson)

COAL MINING

Northeast Pennsylvania was once a huge coal mining center that supplied nearly 80 percent of the country. The towns of Hawley and Honesdale were major distribution centers that funneled the coal to New York via boat or railroad. The areas around Scranton and Wilkes-Barre were among the few places in the world that harbored anthracite, or hard, coal beneath their surfaces. There are no remaining active deep mines left, but a few attractions allow you to get an up-close understanding of this once-mighty industry. For more information, visit www.pacoalhistory.com.

Lackawanna County Coal Mine Tour (570-963-6463), McDade Park, Scranton. Open daily April through November, except Easter and Thanksgiving; $10 adults; $7.50 kids. Informative hour-long tours are led by former mine workers and take you via a yellow transport car 300 feet down into an underground city of offices, stables, and hundreds of rooms; be prepared to walk about 0.25 mile. Before or after your tour, stop by the adjacent **Pennsylvania Anthracite Heritage Museum** (570-963-4804) to round out your visit, well worth the $6 admission.

No. 9 Coal Mine and Museum (570-645-7074; www.n09mine.com), 9 Dock Street, Lansford. Open Wednesday through Sunday; museum and mine tour $8; museum only $3. About 10 miles southwest of Jim Thorpe, this deep mine produced coal for more than a century before closing in 1972. It reopened as a tourist attraction in the 1990s, and offers hour-long underground tours by enthusiastic guides. The museum displays include an armored coal car and the mine's original elevator shaft.

Eckley Miners' Village (570-636-2070; www.eckleyminersvillagemuseum .com), Freeland. Open daily, except some holidays; $6 adults, $4 ages 6–12. About 30 minutes from either Jim Thorpe or Wilkes-Barre, Eckley is an authentic anthracite coal mining "patch town" and is worth the

among its clientele. All sorts of cut, enameled, etched, and gilded glass are displayed among period antiques and artifacts from the glass factory. The gift shop sells phenomenal Christmas ornaments, as well as paperweights, jewelry, and a wide assortment of glassware. The museum is surrounded by the Dorflinger-Suydam Wildlife Sanctuary (see also Green Space).

ECKLEY MINERS' VILLAGE

effort it takes to get here. The coal operation closed in 1971, but the town was saved from demolition by the 1970 Sean Connery film *The Molly Maguires,* which filmed many scenes here and in Jim Thorpe; several movie props such as a general store and a mini-coal breaker remain. Exhibits in the visitor center demonstrate the dangers, misery, and class divisions endured by miners and their families; check these out and then stroll down the main street and see how the workers' homes were ranked by skill level and religion; about 50 descendants of the miners, mostly widows and offspring, still live in many of the homes. Guided tours are offered daily and included in the admission fee. Bring a map and detailed directions; this is definitely off the beaten path.

NORTHEASTERN PENNSYLVANIA

✳ To Do

Roebling's Delaware Aqueduct (570-729-7134) in Lackawaxen is the oldest existing wire suspension bridge in the country; it runs 535 feet from Minisink Ford, New York, to Lackawaxen, and is known locally as Roebling Bridge. Begun in 1847 as one of four suspension aqueducts on the Delaware and Hudson Canal, it was designed by John A. Roebling, the future engineer of New York's Brooklyn Bridge. Its suspension design allowed more room for ice floes and river traffic than conventional bridges and it was considered a huge time-saving success during its 50 years of operation. There is a small parking lot and information kiosks on the Pennsylvania side, and a pedestrian walkway across that affords terrific views of the river.

FOR FAMILIES ✐ **Claws 'N' Paws Wild Animal Park** (570-698-6154; www.clawsnpaws.com), PA 590, Hamlin. Open daily May through October; $15, $12 ages 2–11. This private zoo is home to more than 120 species of animals, including a white tiger, snow leopard, and the usual allotment of monkeys, reptiles, and meerkats. There are lots of hands-on activities that let kids feed parrots and giraffes, mingle with turtles, and participate in a fossil dig.

✐ **Stourbridge Railway** (570-253-1960; 800-433-9008; www.wayne countycc.com), 303 Commercial Street, Honesdale. On August 8, 1829, the Delaware & Hudson Railroad launched the first commercial locomotive on rails in the western hemisphere. Diesel passenger trains still leave from this spot on themed excursions late spring through early December. Check the Web site for a schedule. The cost usually ranges from $15–18 per ride. They also run weekday rides for groups in summer and fall, and there is usually extra seating for individuals. The rides last about 90 minutes and cost between $5 and 8.

SCENIC DRIVES For breathtaking scenery, head to NY 97, at the intersection of US 6 and US 209 in Port Jervis, and follow it north a few miles to the hamlet of **Sparrow Bush.** Continue on 97 to a dramatic section of the road known as **Hawk's Nest,** a stunning and winding road perched high above the Delaware on rocky cliffs that has been featured in many car commercials. Continue on to Barryville, New York, where you can cross back over the river to Pennsylvania and follow Twin Lakes Road to US 6 back to Milford.

✳ Outdoor Activities

BICYCLING Bicycling along the **Lackawaxen River** affords level terrain and a pretty river view on the lightly traveled road known as the Towpath.

There are few bike rental shops in the area, so you might want to consider bringing your own.

BOAT EXCURSIONS/RENTALS In **Promised Land State Park** (see also Green Space), a boat concession off PA 390 (570-676-4117) offers rowboat, canoe, and kayak rentals. Electric motors are also available. On Lake Wallenpaupack, **Pocono Action Sports Marina** (570-226-4556) at Tanglewood Lodge rents power boats, sailboats, canoes, and jet skis. **Wallenpaupack Scenic Boat Tour** (717-226-6211) offers 30-minute cruises by patio boat daily from the end of June through September and weekends in spring and fall. $14 adults, $10 ages 12 and under.

FISHING Between Dingmans Ferry and Promised Land State Park is a hidden anglers' paradise known as **Pecks Pond.** There's not much here, just a rustic inn and tavern and a natural shallow pond filled with bass, pickerel, perch, and other panfish. **Pecks Pond Backwater Adventures,** a small outfitter (570-775-7237; www.peckspond.com), rents rods and reels and all kinds of boats.

Also: the **Lackawaxen River** is stocked with rainbow, brook, and brown trout in the spring and fall. For condition updates and supplies, visit or call **Angler's Roost** (570-685-2010), 106 Scenic Drive, Lackawaxen. They also run canoe and rafting trips for small and large groups.

Rivers Outdoor Adventures (570-943-3151; www.riversfly fishing.com), runs trips to the Upper Delaware River, where smallmouth bass, trout, shad, and walleye are popular catches. Fishing this region requires either a New York or a Pennsylvania license.

GOLF Cliff Park Golf Course (570-296-6491), 155 Cliff Park Drive, Milford. The country's second-oldest golf course has 9 challenging holes stretching over 3,153 yards.

STREAM NEAR DINGMANS FERRY

Country Club at Woodloch Springs (570-685-8075), 1 Woodloch Drive, Hawley. Serious golfers love this challenging 18-hole par-72 course, though it's accessible only to guests of nearby Woodloch Pines and a few other resorts in the area.

Cricket Hill Golf Club (570-226-4366), US 6, Hawley. More than 10 ponds dot this 18-hole public course with tees to 5,790 yards.

HIKING **Promised Land State Park** has some of the region's best hiking trails, from easy to strenuous (see Green Space). In Milford, folks like to hike up to the **Knob,** an overlook with views of the entire town and surrounding valley. Access it via the Mott Street Bridge off Harford Street. For light exercise, there's the **Bingham Park River Walk** in Hawley.

HORSEBACK RIDING **Black Walnut Stables** (570-296-9336) at the Black Walnut Inn in Milford offers one- to three-hour trail rides starting at $35 an hour.

Malibu Dude Ranch (570-296-7281; www.malibududeranch.com) in Milford has hourly rides starting at $30, as well as pony rides and guided day trips through the countryside.

SWIMMING **Lake Wallenpaupack** has a public beach where swimming is allowed; it's just south of the visitor center off US 6/PA 507; you can also swim at designated spots by the lakes in Promised Land State Park. In Milford, a favorite spot is **Milford Beach** (570-729-7134), a former farm overlooking the Delaware River that was spruced up by the National Park Service. There's no sand, but you will find lifeguards (in summer), comfort stations, and picnic areas. There's a small fee to park.

SKIING For a comprehensive list of ski resorts in the region, contact the **Pocono Mountains Visitor Bureau** (800-762-6667; www.800poconos.com).

Elk Mountain Ski Resort (570-679-4400), Union Dale, north of Scranton. One of the largest ski areas in northeast Pennsylvania with 27 trails and a terrain park on the east side of the mountain.

Ski Big Bear at Masthope (570-685-1400; www.ski-bigbear.com), 196 Karl Hope Road, Lackawaxen. This small facility near the New York border caters to families and groups. It has 18 trails, three lifts, snow tubing, and a terrain park. There's also a ski school for first-timers and kids.

WALKING An easy lakefront walking trail can be accessed at the **Wallenpaupack Environmental Learning Center** (800-354-8383; 126 PPL Drive) or the **Lake Wallenpaupack Visitor Center** (570-226-3191) on

VIEW OF LAKE WALLENPAUPACK

US 6. It's about 1.5 miles long and leads to a waterfront overlook. Pick up a trail map at the visitor center.

✳ Green Space

Promised Land State Park (570-676-3428), PA 390, Promised Land Village. The early settlers who named the area mistakenly thought it would be great for farming; yet once you see the place you'll realize the name isn't entirely off base. Located a few miles south of Lake Wallenpaupack, it has two large swimming and boating lakes with sand beaches, several camping areas, and some of the best hiking and cross-country ski trails in the region. Also within the park is Bruce Lake Natural Area, a 2,700-acre natural site including two lakes. The loop around Conservation Island is a popular easy trail; serious hikers can take the Bruce Lake Loop through hemlock and oak forest to a glacial lake, about 9.5 miles round-trip.

Dorflinger-Suydam Wildlife Sanctuary (570-253-1185), White Mills. Acres of scenic forest and meadows surround the Dorflinger Glass Museum (see also Museums). No picnicking or pets are allowed, but visitors may wander along any of the easy nature trails (pick up a map at the kiosk on the way in). The Wildflower amphitheatre is the site of regular summer concerts and an annual wildflower festival.

WATERFALLS The Pocono Mountains region has more than two dozen named waterfalls. Here are a few favorites. There is no charge to see them. Swimming is prohibited.

Dingmans Falls (570-828-7802), Johnny Bee Road, near the junction of US 209 and PA 739. Take the raised boardwalk trail past a slender but pretty cascade of water, then continue another 0.5 mile through a hemlock ravine to the base of the steep and stunning Dingmans Falls. The fit can walk to the top of the falls via a steep trail to the left of the base.

Childs Falls, George W. Childs Recreational Site, Silver Lake Road. A few miles upstream from Dingmans Falls, this three-tiered waterfall in a secluded gorge can be reached via a steep 1.8-mile loop trail framed by sheer rock walls and hemlock forest. Bring a picnic and settle in at one of the tables near the falls.

Raymondskill Falls, Raymondskill Falls Road, off US 209. These exquisite cascades are only 3 miles south of Milford, and some feel that they are the state's most splendid (at 165 feet, they are definitely the highest). It's a very short hike to the Upper Falls, but the best views can be found at the Middle Falls, which require a steep 0.5-mile hike down uneven stairs.

Shohola Falls, off US 6 between Milford and Hawley. Located on state game lands in the Shohola Recreation Area, these pretty falls are challenging to find. Look for the two parking lots on either side of a concrete bridge. It's a short, but very steep walk, past a scenic dammed lake to the falls.

✳ Lodging

BED & BREAKFASTS

Harrington House (888-272-1234; www.harringtonhousemilford.com), 208 W. Harford Road, Milford. Formerly the Hattree Inn, this popular B&B is pet-friendly and within walking distance of downtown Milford. The four rooms with private baths are spacious and elegantly furnished with unique touches such as working fireplaces, oriental rugs, and exposed brick walls. Owner Adriane Wendell (and her dog, Daniel), is a gracious and accommodating host who whips up gourmet breakfasts such as pumpkin spice waffles and herb-cheese soufflés. Rooms $160.

Roebling Inn (570-685-7900; www.roeblinginn.com), 155 Scenic Drive, Lackawaxen. This stately home two doors down from the Zane Grey Museum is nestled in an extraordinary setting overlooking the Lackawaxen River. Each of the five rooms has a private bath, TV, and queen bed; the corner rooms facing the river are especially nice and have fireplaces. A cute one-bedroom cottage nearby sleeps three and allows children under 12. Owners JoAnn and Donald Jahn know the area well and are happy to proffer sightseeing advice. Rooms $99–145. Cottage: $129–185, with a two-night minimum.

INNS & RESORTS

Milford
Cliff Park Inn (570-296-6491; 800-225-6535; www.cliffparkinn .com), 155 Cliff Park Road. This is the only B&B in the 70,000-acre Delaware Water Gap National Recreation Area, and its views alone are worth the price of a night or two. All 14 rooms have private baths, TVs, luxury linens, and wireless Internet access; some have sun porches, claw-foot tubs, and king beds. The restaurant on the premises serves lunch, dinner, and Sunday brunch, and has been (along with the inn) awarded three stars by the *Mobil Travel Guide*. There's a challenging 9-hole golf course (for an extra fee), there's a wide front porch with rocking chairs, and there are 7 miles of hiking trails with river overlooks. No children under 12. Standard rooms $141–204, premium and deluxe rooms $204–268, with a two-night minimum on weekends May through October.

& **Hotel Fauchere** (570-409-1212; www.hotelfauchere.com), 401 Broad Street. Step through the doors of this sophisticated 19th-century inn and you might think you've been transported to a boutique hotel in SoHo. New Yorkers love it here, perhaps because of its connection to the famous Delmonico's Restaurant

(see Dining Out) or because owner Sean Strub is a tireless promoter of Milford's beauty and amenities. Luxuries abound: Kiehl's bath products, luxury Frette linens, heated bathroom floors and towel racks, and complimentary wine. The 2 second-floor rooms with large balconies are especially nice. Rooms $275–425, including breakfast. Rates drop November through April.

Malibu Dude Ranch (570-296-7281; www.malibududeranch .com), 401 Broad Street. Horse lovers and families will want to check out this all-inclusive dude ranch next to a pretty lake. Rates include all meals, clean and rustic accommodations (no TV or A/C), and all activities such as volleyball, swimming, and horseback and pony riding. New owners took over in 2010 and renovated rooms in the lodge. There are several buildings (the Boat House is a favorite) and 16 cabins on the property that sit apart from the main lodge; they tend to be quieter. Daily rates start at $109–135 per person; weekly rates are $610 per person (kids 5–12 are half price).

Hawley
The Ledges (570-226-1337; www.ledgeshotel.com), 120 Falls Avenue. Hawley's newest inn opened in a former silk mill complex in 2011. The rooms and suites are modern, comfortable, and environmentally friendly, but the standout attraction here is the

views of the waterfall and river gorge out back. Multi-tiered decks and a welcoming great room provide the best vantage points; if the weather is good, you may never want to leave the grounds. A wine bar serves drinks and small dishes in the evening, and there's a breakfast café next door (See Eating Out). A trail out back leads to Lake Wallenpaupack, which is less than a mile away; ask the front desk for details. Getting to the hotel is the hardest part: Look for the unmarked road off US 6 that winds behind the Silk Factory complex. Rooms $120–160, suites $225–260.

✍ & **Woodloch Pines** (570-685-8000; 800-572-6658; www.woodloch.com), PA 590 east. This popular lakefront resort outside Hawley bills itself as being "like a cruise on land." Indeed, you'll never have to leave the complex if you don't want; there are indoor and outdoor pools, a 9-hole golf course, and plenty of morning-till-night organized activities, from movies and boat rides to bocce and scavenger hunts. It also helps that the lake-and-forest setting is gorgeous and shouts "getaway" from the tips of its blue spruce trees. Standard rooms in the main lodge sleep up to four with small sitting areas and fold-out couches. Deluxe lakeview rooms are spacious with two queen beds, a pullout couch, and small balcony. There are also large homes available for rent a few minutes' drive away in the Woodloch Springs golfing community. Rates typically start at $350 a night per person and include three meals and most activities.

Settler's Inn (570-226-2993; 800-833-8527; www.thesettlersinn.com), 4 Main Avenue. First-class

ENTRANCE TO SETTLER'S INN

all the way, from the 20 stylish guest rooms to the attentive service and excellent on-site restaurant. Weather permitting, breakfast is served on the terrace and usually includes a choice of four different entrées, house-made granola, and fresh fruit. Standard rooms are $166–296, while deluxe rooms, many of which have Jacuzzi tubs and fireplaces, run $180–395. They also offer room and dinner packages.

MOTELS ✥ Myer Country Motel (570-296-7223; 800-764-6937; www.myermotel.com), 600 US 6 and 209, Milford. This 1940s-style cabin motel is one of the best values in Milford. Located just outside of town near the New Jersey border, it has been in the same family for generations and features 19 separate cottage units. The decor is more appealing than the usual standard motel offering, and all rooms have TVs, refrigerators, and front porches. There are smoking and nonsmoking rooms, and coffee and juice are available in the office each morning. The place fronts a busy road, but is surrounded by several acres of blue spruce and pine trees. Reserve early; these rooms go fast. Rooms $66–81 weekdays, $86–101 weekends, May through October; prices drop in the off-season.

East Shore Lodging (570-226-3293; www.eastshorelodging.com), US 6, Hawley. It doesn't look like much from the outside, but this friendly motel right on Lake Wallenpaupack is a terrific value. Rooms are bright and attractive with one or two queen beds, private baths, and TVs. Rooms $69–135; suites $85–175, includes breakfast.

Ehrhardts Waterfront Resort (800-678-5907; 570-226-4388; www.ehrhardts.com), 205 PA 507. This family-owned operation includes a motel, cottages, and popular restaurant—all framed by views of Lake Wallenpaupack. Don't expect luxury, but rooms are clean with small fridges and microwaves, and many were updated in 2011. Rates include the use of paddleboats, canoes, two swimming pools, and boat slips, but my favorite amenity might be the many Adirondack chairs thoughtfully placed all over the property with prime views of the lake. Rates drop considerably in winter and fall. Rooms $81–187, cottages that sleep four to six $131–242.

CAMPGROUNDS Promised Land State Park (570-888-7275), (see also Green Space) offers nearly 500 camp sites on its property. Centrally located Pickerel Point and Deerfield areas have more than 200 primitive tent sites; many walk-in sites overlook Promised Land Lake. Sites at Lower Lake Campground at the lake's western edge have hot showers and electricity hookups. Pickerel Point is open year-round. Tent sites: $9–25.

Wilsonville Recreation Area
(570-226-4382; www.wilsonville
campground.com), has 160 wooded tent and RV sites with electric
and water hookups for $22–30 per
night. It's right on Lake Wallenpaupack and within walking distance of the lake's only public
beach.

✳ Where to Eat

DINING OUT

Milford
& ᵞ **Delmonico Room** (570-409-
1212), 401 Broad Street. Dinner
Thursday through Sunday; Sunday
jazz brunch. It's easy to picture
Theodore Roosevelt or Mary Pickford enjoying frog legs in aioli or
Alsatian country pate in the grand
formal dining room of the Hotel
Fauchere. They were among the
famous who patronized the hotel
when it was owned by Louis
Fauchere, a well-known chef at
Delmonico's in New York. Today,
the dining room stays true to its
haute cuisine roots, offering a
prix-fixe menu featuring items
such as crown roast of lamb and
roasted red snapper pot-au-feu.
For a more casual meal, try the
downstairs Bar Louis, which
serves a delectable sushi pizza.
Tasting menu: $85–115; Bar Louis
menu: $10–34.

ᵞ **Jorgensen's at the Dimmick
Inn** (570-296-4021), 101 E. Harford Street. Lunch and dinner
daily. The wide front porch of this
19th-century establishment is
among the most coveted people-

watching spots in town. Menu
specialties include St. Louis-style
barbecue ribs and charcoal-grill
sirloin fillets; the large menu also
includes ostrich steak, Maryland-
style fried chicken, sandwiches,
and several seafood and pasta
options. Leave room for dessert;
the peanut-butter pie is divine.
Sandwiches: $8–11; entrées:
$11–29.

🍴 ᵞ **WaterWheel Café** (570-296-
2383; www.waterwheelcafe.com),
150 Water Street. Breakfast and
lunch daily; dinner and bar menu
Thursday through Saturday.
Located in a beautiful creek-side
location near Grey Towers, this
multifaceted eatery features a
café, restaurant, bakery, and a bar
with live music Thursday through
Sunday. It's a great spot for lunch;
sit on the deck overlooking the
creek and choose from a long list
of specialty sandwiches including
fresh-roasted turkey and duck-
liver mousse with port. Inside, you
can watch the three-story-high
water wheel in action behind a
glass wall. Dinner specialties
include crispy hazelnut pork chops
and several tasty Vietnamese dishes. Reservations are recommended at dinner. Dishes $4–10; dinner
entrées: $18–28.

Hawley area
French Manor (877-720-6090;
www.thefrenchmanor.com), 50
Huntingdon Drive, South Sterling.
Many view this as the finest
restaurant in the Pocono Mountains. Classic French cuisine is

served in a candlelit dining room with a high-vaulted ceiling; specialties include Chateaubriand for two, grilled rack of lamb with curried ratatouille, and slow-rendered Muscovy duck breast with macadamia nut tapenade. The cheese and dessert cart is a spectacular indulgence. Proper attire required. Entrées $36–52.

Settler's Inn (570-226-2993; www.thesettlersinn.com), 4 Main Avenue, Hawley. Breakfast and dinner daily; call for lunch hours. One of the town's top restaurants, with a farm-to-table menu that might include zucchini lavender soup, miso-glazed salmon with orange fennel salad, or black truffle chicken roulade. There's an extensive and thoughtful wine and beer selection. You can also opt for a more casual and inexpensive meal in the cozy tavern. Dinner entrées $24–40, tavern menu $9–18, brunch $9–15.

EATING OUT ❦ **Trackside Grill** (570-253-2462), Honesdale. Breakfast and lunch Monday through Saturday. This small diner near the Stourbridge Railway station serves hearty sandwiches such as hot turkey and French dip, plus salads, homemade soups, and a kids' menu. Breakfasts start at $2.25 for two eggs with toast and go up to $5.25 for creamed chip beef. Nothing on the lunch menu costs more than $8.

❦ **Ledgedale BBQ Pit** (570-689-2200), Ledgedale Road and Goosepond Road, Lake Ariel.

Reasonably priced sandwiches and platters of pork ribs, half chickens, crab cakes, and clam strips. The $5 hot dog hero (three dogs with bacon, sauerkraut, and mustard on a toasted roll) is legendary. Sit in the small dining room or outside at a picnic table. Dishes $5–14.

Milford Diner (570-296-8611), 301 Broad Street, Milford. Open daily 6 AM–10 PM. Classic diner with friendly service and hearty dishes such as pork and sauerkraut, beef goulash, and stuffed cabbage. Expect long waits for breakfast on weekends. Dishes $3–17.

Hawley

❦ & ⅄ **The Boat House** (570-226-5027), PA 507. Lunch and dinner daily. This casual nautical-themed restaurant overlooks Lake Wallenpaupack and has a huge menu featuring appetizers, salads, hot and cold sandwiches, and burgers, plus grilled seafood and steak dinners. Reservations are recommended in summer. There's live music on Friday nights. Sandwiches: $8–12. Platters $10–20.

Cocoon Coffeehouse (570-226-6130), US 6 and Belmont Avenue, Hawley. Open daily 7 AM–6 PM. Stop here for blueberry coffeecake, ginger peach iced tea, and savory sandwiches on the menu. You can also surf the Web, lounge on the comfy couches, and admire the artwork on the walls. It's next door to the Ledges Hotel in the Silk Mill complex. Dishes $3–8.

&. ※ **Cora's 1850 Bistro** (570-226-8878), 525 Welwood Avenue. Lunch and dinner daily; Sunday brunch. Housed in a former hotel and run by two Culinary Institute of America graduates, this attractive yellow-walled eatery seems to have something for everyone on its menu, from burgers and salads to a long list of appetizers and a $5 kids' menu. Entrées include chicken Oscar, Cajun cowboy rib steak, grilled portabella puttanesca, and sesame-seared tuna. There are regular weekday specials, such as all-you-can-eat wings or steak and Alaskan King crab legs. Sandwiches and appetizers $6–9; entrées $14–26.

&. **Hawley Diner** (570-226-0523), 302 Main Avenue. Breakfast, lunch, and dinner Monday through Saturday, breakfast and lunch Sunday. Old-school diner that was serving good jumbo Belgian waffles and other typical diner fare long before tourists discovered the area. It fills up on weekends. Breakfast and lunch $2–5; dinner dishes $8–13.

Lunchbox Café (570-226-0300), 215 Main Avenue. Unlimited coffee refills, good homemade soups, and quality deli sandwiches make this a favorite breakfast and lunch spot. Friendly service, too.

BYO Where to buy wine in the northern Pocono Mountains region:

There are **Wine & Spirits** stores in Milford at 106 W. Harford Street (570-296-7021) and in

Hawley at the **Village** shopping center on PA 739 (570-775-5010).

❋ Entertainment

MUSIC If you're not staying at an all-inclusive resort like Woodloch Pines, your best bets for late-night action in this area are the bars and lounges of popular restaurants and hotels. **The Pub in the Apple Valley Restaurant** (570-296-6831; US 6, Milford) hosts karaoke or live bands most weekends. **The WaterWheel Café** in Milford and the **Boat House** in Hawley also feature live music on weekends.

MOVIES & THEATER Cinema **6** (570-251-3456), 1199 Texas Palmyra Highway, US 6, Honesdale. First-run and 3D films in a modern setting.

Ritz Company Playhouse (570-226-9752; www.ritzplayhouse .com), 512 Keystone Street, Hawley. A 1930s movie house, now a nonprofit community theater, stages five shows each summer, mostly comedies and children's plays.

❋ Selective Shopping

Antiques are the main inventory of stores around here. Hawley, Honesdale, and Milford all have a robust selection of shops selling furniture, crafts, and other items. The granddaddy of the area's antiques shops is **Castle Antiques & Reproductions** (570-226-8550), 230 Welwood

Avenue, Hawley, a former lingerie factory on the edge of town that is now home to a massive selection of ceramic vases, cast-iron toys, old tools, cut glass, and every type of furniture imaginable. **Timely Treasures** (570-226-2838) off US 6, between Hawley and Lake Wallenpaupack, also has a good selection of furniture, garden items, and unusual gifts. In Milford, **Forest Hall Antiques** (570-296-4299), 214 Broad Street, occupies the upper floors of a French Normandy-style building that once housed Yale's School of Forestry, with wares such as Victorian chairs, pewter pitchers, porcelain china, and film posters. Milford also happens to boast two terrific book stores. **Books & Prints at Pear Alley** (570-296-4777), 220 Broad Street, has an excellent collection of used and out-of-print books, many of them gleaned from private collections. **Books n' Stuff** (570-409-6882; www.books nstuff2.com), 115 7th Street, sells used books on all subjects, plus audio books, computer and video games, and old-fashioned board games. It's in the quaint Old Lumberyard Shops complex, which is also home to a café and **Old Lumberyard Antiques** (570-409-8636), 113 7th Street, a browser's paradise of furniture, quilts, toys, china, vintage advertisements, and more.

✳ Special Events

January: **Eagle Fest** (second or third weekend), Narrowsburg, New York, across from Beach Lake, Pennsylvania—Winter is the best time to spot eagles here, and the area welcomes them with a festival featuring live birds of prey demonstrations, lectures, films, and staffed observation areas. Contact the Eagle Institute for more information: 570-685-5960.

February: **Crystal Cabin Fever** (last two weeks), PA 590, between Hawley and Hamlin—the area rids itself of winter cabin fever with detailed ice sculptures, a life-size ice cabin, carving contests, and a giant ice slide that will thrill kids. There's also plenty of hot chocolate. For more info, visit www.crystal cabinfever.com.

June: **Milford Music Festival** (second weekend), Ann Street Park, Milford—a mix of jazz, blues, rock, and classical performers take the stage over three days during this popular celebration of live music.

August: **Festival of Wood** (second weekend), Grey Towers National Historic Site, Milford—wood carving demonstrations, forestry walks, and live music.

October: **Black Bear Film Festival** (second weekend), Milford—independent films, lectures, plus displays of life-size bear sculptures. Visit www.blackbearfilm festival.com.

INDEX